Indigenous Peoples

ISBN 90 5166 978 X

Eburon Academic Publishers
PO Box 2867
2601 CW Delft
The Netherlands
Fax: (+31) 15 2146888 / Phone: (+31) 15 2131484
www.eburon.nl / info@eburon.nl

Cover design: Hans Ragnar Mathisen
Graphic design: Bjørn Hatteng

Indigenous Peoples:
Resource Management and Global Rights

Svein Jentoft, Henry Minde and Ragnar Nilsen

Eburon Delft
2003

In memory of Aslak Nils Sara (1934-1996)
– Sami chief and true environmentalist

Contents

The Land

Acknowledgements

The present volume is partly the outcome of the special session on Indigenous Peoples at the 7th Circumpolar Universities Co-operation Conference "When Distance is a Challenge", held at the University in Tromsø 19-21 August, 2001. Most of the essays presented at this session are included here, whilst a number of other chapters have been commissioned for inclusion in this book.

We are grateful to the Centre for Sami Studies at the University of Tromsø for its support. We particularly acknowledge the skilled assistance of graphic designer Bjørn Hatteng; and Mary Katherine Jones, who helped us prepare the manuscripts and translated Chapters 5, 9 and 15. Thanks also to the Sami artist Hans Ragnar Mathisen, for allowing us to use one of his paintings as a cover design. We are also grateful to Marine Policy for permission to reprint the article by Anthony Davis and Svein Jentoft as a chapter in this book.

The Norwegian Science Council provided financial support through the project *The Challenge of Indigenousness: Politics of Rights, Resources and Knowledge*. This book is the first in a series of publications from this project.

Tromsø, June 2003.
Svein Jentoft, Henry Minde and Ragnar Nilsen

Introduction

Svein Jentoft

We are now at the end of the UN International Decade of the World's Indigenous People and more than ten years have passed since the World Summit on Sustainable Development in Rio. What has been accomplished? Are indigenous peoples better off now than they were ten years ago? Have expectations been met? There are no clear answers to these questions. At this point in time it is also a little premature to make any final judgement. But the answer is most likely to be both yes and no. In some areas things have really advanced for indigenous peoples around the world, while in others they have deteriorated. Likewise, for some indigenous groups the situation has improved, while for others it has worsened. The question is, how it all adds up, how the positive developments compare to the negative ones.

It certainly takes more than a decade to rectify all the injustice that centuries of colonisation and imperialism have wrought upon indigenous peoples. As Peter Jull points out in this publication (Chapter 2),

> What we can say is that the political and policy frameworks required to replace colonialism, dispossession and marginalisation are now clearly visible, and are in various stages of negotiation or implementation. This is a process, and as such takes some time; after all, discussion and mutual understanding are required.

However, there is still a considerable urgency related to this process, as indigenous peoples cannot afford to wait for a long time to have their human rights guaranteed and their culture secured. In an age of globalization they are exposed to external forces as never before. In addition, as Erica-Irene Daes points out in Chapter 4, "indigenous peoples challenge the fundamental assumptions of globalization. They do not accept the assumption that humanity will benefit from the construction of a world culture of consumerism." This means that their situation must be addressed at all levels. What happens at the level of the community is of no less importance than what occurs at national and international levels. What occurs globally also has a great impact on what occurs locally.

It was a substantial victory when the United Nations' World Summit on Sustainable Development (Rio+10), held in Johannesburg, South Africa in August/September 2002 unanimously declared: "We affirm the vital role of indigenous peoples in sustainable development." This was the first time in UN history that the unqualified term "indigenous peoples" had been adopted unconditionally in an official UN document. Notably, there was no quarrel about the plural 's' in peoples, which on previous occasions has stirred controversy. It remains to be seen what implications this statement will have. The first test was in December 2002, when delegates met in Geneva to discuss the UN Declaration on the Rights of Indigenous Peoples and the Principles and Guidelines for the Protection of the Heritage of Indigenous Peoples. Interestingly, the delegates had few reservations regarding this term.

Other positive developments are worth mentioning. In 2002, a UN Permanent Forum for Indigenous Issues was established, chaired by the former president of the Sami Parliament, Ole Henrik Magga. The Forum is in itself an important recognition by the world community of the particular problems, interests and aspirations of indigenous peoples. Only time will tell what difference this new institution will make for indigenous peoples, and whether expectations will be met. The inadequate resources at the Forum's disposal give cause for concern, but then, Rome wasn't built in a day.

Communal Rights of Property

When assessing the results of the International Decade of the World's Indigenous People, some landmark court rulings in favour of indigenous peoples should also be mentioned. For instance, the case of the Mayagna Awas Tingni community in Nicaragua is now attracting international attention. Here, the Inter-American Court of Human Rights ruled that Nicaragua had violated the property rights of this community by permitting a foreign company to log within the community's traditional lands and otherwise failing to provide adequate recognition of the community's land tenure. The verdict makes reference to the communal property of indigenous peoples in general, and thus applies to all of Nicaragua's indigenous communities. It is also important to note that the court stressed that the rights expressed in international human rights law have "autonomous meaning that cannot be limited by the meaning attributed to them in domestic law".

The ruling in the Mayagna Awas Tingni case is strikingly similar to the Norwegian Supreme Court's decision concerning Sami collective grazing, fishing and hunting rights in the Svartskogen valley in northern Norway. In this case, the state argued that the territory was *terra nullius*; that it is not occupied by anyone in particular and thus was subject to government control and management. Contrary to this view, the Sami population residing in the area claimed that they had always used the land, assuming that it was theirs. With reference to domestic as well as international law, the court supported the local Sami position.

At the end of the International Decade for the World's Indigenous People, there are indeed some accomplishments. The reader of this book will learn about other examples that are encouraging to indigenous peoples, such as New Zealand's fisheries management settlements involving the Maori, depicted by Bjørn Hersoug in Chapter 7, and the Rama people's successful claim to be represented in the evaluation process of the so-called "Dry Canal" mega-project in Nicaragua (María Luisa Acosta, Chapter 11). Furthermore, Henry Minde (Chapter 5) links the creation of a Sami political institution to the events – in his words, a "silent revolution" – that occurred in the wake of the Alta River dam construction project in the Sami heartland of Norway. In addition, the Nunavut Inuit territory, recently established in Northern Canada, which is referred to in several chapters (Barsh and Henderson, Chapter 3; Jull, Chapter 2) must be listed as a positive achievement.

However, as Jull makes clear in Chapter 2, it should not be forgotten that these improvements have not come easily, rather from a hard, grassroots struggle within the indigenous communities. National governments have mostly been reluctant supporters, if not vociferous antagonists to these developments, where issues have had to be settled in court rather in national assemblies. No-one should for a moment believe that the struggle is over, even if the working process with the new Declaration should finally reach a positive conclusion. It is not for nothing that the Declaration has remained in draft form without much movement for ten years now. The Geneva meeting was a positive step forward, but much work still remains. Considering that the Draft Declaration contains articles such as the one that follows, perhaps it should not come as a surprise that the process is far from straightforward. Yet this was among the less controversial paragraphs in Geneva.

Article 26
Indigenous peoples have the right to own, develop, control and use the lands and territories, including the total environment of the lands, air, waters, coastal seas, sea-ice, flora and fauna and other resources which they have traditionally owned or otherwise occupied or used. This includes the right to the full recognition of the laws, traditions and customs, land-tenure systems and institutions for the development and management of resources, and the right to effective measures by States to prevent any interference with, alienation of or encroachment upon these rights.

This is indeed progressive language, which will inspire indigenous peoples to make further claims on national governments. But is important to remember that legislation, which already exists – such as the ILO Convention 169 and the Biodiversity Convention – has been successfully invoked to protect the rights of indigenous peoples. Another piece of legislation is the International Covenant on Civil and Political Rights, which confirms the rights of self-determination and cultural integrity, and the International Convention on the Elimination of All Forms of Racial Discrimination. Then there are a number of regional human rights' treaties that apply to non-indigenous and indigenous peoples alike, for instance the African Charter on Human and Peoples' Rights, the American Convention on Human Rights, and the equivalent European Convention. Notably, these instruments were phrased in terms of individual rights but are now increasingly being interpreted also to support the collective rights of indigenous peoples (Anaya, 2002). The Mayagna Awas Tingni case is an illustration of this point. For indigenous peoples, this is no doubt positive; the negative side is that court rulings are needed to make governments adhere to these conditions. But governments change and some prove more supportive of indigenous claims than others.

So, statements by governments regarding the rights of indigenous peoples are sometimes nothing more than 'window dressing' – merely intended to display good but lofty intentions. States are supportive of global principles in favour of indigenous peoples, but their reluctance is evident when it comes to merging international with national law. For example, Norway has long been a champion of indigenous peoples' rights in international forums. Norway was instrumental in forming the ILO convention 169 and was also first to ratify it (cf. Minde, 2001, and Chapter 5 in this volume). Article 14 of the ILO convention 169 states that "rights of ownership and possession of the peoples concerned over the lands which they traditionally occupy shall be recognized ... Particular attention shall be paid to the situation of nomadic peoples and shifting cultivators in this respect." The language could not be more fitting to the Sami of the Nordic countries, but here the issue is still pending – in the case of Norway, due to government insistence on a more lax interpretation of the ILO convention (Nilsen, Chapter 9). Norway is not the only country dragging her feet, however. As yet, only twelve countries have ratified this convention. Sweden, Finland and Russia, who also have Sami populations, have not done so. In all of these countries – Norway included – the issues of indigenous self-determination, and particularly the collective property rights concerning land and water, are the main obstacles (cf. Tuulentie, Chapter 14).

The Biodiversity Convention also remains still very much a castle in the air in many countries. With regard to Canada, Barsh and Henderson (Chapter 3) conclude that the "positive image of Canadian leadership in the empowerment of indigenous peoples is not reflected ... in Canada's response to its own legal obligations under the Convention on Biological Diversity"... Canada is certainly not alone in falling short of fulfilling the demands of a convention. In some instances, not even domestic legislation seems to make an impact. Nicaragua, for example, has one of the most advanced domestic legislations with regard to indigenous peoples. Yet the government's readiness to comply with its own rules is questionable, as has been demonstrated in the Mayagna

Awas Tingni case and in Dry Canal case described by Acosta in this publication (Chapter 11).

The question of how nation states are living up to international human rights principles and their obligations regarding indigenous collective rights to their traditional territories, and their terrestrial and marine resources, is one requiring further research. This book should be seen as a small contribution that highlights some of the key questions.

Rights to Culture

At the end of the International Decade, perhaps the most worrying concern is that indigenous peoples continue to be under heavy pressure from global market forces that are not under indigenous, national or international control. Indigenous peoples are increasingly affected by the impact of the demand for natural resources, industrialization and modernization, trade, and migration (cf. Nilsen, Chapter 9; Jan Åge Riseth, Chapter 12). Examples may be drawn from many parts of the world and have a prominent place in this book: the extraction of mineral oil in the Northern territories of Canada and Alaska (Rober Snyder, Daniel Williams and George Peterson, Chapter 6; Jull, Chapter 2), the interests of pharmaceutical companies in exploiting indigenous ecological knowledges (Daes, Chapter 4), logging and de-forestation in Finland (Jukka Nyyssönen, Chapter 13) and Nicaragua (Acosta, Chapter 11), the over-extraction of marine resources in Norway and Canada (Anthony Davis and Svein Jentoft, Chapter 10; Einar Eythórsson, Chapter 8) and New Zealand (Hersoug Chapter 7), water-powered mega-projects, such as in Norway (Minde, Chapter 5; Nilsen, Chapter 9) and the planning of an inter-oceanic railway in Nicaragua (Acosta, Chapter 11).

Legislation at an international and national level is essential for shielding indigenous communities from some of these forces, but legal instruments are scarcely sufficient, for the simple reason that governments, for instance, often ignore these if it is in their interests to do so. As Daes points out in Chapter 4, the Convention of Biological Diversity was a crucial step, insofar as it recognizes the need to "respect, preserve and maintain" the ecological knowledge of indigenous peoples and to ensure that the benefits of commercial applications are shared equitably. But enforcement is of crucial importance, since it is private multinational companies, and not nation states, who are involved. In Chapter 11 Acosta describes a case in point, where the Nicaraguan government was censured for disregarding the communal rights of indigenous peoples, as codified in Nicaraguan law.

What must be understood is that these trends often have detrimental, irreversible consequences for the indigenous communities affected, which generous compensation schemes can never rectify. Indigenous communities do not only suffer economic loss, when they are driven off their land and have to live with the ecological degradation that follows. Indigenous peoples also suffer "culture loss" (cf. Peterson, Williams and Snyder, Chapter 6). The intimate economic, social and cultural relationship that indigenous peoples have with their traditional land and waters makes this point a particularly important one. As Watters (2001/2002, 239/40) makes clear "...culture and the environment are intertwined for many indigenous peoples, they are indivisible. Any harm to one is almost certain to damage the other and injury to both is a substantial threat to identity and therefore even survival"... Stevens (1997, p. 3) also argues that

> To a considerable degree, the state of the land and their continued rights to inhabit and live from it are intrinsic not only to many indigenous peoples' welfare, but also to their cultural survival. Often their ways of life and identity are tightly linked to particular territories and places, and to specific ecosystems and natural and cultural resources. Their ways of life and their continued existence as peoples are threatened by loss of autonomy over their lands and their livelihood and by the destruction of the environmental basis of their distinctive cultures and identities.

So, if Watters and Stevens are correct, and there is no reason to believe that they are not, how do we estimate in money terms the loss of belonging, the intimate bonds and sense of place? It is, of course, much more difficult to assess and value culture loss than economic and nature loss, for instance within the framework of a compensation programme. The market mechanism provides little guidance in settling the issue. According to Snyder, Williams and Peterson (Chapter 6), the problem was raised in connection with the Exxon Valdez oil spill in Alaska. But it equally relevant in, for instance, the case of the Dry Canal in Nicaragua described by Acosta in Chapter 11, and the Alta river case described by Minde in Chapter 5. Obviously, there are things for which money cannot compensate – which do not mean, of course, that indigenous peoples should not be compensated when they become victims of culture loss. Social research has a role in providing an insight into the complex links that exist between indigenous society, culture and nature, including the complicated issue of culture loss assessment. Typically, as Snyder, Williams and Peterson point out, this would require in each case an inter-disciplinary research approach.

Resource Management
Ironically, well-intentioned state management regimes, which were established to conserve natural resources and secure sustainable development, have in many instances affected indigenous peoples negatively. As Kaul (2002, p.13) notes:

> Many environmental agreements have been adopted pertaining to the Arctic—seeking to limit "tragedies of the commons" that were not necessarily caused, or at least,

not caused alone by local people. Thus, local people find their development options curtailed due to past forms of resource over-utilization (e.g. over-fishing and over-hunting); and they find themselves at the receiving end of current forms of over-utilization (e.g. the effects of global warming).

Indigenous peoples are often among those locals most severely affected by efforts to protect the environment, because their stakes and aspirations are basically disregarded. With reference to the Arctic, Nuttall (1998, p.1) claims that "science-based resource management systems designed to safeguard wildlife and the Arctic environment have, for the most part, ignored indigenous perspectives". But in some instances, steps have been taken to rectify the errors made. A case in point is the 1999 ruling of Canada's Supreme Court respecting centuries-old treaty rights between the British government and the Mi'kmaq nation (Davis and Jentoft, Chapter 10). Here, the Mi'kmaq successfully argued that the treaty protected them from government interference in their subsistence and commercial fishing practices. In Norway, the introduction of the vessel quota system in 1990 provoked similar reactions from the Sami parliament, which led to changes – albeit small ones – in the fisheries management system (Nilsen, Chapter 9). In New Zealand it took a long time, and lot of political activism, before the Maori fisheries' rights and interests were recognised as something that the government-installed quota system would have to take into account. As in Canada, Maori fishermen were able to invoke a treaty with the colonial power (Hersoug, Chapter 7).

Inspired by the World Commission on Environment and Development (Brundtland Report) and Agenda 21, which resulted from the first World Summit on Sustainable Development in Rio in 1992, we have witnessed a growing appreciation of the need for the stronger involvement of indigenous organisations and communities in natural resource management decision-making. "Co-management" regimes are currently being introduced in many countries around the world (Wilson et al, 2003) and these hold much promise for indigenous peoples (cf. Jull, Chapter 2; Jentoft, 1998). Agenda 21 stated that "…indigenous people and their communities and other local communities have a vital role in environmental management and development because of their knowledge and traditional practices." (UN, 1992). In other words, top-down management regimes, where indigenous communities are left to play a passive receiving role of rules and regulations, should be avoided. No doubt, if taken seriously and implemented in practice, the recommendation will result in a major management reform in most countries that have indigenous peoples within their borders.

It is important to note that Agenda 21 has also made state governments responsible for enabling the effective participation of indigenous peoples in achieving sustainable development. Decision-making processes must become more inclusive of indigenous peoples' interests and concerns. Secure rights are important, but only as a first step. Watters argues, with respect to the Sami:

> These concerns highlight the necessity for the state to examine its decision-making processes with an emphasis on shared governance and participation, while ensuring access to justice to administrative and juridical review. It is only by institutionalising governance and participation, especially in agency decision-making, that rights retain meaning. Moreover, it is the duty of the state to meet these standards. The burden is not on the Sami to justify them. (Watters, 2001/2002, p. 301)

The Nordic countries are not alone in failing to meet such principles. At best, states adopt a passive, reactive position. These issues never surface unless indigenous peoples introduce them onto the public agenda. However, this should not always be interpreted as bad will, so much as a lack of imagination regarding exactly what needs to be done and who is capable of doing whatever is required to be done. Community-based management is not all that common in non-indigenous settings, either. Typically, natural management regimes work from the top down based on a command and control principle (Jentoft, 2000). A policy brief from the World Resources Institute conference held in Italy in 2002 may provide some helpful guidelines for management reform in both indigenous and non-indigenous situations. The conference concluded that, in order secure full democratic participation in resource management, the following strategy should be employed (cf. Ribot, 2002):

1. Work with democratic local institutions as a first priority
2. Transfer sufficient and appropriate powers
3. Transfer powers in the form of secured rights
4. Support equity and justice
5. Establish minimum environmental standards
6. Establish fair and accessible adjudication
7. Support local civic education
8. Give decentralization time
9. Develop indicators for monitoring and evaluating decentralization and its out comes.

Indigenous peoples are not explicitly referred to in this brief, but since much of the human rights legislation that has been invoked in support of indigenous peoples is of a general nature; these recommendations would apply no less to indigenous peoples than to non-indigenous peoples. However, some of these points require comment from an indigenous peoples' perspective.

The first remark regards the rights issue. As stated in ILO convention 169, indigenous peoples have rights of property concerning their communal lands and waters, not only rights of use. Consequently, as Barsh and Henderson remind us (Chapter 3), indigenous peoples are not simply 'stakeholders' within their territories, as this term is commonly defined. They argue that a stakeholder can be anyone – an institution, an individual or a group that expresses interest in a particular government decision: "The notion of 'stakeholders' … admits no levels, or degrees of rights or interest, it is merely an euphemism for 'general public' and enables bureaucrats to collapse all the groups competing for their attention into a single, undifferentiated mass."

However, as in the case of Sami coastal fishermen in northern Norway (Chapter 8), Eythórsson holds that indigenous resource users are not even considered as stakeholders with a right to be heard in the decision-making process. Their ethnic status is not considered an issue at all, and is certainly not something that should grant indigenous communities the right of representation at the management decision-making table. It is only very recently that Sami interests and aspirations have become legitimate concerns vis à vis state fisheries authorities (Nilsen, Chapter 9). However, within the prevailing management institutions they do not have the necessary power to make much of an impact. As Davis and Jentoft point out in Chapter 10, the future does not hold out much promise that things will change in favour of the Sami fishermen, as the government keeps insisting that Sami fisheries must continue to be managed within the prevailing system that applies to all fishermen in Norway – indigenous and non-indigenous alike.

Non-indigenous resource users often invade and gradually take over indigenous lands, leading to resource depletion, ecosystem degradation and loss. This is now the situation in Nicaragua, with the agricultural frontier in Nicaragua moving east into the rainforest and the coastal estuaries and plains. Little by little, therefore, indigenous peoples become a minority, even within their traditional territories. Thus, demarcation of indigenous lands is essential, as is stressed in the Mayagna Awas Tingni case. As indigenous territories become ethnically mixed, and non-indigenous groups become dependent on indigenous natural resources for livelihoods and profit, governments become less willing to protect indigenous interests and safeguard indigenous rights.

The ambivalence of governments with regard to ILO convention 169 must be understood in this perspective. Tuulentie (Chapter 14) also highlights this issue, in the case of Finland and the Sami Bill of 1990:

Traditional livelihoods among the indigenous people, such as fishing, hunting and reindeer herding, were regarded as an integral part of the Sami culture in the legislation proposal. The problem is that those "traditional Sami livelihoods", particularly hunting and fishing, are also regarded as an important part of Finnish national identity. … The wilderness, as a symbol of freedom from authority and modern civilisation, is related directly to this view, and taking away this kind of freedom is seen as controverting the ideas of equality.

Partly for this reason, indigenous communities should at least consider sharing management responsibilities, with the aim of reaching agreement on environmental standards, extraction practices and adjudication procedures, and tapping into the management expertise and support that state management agencies may provide. As Jull argues (Chapter 2), "[o]nly the partnership and co-management of indigenous and senior governmental authorities will bring adequate power and funds to bear on the problem".

Secondly, the issue of adjudication is worth noting. Although crucial in its own right, securing the rights to land and water is only one step on the way to sustainable development. Effective management is also a prerequisite. Management measures must be put in place to prevent fragile ecosystems from being harmed, due to over-exploitation or otherwise ecologically unsound behaviour. Rules must be developed and enforcement put in place. In addition, a proper organization for carrying out these functions must be established, one that is representative of the user groups affected by management decisions. As Berkes (2000, p.125) contends, " [a]ll systems of management require appropriate institutions. That is, for a group of interdependent hunters to function effectively, there has to be a social organization for co-ordination, co-operation, rule making and rule enforcement." His remark also applies to users of other common-pool natural resources.

Management structures of this kind are inherently confrontational because they restrict people's access to, and extraction of, natural resources. Indigenous communities must themselves agree upon the rules of the game and they must themselves become involved in, and be made responsible for, management decision-making and conflict resolution. The New Zealand aboriginals have gained substantially in securing their collective rights to marine resources, but they are still struggling to sort out their internal differences on how to share them in an equitable fashion (cf. Hersoug, Chapter 7). Institutional mechanisms for the resolution of conflict within indigenous communities must also, therefore, be put in place. Collective rights to natural resources are important, but they can only do part of the job. Where there is scarcity, decisions and rules must be established concerning the sharing of that which is collectively owned and controlled. But such rules should not be unilaterally imposed upon an indigenous community by a central authority.

Thirdly, local indigenous communities are not always well organised and otherwise equipped to assume management responsibilities. In many instances, communities are ridden with conflicts, inequity and an inability to co-operate. These are problems that must be addressed as a pre-condition for, or integral part of, the management reform process. Community-based co-management systems can only work if indigenous communities are sufficiently organised to exercise regulatory functions based on "secure rights" (cf. Riseth, Chapter 12). In order to achieve this, their civic institutions must be strengthened, including educational ones, as expressed in Ribot's brief, referred to earlier in this article. Indigenous peoples must organize themselves. They cannot wait until the state authorities take the initiative. Indigenous community-based management organizations must rely on voluntary local support, and cannot successfully operate if they are enforced externally on communities. As Kaul (2002, p. 7) observes,

> ... as experience has shown, where development is not 'home-grown' and is not rooted in local politics, policy co-ordination among local interests tends to be relatively weak. Supply-driven – as opposed to local, demand-driven – development may also have a negative impact. It may skew incentive structures and initiate dependency on outside support or certain negative development trends that may not support local development in the long run.

The state can, and should, provide organisational support, but the primary agent must be the indigenous community (cf. Hersoug, Chapter 7). The community may seek assistance from the government, from non-governmental organizations (NGOs) or from universities, but they must themselves carry the main burden, for the simple reason that organization is something that cannot be imposed on them. As Nyyssönen argues (Chapter 13), to be effective, a management system must be regarded as legitimate among the resource users. A sense of ownership of the management system among the users is crucial. For that, participation, democracy and transparency are essential.

This Book

The chapters of this volume are organised in three sections: In the first section the authors are addressing indigenous people's issues that have appeared in recent years in international fora, such as the UN, that pertain to human rights. A common theme is the development that has occurred in the aftermath of the Rio meeting on sustainable management and the advent of ILO Convention 169 concerning the rights of indigenous peoples. The second section contains contributions from authors, who focus particularly on indigenous rights to, and the use and management of, marine resources. In most instances, indigenous peoples' fish harvesting practices are managed within a legal and institutional framework that is not their own making, and over which they have little, if any, control. The conflicts that are bound to appear as a consequence are a theme running through several chapters here. These draw on Norwegian, Canadian, New Zealand and US experiences. The third section is made up of chapters that examine similar rights, use and management relating to communal land and terrestrial resources in countries such as Nicaragua, Norway and Finland. In all

these countries, indigenous peoples are experiencing an increasing encroachment of external forces on their traditional territories.

In Chapter 2, Peter Jull observes that in the world's hinterland regions, including much of Australia, northern Norway, northern Canada, and the circumpolar region as a whole, the post-1945 collision of the white man's industrial
culture and indigenous 'sustainable development' values has led to a negotiation of new forms of political economy. The need for such an accommodation,
and for respite from the Western world's restless and relentless energy, has
found surprising recognition through the recent environmental movement, even
in its most formal documents such as the Brundtland Report of 1987. Now, Jull
argues, it is becoming clear that indigenous peoples are not only rescuing their
traditional territories from the political and developmental vagaries of outsiders, but are providing new models of governance and inter-cultural reconciliation in their stubborn fight for the protection of their lands, fresh water and seas.
Jull points to the fact that, despite their social-economic and economic disadvantage, indigenous peoples are achieving what highly paid official experts and
research bodies have been unable to do, and reminds us that the key to environmental protection and human rights is political will, not wealth or expertise.

Russel Lawrence Barsh and James (Sakej) Youngblood criticize Canada's
follow-up strategy of the Convention of Biological Diversity, in Chapter 3. For
these two authors, it is a great paradox that Canada plays a very progressive
role in international fora when indigenous rights are on the agenda, but is rather
passive on the home front when it comes to implementing its commitments, for
instance those regarding indigenous communities' rights to manage their own
lands and control their own development process. They argue that Canada still
has a long way to go to comply with the international law, for example when
it comes to recognizing indigenous peoples' traditional ecological knowledge;
protecting their customary resource use practices; providing support for educational institutions in indigenous communities; and establishing the necessary
mechanisms that will allow indigenous peoples to participate in decision-making processes where they have high stakes.

Indigenous peoples' experience of globalization is Erica-Irene Daes' main
concern in Chapter 4. While globalization creates an immense market for the
dissemination of ideas and new voices, it also makes it easier for one voice to
suppress the voice of others. She argues that globalization is threatening the
"confidentiality of indigenous peoples' most private and sacred knowledge".
In her view, the Internet is a mixed blessing, as it makes it much easier to appropriate illicitly for the purpose of economic gain the special knowledge that
indigenous peoples possess. The legislation that can secure indigenous peoples'
intellectual property is not in place in most countries, with a few notable ex-
ceptions. As the Special Rapporteur of the UN Sub-Commission on Promotion
and Protection of Human Rights, Professor Daes drafted a set of guidelines that

will provide indigenous peoples with the authority to license or veto research and affirm the applicability of customary law as the ultimate determinant of indigenous cultural and intellectual property rights. Although internationally accepted principles are important, the most critical factor, and her gravest concern, is their effective enforcement.

In Chapter 5, Henry Minde depicts the events and developments relating to the Alta River hydro-electric project in the Sami heartland of Norway, which in many ways represented a watershed in the relationship between the Sami and the Norwegian state. He raises two historical questions: why did the project become so politically inflamed concerning Sami issues, and how did the Norwegian political system towards the Sami claims of land rights and self-determination change in consequence? Minde employs the 'domain' concept to demonstrate the power structure of minority politics relating to the Sami before and after the Alta affair. He argues that over time such a domain can develop its own standards, which take more account of particular interests within its own domain than of overall national or universal interests. He argues that the Norwegian assimilation policy, the development of an international indigenous movement, and the outcome of the Alta affair, can be analysed as contributing factors to the fall of the old domain. It led to the Norwegian authorities' acceptance, during the process of revision of ILO Convention 107 (concerning indigenous and tribal peoples), that the Sami movement was different from ordinary interest groups within the liberal political system. Minde concludes that, as a key actor in reaching the compromise that led to ILO Convention 169, and as the first state to ratify the convention, Norway has a special global responsibility to defend the human rights status of indigenous peoples.

Robert Snyder, Daniel Williams and George Peterson examine, in Chapter 6, some of the debates regarding indigenous peoples that have surfaced in the aftermath of the Exxon Valdez oil spill in Alaska in 1989. Past attempts by economists and anthropologists to conceptualize and value culture loss suggest, according to the three authors, that greater effort is needed to open up new dialogues that recognize the perspectives of all those participating in resource valuation processes. They argue that economic methods employed to value social and material goods associated with indigenous peoples' 'sense of place' in the Arctic region develop only a portion of a more holistic problem of resource valuation for indigenous peoples practising subsistence-based livelihoods. Anthropological approaches to culture loss and valuation attempt a more holistic understanding of an indigenous people's sense of place, highlighting the uneven power relations embedded in the politics of resource valuation. They discuss these issues in the context of economic efforts to conduct an Environmental Resource Damage Assessment (ERDA) of the Exxon Valdez oil spill for the value of the losses suffered by indigenous cultures affected by the spill.

In Chapter 7, Bjørn Hersoug depicts the fisheries management system in New Zealand, as it relates to the Maori. In 1986, New Zealand introduced a Quota Management System (QMS) based on Individual Transferable Quotas (ITQs), without the fisheries authorities paying much attention to aboriginal rights represented by Maori claims (dating back to 1840). By mobilizing round the Treaty of Waitangi of 1840, Maori tribes managed to strike a beneficial deal with the Ministry of Fisheries and the existing industry, granting them ten per cent of all ITQs, plus a financial compensation. Nearly two decades later, the Maori control one third of the entire fishing industry. However, Hersoug observes, further allocation of the quotas to eighty different tribes has proved very difficult. It can be claimed that the solution of the 'Maori problem' was an absolute precondition for the successful establishment of the ITQ system. On the other hand, he argues, the QMS provided the 'currency', making it possible to sort out the Maori commercial claims. Finally he claims that the provision of the separate sphere of Maori customary fishing is an innovative attempt to establish the best of both worlds, keeping the Maori in touch with their cultural fishing roots, whilst also participating in the modern commercial sector. What makes New Zealand special, so that in many ways it may be regarded as a success story of indigenous resource rights claims, is that Maori interests now have large stakes in all the fisheries sectors: commercial, customary and recreational fisheries, as well as aquaculture.

In Chapter 8, Einar Eythórsson explains the virtual disappearance, in cultural terms, of Norway's coastal fishing Sami. Over the past century, the Sami speaking people along the northern Norwegian coast have vanished as a group with their own distinct culture. The author shows how the ethnic identity of the coastal Sami has been suppressed, resulting in a pariah status. Eythórsson uses Foucault's distinction between power relation and domination, and characterises the relation between the Sami minority and the Norwegian majority as one of Norwegian domination, i.e. as a fundamentally oppressive relationship that does not leave room for Sami resistance. As a consequence, the coastal Sami indigenous identity has not only been rendered irrelevant in the larger Norwegian society: it has also come to be regarded as a heavy stigma, preventing ethnic identity formation and hindering resistance against racial oppression. Eythórsson shows how the ethnic taboo was broken through what might be characterized as a coastal Sami revolt. Through this revolt, the coastal Sami identity was transformed and made relevant in different fields of action, including struggles over natural resources such as fish in northern Norway. Eythórsson finds that the coastal Sami are no longer a pariah group, dominated by the Norwegian majority population, as they once were. Rather, they have become an actor playing an increasingly important part in the political process of fisheries resource management.

Ragnar Nilsen, in Chapter 9, analyses the consequences of the Norwegian fishery policy in the coastal Sami area during the period after the Second World War. In spite of open access to fish resources, coastal Sami families have given up their fish adaptations in the modernization process, as it turns out to be very difficult to combine seasonal small-scale fishing and small-scale agriculture. Stimulated by the state industrialization policies, the cod-fish resource has, to a large degree, been taken over by trawler and industry companies. A more general Sami struggle to achieve greater recognition of their indigenous political and human rights, at the beginning of the 1980s, stimulated the coastal Sami protests against these policies. Nilsen finds that Sami fisheries politicians are pursuing a double strategy: on the one hand, they have demanded a thorough investigation into their legal rights and status as an indigenous people in Norway. On the other hand, they have worked to establish political and economic institutions, to support the Sami economic and cultural development. These measures have included public support for small fishing vessels and landing facilities in coastal Sami areas.

In Chapter 10, Anthony Davis and Svein Jentoft observe that access to and use of natural resources as a cornerstone in sustaining indigenous cultures has recently obtained considerable international attention. Access to marine resources has become a key issue for many aboriginal peoples struggling to move from dependency on the nation state to self-determining agency. Their chapter describes and compares recent developments concerning Eastern Canadian Mi'kmaq and northern Norwegian Sami initiatives to achieve a recognition and realization of their aboriginal entitlements. They outline and discuss the core characteristics of the Canadian and Norwegian nation state responses to these initiatives, with an emphasis on the implications of aboriginal entitlements for the present 'privilege allocation' premise, and the paternalistic nature of fisheries management systems. The authors conclude with a discussion of the potential for an alliance between coastal zone non-indigenous peoples and indigenous peoples, for the purpose of developing an alternative approach to fisheries management that will enhance local agency in, and the ecological sustainability of, fisheries livelihoods.

In Chapter 11, María Luisa Acosta describes the situation for the various indigenous peoples of Nicaragua's Atlantic provinces, and their ability to protect their legal rights to communal lands. Her case study is a recently proposed plan to build a double track railway – the so-called Dry Canal – across the continent. This is indeed a mega-project that will cut deeply into indigenous territories, in this case those belonging to the Rama Indians. The paradox, however, is that indigenous peoples should from a legal perspective be well protected from encroachment of their land. The fact of the matter is that the Nicaraguan government has been dragging its feet by only reluctantly – if at all

– enforcing the constitutional rights of its indigenous peoples. The Dry Canal affair is no exception to this rule. Acosta explains the content of the domestic legal framework regarding indigenous peoples, the violations committed by the government, and the advancements made by indigenous communities in gaining a stronger voice in the political process. She argues that their situation is not a hopeless one.

Jan Åge Riseth's topic, in Chapter 12, is the local management strategies among Sami reindeer herders in two regions in Norway. Riseth demonstrates that there are striking regional differences in herd productivity. In the south, the herders have, through a sustainable herding strategy, managed to maintain an acceptable level of meat production. This is founded on a long-lasting co-operation between herders and the local reindeer administration. The strategy involves protecting winter lichen pastures, by exploiting them only during the winter season. In the north, the herders have started to make use of the winter lichen pastures in the autumn as well, causing a deterioration of these pastures in large areas of the inner Finnmark region. The author explains how the different pasture strategies in the south and north are caused by an interplay of different factors. These include ecological factors, such as easy access to winter pastures during the autumn in the north. In addition, the relations between the herders and the reindeer administration are different in the two regions. Finally, the strategies for productivity optimization are dissimilar: in the south, the Sami reindeer herders have tried to increase meat production per animal. In the north, the herders have increased the number of animals, with a negative consequence for the natural resources and the herders' incomes.

In Chapter 13, Jukka Nyyssönen analyses the environmental efficiency of the institutions responsible for forestry and reindeer herding resource management in the Inari region in Finland. Forest Government and the reindeer herding co-operatives are studied as property rights regimes. Nyyssönen argues that, on the surface, the case of Inari is one of a sustainable indigenous economy replaced by a state-driven over-use of formerly common resources, now claimed to be state property. The forestry industry is still the major threat to the reindeer winter pasturelands. Inefficient management by the herding co-operatives has also worsened the pastureland situation. The Sami response has been to increase their stock of reindeer, but this has only exacerbated the problem. The power structure in the Inari resource management has also hindered the Sami from becoming involved and exercising any influence over resource management that, according to Nyyssönen, has led to a collapse of the legitimacy of both the resource management and the land ownership structure. He argues that the main reason for resource over-use is the régime structure, as well as an unsuccessful Sami strategy.

Seija Tuulentie's point of departure, in Chapter 14, is the observation that national identity is firmly embedded in our entire view of the world. Nationalism, as a cultural and collective identity, shapes the relationship of the majority and the minority in a nation state. She explores how Finlands's majority population has constructed their own national identity when dealing with the legal rights claims of the indigenous Sami (former Lapp) minority. Her main finding is that national identity is maintained through an omnipresent discourse and through the rhetorical strengthening of the existing situation. For the majority population, not only the question of Sami land ownership, but also the issue of Sami language rights, are contentious issues. Those who belong to the majority take the nation state for granted. For the Sami minority, it has been necessary to adopt the same national rhetoric in order to make their voice heard.

In their summary chapter (Chapter 15), Henry Minde and Ragnar Nilsen depict the main barriers that prevent indigenous peoples from managing their own natural resources. They point out that there exist, among nation states, significant variations in indigenous self-government, and in the degree of control over these resources. In some countries, indigenous groups have managed to establish a certain degree of autonomy through elected assemblies and through delegated autonomy or co-management arrangements. In other countries, indigenous peoples have been far less successful in gaining management control. The two authors conclude that political mobilization through global indigenous networks appears to have been instrumental in modifying the central power structure, in the case of certain national states and in some fields of resource use. Indigenous empowerment does, however, meet considerable obstacles, particularly at the level of national state. They argue that it is essential for future research to focus on the interplay between the indigenous peoples' struggle for self-determination and the structures of power that exist in national states.

References

Anaya, James: "The Developing International Jurisprudence of Indigenous Rights within the U.N. Treaty Bodies and the Inter-American Rights Institutions." Presentation at the Conference on Indigenous Politics: Aspects of Power and Democracy. Tromsø, 3-5 October 2002.

Berkes, Fikret: "Indigenous Knowledge and Resource Management in the Canadian Sub-arctic." In F. Berkes and C. Folke: *Linking Social and Ecological Systems: Management Practices and Social Mechanisms for Building Resilience*. Cambridge: Cambridge University Press, 2000.

Jentoft, Svein (ed.): Commons in a Cold Climate. Coastal Fisheries and Reindeer Pastoralism in North Norway. The Co-management Approach. Casterton Hall: The Parthenon Publishing Group, 1998.

Jentoft, Svein: "The Community: A Missing Link of Fisheries Management." *Marine Policy*, 24, pp. 53-59, 2000.

Kaul, Inge: Challenges of Human Development in the Arctic. New York: UNDP - United Nations Development Program, 2002.

Minde, Henry: Sami Land Rights in Norway: a Test Case for Indigenous Peoples. *International Journal on Minority Group Rights*. Vol. 8, pp. 107-125, 2001.

Nuttall, Mark: Protecting the Arctic: Indigenous Peoples and Cultural Survival. Amsterdam: Harwood Academic Publishers, 1998.

Ribot, Jesse C.: Democratic Decentralization of Natural Resources: Institutionalizing Popular Participation. World Resources Institute, 2002.

Stevens, Stan: "Conservation Through Cultural Survival. Indigenous Peoples and Protected Areas." Washington D.C., Island Press, 1997.

UN, Principle 21, Agenda 21: Report of the United Nations Conference on Environment and Development. Rio de Janeiro, 3-4 June 1992.

Watters, Lawrence: Indigenous Peoples and the Environment: Convergence from a Nordic Perspective. *UCLA Journal of Environmental Law and Policy*, Vol. 20, 2001/2002, No. 2, pp. 237-304).

Douglas Clyde Wilson, Jesper Raakjær Nielsen and Poul Degnbol (eds.): The Fisheries Co-management Experience: Accomplishments, Challenges and Prospects. Kluwer, Dordrecht. 2003.

The World

CHAPTER 2

The Politics of Sustainable Development: Reconciliation in Indigenous Hinterlands

Peter Jull[1]

Introduction: The 'Brundtland Report'

In April 1987 the report of the World Commission on Environment and Development, or 'Brundtland Report', was released (Brundtland 1987). It had tremendous impact around the world as the strongest set of propositions yet made by an official body on the world environment and its interlocking sets of problems and needs. It established the term 'sustainable development' at once as a goal, a standard, and, too often, an empty cliché used by governments, policy-makers, and commentators everywhere. It also had immediate effect among Arctic indigenous peoples. For instance, on that April 1987 morning Inuit Circumpolar Conference (ICC) president Mary Simon was flying from Ottawa to Greenland for important meetings and community visits on sensitive environmental and related issues and briefed herself en route from press reports of the report's release (Jull 1991b; 1991c; 1999a). When she arrived in Greenland's capital Nuuk she began at once to talk up the report's importance, as well as its findings and recommendations. It would be some days or weeks before full texts of the Brundtland Report reached the far corners of indigenous hinterlands.

Even now Brundtland's powerful brief section on indigenous peoples, 'Empowering Vulnerable Groups', is too little known (1987, 114-117). First it notes that 'processes of development' gradually integrate local communities into larger social and economic frameworks.

> But some communities – so-called indigenous or tribal peoples – remain isolated because of such factors as physical barriers to communication or marked differences in social and cultural practices. Such groups are found in North America, in Australia, in the Amazon Basin, in Central America, in the forests and hills of Asia, in the deserts of North Africa, and elsewhere.

---

[1] The author wishes to thank Louise Harrold for discussions of her research on co-management which were stimulating aids to the writing of this paper.

Northern Scandinavia, i.e., Sápmi, and Northern Russia could have been added to that list. Then the report turns to the importance of indigenous eco-cultural systems.

> The isolation of many such people has meant the preservation of a traditional way of life in close harmony with the natural environment. Their very survival has depended on their ecological awareness and adaptation. But their isolation has also meant that few of them have shared in national economic and social development; this may be reflected in their poor health, nutrition, and education. These communities are the repositories of vast accumulations of traditional knowledge and experience that links humanity with its ancient origins. (...) It is a terrible irony that as formal development reaches more deeply into rain forests, deserts, and other isolated environments, it tends to destroy the only cultures that have proved able to thrive in these environments. (Brundtland 1987, 114-115)

Rarely has the connection between intact indigenous societies and remaining 'wild' areas been so well made. The report then goes on to make the only recommendations it logically can.

> Hence the recognition of traditional rights must go hand in hand with measures to protect the local institutions that enforce responsibility in resource use. And this recognition must also give local communities a decisive voice in the decisions about resource use in their area. (Brundtland 1987, 115-116)

The report calls for social and economic programs to enhance the well-being of indigenous peoples in these hinterland areas – something which Brundtland's Norway has done more successfully since 1945 than any other country – before concluding:

> In terms of sheer numbers, these isolated, vulnerable groups are small. But their marginalization is a symptom of a style of development that tends to neglect both human and environmental considerations. Hence a more careful and sensitive consideration of their interests is a touchstone of a sustainable development policy. (Brundtland 1987, 116)

This important defence of sparsely populated hinterlands remaining sparsely populated hinterlands, with their unique cultures intact is too rarely made in official documents. It remains an astonishing idea to many governments.

The World of 'Northern Territories' since 1945

The subject of this paper is the process of resistance and political activism of previously 'invisible' indigenous peoples in national hinterlands vis-à-vis national and international development policies. Through their defence of home-lands and culture, and the search for more power in their lives and in the protection, management, and development of land and sea territories, Sami, Inuit, and other peoples of Northern Eurasia and North America, as well as Australia's Aboriginal peoples and Torres Strait Islanders, have been shaping new political institutions and political cultures. This has been a negotiation, sometimes implicit and visible in hindsight, sometimes explicit.

Circumpolar governments were drawn into national northlands during and after World War II. This was particularly true in North Norway, Russia, Alaska, Northern Canada, and Greenland – and also in Northern Australia. After the agonies of world Depression and War, there was a too-simple faith in material solutions to problems. The official emphasis in all these areas was construction and material improvement, usually in expectation of large profits from large projects to follow. Defence, mining, oil and gas development, hydro-electric power, or physical incorporation of the hinterland into the nation-state through road, rail, and port building, not to mention school, health, and administration facilities, were often carried out in massive assault-style D-Day operations.

Not surprisingly these intrusions have often been felt by indigenous peoples and other long-established locals as an assault. In a 1966 film designed to encourage northern investment and development, *The North has Changed,* Canada's Department of Indian Affairs and Northern Development (DIAND) began with a fur-clad indigenous person gliding over a lake or bay in a traditional kayak, whereupon the screen goes blank in an explosion and we find, next, great machines and trucks ripping into the sub-surface to fast-throbbing music of excitement! However, it is noteworthy that a major initial catalyst for political mobilization among indigenous peoples in North Norway, Northern Canada, and Greenland was not so much outsiders' resource exploitation but large-scale projects to better the material living conditions and facilities available to northern people themselves. These were carried out, initially, with little regard to the wishes or expressed needs of indigenous peoples, and brought many forms of dislocation, from influxes of transient work forces, to physical relocation from long established camping and hunting grounds, to bewildering new lifestyles and official controls. In other words, pace and shape of change were initial problems and political motivations in many areas *before* land, sea, and resource rights in the narrow sense, or environmental protection, became central. However, all were intimately related because the new social ways indigenous peoples were expected to adopt were intended to prepare a new indigenous proletariat to service the activities of industrial societies moving northwards.

When it became clear that the White Man intended to make new uses of water and land incompatible with traditional livelihoods, or with the maintenance of viable species habitat for such livelihoods, a critical political bonding took place. If the young and school-educated indigenous had the big ideas and angry words to talk back to the White Man while their parents and grand-parents cowered, the elders knew the ancient territory and its capacities, and were outraged at the arrogance and vandalism of governments and the developers they licensed. Tracked vehicles tearing up tundra, ships smashing through previously ice-fast seas, aircraft buzzing around reindeer (caribou) herds, explosions set off in wildlife habitat for seismic surveys – it was all a form of madness, and proved that the governments and experts from far away were not morally or intellectually competent to govern the North.

Governments have experienced the new messages from the hinterland in various ways. Some in national capitals have appreciated the inevitable maturing of regional opinion and desire for equal social and political rights, and seen this as a success story for public programs and policies. Many others have seen it as ingratitude by people on whom many good and costly things were being bestowed. Some have seen it as an affront to the dignity and authority of national institutions, or to the self-esteem and good intentions of the majority national culture. Most have failed, at least initially, to recognise that the challenge contains elements such as a knowledge revolution (especially in relation to understanding nature's processes in exotic environments); a demand for *better* public policy no less than for *more* public benefits and *more* local control of policy; serious proposals or demands for alternatives to resource extraction with its socio-environmental costs; and the call for policies focused on the needs of hinterland society rather than the national economy – or to recognise that these could be legitimate perspectives. Perhaps most difficult has been the demand that hitherto lowly regarded or rustic ways in marginal areas amount to living cultures and languages worth maintaining in themselves, richly meaningful to those who share them even if short of monuments in travel guidebooks.

In respect of sustainable development, by which we mean here *ecologically sustainable development* (ESD), what natural processes will bear without depletion so that they will continue to serve future generations (a central concept of all the indigenous peoples of hinterlands, of course), hinterland peoples frequently have found strong support from environmental science and environmental advocacy groups. The 'old' lore of hinterland peoples is actually 'new' for the White Man who has previously attempted to commodify landscapes as private property and industrial resources. This may also create problems because in the political activism phase indigenous peoples may have the best state of the art advice and advisers, while after winning control of regions or public bodies they may hire the bad old boys from officialdom (not least to show them who's boss now!) or imitate the bad old ways, having seen no other models in their regions. Similarly, social justice won in remote areas may too much resemble the numbing clerical culture of remote offices of the former national northern administration. Part of the disadvantage of the hinterland is the lack of knowledge, e.g., of actual options available or alternatives possible.

Indigenous Internationalism

The era of indigenous internationalism began in 1973 at the Arctic Peoples Conference with Greenlandic, Sami, and Northern Canadian indigenous hinterland peoples sharing their experiences of 'frontier' resource development pressure and other aspects of their marginalisation by government and industry. That event often recognised as the beginning of indigenous internationalism (Kleivan 1992; Jull 1998a; 1998b). Those peoples attending were under pressure in their 'first world' homelands from national resource development and socio-political assimilation or integration policies. The White Man[2] was also feeling pressure. The Yom Kippur War between Israel and Arab countries some weeks earlier and related oil politics were ending the long Post-War economic boom, while Copenhagen itself was dimly lit and chilly as it entered the winter dark thanks to energy restrictions during an Arab oil boycott imposed on Denmark. The main concern of the peoples at the conference was how to survive the 'frontier energy' development policies of governments and industry, to have their livelihoods and vital environments recognised and protected, and to gain real influence in policy-making for their regions.

Building on that experience the Sami and Greenlanders were major participants in the founding of the World Council of Indigenous Peoples (WCIP) in Port Alberni, British Columbia, Canada, in late 1975 (Sanders 1977).[3] That meeting made the shared experience of industrial, government, and settler pressure on lands, waters, and resources of all kinds – i.e., dispossession and *un*sustainable development – the basic currency of world indigenous cooperation and understanding.[4] It was well understood that the pressures on indigenous territories in countries like Paraguay and Guatemala were a good deal less

---

[2]   'The White Man' is a term well understood by indigenous and non-European peoples around the world as an historical term for European domination, almost always by white males. It is not a slip into ill-chosen language, but is carefully chosen.

[3]   Unfortunately Canadian Inuit are usually reluctant to join in projects and gatherings led by Canadian First Nations ('Indians'). Despite the tact of Chief George Manuel and his team before and after Port Alberni, Canadian Inuit did not participate. Indians are patronising and uninformed about Inuit realities and politics, in the Inuit view, a sense constantly reinforced by Indian leaders and representatives misrepresenting (albeit from ignorance as much as intention) the Inuit land/sea and political settlements such as Nunavut, while Inuit organizations make little effort to differentiate among the loudmouths and well-intentioned persons on the Indian side. Inuit uffishness has sometimes weakened indigenous political clout at national and regional levels, but arguably never to the specific disadvantage of Inuit. By speaking quietly Inuit leaders have often been seen by others as more reasonable, despite similar political and territorial objectives to Indian first nations.

[4]   The prologue to the fine new book on British Columbia indigenous-white history, *Making Native Space,* is an evocative account of the initial white arrival and land takeover at the site of Port Alberni (Harris 2002).

'gentlemanly' than in Canada or Norway. The meetings had to be conducted in secrecy and high security to protect Latin American Indian delegations, although some countries, e.g., Paraguay, managed to seize and jail delegates on their return home.

In mid-1977 when the Inuit Circumpolar Conference (ICC) united the Inuit 'nation' of the Arctic for the first time, ever, the host Mayor Eben Hopson of the Inuit North Slope Borough, Barrow, at Alaska's northernmost point, said that the people gathered must have two priorities: protection of the Arctic environment from government and industry, and achievement of maximum regional self-government or home rule powers in their home areas to make that protection and the survival of Inuit culture active and successful (Lauritzen 1983). Since then the Inuit working through ICC have played a major role in indigenous and world environmental advocacy and action, *mirabile dictu,* and the individual Inuit regions, apart from Chukotka, have achieved new tailor-made governments (often with supplementary quasi-government authorities) to assert environmental and other values vis-à-vis the surrounding industrial nation-states which have always threatened to swallow them. This Inuit activism has been an important background factor in establishing the culture and tone of the Arctic Council of which ICC is a founding indigenous member. (National governments of USA, Russia, the five Nordic countries, and Canada form the core of the Council with indigenous peoples including Sami Council, ICC, Aleuts, et al. as Permanent Participants.)

Thirty years after Copenhagen, Sami politics at home and internationally, and elected Sami parliaments in Finland, Norway, and Sweden, have increased recognition of rights and needs, and sharpened the search for political solutions to territory and resource management of land, freshwater, and sea between Sami and non-Sami (IWGIA 1996; Minde 1984; 2001). Greenland Home Rule has brought Inuit control of that country and provided an international case study in leading edge interaction between European liberalism and indigenous self-determination (Close 2002; Kalhauge Nielsen 2001; Jull 1986a). In the Yukon and Northwest Territories (NWT) negotiated land claims settlements, resource management structures, and self-governance have been proceeding or are implemented, while the NWT now has its 7th indigenous premier in office (Jull 2001d). The Inuit eastern half of the NWT has its own land and sea claims settlement and since 1999 has been reconstituted as the self-governing territory of Nunavut (Dahl et al. 2000; Jull 2001a; 2001b; 2001d). These achievements, and those of other peoples around the Arctic and Sub-Arctic, have provided dynamic models and experience for peoples all over the world. No less important has been the impact of these changes on wider public policy and political culture in the strong and wealthy industrial nation-states where they have taken place, and the flow-on effect on national behaviour in international forums.

Important changes since the 1973 conference have included the global surge of environmental understanding, especially that embodied in the Brundtland Report with its call for 'sustainable development'; the collapse of public administration and services in many regions of Russia creating new indigenous opportunities in principle but also many problems or crises in fact (Pika et al. 1996); the spread of neo-liberal economics and 'globalisation'; and the increase in exchanges, cooperation, and networking among the peoples and regions of the Arctic and Sub-Arctic regions, e.g., as practised in the Arctic Council. Another important development, of course, has been the success and spread of international indigenous contacts and mutual support, i.e., *indigenous internationalism,* and the greater focus of world bodies and news/information media on indigenous issues as a result (Jull 1998a; 1998b). Most recently the United Nations Permanent Forum has met for the first time, in 2002, choosing long-time Sami leader Ole Henrik Magga, representing Sami and Inuit at the Forum, as its first Chair.

The submission to the UN 2002 Earth Summit 2002 from the Commonwealth Policy Studies Unit, London, in support of the 54 Commonwealth of Nations (former British Empire) member countries' indigenous peoples, aptly took its title from the uncomfortable indigenous peoples' status as 'the miner's canary' in the world environment, the first to feel the effects of a planet or policies gone wrong. It usefully reviews indigenous sustainable development needs in international relations context (Havemann & Whall 2002).

In the early years after the Brundtland Report was published the central place of indigenous peoples was much highlighted in public events relating to the ethic of sustainable development. That seems to have changed now, with indigenous peoples given all too little attention at the 2002 Earth Summit, as the new ICC president Sheila Watt-Cloutier found (e.g., ICC Canada Press Release, 2-9-2002). It is important for indigenous peoples, especially experienced and well resourced groups in 'first world' countries like Norway, Canada, and Australia, to restore that high indigenous profile.

Canada's Northwest Territories and Nunavut

The Northwest Territories (NWT) and Nunavut make up 34% of Canada's land area, in 1996 having 64,125 people of whom 40,000 were indigenous (in a total Canadian population of 28.5 million then, now over 30 million). Until recent times this huge region was considered by most Canadians, including governments, as (1) a national treasury of undiscovered or unextracted sub-surface wealth in minerals, oil, and gas, and (2) a stark place of unspoiled exotic nature where some isolated peoples continued to practice ancient hunting cultures. Because the region was so vast it was not understood that there might be a basic conflict between these two northern identities. When indigenous peoples

27

and non-indigenous experts with whom they worked began to explain that the North was not a vast undifferentiated mass but a network of intricately inter-related systems, and that damage in particular places might be very widely felt, this was a surprise. Together with growing public awareness of the differing indigenous peoples and ways of life of the North – an awareness largely born of political conflict over lands, waters, and resource development – the blank emptiness awaiting the White Man's transforming imagination suddenly seemed very different. The challenge was not for Canadians to create something new or extend their Southern ways into the North, but to recognise that something 'rich and strange' already existed, and, furthermore, to value and protect it. Or, in terms of the late Northrop Frye's discussions of Canadian society and culture, Canadians are at last overcoming their 'garrison mentality' and venturing out from their imperial outposts into the forests and tundras, getting to know the original inhabitants (Frye 1971 on garrison mentality).

This is being achieved in two main ways. First of all, the whole huge region is being politically re-organised (Dacks 1990; Dickerson 1992; Cameron & White 1995; Jull 1981; 1984; 1991a; 1991d; 1994; 1995; 1999c; 1999d; 1999e; 2000a; 2000b; 2001a; 2001b; 2001c; 2001d). Each people or ethno-region within it negotiates a land/sea claims settlement with the national government, including creation of new bodies to make decisions about resources and environment in a people's entire homeland. Of course, the few towns with largely white populations such as Yellowknife and Hay River are little affected. The claims settlements create the general rules for development and the environment, a fact accepted happily by mining and other industries who want predictable operating procedures. These regional agreements include self-government arrangements. For instance the whole of Nunavut is now a self-governing territory like the whole NWT or Yukon, similar to one of Southern Canada's provinces in its wide powers, while within the NWT the Deh Cho ('Slavey') or Dogrib (Tlicho) or Inuvialuit region works out local and regional self-government arrangements in addition to the existing NWT government. In other words, local and regional governments reflecting the human culture and ecological character of the region are able to express and defend those identities and imperatives, while gaining access to the financial resources and political powers distributed through Canada's federal system of government. The negotiated indigenous arrangements become part of Canada's national Constitution and cannot be amended at the whim of white majorities in Yellowknife or Ottawa.

The second special feature is *co-management* (Harrold 2002; Freeman & Carbyn 1988; Pinkerton 1989; Alternatives 1991; Inglis 1993). Within the large region covered by each agreement new bodies to make decisions for – and to manage – wildlife, water, development, etc. are created with equal numbers of indigenous representatives chosen by the indigenous birthright corporation and of government environment specialists. The decisions made can only be overruled by the national government under very narrow rules in very special circumstances within a short time period. In other words, these new bodies really are making the decisions. What is more, they are an attempt to combine indigenous ecological knowledge or IEK with knowledge generated by the Western scientific tradition to achieve the best results both traditions can offer, and also to give legitimacy to decisions which, after all, will bind the indigenous party who depend on the region for food and livelihoods. The rise of indigenous-white co-management over the past two decades has been so rapid as both an intellectual tradition and policy tool that it seems like a revolution to some; although it will be improved with time and experience, it has been remarkably widely and well accepted to date (Harrold 2002; Inglis 1993; Pinkerton 1989). One may see co-management as either a new intellectual and scientific current, a belated recognition of the knowledge and wisdom of peoples who have relied on their natural surroundings for centuries for all the necessities of life, or an acceptance by the White Man that for all his expensive and clever ideas for managing nature and development, he has no credibility in these matters with indigenous peoples. The latter have seen him systematically ruin that nature, bring hardship and hunger to locals thereby, and make all sorts of wrong decisions and assumptions in trying to correct matters. The Canadian government realized that its claims to the territories of the North would not be accepted in northern opinion or in law unless and until it shared power and accepted the expertise of indigenous societies. However, that being said, the concept and practice have been largely welcomed now by governments for a whole range of reasons. Like northern claims settlements themselves, after governments had been dragged into them kicking and screaming, they discovered that they quite liked them and now travel the world boasting about what fine and clever Canadian discoveries they are!

Australia's Torres Strait Islands, and 'Saltwater People'

The many small islands and coral reefs between the north-eastern point of Australia and Papua New Guinea are home to a Melanesian people, the Torres Strait Islanders living in some 19 communities (TSRA 2001; Lui1994; 1995; Beckett 1987; Singe 1989; Sharp 1992; 1993; 1996; and Jull 1997). In a regional population of *c.* 8000, some 6000 identify as indigenous Islanders. Today the Islanders are working slowly towards a system which will provide both a strong *regional* government and relatively autonomous *local* island councils, together with protection and political inclusion of the Strait's non-indigenous residents (TSRA 2001; Jull 1997). Also a minimal recognition of island native title by Queensland has been proceeding, island by island, since the landmark *Mabo* decision of the High Court in 1992 recognized native title in the easternmost Torres Strait Islands – and thus in Australia for the first time (Bartlett 1993).

The biggest issue remains the Islanders' vast and rich sea territory scattered across a region of forbidding coral reefs. Islanders feel no less passionately their marine ownership and rights here than in the 18th and 19th centuries when British and other explorers, or ships full of British families sailing to or from the Australian colonies, ended their lives here in large numbers, wrecked or skirmishing with the Islanders. A recent court decision has seen Islanders acquitted after seizing the catch of outsiders fishing near their island, the court finding that they sincerely believed it was their right. The Strait is rich in fish, turtles, dugong (a sea mammal much prized by Islanders), and shellfish, but most of the work and profits go to outsiders, although Islander subsistence fishing is the main source of food. The Strait is an international waterway, and a very dangerous reef-strewn one, while major resource extraction and industrial projects in adjacent Indonesia and PNG, all provide serious environmental threats. Australian governments have often regarded the Islanders, patronisingly and wrongly, as 'moderate', i.e., malleable. The inevitable collision over marine rights and environmental protection will change that when passionate Islanders find that development projects in or near their region, or pollution accidents, find them almost powerless in law, left with the costs but not benefits of development.

In a new book, *Saltwater People,* the Melbourne-based academic Nonie Sharp (2002) takes up the situation of Torres Strait and that of other indigenous sea peoples and their regions across the north of Australia. Her comparative background research included visits to the Sami coast of Northern Europe, to Nunavut, and to coastal British Columbia, as well as to areas of Western Europe where older coastal traditions remain. In her six Tropical Australian case studies Sharp shows the range and depth of marine consciousness and knowledge, of the total shaping role of local marine ecology, in indigenous cultures. Anyone concerned about the indigenous self-reliance, local economy, and environment of the Tropical coasts would see that strengthening these local societies and their power would be the best public policy. However, that would require a very great mental leap for the state or federal governments in Australia who still see the world through old-fashioned industrial age lenses. Of course there are officials and even some offices in governments who try to do the right thing, and various inquiries and reports have shown the way, but one can only be fearful for the future (RAC 1993; Smyth 1993; Jull 1993).

The only hope may be concerted action by Tropical coast peoples, supported by non-indigenous allies. For instance, in North America the Inuit from Alaska across Canada, right down the Labrador coast, and across to Greenland, revolutionised thinking about Arctic seas, coasts, and environment from the 1970s (CARC 1984; Lauritzen 1983; Jull 1987; Anjum 1984; Brower & Stotts 1984). That is, by working within their own regions and regional organizations, as well as at national and international levels, they forced governments and industry, as well as the international community, to defend their development proposals and end their ignorance about the Arctic. This produced years of intelligent discussion, of official proposal and Inuit and public counter-proposal, and vastly increased the country's grasp of Arctic realities and needs. Inuit led Canada in the 'discovery' of its third ocean in an intelligent and conscious way which the Atlantic and Pacific had never received.[5] Through these processes Inuit built up strong credibility which spilled over into their political aspirations generally – e.g., all Inuit in those three countries now have their own governments or other significant regional self-governing institutions. At home, however, many organizations, institutions and official bureaux recognized the positive benefits for all citizens in the Inuit initiatives and supported and even joined them. Something similar happened with the path-breaking work of Monica Mulrennan in Torres Strait in the early 1980s (Mulrennan & Hanssen 1994). Dialect differences, very different traditions of indigenous-government relations, etc. made Inuit marine cooperation difficult. Obstacles are not greater in Outback Australia, in my view (e.g., Jull & Craig 1997). For years various indigenous and non-indigenous bodies have recommended indigenous workshops among Sami, Inuit, Torres Strait Islanders, and Tropical coast Aboriginal peoples to discuss marine and coastal issues. Such contact is needed.

Other Illustrations

There is much activity, meanwhile. All across Canada and hinterland Australia there are indigenous peoples working to regain control of productive territory as a means to restoring healthy communities. For instance, Australia's northeastern point, the great Cape York Peninsula, has attracted much recent attention thanks to work by local leader Noel Pearson working with the Queensland government to development 'partnership' arrangements to tackle the systemic dysfunction and crisis of violence in indigenous communities (Pearson 2002; Fitzgerald 2001; Robertson 1999). The region includes some of the richest intact eco-systems in Australia.

The future of Australia's Northern Territory remains contested. The only real meeting point is that NT statehood-seeking whites and Aborigines both agree that the present system is a failure and should be replaced. That could be a valuable political resource for future negotiated reconciliation. Whereas in other 'first world' countries national capitals and opinion, e.g., political parties, have insisted that their hinterland connections maintain some standards in words and actions vis-à-vis indigenous peoples and all other minorities, Australia has too often been passive at national level. Furthermore, indigenous

---

[5]   Inuit were well assisted by advisers like Milton Freeman, Peter Usher, the late Randy Ames, Lorraine Brooke, Judy Rowell, Terry Fenge, Peter Jacobs, Marc Stevenson, and many others, and by the Canadian Arctic Resources Committee, an independent Arctic policy think-tank especially under Murray Coolican, Peter Burnet, John Merritt, and their successors.

issues are largely governed by the states and territories.[6] The states, predictably, viewed Aborigines as an obstacle to land and resource development and treated them in largely brutal, authoritarian, and arbitrary style until very recently, leaving a huge contemporary backlog of social dysfunction in indigenous communities and families (Haebich 2000; Kidd 1997). Apart from some personally non- or anti-racist premiers, policy and politics in respect of race have tended to move at the pace of the more backward opinions, although some policy trends seemed positive. However, since 1996 Australia has had a national government led by John Howard which, uniquely among 'first world' countries, has *actively* cultivated community xenophobia as a party and electoral strategy (Markus 2001; Rundle 2001). The world had a glimpse of this with Howard's personal handling of the Norwegian ship *Tampa* and its rescued asylum seekers in August 2001 (Beeson 2002; Charlton 2002; Ward 2002; Marr & Wilkinson 2003).[7] In August 1998 Howard endorsed an NT plan for statehood which had been designed aggressively to shut out Aboriginal peoples, rights recognition, and interests so completely that it failed at referendum two months later. Howard himself would have little sympathy for indigenous survival or sustainable development for their own sakes. He laments the fact that many Aborigines live in isolation, maintain their cultures, and are not 'fully integrated', rather than assimilated into industrial society and the general workforce ('Secret life of city blacks' by George Megalogenis, *The Weekend Australian, 28-29/9/02).*[8] However, one or two of his ministers seem prepared to support hinterland indigenous self-help projects provided these are accompanied by ostentatious anti-socialist rhetoric.

In Canada the Deh Cho (Slavey) people of the south-western NWT have been an almost classical model of how principle and practice can bring good results in their work with the federal and NWT governments assisted by facili-

---

[6] The two mainland territories are the Australian Capital Territory, i.e., Canberra, and the NT. While the former has relatively few Aborigines, it tends to be the most socially progressive jurisdiction in Australia (and the best educated), and has made many positive steps in the spirit of Aboriginal Reconciliation since becoming self-governing a decade ago.

[7] And another glimpse with war against Iraq apparently looming. In *The Australian,* 7-Oct-2002, California-based academic Tom Plate writes: '[Howard] chose … in his remarks before the American Chamber of Commerce, to becloud, if not befoul, his position when he added that, whatever the pros and cons of an Iraqi attack, *Australia needed to support the Americans and the British because of their similar values and "similar … view of life".* That sounded racist – and it was most unfortunate. Consider that all the targets now under consideration by the West – the terrorists, Iraq, Iran – are Muslim. What Howard in effect did was to invoke the us-against-them, white-against-non-white, Western v Islamic showdown that makes one shiver.' [emphasis added]

[8] The most disturbing aspect of Howard's view is the implication here, and elsewhere, that Aborigines are failing to become good Australians. Like the populist xenophobe Pauline Hanson, he tries to undermine and usurp the moral cachet of the first inhabitants.

tator Professor Peter Russell, one of the world's ablest non-indigenous observers and practitioners in indigenous constitutional work. Like other Canadian peoples the Deh Cho have much documentation online, the federal government's Indian and Northern Affairs Canada site being a good starting-point (http://www.ainc-inac.gc.ca/index_e.html). Other NWT peoples also have regional agreements complete or under negotiation or implementation. Labrador Inuit on the Atlantic coast and Nisga'a villages by the Pacific have also reached important regional agreements on land, marine, and self-government issues in recent years. Many other indigenous locales and regions large and small across Canada are working actively to similar ends.

Quebec Inuit live along the coasts of Ungava Bay, Hudson Strait, and north-eastern Hudson Bay in 15 villages including *c.* 9200 Inuit of a total population of 9900. In 1975 with Cree they negotiated the 1975 James Bay and Northern Quebec Agreement to cope with hydro-electric power development in the southern regions of their territory, Nunavik. However, they wanted more reforms. Since the early 1970s Quebec has learned that futile suspicions among Inuit, Indian, and Francophone peoples, and confrontations over development issues, bring nothing but trouble at home and international censure. By 1989 the Inuit had ready a united front of Nunavik organizations pressing a reform agenda. However, more years elapsed before the full Nunavik Commission was established. Now, *Amiqqaaluta/ Partageons/ Let Us Share,* the March 2001 report of that Commission – a tri-partite body comprising Inuit, the Government of Quebec, and Government of Canada – has proposed creation and structures of a Nunavik territory for Quebec. The proposals are unprecedented for any Canadian province, but what is more, they draw deliberately on the experiences of other Inuit regions in Canada and abroad. (The report is online in English, French, and Inuktitut, the English text being Nunavik Commission 2001. See also Jull 2001c for comments.) In April 2002 a further development occurred: Inuit and Quebec reached a major agreement or treaty on how to conduct their future relations and on how to share development benefits and procedures (Makivik-Quebec 2002). Earlier Quebec had reached a similar agreement with the Cree. Quebec had taken a view for many years that it could simply knock the northern and other indigenous peoples into line, an approach which generated much conflict and extremely bad publicity for the Quebec government and Quebec aspirations. Now all that was ended, formally, as it had been ended for many years in fact.

Across Northern Russia and Siberia some 40 indigenous nations totaling *c.* 200,000 people are grouped in RAIPON, the Russian Association of Indigenous Peoples of the North, with a useful website (http://www.raipon.org/english/index.html). A support group for the Russian peoples, ANSIPRA, provides useful information and contact (http://www.npolar.no/ansipra/english/index.html) from its base in theNorwegian Polar Institute, Tromsø. RAIPON president Sergey Haruchi told the ICC assembly in Kuujjuaq, Canada, in August 2002 that sustainable development was the next big priority. Greenland's Inuit home rule government in place since 1979 serves 56,540 people of whom 80% are native speakers of the Inuit Greenlandic language. Fishing and related marine issues have been central to political and national development over recent decades, so an attack on Greenland's wildlife policy by a Danish writer has been the more bitterly felt. Meanwhile Greenland has provided moral and intellectual leadership internationally in sustainable development discussions, e.g., Lynge 1992; 1998. New Zealand/Aotearoa has also seen dramatic renegotiation of national identity and environment and land use issues in recent years between the *c.* 615,000 Maori and Pakeha (non-indigenous New Zealanders), the total population being 3.94 million (Walker 1990; Orange 1992; 1995; Fleras & Spoonley 1999).

In Alaska the dramatically fluctuating population, c. 635,000 in 2001, includes about 16% indigenous people, but they are the great majority of the 2000 indigenous villages around the large state while the non-indigenous are grouped in a few cities and worksites. The fight for the 1971 Alaska claims settlement was a spectacular battle centred on land, seas, and resources, and the issues continue to centre state politics (Mitchell 2001). The gusto with which Alaskan Natives like the Inupiat of the North have confronted the US government and military, and Big Oil, is a reminder that even remote isolated hunter-gatherer people are a match for anyone given the political will (McBeath & Morehouse 1980; Jull 1986b).

Some indigenous leaders may become so focused on the rhetoric and legal fine points of their own political negotiations or aspirations that they create obstacles to mutual understanding and cooperation by demonising or dismissing other groups or regions at home or abroad. This overlooks the realities that in most matters, including environmental protection and sustainable development, there are many useful practices and precedents widely scattered, and that indigenous peoples everywhere share similar concerns. All are engaged in building or re-building regional structures and identities, and trying to defend and recover sacred, productive, or other significant territory. A network of indigenous peoples and regions dedicated to sharing and developing their practical expertise is long overdue (Jull 1999b). Meanwhile, it is heartening to see fine new books like Nettheim, Myers and Craig (2002) which not only examine the resource, environment, and self-government needs of indigenous peoples across a continent but with detailed chapters looking at issues in relation to, e.g., Sami, Greenland Inuit, Canadian Inuit, and Alaskan experience.

Sápmi (Northern Scandinavia)

'Lapland' used to be clearly identified on English-language maps as an international region covering the north of the three Scandinavian countries. Although large by European standards, the very finite national regions which make up Sápmi ('Lapland') each have their road and rail ambitions, their national governments interested in resource extraction and in military security vis-à-vis the heavily militarized Russian Kola, and local people eager for jobs in regions where the government is and must remain a very significant employer, e.g., through construction and maintenance projects. Also, northern residents of all sorts want the very high quality of life which is taken for granted in the southern regions of those countries. Sami and Sami traditions of life face almost impossible pressures from development. Governments, for their part, have been happy to talk about balanced development and respect for the environment – in which Norway had always looked particularly good in international comparison, at least until the higher standards set by their former Prime Minister, Ms Brundtland – but they have been very evasive in recent times about recognizing Sami rights to land, water, and resources despite accepting a Constitutional commitment. That is, the recent Norwegian Constitutional amendment has in-built the commitment to assure to Sami the material basis of their cultures, e.g., lands, freshwater, and seas for practice of their traditional livelihoods (Smith 1987). Even a rash of embarrassing cases brought especially from Finland and Sweden to UN human rights mechanisms have failed to look at the Sami situation whole. Rather, the Sami are experiencing death by a thousand small cuts, cuts of incrementalism eroding their actual position bit by bit. Tied closely to this is language loss, a loss of the ways of discussing and recording hinterland environments (Minde 2003, see also Brody 2001 on Inuit).

If the wealthy educated countries like Norway, Sweden, and Finland with reputations for finding reasonable solutions to new problems and maintaining healthy Nature alongside healthy Society continue to be unable or unwilling to understand and work through sustainable development and its implications at home, what hope is there for the rest of the world? Of course, Norwegians know little or nothing about their own North, being rather more aware of Los Angeles or Las Palmas, but it is time that they learned about it. Sami can help them. Meanwhile, Norwegians are able to be helpful fixers from Sarajevo to Sri Lanka, and the Middle East, amid the most bitter and intractable conflicts, but they have been less ready to come to grips with the thousand-year-old conflicts in national territory they claim in North Norway.

Conclusions

Sustainable development is not an idea, let alone a White Man's idea, imposed on indigenous peoples or their territories – it is a daily lived reality, an organic part of evolved and evolving indigenous economies, societies, cultures, and self-identifying political communities. Sustainable development did not need world reports or even written language to be established in hinterlands, being integral to indigenous oral knowledge and sheer survival (Henriksen 1973;

Brody 2001). The advent of modern environmental science, and its recognition by powerful international agencies and in powerful documents like the Brundtland Report, has given indigenous peoples a means and vocabulary of communicating the sustainable development concept and its implications to non-indigenous authorities and experts. Of course, not a little indigenous culture is lost in that translation process, and government departments or experts are apt to pick out the bits they find useful (Harrold 2002). Of itself sustainable development has turned the tables on the White Man's previously assumed cultural superiority and knowledge, e.g., by revealing that old illiterate hunters from the High Arctic in Greenland or Canada may know quite a lot which gobsmacks and re-orients dark-suited and expensive regulatory board project inquiries full of university experts and Toronto professionals.

The emergence of northern hinterlands has been a success story in its impact on political culture as a whole and the life of countries. It has opened national society to the political economy of sustainable development and to reconciliation with indigenous peoples and cultures, greatly expanding the sense and pride of nationhood. However, it is too early to say it has been sufficiently successful in many of the indigenous milieux where the political strategy was devised. All the problems of recent social change cannot be healed at once. To keep up or to consolidate these new societies it may be necessary to endure more change. What we can say is that the political and policy frameworks required to replace colonialism, dispossession, and marginalisation are now clearly visible, and are in various stages of negotiation or implementation. This is a process and as such takes some time; after all, discussion and mutual understanding are required.

Unlike the days of *modernizing* the North by massive assault, when the views of the old and indigenous were obstacles to be overcome – always in their own best interests, of course! – now indigenous people old or young are 'worth listening to'. They have won respect as they have won or undermined power. Most of this change has been implicit. However, in countries like Norway, Australia, and Canada with strong environmental currents in modern times, the indigenous case could and should be presented more explicitly in sustainable development terms. The search for continuing marine-oriented livelihoods in Torres Strait and across the north coasts of Australia is an obvious example. Governments talk a great deal about the need for indigenous self-reliance but usually seem unable to imagine or assist any future except on the margins of an industrial economy.

One may even see sustainable development as a comprehensive political program in indigenous hinterlands, albeit one usually unstated. It has been the driving force and core of broad indigenous resistance to the assimilation of their homelands into the industrial economy, while providing also an ethic and rationale for the small-scale local control, knowledge, and cultural distinctiveness which indigenous societies represent (Jull 1986b). It is a coherent intellectual response to the fading lustre of industrial frontier economics, while, as the Brundtland Report shows above, it provides a framework for recognising the uniqueness and unique politico-cultural imperatives of indigenous hinterlands or 'sparselands'.[9] Finnmark or Nunavut or Central Australia need not be developed like Southern Ontario or Sjælland or Sydney, and there are good reasons for not doing so.

Indigenous people have a long-term commitment to the hinterland. If resource boomtowns come and go, and transient populations fluctuate widely, indigenous people and the small population of others who have chosen to make permanent homes among them – sometimes for generations – are essential to the stability of place. They are very much a permanent population. Although indigenous peoples are often minorities in their home regions, the rapid throughput of transient outsiders and different living areas does not change a region's indigenous character or imperatives.

> Only determined resistance by indigenous peoples in hinterlands to industrial nation-state thinking and projects will save these large regions for the world and for themselves.

The reflexes and *idées fixes* of industrial nation-states make them much too slow, even if they have some goodwill and stated sustainable development policies. Indigenous peoples are not just canaries in the mine but must also be, as the Greenland premier put it to me over 20 years ago, the soldiers and police protecting the Arctic environment (Jull 1981). But rarely can they act alone.

> Only partnership and co-management of indigenous and senior governmental authorities will bring adequate power and funds to bear on the problem.

In quiet times the two sides may even choose too cooperate, out of wisdom rather than fear, and one may hope that it becomes habit-forming.

> Only formal recognition of indigenous rights and political communities in respect of hinterlands will protect their physical environments.

One may read the history of Canadian Arctic marine and coastal policy from the 1960s in this way, i.e., as unrelenting Inuit rights activity providing the relatively strong outcomes falling into place today.

---

[9] I am indebted for this useful word to the writings of Professor John Holmes, Geography, University of Queensland.

In 'first world' countries there is much money lavished by governments on official expertise and outside research as well as expensive and handsome publications in the name of environmental protection and sustainable development. Unfortunately there are not always very significant outcomes. However, where there are remote, disadvantaged, even little educated, and often semi-literate indigenous hunter-gatherers, their understanding and determination have forced governments to re-consider their policies and institutions to accommodate sustainable development and protect important eco-systems. Indigenous peoples have had the political will which the majorities in industrial countries have not. If the 'native movement' seemed quixotic, irritating, or dangerous to many in national capitals in the 1960s and 1970s, it has since won wider support as the White Man has come to understand and accept sustainable development and the limitations of 'gold rush' thinking. The sensible future is for national and sub-national governments to accept the wisdom and value of indigenous agendas and to work with indigenous peoples, *in the national interest.*

References

Alternatives, 'Aboriginal Peoples and Resource Development: Conflict or Co-operation?', Special Issue, Vol 18, No 2, Faculty of Environmental Studies, University of Waterloo, Canada, Sept-October 1991.

Anjum S, 'Land-use Planning in the North Slope Borough', in CARC 1984, 269-289.

Arctic Council, *Inari Declaration* on the occasion of the Third Ministerial Meeting of the Arctic Council, Inari, Finland, 2002 online: http://www.arctic-council.org/whatsnew.asp

Arthur WS & McGrath V, *Torres Strait development study, 1989,* Australian Institute of Aboriginal Studies, Canberra 1990.

Babbage R et al., *The strategic significance of Torres Strait,* Strategic and Defence Studies Centre, Australian National University, Canberra 1990.

Bartlett RH, 1993. *The Mabo Decision* with commentary ... and full text of the decision, Butterworths, Sydney 1993.

Beckett J, *Torres Strait Islanders: custom and colonialism,* Cambridge University Press 1987.

Beeson M, 'Issues in Australian Foreign Policy, July to December 2001', *Australian Journal of Politics and History,* Vol. 48, No. 2 (June 2002), 226-240.

Bjørklund I *et al., Sápmi – becoming a nation,* Tromsø University Museum, Tromsø, Norway 2000.

Brantenberg OT, 'The Alta-Kautokeino Conflict: Saami Reindeer Herding and Ethnopolitics', *Native Power: The Quest for Autonomy and Nationhood of Indigenous Peoples,* Universitetsforlaget, Oslo 1985, 23-48.

Brantenberg OT, 'Norway: Constructing Indigenous Self-Government in a Nation-State', *The Challenge of Northern Regions,* ed P Jull & S Roberts, Australian National University North Australia Research Unit, Darwin 1991, 66-128.

Brantenberg OT, 'Murky Agenda in the Mørketid: Norwegian Policy, Sami Politics and the Tromsø Conference', in Brantenberg OT et al (eds), 1995, 27-38. Online: http://www.uit.no/ssweb/dok/series/n02/en/004brant.htm.

Brantenberg OT, Hansen J & Minde H (eds), *Becoming Visible: Indigenous Politics and Self-Government*, The Centre for Sami Studies, University of Tromsø, Norway 1995.

Brody H, *The Other Side of Eden: Hunter-Gatherers, Farmers and the Shaping of the World*, Faber and Faber, London 2001.

Brower E & Stotts J, 'Arctic Policy: The Local/Regional Perspective', *United States Arctic Interests: The 1980s and 1990s*, ed. WE Westermeyer and KM Shusterich, Springer-Verlag, New York 1984, 319-344.

Brundtland GH et al., 1987. *Our Common Future: [Report of the] World Commission on Environment and Development*, Oxford University Press.

Cameron K & White G, *Northern Governments in Transition: Political and Constitutional Development in the Yukon, Nunavut, and the Western Northwest Territories*, Institute for Research on Public Policy, Montreal 1995.

CARC, *National and Regional Interests in the North: Third National Workshop on People, Resources, and the Environment North of 60°*, [ed. D Leamann], Canadian Arctic Resources Committee, Ottawa 1984.

Charlton P, 'Tampa', *Howard's Race*, ed. Solomon, Sydney 2002, 79-107.

Close S, 2002. *Re-Imagining Fourth World Self-Determination: Indigenous Self-Governance in Greenland and Torres Strait*, Research paper, School of Political Science & International Studies, University of Queensland, Brisbane 2002.

Dacks G (ed), *Devolution and Constitutional Development in the Canadian North*, Carleton University Press, Ottawa 1990.

Dahl J, Hicks J & Jull P (eds), *Nunavut – Inuit regain control of the lands and their lives*, International Work Group for Indigenous Affairs, Copenhagen 2000.

Dickerson MO, *Whose North? Political Change, Political Development, and Self-Government in the Northwest Territories*, Arctic Institute of North American and University of British Columbia Press, Vancouver 1992.

Downing J, *Ngurra Walytia: Country of My Spirit*, Australian National University North Australia Research Unit, Darwin 1988.

Eidheim H, *Aspects of the Lappish Minority Situation*, Universitetsforlaget, Oslo 1971.

Fitzgerald A, Cape York Justice Study, 3 vols., Department of the Premier and Cabinet, Government of Queensland, Brisbane, November 2001, Online: http://www.premiers.qld.gov.au/about/community/capeyorkreport.htm

Fleras A & Spoonley P, *Recalling Aotearoa: Indigenous Politics and Ethnic Relations in New Zealand*, Oxford University Press, Auckland 1999.

Freeman MMR & Carbyn LN (eds), *Traditional Knowledge and Renewable Resource Management in Northern Regions*, IUCN Commission on Ecology and Boreal Institute for Northern Studies, Edmonton 1988.

Frye N, *The Bush Garden: Essays on the Canadian Imagination*, Anansi, Toronto 1971.

Ganter R, *The Pearl-Shellers of Torres Strait: Resource Use, Development and Decline, 1860s-1960s*, Melbourne University Press 1994.

Haebich A, *Broken Circles: fragmenting indigenous families 1800-2000*, Fremantle Arts Centre Press, Fremantle, WA 2000.

Harrold L, *Co-Management or Eco-Colonialism? Recognising Indigenous Ecological Knowledge in Canada*, Research paper, School of Political Science & International Studies, University of Queensland, Brisbane 2002.

Harris C, *Making Native Space: Colonialism, Resistance, and Reserves in British Columbia* , University of British Columbia Press, 2000.

Havemann P & H Whall, 2002. *The Miner's Canary: Indigenous Peoples and Sustainable Development in the Commonwealth,* Memorandum for Commonwealth governments attending the World Summit on Sustainable Development, Commonwealth Policy Studies Unit, University of London 2002, online: http://www.cpsu.org.uk/downloads/CPSU_MEM.pdf

Helander E, *The Sami of Norway,* Hand-out, Ministry of Foreign Affairs, Oslo 1995. Online: http://odin.dep.no/odinarkiv/norsk/dep/ud/1997/annet/032005-990462/index-dok000-b-n-a.html

Henriksen G, *Hunters In The Barrens: The Naskapi on the Edge of the White Man's World*, Memorial University of Newfoundland, St. John's 1973.

Høeg P, *Miss Smilla's Feeling for Snow,* trans. F David, Flamingo HarperCollins, London 1994.

Inglis J (ed), *Traditional Ecological Knowledge: Concepts and Cases, International Program on Traditional Knowledge,* Canadian Museum of Nature and International Development Research Centre, Ottawa 1993.

IWGIA, *Self Determination and Indigenous Peoples: Sami Rights and Northern Perspectives,* IWGIA Document No. 58, International Work Group for Indigenous Affairs, Copenhagen 1987.

IWGIA, *Indigenous Affairs,* Special Sami issue, 2/1996 (April-June).

Jull P & Bennett K, 'Unwept, Unburied in Howard's Australia', *The Northern Review* (Canada) No. 21, Summer 2000, 156-171.

Jull P & Craig D, 'Reflections on Regional Agreements: Yesterday, Today and Tomorrow', *Australian Indigenous Law Reporter,* Vol. 2 (1997), No 4, 475-493. Online: http://www.austlii.edu.au/au/journals/AILR/1997/48.html

Jull P & Kajlich H, 'First Peoples, Late Admissions: Recognising Indigenous Rights' (Chapter 21), *Beyond the Republic: Meeting the Global Challenges to Constitutionalism,* ed C Sampford & T Round, The Federation Press, Sydney 2001, 257-269 (and Appendix 2, 303-305).

Jull P & Reinke L (eds), *Living Indigenous Nations,* being a special issue of *Arena Magazine,* No 45, February-March 2000.

Jull P & Roberts S (eds), *The Challenge of Northern Regions,* Australian National University North Australia Research Unit, Darwin 1991.

Jull P & Rutherford J, 'Australia', *The Indigenous World, 1999-2000,* International Work Group for Indigenous Affairs, Copenhagen 2000, 153-168.

Jull P, 'Aboriginal Peoples and Political Change in the North Atlantic Area', *Journal of Canadian Studies,* Vol. 16 (1981), No. 2, 41-52.

Jull P, *Political Development in the Northwest Territories,* Background Paper No. 9, Government of Alberta, Edmonton, Canada, February 1984, 33 pages.

Jull P, 'Greenland's Home Rule and Arctic Sovereignty: A Case Study', Conference paper, *Sovereignty, Security and the Arctic,* York University, Toronto, May 1986, 24 pages (1986a).

Jull P, *Politics, Development and Conservation in the International North,* Canadian Arctic Resources Committee, Ottawa 1986, 107 pages (1986b).

Jull P, 'Inuit Politics and the Arctic Seas', *Politics of the Northwest Passage,* ed. Franklyn Griffiths, McGill-Queen's University Press, Montreal, 1987, 46-63 [notes 278-281].

Jull P, 'Canada's Northwest Territories: Constitutional Development and Aboriginal Rights', in Jull & Roberts 1991, 43-64 (1991a).

Jull P, 'Lessons from Indigenous Peoples', *Social Alternatives,* Vol. 9 (1991), No. 4, January 1991, University of Queensland, 47-49 (1991b).

Jull P, 'Lessons from Indigenous Peoples', *Sweet Promises: A Reader on Indian-White Relations in Canada,* edited by J.R. Miller, University of Toronto Press, 1991, 452-457 (1991c).

Jull P, *The Politics of Northern Frontiers,* North Australia Research Unit, Australian National University, Darwin 1991, 90 pages (1991d).

Jull P, *A Sea Change: Overseas Indigenous-Government Relations in the Coastal Zone,* Resource Assessment Commission, Commonwealth of Australia, Canberra, September 1993, 156 pages.

Jull P, 'Emerging Northern Territory Constitutions in Canada: National Policy, Settler Hegemony, Aboriginal Ethno-Politics, and Systems of Governance', *Constitutional Change in the 1990s,* edited by R. Gray, D. Lea & S. Roberts, Northern Territory Legislative Assembly Sessional Committee on Constitutional Development and Australian National University North Australia Research Unit, Darwin 1994, 94-116.

Jull P, 'Politics & Process: The Real World of Regional Agreements in the Northern Hemisphere', *ATSIC Regional Agreements Seminar, Cairns, 29-31 May 1995,* Proceedings, Aboriginal and Torres Strait Islander Commission (ATSIC), Commonwealth of Australia, Canberra 1995, 17-47.

Jull P, 'The political future of Torres Strait', *Indigenous Law Bulletin,* Vol 4, No 7 (November 1997), 4-9. Online: http://www.austlii.edu.au/au/journals/ILB/1997/39.html

Jull P, ,'First world' indigenous internationalism after twenty-five years', *Indigenous Law Bulletin,* Vol 4, No 9 (February 1998), 13-16, (1998a).

Jull P, 'Indigenous "Stunts" Abroad', *Arena Magazine,* No. 33 (February-March 1998), 37-38, (1998b).

Jull P, 'Bridging the Indigenous Gulf', *Arena Magazine,* No. 43, October-November 1999, 33-34 (1999a).

Jull P, 'Indigenous Internationalism: What should we do next?', *Indigenous Affairs,* 1/1999 (January-March), International Work Group for Indigenous Affairs, Copenhagen, 12-17, (1999b). Online: http://www.yukoncollege.yk.ca/~agraham/nost202/jullart1.htm

Jull P, 'Negotiating Indigenous Reconciliation: Territorial Rights and Governance in Nunavut', *Arena Journal,* New Series, No. 13, 1999, 17-23, (1999,c).

Jull P, 'Reconciliation & Northern Territories, Canadian-Style: The Nunavut Process and Product', *Indigenous Law Bulletin,* Vol. 4 (1999), No. 20, 4-7, (1999d).

Jull P, 'New Deal for Canada's North', *North,* 1/1999, Vol. 10, published by Nordregio, Stockholm 1999, 5-10, (1999e).

Jull P, 'Inuit and Nunavut: Renewing the New World', *Nunavut – Inuit regain control of the lands and their lives,* ed. J Dahl, J Hicks & P Jull, International Work Group for Indigenous Affairs, Copenhagen 2000, 118-136 (2000a).

Jull P, 'Resource Management Agreements with Aboriginal Communities in Canada: Regional Agreements', *Integrated Water and Land Management: Essays on Comparative Approaches to the Integration of Water and Land Management,* ed. DE Fisher & N McNamara, Faculty of Law, Queensland University of Technology, Brisbane 2000, 453-485 (2000b).

Jull P, 'Negotiating Nationhood, Renegotiating Nationhood: Canada's Nunavut and Nunavut's Canada', Conference paper, *Re-Thinking Indigenous Self-Determination,* School of Political Science & International Studies, University of Queensland, Brisbane, [forthcoming in *Balayi* journal], (2001a).

Jull P, 'Nunavut: The Still Small Voice of Indigenous Governance', *Indigenous Affairs* 3/01, 42-51, (2001b).

Jull P, *The Making of Northern Territories & Canada's Indigenous Hinterlands,* Unpublished working paper, School of Political Science & International Studies, University of Queensland, Brisbane, November 7, 2001, 54 pages, (2001c). Online under 'Various Articles' at ANSIPRA site: http://www.npolar.no/ansipra/english/index.html

Jull P, *"'Nations with whom We are connected": Indigenous Peoples and Canada's Political System',* 3rd ed., School of Political Science and International Studies, University of Queensland, Brisbane, September 15, 2001, 55 pages, [Abridged in two parts, *Australian Indigenous Law Reporter,* 6(2) & 6(3), 2001.], (2001d).

Kaalhauge Nielsen J, *Greenland's geopolitical reality and its political-economic consequences,* DUPI Working Paper No 2001/6, The Danish Institute of International Affairs, Copenhagen 2001.

Kehoe-Forutan S, *Torres Strait Independence: a Chronicle of Events,* Department of Geographical Sciences, University of Queensland, St. Lucia 1988.

Kidd R, *The Way We Civilise: Aboriginal Affairs – the untold story,* University of Queensland Press, Brisbane 1997.

Kidd R, *Black Lives, Government Lies,* Frontlines series, University of New South Wales Press, Sydney 2000.

Kleivan I, 'The Arctic Peoples' Conference in Copenhagen, November 22-25, 1973', *Études Inuit Studies,* Vol. 16 (1-2), 1992, 227-236.

Lauritzen P, *Oil and Amulets: Inuit: A People United at the Top of the World,* Breakwater, St. John's, Newfoundland 1983.

Laxness HK, *The Atom Station,* Permanent Press, 1983.

Lefort R, 'Minorities: Challenging the State to Evolve', *UNESCO Sources,* No. 74, November 1995.

Lui G, 'A Torres Strait perspective', *Voices from the Land: 1993 Boyer Lectures,* Australian Broadcasting Corporation, Sydney, 1994, 62-75.

Lui G, 'Torres Strait Self-Government and the Australian Nation State', *Becoming Visible: Indigenous Politics and Self-Government,* ed. OT Brantenberg, J Hansen & H Minde, The Centre for Sami Studies, University of Tromsø, Norway, 1995, 211-227. Online: http://www.uit.no/ssweb/dok/series/n02/en/211luig.htm

Lynge F, *Arctic Wars: Animal Rights, Endangered Peoples,* trans. M Stenbæk, Dartmouth College & University Press of New England, Hanover, NH, 1992.

Lynge F, 'Subsistence Values and Ethics', *Indigenous Affairs,* 1998/3 (July-September 1998), 22-25.

Makivik, 25th Anniversary of James Bay and Northern Quebec Agreement, *Makivik Corporation,* Website, Kuujjuaq & Montreal, Québec 2000. http://www.makivik.org/

Makivik-Quebec, *Partnership Agreement on Economic and Community Development in Nunavik,* Makivik & Government of Quebec, Quebec City, April 2002, online: http://www.cex.gouv.qc.ca/w/html/w2160001.html

Markus A, *Race: John Howard and the remaking of Australia,* Allen & Unwin, Sydney.

Marr D & M Wilkinson, 2003. *Dark victory: the military campaign to re-elect the Prime Minister,* Allen & Unwin, Sydney.

Masiel D, 2002. *2182 kHz,* Random House, New York.

McBeath GA & Morehouse TA, 1980. *The Dynamics of Alaska Native Self-Government,* University Press of America, Lanham, Maryland 1980.

Minde H, 'The Saami Movement, the Norwegian Labour Party and Saami Rights', *L'image de l'autre: étrangers, minoritaires, marginaux,* Vol 2, ed. Ahrweiler, Stuttgart 1984. on-line: http: //www.uit.no/ssweb/dok/Minde/Henry/84cont.htm#x0

Minde H, 'Sami Land Rights in Norway: A Test Case for Indigenous Peoples', *International Journal on Minority and Group Rights,* Vol. 8, Nos. 2-3, 2001, 107-125.

Minde H, 'Assimilation of the Samis – Implementation and Consequences', *Acta Borealia,* vol. 20 (2003), [forthcoming].

Mitchell DC, *Take My Land, Take My Life: The story of Congress's Historic Settlement of Alaska Native Land Claims, 1960-1971,* University of Alaska Press, Fairbanks, AK, 2001.

Mulrennan M & Hanssen N (eds), *Marine Strategy for Torres Strait: Policy Directions,* Australian National University North Australia Research Unit, Darwin, and Island Coordinating Council, Torres Strait, 1994.

Mulrennan M & Hanssen N (eds), *Marine Strategy for Torres Strait: Policy Directions,* Australian National University North Australia Research Unit, Darwin, and Island Coordinating Council, Torres Strait, 1994.

Mulrennan M & Scott C, 'Indigenous Rights and Control of the Sea in Torres Strait', *Indigenous Law Bulletin,* Vol. 5, No. 5 (January 2001), 11-15.

Mulrennan ME, 'Great Whale: Lessons from a Power Struggle', *A Casebook of Environmental Issues in Canada,* John Wiley & Sons, New York 1998, 15-31.

Nettheim G, Myers GD & D Craig, *Indigenous Peoples and Governance Structures: A comparative Analysis of Land and Resource Rights,* Aboriginal Studies Press, Canberra, 2002.

Nicholls C, 'Risking Linguistic Genocide', *Arena Magazine,* No. 51 (February-March 2001), 17-20.

Nunavik Commission, *Amiqqaaluta / Partageons / Let Us Share: Mapping the Road Toward a Government for Nunavik,* Report of the Nunavik Commission, Tri-lingual Inuttitut, French & English in one volume [Quebec City, Québec], March 2001. Online (English and Inuit language texts): http://www.ainc-inac.gc.ca/pr/agr/nunavik/lus_e.html

Nuorgam A, Speech, 10th Anniversary of AEPS [Arctic Environment Policy Strategy], Rovaniemi, Finland 2001. Online: http://www.saamicouncil.org/english/statements.php

Nystø SR, 'Citizenship, self-government, self-determination: A comparison of Aboriginal peoples in Canada and Saami people in Norway', Presentation by President of the Sami Parliament of Norway to *Seminar on self-determination,* Ministry of Local Government and Regional Development, & Embassy of Canada, Oslo, November 5, 2001.

Orange C, *The Treaty of Waitangi,* Bridget Williams Books, Wellington 1992.

Orange C, 'Two Peoples: One land', *Northern Perspectives,* Vol. 23 No. 2 (Summer 1995), [Canadian Arctic Resources Committee, Ottawa], 2-12.

Paine R, *Dam a River, Damn a People? Saami (Lapp) Livelihood and the Alta/Kautokeino Hydro-electric* Project and the Norwegian Parliament, IWGIA Document 45, International Working Group for Indigenous Affairs, Copenhagen 1982.

Pearson N, Noel Pearson Priority Papers, Cape York Partnerships website, 2002: http://www.cap eyorkpartnerships.com/noelpearson/index.htm

Peterson N, "Capitalism, culture and land rights", Social Analysis, 18, December, 1985-101.

Pika A, Dahl J & Larsen I (eds), *Anxious North: Indigenous Peoples in Soviet and Post-Soviet Russia: Selected Documents, Letters, and Articles,* IWGIA Document No 82, International Work Group for Indigenous Affairs, Copenhagen 1996.

Pinkerton E (ed), *Co-Operative Management of Local Fisheries: New Directions for Improved Management and Community Development*, University of British Columbia Press, Vancouver 1989.

RAC, 'The Role of Indigenous People', *Coastal Zone Inquiry: Final Report*, Resource Assessment Commission, Commonwealth of Australia, Australian Government Publishing Service, Canberra 1993, 165-189.

Robertson B *et al., Aboriginal and Torres Strait Islander Women's Task Force on Violence*, Office of Women's Policy, Government of Queensland, Brisbane 1999. Online: http://www.qldwoman.qld.gov.au/publications/main.html

Rundle G, *The Opportunist: John Howard and the Triumph of Reaction*, Quarterly Essay, Black Inc, Melbourne 2001.

Sanders DE, *The Formation of the World Council of Indigenous Peoples*, International Work Group for Indigenous Affairs, Copenhagen 1977.

Sanders W, 'Reshaping Governance in Torres Strait: The Torres Strait Regional Authority and Beyond', *Australian Journal of Political Science* (1995), Vol. 30 (1995), 500-524

Scott C, *Political spoils or political largesse? Regional development in northern Quebec, Canada and Australia's Northern Territory*, Discussion Paper No. 27, Centre for Aboriginal Economic Policy Research, Australian National University, Canberra 1992.

Sharp N, *Footprints Along the Cape York Sandbeaches*, Aboriginal Studies Press, Canberra 1992.

Sharp N, *Stars of Tagai: The Torres Strait Islanders*, Aboriginal Studies Press, Canberra 1993.

Sharp N, *No Ordinary Judgment: Mabo, The Murray Islanders' Land Case, Aboriginal Studies Press*, Canberra 1996.

Sharp N, *Saltwater People: The Waves of Memory*, Allen & Unwin, Sydney, & University of Toronto Press, Toronto 2002.

Shnukal A, 'Pacific Islander immigrants in Torres Strait', *Voices*, Winter 1992, 5-14.

Singe J, *The Torres Strait: People and History*, University of Queensland Press, St. Lucia 1989.

Smith C, 'The Sami Rights Committee: An Exposition', in IWGIA 1987, 15-55.

Smyth D, *A Voice In All Places: Aboriginal and Torres Strait Islander Interests in Australia's Coastal Zone (Revised Edition)*, Resource Assessment Commission, Canberra 1993.

TSRA, *A Torres Strait Territory Government*, Statement from Bamaga Meetings, being *TSRA News* No. 40 (October 2001), Torres Strait Regional Authority, Thursday Island, Qld. Online: http://www.tsra.gov.au/4001.pdf

TSRA, 'Queensland Government Responsible for Native Title Debacle, Press Release, Torres Strait Regional Authority, 12-9-2002, http://www.tsra.gov.au/Press.html

Walker R, *Ka Whawhai Tonu Matou / Struggle Without End*, Penguin, Auckland 1990.

Ward I, 'The Tampa, wedge politics and political journalism', *Australian Journalism Review*, Vol. 24 (1), July 2002, 21-39.

Yevtushenko Y, *Bratsk Station and Other New Poems*, Doubleday, New York 1967.

CHAPTER 3

Biodiversity and Canada's Aboriginal Peoples

Russel Lawrence Barsh and James (Sakej) Youngblood Henderson

Indigenous peoples ("Aboriginal peoples" in the language of Canada's *Constitution Act*, 1982) were an integral part of the world mobilization of grassroots movements leading up to the "Earth Summit" at Rio de Janeiro ten years ago. They were heaped with great praise for their ecological wisdom, respect for natural processes, and sanity in the face of crass consumerism. Six months after Rio, the United Nations Secretary-General inaugurated the International Year of the World's Indigenous People by calling on all governments to "listen to, and work with indigenous peoples."(Barsh 1994:67). The chairperson of the UN Working Group on Indigenous Peoples, Erica-Irene A. Daes, told the General Assembly: "Henceforth, indigenous peoples should not only have a decisive voice in decisions that affect them directly, but share in all of the decisions that will shape the future of our planet." (UN Document A/49/444 (1994)). Indeed, the theme adopted for the final year of the International Decade of the World's Indigenous People (1995-2004) is "partnership in international action."

Canada has publicly welcomed the emergence of indigenous peoples as a priority concern of the international community, and as direct participants in global affairs. Canadian diplomats introduced the General Assembly resolutions proclaiming the International Year and International Decade. This positive image of Canadian leadership in the empowerment of indigenous peoples is not reflected, however, in Canada's response to its own legal obligations under the Convention on Biological Diversity. On the contrary, Canada would not be in compliance with relevant provisions of the Convention even if it fully implemented the Canadian Biodiversity Strategy (CBS), which remains a discussion paper without legislative status eight years after its first publication.[1] Indeed, the CBS fails to respect other applicable international norms, as well as Canada's own constitution.

Biodiversity and Aboriginal peoples

Historically, Aboriginal peoples not only utilized the naturally occurring biodiversity of North America for food, medicine, materials, ceremonial and cultural

---

[1]   Available at http://eqb-dqe.cciw.ca/eman/reports/ (last visited 24 March 2002).

life but also routinely took steps to increase the biodiversity of their territories. In the boreal forest, for example, controlled burning was used to create pastureland, berry patches, and greater forest-edge effects for wildlife (Lewis and Ferguson 1988). The temperate forests bordering the Great Lakes were also carefully burned to increase pastureland for wildlife and create rich, sunlit patches for gardens; rainforests along the Northwest Coast were burned to promote the growth of "wild" food plants such as *camas*, a lily with a potato-like starchy root (Boyd 1999). Except where they were heavily plowed by European settlers, anthropogenic meadows and parklands quickly regenerated into "natural" oligarchic forests (Williams 1999). The role of indigenous peoples in shaping important "natural" ecosystems has only barely been studied yet in North America (compare Morauta et.al., (eds.) 1980; Sponsel 1986).

Aboriginal peoples' continuing dependence on biodiversity for food and medicine has been documented extensively, however, particularly in the far North and the Pacific Northwest. Other related concerns include the use of plants and animals as materials, protection of sacred sites, and maintenance of traditional knowledge.

Harvesting food

Aboriginal peoples in Canada continue to harvest a wide variety of wildlife and plants for food, and the role of harvesting in maintaining adequate nutrition is a major concern (Barsh 1997a; Royal Commission 1986: 219). Aboriginal people generally cannot afford an adequate store-bought diet, and are healthier in places where they continue to have access to traditional foods. The cultural appropriateness of foods, and the role of certain foods in community feasts, religious ceremonies and exchanges of gifts used to reinforce kinship ties are also concerns (Robertson 1990; Kuhnlein and Turner 1991). In the Pacific Northwest, community business cannot be conducted without salmon and other traditional feast foods. In western Ontario and Manitoba, there is an essential link between Anishinabe ("Ojibway") identity and the annual harvest of *mahnomen* (wild rice) (Vennum, Jr. 1988). Amongst the Newfoundland Míkmaq, and the Innu of Labrador, seasonal moose and caribou hunts are as central to social relations and personal identity as they are to human health. A steep drop in Inuit hunting in the 1980s, triggered by a European Community ban on sealskin imports, had a significant impact on Inuit health and culture (Wenzel 1991).

Harvesting obviously requires large, healthy populations of useful animals and plants, and access to places where animals and plants can be collected efficiently at appropriate seasons of the year. Private land ownership increasingly limits Aboriginal peoples' opportunities to harvest what they need, while the "development" of land for industry and human settlements continues to reduce the size of many important populations of animals and plants. Non-Aboriginal people value many increasingly scarce or threatened species for recreational purposes (e.g. moose, Atlantic salmon) or for aesthetic reasons (harp seals). They argue that Aboriginal people must share a larger proportion of valuable species, or stop harvesting them altogether. While Aboriginal people contend that they have a right to harvest whatever they need for a livelihood, and a right to sell what they do not eat, many other Canadians demand "equal rights" to fish and wildlife. In practice, "equal rights" means that everyone has a limited opportunity to harvest small quantities of wildlife for sport.

Particular harvesting methods, such as the use of dip-nets and spears for salmon in the falls of Northwest Coast river systems, can have great social and cultural significance. People must also be free to use more efficient, less wasteful technologies if they choose, of course: traditional weirs are the most efficient method of intercepting migrating salmon (Barsh 1982), but there is little disagreement about the superiority of high-power rifles for hunting large animals. Without the right to sell what they harvest, however, Aboriginal people cannot afford "modern" equipment such as rifles, nylon nets, snowmobiles, or gasoline powered boats (Freeman 1993).

Harvesting is interrelated with the planning of human settlements. Aboriginal peoples must live reasonably close to routine harvesting places. Distance increases costs: dependence on the use of motor vehicles (autos, snowmobiles, power boats) and purchased fossil fuels. Even if harvesting activity is maintained, it requires larger amounts of cash. Either people need wage employment to meet this cost—reducing the time they can devote to harvesting—or they must engage in additional harvesting for sale. This was the dilemma for Inuit in the 1980s, facing growing distances between jobs in centralized towns and hunting areas, as well as a declining world market for sealskins.

At the same time, Aboriginal peoples are concerned about health hazards from the chemical contamination of animals and plants. Although there are more point sources of industrial pollution in southern Canada (such as pulp and paper mills, mines, and fossil fuel burning power generators), Aboriginal peoples in Arctic Canada traditionally eat more fatty mammals such as seals that tend to accumulate toxic chemicals such as PCBs in their blubber. Pollution therefore threatens Aboriginal people as well as biodiversity.

The diets of animals affect the palatability, acceptability, and nutritional value of their flesh. After switching to different forage, otherwise healthy herbivores may taste different, a phenomenon certainly understood by careful Canadian shoppers and chefs. Hence the integrity of the ecosystem as a whole determines the nutritional value and taste of wildlife and fish, as well as their safety for human consumption. Reduced biodiversity may force Aboriginal peoples to eat lower-quality food, and may undermine their physical health and cultural survival.

Medicines and materials

Numerous inventories have been made of medicinal plants used by the Aboriginal peoples of Canada and adjacent parts of the United States.[2] The efficacy of traditional medicine is rapidly gaining credibility, moreover; one study confirmed that 82 out of 96 medicines used by Aboriginal peoples in British Columbia are effective antibiotics, for example (McCutcheon et.al. (eds.) 1992; also see, generally Barsh 1997b).

Medicinal plants are frequently found in small, highly sensitive ecological niches such as stream margins, marshes, and isolated stands of very ancient trees. The potency of a medicine can be affected by soil chemistry, microclimate, associations with other plant species, and the time and season of harvesting. Aboriginal peoples not only need to maintain access to sites where medicinal species flourish, but access to the relatively high-potency gathering sites, at the seasons of the year when medicinal potency is greatest. They also need protection of high-potency sites from chemical contamination or disturbances. Water quality, a crosscutting issue for all of the concerns expressed by Aboriginal peoples, is particularly relevant to medicinal plants. Since traditional healers depend on large numbers of widely dispersed plant species to secure all of the compounds they need,[3] the degradation of any ecosystem is likely to destroy part of the local Aboriginal pharmacopoeia and adversely affect Aboriginal peoples' health (Anyinam 1995).

Plants and animals continue to be used as materials as well as food and medicine: cedar and sweet grass for baskets, for example, and furs for clothing (Turner 1998 [1979]). Increasingly, these uses are related to income and diet, and hence to human health. Aboriginal communities are using more imported and manufactured materials for everyday purposes while using traditional locally harvested materials to make artisanal products for sale. Cash income is often needed for hunting and fishing equipment or for purchasing food when traditional diets can no longer be harvested locally.

Sacred sites and landscapes

It is commonplace today for Canadians to recognize the existence of Aboriginal "sacred sites" and other places of particular historical and cultural significance to Aboriginal peoples. The full complexity of the sacred geography in Canada is still poorly understood, however. Although Bruce Chatwin's popular personal narrative, *Songlines*, drew wide public attention to the linkages between songs, sites, landscapes, and elders' periodic journeys around the countryside

---

[2]   Traditional medicines may include insects, vertebrate animals, and inorganic minerals, although plants generally form the largest proportion of the pharmacopoeia.

[3]   For example, the Warao of Venezuela prepare 292 different drugs from 100 plant species found in a wide variety of habitats (Wilbert and Haiek, 1991).

of Australia, this conception of the ecosystem as a sacred whole has not yet been applied in a Canadian context. Even Hugh Brody's widely read *Maps and Dreams* described the Northern Aboriginal spirit world as if it did not relate directly to physical landscapes.

For Aboriginal peoples, the sanctity of landforms, ecosystems and species is all a matter of degree (Vecsey 1980; Barsh 2000). All species are regarded as kinfolk, and, like human kin, stand in varying individual and historical relationships to one another. Those with an especially close and important relationship may be regarded as the most sacred, but no element of the environment lacks some form of potentially significant, and useful power. Similarly, certain features of the landscape may be regarded as critical nodes in the ecosystem, where relationships between species converge and can be understood, and where their power is felt. Sacred sites often do, in fact, contain important habitats that serve as life-cycle bottlenecks, such as nurseries, nesting areas, groves of trees that act as central points for the continued dispersal of seeds, and migration landmarks. Ancient stands of red cedars in Northwest Coast rainforests are an example of sacred sites that serve important ecological functions.

Sacred sites are not limited to ceremonial places, or places that are periodically used to for purification or healing. Many are simply known, respected, and left relatively undisturbed. They may therefore function as refugia, and help maintain the populations of many species over a wider area. For instance, the Cypress Hills and other isolated mountain ridges and peaks on the Canadian Prairies maintain important island ecosystems with animals and plants not found elsewhere in that vast region of the country. Most are also considered sacred by Aboriginal peoples, and were used sparingly and cautiously.

Concerns for Aboriginal peoples include unrestricted access to sacred sites for ceremonial and healing purposes; protecting sites from any disturbance, contamination, or inappropriate human activities; privacy when visiting or using sites; and the continuing integrity of the larger ecosystems with which sites are connected. Sites tend not to be publicly identified until they are threatened by some project, because Aboriginal people fear that public knowledge, demarcation, and government supervision will lead to restrictions on Aboriginal peoples' own activities, as well as to increases in non-Aboriginal traffic.

Traditional knowledge

Indigenous peoples throughout the world regard their traditional ecological and medical knowledge (TEK) as proprietary and confidential (Daes 1993; UNDP 1994).[4] The protection and wider application of TEK involves three

---

[4]　Current documentation of the continuing international policy debate over the legal status of traditional knowledge can be found on websites maintained by the Secretariat of the Convention on Biological Diversity, http://www.biodiv.org, and the World Intellectual Property Organization (WIPO), http://www.wipo.int/traditionalknowledge/.

related issues, from the perspective of Aboriginal peoples in Canada: (1) identification of the traditional owners under Aboriginal peoples' own systems of law; (2) respect for customary procedures required for the learning and use of TEK; (3) compensation for the right to learn and use TEK. Traditions for the transmission and use of TEK are highly localized. Two generalizations can be made about the customary laws applicable to TEK. The traditional owners may be individuals, societies, family groups (clans or lineages), or whole nations, depending on the kind of knowledge involved and the culture of the peoples concerned. Assuming that "bands" established under the *Indian Act* are the true owners is a gross oversimplification that would do injustice to the beliefs and feelings of most Aboriginal people who actually possess and use TEK.

The second generalization is that few indigenous legal systems accept the possibility of ever alienating TEK completely. Like the land itself, a people's collective knowledge of the land and its biological diversity remains connected with them forever TEK can be shared with properly trained outsiders under certain circumstances, but the borrowers must accept the continuing supervision of the original owners (Barsh 1999; Battiste and Henderson 2000). TEK is not a commodity or "right," in the familiar Western legal sense, but rather it is a *responsibility* that is associated with living on the land.

Applicable legal standards

Canada must not only comply with Convention on Biological Diversity (CBD), but with its domestic constitutional law, and with United Nations instruments defining the rights of indigenous peoples globally. For the sake of brevity and simplicity, this review will focus on the domestic and international recognition of three legal principles: (1) indigenous peoples' right to exercise control over their traditional lands or territories; (2) indigenous peoples' right to continue harvesting those living resources that they have traditionally used; and (3) indigenous peoples' right to control, and benefit from the use of their traditional knowledge. Territorial control, resource use and the right to maintain and benefit from traditional knowledge have all been affirmed to a greater or lesser extent by international instruments applicable to Canada, and by Canadian domestic courts.

Canadian domestic law

Exclusive jurisdiction over "Indians, and Lands reserved for the Indians," was allocated to Canada's national parliament by section 91(24) of the *Constitution Act, 1867*. This has long been interpreted to apply to Inuit as well as "Indians" (Re *Eskimos*, [1939] S.C.R. 104). Provincial governments may exercise authority over Aboriginal peoples only to the extent of a lawful delegation of the federal power, for example in accordance with section 88 of the *Indian Act* (applying provincial laws to Indian reserves except where *prohibited* by Indian treaties or federal laws).

The federal power itself has been limited by section 35 of the Constitution Act, 1982, which declares: "The existing aboriginal and treaty rights of the aboriginal peoples of Canada are hereby recognized and affirmed." Respect for these rights is a condition of Canada's independence from the United Kingdom. In *Indian Association of Alberta (R. v. Secretary of State for Foreign and Commonwealth Affairs ex parte Indian Association of Alberta*, (1982) 2 W.L.R. 641), Lord Denning concluded that the United Kingdom has delegated its responsibilities to its Aboriginal allies and treaty-partners to Canada. However, he found that section 35 "does all that can be done to protect the rights and freedoms of the aboriginal peoples of Canada" by making them part of the constitution "so that they cannot be diminished or reduced". Lord Denning added:

> No Parliament should do anything to lessen the worth of these guarantees. They should be honoured by the Crown in respect of Canada "so long as the sun rises and the river flows." That promise must never be broken.

The nature and content of the rights thus secured, and the extent to which parliament may continue to regulate their exercise, has been the subject of considerable litigation since 1982. The Supreme Court has addressed only some of the issues in dispute. Section 35 refers to two distinct categories of rights: rights of "aboriginal" origin, and rights derived from specific treaties. These rights became "entrenched" (protected against parliament) constitutionally, if they still "existed" on the date the *Constitution Act, 1982*, came into force.

With respect to "aboriginal" rights, the Supreme Court in *Sparrow* concluded that "the test of extinguishment ... is that the Sovereign's intention must be clear and plain if it is to extinguish an aboriginal right." (*R. v. Sparrow* [1990] 1 S.C.R. 1075). In the case of traditional fisheries in British Columbia, no federal or provincial action prior to 1982 evinced "a clear and plain intention" to reduce Aboriginal peoples to an equal legal footing with non-Aboriginal Canadians. Aboriginal fisheries had been regulated to a limited extent, but the underlying historical right was never explicitly abolished. It therefore still "existed" in 1982. Since the relationship between the Crown and Aboriginal peoples is fiduciary rather than adversarial, the term "aboriginal rights" should always be given "a generous, liberal interpretation" in Aboriginal peoples' favor.[5]

"Rights that are recognized and affirmed are not absolute," however. The federal fiduciary duty towards Aboriginal peoples must be "reconciled" with other government responsibilities, such as the conservation of wildlife and public safety. "The best way to achieve that reconciliation," the Supreme

---

[5] The original source of this principle is *Guerin v. The Queen*, [1985] 2 S.C.R. 335.

Court concluded in *Sparrow*, "is to demand the justification of any government regulation that infringes upon or denies aboriginal rights." The Supreme Court elaborated a three-step test for justification, once the existence of an "aboriginal right," and interference by government have been demonstrated by the Aboriginal party. Ottawa must prove that a restriction is "reasonable," that it does not impose an "undue hardship" on Aboriginal people, and that it does not prevent them from exercising their rights "by their preferred means". Even if there exists a reasonable justification for regulating the exercise of an aboriginal right, Ottawa must adopt the least restrictive alternative. In the case of preserving salmon species in British Columbia, the Supreme Court concluded that more could be done to reduce non-Aboriginal fishing before reducing Aboriginal harvesting. The Court reminded Ottawa that "the honour of the Crown is at stake in dealings with aboriginal peoples," so that in conflicts involving Aboriginal and non-Aboriginal people, the "special trust relationship and the responsibility of the government vis-a-vis aboriginals must be the first consideration."

Sparrow did not offer much guidance for determining the contents of the box of "aboriginal rights," although the Court reasoned that section 35 "must be interpreted flexibly" so as to permit a certain degree of "evolution" of its coverage—for example, fishing with new kinds of fishing gear. Six years later, in the *Van der Peet case (R. v. Van der Peet*, [1996] 2 S.C.R. 507), the Supreme Court imposed a very high threshold test on assertions of aboriginal rights: the right claimed must relate to an activity or practice that had been "a central and significant part of the [particular Aboriginal] society's distinctive culture" before the establishment of the Canadian state. Moreover, the right claimed must be "cognizable to the non-aboriginal legal system" and is subject to "reconciliation" with Canada's English legal traditions.[6] We have argued elsewhere that these additional tests place a heavy burden on Aboriginal peoples (Barsh and Henderson 1997). The Supreme Court appears to be saying that there is no general aboriginal right to harvest wildlife for food, for example; whether an aboriginal right exists will differ from community to community and from species to species, depending on the Canadian courts' conclusions about the centrality of each species to each community's ancestral culture and identity.

In separate decisions, the Supreme Court has addressed parliament's power to continue to regulate the exercise of "treaty rights". Before 1867, the British Crown made treaties of peace with most of the Indigenous nations of Atlantic Canada and the Great Lakes; between 1869 and 1929 the Canadian government made 11 more treaties with Indigenous peoples of the Great Lakes, Prairies, and Northwest Territories involving land cessions as well as political arrange-

---

[6] In *Delgumuukw v. The Queen*, [1997] 3 S.C.R. 1010, however, the Supreme Court recognized the relevance of Aboriginal customary laws to a determination of the character and geographical extent of aboriginal land rights.

ments.[7] In the *Simon* case (*Simon v. The Queen*, [1985] 2 S.C.R. 387), the Court ruled that the rights reserved by Indian treaties "should be given a fair, large and liberal construction in favour of the Indians." Accordingly, the Court would "demand strict proof of the fact of extinguishment in each case where the issue arises". In *Sioui* (*R. v. Sioui* [1990] 1 S.C.R. 1025), moreover, the Court characterized Indian treaties as "sacred" in law: "it impossible to avoid the conclusion that a treaty cannot be extinguished without the consent of the Indians concerned."

Nevertheless, a recent Supreme Court decision has left the legal status of Canada's Indian treaties in some doubt (*R. v. Marshall*, [1999] 3 S.C.R. 456; *R. v. Marshall*, [1999] 3 S.C.R. 533). In 1999, the Court ruled that treaties between the Crown and the Míkmaq of Canada's Atlantic seacoast had not only reserved the right of Míkmaq people to harvest eels for food, but (by necessary implication of the historical circumstances of the treaties) their right to sell enough eels to enjoy "a moderate livelihood". The Court could find neither any express legislative extinction of Míkmaq fishing rights before 1982, nor any justification for limiting Míkmaq fishing in order to conserve Atlantic fish stocks. The federal fisheries minister was advised to incorporate the Míkmaq treaty right to a "moderate livelihood" into the applicable regulations.

Federal and provincial officials publicly criticized the Supreme Court and predicted that the Court's decision would wreak chaos in the Atlantic fishery (Barsh and Henderson 2000). Non-Míkmaq fishermen requested a re-hearing of the case. Instead of granting a new hearing, the Supreme Court took the exceptional step of issuing a revised decision in which it reaffirmed both the treaty right, but also the authority of the fisheries minister to regulate Míkmaq fishing. The Court also explained its decision applied only to eel fishing by one Míkmaq community. The full scope of the treaty right, according to the Court, would have to be determined case by case, species by species, community by community—inevitably a very arduous and expensive process.[8] Meanwhile, the federal minister has negotiated agreements with most Míkmaq communities that they will continue to fish under existing rules with some increases in their harvest quotas, while Ottawa purchases up to 10 percent of existing licenses from non-Míkmaq fishermen and transfers them to Míkmaq fishermen. Some communities refused to agree to this solution, resulting in confrontations with federal police for the past three years.

Aboriginal peoples throughout Canada maintain that they continue to enjoy "aboriginal" or treaty rights to harvest all of the resources they traditionally

---

[7] The best overview and analysis of treaties with Aboriginal peoples in Canada may be found in the Royal Commission, 1996.

[8] Nearly 30 Míkmaq and Malecite communities assert rights under the treaties to salmon, cod, eels, lobsters, crabs, and other marine species as well as waterfowl and terrestrial animals such as moose (Barsh [in press]).

utilized, by the most efficient available methods, throughout their traditional territories and under their own systems of management. They also assert the right to continue to enjoy access and privacy in relation to sacred sites, and the right to retain total control of their traditional knowledge. Parliament has never expressly extinguished any of these rights hence any exercises of federal regulatory power must meet the justification test in *Sparrow*. The regulation must address a legitimate objective, such as conservation, by the least restrictive means. If the objective can be met by imposing additional restraints on non-Aboriginal people, the Crown is bound to do so. Even the Mikmaq treaty fishing decisions are consistent with this summary of Canadian constitutional law.

The Convention on Biological Diversity

The CBD makes several express references to "indigenous and local communities," as well as "local populations" and "customary uses" of biological resources "in accordance with traditional cultural practices". All of these references clearly apply to "the Aboriginal peoples of Canada," as they are defined in section 35 of the *Constitution Act, 1982*. As a party to the CBD, Canada has an obligation to implement these provisions in its domestic laws, but has thus far failed to do so.

In its preamble, the convention recognizes "the close and traditional dependence of many indigenous and local communities embodying traditional lifestyles on biological resources, and the desirability of sharing equitably benefits arising from the use of traditional knowledge, innovations and practices relevant to the conservation of biological diversity". This identifies two of the rights of indigenous peoples—resource use and traditional knowledge—which are addressed separately in articles 10(c) and 8(j) of the convention, respectively. Environmental rehabilitation, mentioned in article 10(d) of the convention, strengthens the right of continued traditional use of resources.

The most important provision of the convention from a Canadian viewpoint is article 10(c), directing states to "protect and encourage customary use of biological resources in accordance with traditional cultural practices that are compatible with conservation or sustainable use requirements" –in other words, "aboriginal rights" as defined by the Canadian Supreme Court in *Sparrow*. It may be argued that article 10(c) of the CBD makes Canada accountable to the international community for its implementation of "aboriginal rights". At the same time, Canadian courts must interpret the CBD in the light of *Sparrow*. For example, *Sparrow* places the burden of proving "justification" on the state, instead of requiring Aboriginal peoples to prove that state restrictions are not justified.

Article 10(d) of the convention directs states to "support local populations to develop and implement remedial action in degraded areas where biological diversity has been reduced." In the Canadian context, this implies that Aboriginal communities have the right to financial support from Ottawa when they take initiatives to reverse environmental degradation in their ancestral territories. In this respect, the CBD appears to add something to "aboriginal rights" as construed by *Sparrow*. *Sparrow* interprets "aboriginal rights" as *negative* rights—that is, rights to be free from interference by the state. Article 10(d) of the CBD contains a *positive* right to state support such as funding.

Article 8(j) of the CBD directs state parties to "respect, preserve and maintain knowledge, innovations and practices ... embodying traditional lifestyles relevant for the conservation and sustainable use of biological diversity and promote their wider application with the approval and involvement of the holders of such knowledge". The phrase "preserve and maintain" implies an important *positive* right to financial resources, for example funding for bilingual schools to help maintain indigenous languages. Article 8(j) also makes an express reference to "approval," which introduces the principle of prior informed consent, and suggests that knowledge is an enforceable property right. However, there is an important limitation on the scope of the right (the knowledge must be relevant to conservation of biodiversity), and a substantive condition on its enjoyment (it must "embody traditional lifestyles"). Hence article 8(j) falls considerably short of the concept of indigenous peoples' "heritage" as defined by the United Nations (Daes 1993). On the other hand, Canada does not yet have any domestic legislation or policies protecting traditional knowledge *or* heritage, and it is unclear whether the Canadian courts would regard knowledge as an "aboriginal right".

Finally, article 14.1(a) of the CBD requires "public participation" in environmental impact assessment procedures. Canadian officials are very fond of multi-stakeholder consultations, but the collection of public comments arguably has little effect on government decision-makers. In light of article 10(c) of the convention, and section 35 of the *Constitution Act, 1982*, however, Aboriginal peoples in Canada must be regarded as distinct from the "public". They have unique legal rights to living resources, and should enjoy a larger voice in impact assessment.

Other international standards
The CBD is expressly subject to "the Charter of the United Nations and the principles of international law" (article 3), and does not disturb states' previous obligations under international agreements except where they threaten biological diversity (article 22). International law and prior agreements include legal standards that are arguably more favorable to indigenous peoples than the CBD itself.

One important source of standards applicable to the CBD is Agenda 21, adopted without a vote by the 174 states attending the United Nations Conference on Environment and Development in 1992. Although it is not a legally binding convention, the consistency and virtual unanimity of inter-governmental support for Agenda 21 provide a sound basis for arguing that it has achieved, or is very close to achieving, the status of customary international law.[9] Its customary-law status is continually being reinforced by its role as the basic operating program for the UN Commission on Sustainable Development. The most relevant provisions of Agenda 21 are found in paragraph 26.3, which calls on governments to take measures, "in full partnership with indigenous people and their communities," that include:

> Recognition that the lands of indigenous people and their communities should be protected from activities that are environmentally unsound or that the indigenous people concerned consider to be socially and culturally inappropriate;

> Recognition that traditional and direct dependence on renewable resources and ecosystems, including sustainable harvesting, continues to be essential to the cultural, economic and physical well-being of indigenous people.

In the same spirit, paragraphs 17.80-17.83 of Agenda 21 call upon states to take account of the "special needs and interests" of indigenous peoples in fisheries, including "nutritional and other development needs," and to protect "their right to subsistence" in all international fishing treaties. Paragraph 11.12(e) calls for the adoption of national forest-management policies that "support the identity, culture and the rights of indigenous people," including their right to "adequate levels of livelihood and well-being".[10]

As such, Agenda 21not only strengthens the principle that Aboriginal peoples have a right to continue harvesting living resources for their subsistence, but goes farther than either the CBD or Canadian law by requiring the protection of Aboriginal territories from environmental degradation or unwanted development. The International Conference on Population and Development in 1994 reaffirmed that states should "protect and restore the natural resources and ecosystems on which indigenous communities depend for their survival and well-being and, in consultation with indigenous people, take this into account in the formulation of national population and development policies." (Paragraph 6.27 of the Programme of Action).

Much stronger language can be found in the International Labour Organisation *Convention on Indigenous and Tribal Peoples*, 1989 (No. 169). No gov-

---

[9] The Universal Declaration of Human Rights, which was adopted by the General Assembly in 1948, is an example of widely respected UN resolution that has become recognized as customary international law.

[10] The quotation is from section 5 of the "non-binding authoritative statement of principles" on forestry, annexed to the conference report and incorporated by reference into section 11.12(e) of Agenda 21.

ernment voted against the adoption of Convention No. 169 at the 76th International Labour Conference, but only 14 states have ratified it thus far. Canada is not one of them. Agenda 21 appealed for wider ratification of this convention, because of its focus on land rights (Paragraphs 26.2 and 26.4(a) of Agenda 21). Convention No. 169 recognizes "the rights of ownership and possession of the peoples concerned over the lands which they traditionally occupy" and their right to continue to use resources on lands which they may not occupy, but traditionally used "for their subsistence and traditional activities" (article 14). Rights include "management and conservation," and the maintenance of traditional land tenure systems (articles 15 and 17). "Traditional activities ... such as hunting, fishing, trapping and gathering, shall be recognized as important factors in the maintenance of their cultures and in their economic self-reliance and development" (article 23), an implied priority for Indigenous peoples over competing users of living resources.

More generally, the convention obligates state parties to respect "the integrity of the values, practices and institutions" of Indigenous peoples (article 5); to provide them with "means for the full development of [their] own institutions and initiatives" (article 6); to consult with them "in good faith ... with the objective of achieving agreement or consent" before taking any action that may affect them directly (article 6); and to allow them "to exercise control, to the extent possible, over their own economic, social and cultural development" (article 7). Special state measures must be taken for "safeguarding the persons, institutions, property, labour, cultures and environment of the peoples concerned," which are consistent with Indigenous peoples' "freely-expressed wishes" (article 4).

While the CBD requires state parties to "protect and encourage" sustainable traditional uses of living resources, Convention No. 169 also protects Indigenous peoples' own institutional system of customary laws and practices, and requires indigenous peoples' consent to the protective regime adopted by the state. In countries such as Canada that have not yet ratified it, Convention No. 169 provides guidance for a progressive interpretation of the CBD. It is consistent, at least, with what the Supreme Court of Canada has said about the importance of customary law as a framework for the identification of "aboriginal rights," including land rights. It is also consistent with statements by federal authorities in Canada that they recognize an "inherent right of self-government" of First Nations, subject to clarification and implementation through negotiations and agreements.

In addition to the CBD, Canada has ratified four human-rights conventions that have been interpreted as having special implications for the land rights of indigenous peoples. Most important is the Convention on the Elimination of All Forms of Racial Discrimination (CERD), which forbids any discrimination in the "right to own property alone as well as in association with others" (article 5(d)). The UN Committee on the Elimination of Racial Discrimination, in supervising state parties' compliance with CERD, has interpreted this provision as a guarantee of secure collective traditional land and resource rights for indigenous peoples, including the prompt settlement of claims (General Recommendation XXIII(51), UN Document HRI/GEN/1/Rev. 5 (2001):192). At its 34th session, CERD requested an explanation of Ottawa's refusal to negotiate Míkmaq land claims to much of Canada's Atlantic seacoast and fisheries (UN Document CERD/C/SR.778 (1987).

Article 27 of the International Covenant of Civil and Political Rights secures the cultural, religious and linguistic freedom of "ethnic, religious or linguistic minorities". Aboriginal peoples do not regard themselves as "minorities," but the Human Rights Committee, which supervises this convention, has held that Canada's commercial development of lands claimed by the Lubicon Lake Cree violated article 27 (*Ominayak v. Canada*, UN Document CCPR/C/38/D/167/ 1984 (1990). A paraphrase of article 27 appears in article 30 of the Convention on the Rights of the Child. Subsistence harvesting and environmental protection may also find support in the International Covenant of Economic, Social and Cultural Rights, which recognizes the right to an "adequate standard of living" including "adequate food," and to the "highest attainable standard of physical and mental health" (articles 11-12). Like the rights of minorities, these principles have been paraphrased in the Convention on the Rights of the Child (articles 23-24). Taken together, the human rights conventions ratified by Canada support, but also go farther than the Supreme Court's reading of section 35 of the *Constitution Act, 1982*. The Court requires a case-by-case proof of the existence of land and resource rights, either in the terms of a treaty with the Aboriginal community concerned, or (as an "aboriginal right") in the central and distinctive elements of that community's aboriginal (pre-European) culture. UN human rights conventions do not contain such limitations—land and resource rights exist by the simple fact of a community's indigenousness.

Draft legislation, such as the draft Declaration on the Rights of Indigenous Peoples, and the draft Principles and Guidelines for the Protection of the Heritage of Indigenous Peoples, elaborates on the norms already applicable to Canada through the CBD, CERD, and (arguably as international customary law) Agenda 21 and ILO Convention No. 169. Unfortunately, the draft Declaration and the draft Principles and Guidelines have been debated in the UN Commission on Human Rights for nearly a decade, without signs of progress towards their adoption. In any event, Canada has a long way to go before it complies fully with existing international instruments.

How Canada performs

Canada's compliance with its CBD obligations towards Aboriginal peoples, and with other relevant international norms, differs considerably amongst the provinces and territories, reflecting the relatively loose and decentralized nature of Canadian federalism as a whole. The greatest level of compliance in practice can be seen in the North, particularly the recently established territory of Nunavut. All three Northern territories remain under the direct control of the national parliament, which settled land claims throughout the region in the 1980s, and delegated substantial powers of self-government to Aboriginal peoples as a part of the settlements. Nunavut is predominantly Inuit, so it is *de facto* an Aboriginal territory and with an Aboriginal government. Claims settlements left Aboriginal peoples with roughly 15 percent of the land northern Canada, with priority rights to fish and wildlife through the North.

At the opposite end of the spectrum are the five Atlantic Provinces,[11] and British Columbia. Aboriginal nations of the Atlantic region made treaties of peace and trade with the French Empire and British Empire in the 17th to 18th Centuries but never made any general cessions of their lands. They still assert land claims and treaty fishing and hunting rights to the entire region. The Supreme Court of Canada has consistently upheld the harvesting rights since 1985, but (as discussed above) there have been serious problems with implementation of the Court decisions. Ottawa consistently refused to consider the land claims until very recently; a framework for negotiations is currently under discussion with Aboriginal leaders (See, generally Henderson et.al. 2000; On Míkmaq treaties, see Handerson 1997).

British settlers seized most of British Columbia without first making treaties or agreements with Aboriginal peoples, and British Columbia First Nations have been agitating for a settlement of their land claims for more than a century (Tennant 1990). After nearly a decade of negotiations, only one claim in British Columbia has been settled (Nishgaa), many First Nations have withdrawn from the process, and the provincial government plans to hold a referendum in 2002 on whether it should continue to participate. An "aboriginal right" to fish was recognized by the *Sparrow* case, however, described above, and the federal fisheries department has implemented this right to a considerable extent, by regulations and management plans, at least with regard to fishing for food. A provincial court has moreover held that provincial authorities must "consult" Aboriginal people before authorizing any development activities on lands that are under claim (*Council of the Haida Nation v. British Columbia and Weyerhaeuser Company Ltd*, 2002 BCCA 147 (2002)).[12]

---

[11] New Brunswick, Nova Scotia, Prince Edward Island, Newfoundland, and the southeastern portion of Québec, which is ecologically and historically part of the same region. Although Newfoundland was settled by English fishermen in the 16th Century and remained as a separate British possession until joining Canada in 1948, the rest of Atlantic Canada was French (Acadie and Nouvelle France) from 1534 to 1749. The Aboriginal peoples of Atlantic Canada (Abenaki, Míkmaq, Malecite, Innu) all speak closely related Algonquian languages.

[12] The defendants have sought leave to appeal to the Supreme Court of Canada.

Canada has not only taken a piecemeal approach to the implementation of section 35 of the *Constitution Act, 1982*, with respect to "aboriginal and treaty rights," but has not yet enacted CBD principles into domestic law, nor applied the CBD explicitly to the rights of Aboriginal peoples. A step in the direction of implementing the CBD was taken in 1994, with publication of the Canadian Biodiversity Strategy (CBS). Government officials characterized CBS as a "blueprint for action," but thus far, it has only led to consultations and studies. A close examination of the text reveals a startling failure to address provisions of the CBD that apply expressly to indigenous peoples.

The ethnocentrism of the CBS is reflected in a box on page 7. It lists five recent medical advances we owe to "scientists' ... study of biodiversity." Four of them were in fact based on the study of TEK. None of them involved recognition or compensation for the traditional holders of this knowledge. The chapter on agriculture ignores the fact that some of the Aboriginal peoples of Canada were traditionally farmers who continue to maintain unique varieties of maize, pumpkins, beans, and other food plants.

Most references to Aboriginal peoples in the CBS are contained in the chapter "Indigenous Community Implementation". It describes what Aboriginal peoples can do to implement the CBD but makes no commitments for federal financial support, legal recognition, or legislative protection for these initiatives. The rest of the CBS speaks as if Aboriginal peoples have no distinct rights in relation to the implementation of the convention by Canada. Three major gaps can be identified: traditional ecological knowledge, traditional resource use, and participation in management.

Traditional knowledge (TEK)
The CBS includes within "traditional knowledge" the harvesting of resources; medicinal plants and other materials; cultigens; and the identification of local biological features and their history. Obstacles to the better utilization of TEK are purportedly scientists' lack of interest, and Aboriginal peoples' reluctance to share their knowledge (At page 35). The fact that TEK has been exploited commercially in the past without Aboriginal peoples' informed consent is not mentioned as one of the reasons why Aboriginal peoples are "reluctant" to share knowledge.

Concretely, the CBS suggests that Ottawa "identify mechanisms" to utilize TEK "with the involvement of the holders," and to "encourage the equitable sharing of benefits" (Strategic Direction 2.3; also see Strategic Direction 1.60). This falls short of the CBD requirement that states "preserve" TEK with the "approval" (i.e., consent) of traditional holders. It is significantly weaker than the customary law principles reflected in Agenda 21, which call upon governments to "ensure" the sharing of benefits from TEK.

The separate chapter of the CBS on "Indigenous Community Implementation" refers to the "maintenance of traditions" and their application to conservation and management, but only to the extent of what Aboriginal peoples can do on their own. Aboriginal peoples cannot alter Canadian intellectual property laws with Ottawa's support; much less strengthen their own local institutional capacity to teach indigenous languages, monitor research within their territories, or negotiate with academic and corporate researchers.[13]

The CBS refers to identifying protected areas through "open and meaningful public and stakeholder participation processes and sound scientific information *and traditional knowledge* to ensure that social, economic, cultural and ecological factors are considered" (Strategic Direction 1.12). A thread of elitism and ethnocentricity can be detected here: TEK must be extracted so that environmental technocrats can make better decisions. CBS likewise suggests including TEK in teaching impact assessment to "professionals" (At page 41), but makes no reference to Aboriginal peoples playing a direct role in evaluating proposed projects that will affect them, or to support for developing their own institutional capacity to conduct research and contribute to policy formulation.

Traditional resource use
Although the CBS quotes article 10(c) of the convention, nowhere does it actually address the obligation to "protect and encourage" traditional uses of living resources. The only reference in the CBS to the fact that Aboriginal peoples have a constitutional right to harvesting living resources is in the separate chapter on "Indigenous Community Implementation" which, as noted above, does not involve any responsibilities on the part of the Canadian government. Aboriginal communities lack the authority or the means to protect their harvesting rights, which continues to be challenged by provincial governments. Defending these rights is Ottawa's responsibility under section 91(24) of the *Constitution Act, 1867*, and section 35 of the *Constitution Act, 1982*, as well as the express terms of CBD and customary international law.

The CBS makes no mention of Aboriginal peoples' subsistence needs or harvesting rights in its chapters on aquatic resources and forests. The chapter of aquatic resources fails to acknowledge that Aboriginal communities are among the most dependent on marine life, especially in the Arctic, and account for an estimated one-third of Canada's entire inland fishery (Berkes 1990). Failure to address these facts implies that Aboriginal peoples are economically and legally "equal" to the average Canadian with respect to biodiversity and the provisions of the CBD, rather than conceding that section 35 of the *Constitution Act, 1982*, and Article 10(c) of the CBD are mutually reinforcing.

---

[13] "It is essential to focus on increasing the capacity of indigenous peoples to supervise research conducted in their territories, and to develop their own institutions for medical and ecological research." (Daes 1993:40).

The only hint in the CBD that Aboriginal peoples have land rights different from those of Canadians generally is a reference to "the development of agreements" to acquire more land from them (Strategic Direction 1.17). The CBS does not treat Aboriginal communities as resource-owners, or as management partners, but merely as a reservoir of relatively unspoiled lands for acquisition by non-Aboriginal people: a classically colonial viewpoint.

Participation in management

In broad terms, the CBS makes a commitment to "enhance the participation of members of the public" and "provide for meaningful public and stakeholder participation" in policy formulation and planning (Strategic Directions 1.35 and 1.85). The modalities for this participatory process are not addressed and the commitment is vague enough to be satisfied by the existing practice of public hearings and consultation, without any sharing of decision-making authority.

For Aboriginal peoples, this not only falls short of the "partnership" standard contemplated by Agenda 21 but does not even take account of the internal jurisdiction of Aboriginal communities under Canada's *Indian Act* and land claims settlements.[14] First Nations governments are a political reality in Canada, although they possess less autonomy and power than they would wish. They are primary land managers within Indian Reserves, and in Northern areas to which Aboriginal interests attach under land claims settlements. The CBS does not refer to them as part of the Canadian inter-governmental system, however.

The CBS refers to collaboration between the federal, provincial and territorial governments in connection with the identification of threatened species, for example (Strategic Directions 1.18-1.22). Aboriginal peoples have important subsistence and ceremonial interests in many threatened species, which may enjoy legal protection as "aboriginal and treaty rights," and lands managed by Aboriginal authorities include critical habitats for threatened species. Aboriginal peoples more than simply "stakeholders" in the way that term is used in Canada. A "stakeholder" can be any institution, individual, or group that expresses an interest in a government decision. With regard to an eagle-nesting site on the banks of the Skeena River, for instance, the "stakeholders" may range from the Aboriginal people who fish salmon amongst the eagles and treat eagles as sacred, to a private environmental research center in Toronto that disagrees with Ottawa's interpretation of recent studies of eagle biology. The notion of "stakeholders" in current Canadian practice admits of no levels, or degrees of rights or interests. It is merely a euphemism for "general public," and enables bureaucrats to collapse all the groups competing for their attention into a single undifferentiated mass.

---

[14] This includes Band Councils under the *Indian Act*, Tribal Councils that function as consortia of Bands, Treaty Organizations, and the Regional Authorities established under comprehensive land claims agreements.

Summary

International recognition of the rights of indigenous peoples to enjoy the continued use of traditional resources, and obtain benefits from the wider application of their traditional knowledge, can best be understood along a gradient from relatively "hard" law to "soft" law. The Convention on Biological Diversity falls into the "hard" category; it has been widely ratified, and is in force in Canada. Agenda 21, while universally endorsed, is best characterized as customary international law. Human rights conventions that are in force in Canada do not speak explicitly to the principles at issue here, but their interpretation by the UN bodies charged with their implementation must be regarded as customary international law. ILO Convention No. 169, while not ratified by Canada, and not ratified by a great many other states, has nevertheless informed the international discourse of indigenous peoples' rights, and may influence the thinking of Canadian jurists in the future.

Current international standards applicable to Canada can be summarized as follows:

(1) *Hard conventional law:* Canada must protect and encourage sustainable customary uses of living resources; preserve and promote the use of traditional knowledge with the approval of the Aboriginal holders; and encourage the equitable sharing of benefits from the use of traditional knowledge.

(2) *Soft, or customary law:* Canada should protect the resources used by Aboriginal peoples from degradation; manage living resources jointly in direct partnership with Aboriginal communities; respect collective ownership; help finance local rehabilitation initiatives; and ensure that Aboriginal peoples share in the benefits from the use of knowledge.

The interpretation given by the Supreme Court of Canada to "aboriginal and treaty rights" under section 35 of the *Constitution Act, 1982*, is narrower than contemporary international "hard" law insofar as the Court has taken a somewhat restrictive case-by-case approach rather than treating all Aboriginal peoples as possessing the same fundamental rights to biodiversity. No ruling of the Court has risen to the level of protection of Aboriginal peoples' rights represented by international customary law.

The CBS remains a policy with no binding legal force within Canada, and does not comply fully with the Convention on Biological Diversity. It does not provide for "maintenance" of TEK, and completely disregards the obligation of Canada to "protect" traditional uses of living resources. It also makes no provision for supporting community initiatives to restore degraded ecosystems. In addition, the CBS is incompatible with the principle of customary international law that indigenous communities have rights to manage their own lands and and control their own development process in partnership or cooperation with national governments.

To achieve a minimum level of compliance with relevant provisions of international law, it would be necessary for Canada to:

(1) Recognize traditional knowledge in its national intellectual property legislation.

(2) Establish a program of financial aid, technical support, and legal recognition to scientific and educational institutions launched by Aboriginal peoples and communities.

(3) Make a commitment to protect Aboriginal peoples' traditional harvesting of resources through federal and provincial legislation, as well as recognition of the jurisdiction of Aboriginal authorities.

(4) Legislatively recognize the right of Aboriginal peoples to be directly represented in all impact assessment decisions, to have adequate resources to conduct their own research on proposed projects affecting their traditional territories, and to veto any project that will affect them directly.

(5) Establish a program of financial aid and technical support to initiatives for restoring the productivity of the ecosystems upon which Aboriginal communities depend for subsistence and medicine.

References

Anyinam, C.: "Ecology and Ethnomedicine: Exploring Links between Current Environmental Crisis and Indigenous Medical Practices," *Social Science and Medicine* 40(3): 321-329 (1995).

Barsh, R.L. and Henderson, J.Y.: "The Supreme Court's Van der Peet Trilogy: Naïve Imperialism and Ropes of Sand," *McGill Law Journal* 42(1): 3-19 (1997).

Barsh, R.L. and Henderson, J.Y.: "Marshalling the Rule of Law in Canada: Of Eels and Honour," *Constitutional Forum* 11(1): 1-18 (2000).

Barsh, R.L.: "The Economics of a Traditional Coastal Indian Salmon Fishery," *Human Organization* 41(2): 171-176 (1982).

Barsh, R.L.: "Indigenous Peoples in the 1990s: From Object to Subject of International Law?" *Harvard Human Rights Journal* 7: 33-86 (1994).

Barsh, R.L.: "Chronic Health Effects of Dietary Change on Hunter-Gatherers: Lessons from North American Indians and Inuit," *Medical Anthropology* 18(1): 1-27 (1997a)

Barsh, R.L: "The Epistemology of Traditional Healing Systems," *Human Organization* 56(1): 28-37 (1997b).

Barsh, R.L.: "How Do You Patent A Landscape? On the Hazards of Dichotomizing Cultural Property and Intellectual Property," *International Journal of Cultural Property* 8(1): 14-47 (1999).

Barsh, R.L.: "Grounded Visions: Native American Conceptions of Landscapes and Ceremony," *St. Thomas University Law Review* 13(1): 127-154. (2000).

Barsh, R.L.: "Netukulimk Past and Present: Mi'kmaw Ethics and the Atlantic Fishery," *Journal of Canadian Studies*, [in press].

Battiste, M. and Henderson, J Y.: *Protecting Indigenous Knowledge and Heritage; A Global Challenge*, Saskatoon, Saskatchewan: Purich Publishing, 2000.

Berkes, F.: "Native Subsistence Fisheries: A Synthesis of Harvest Studies in Canada," *Arctic* 43(1): 35-42 (1990).

Boyd, R. (ed.): *Indians, Fire, and the Land in the Pacific Northwest*, Corvallis, OR: Oregon State University Press, 1999.

Daes, E.-I. (by): *Study on the protection of the cultural and intellectual property of indigenous peoples, Special Rapporteur*, UN Document E/CN.4/Sub.2/1993/28 (1993).

Freeman, M.M.R.: "The International Whaling Commission, Small-type Whaling, and Coming to Terms with Subsistence," *Human Organization* 52(3): 243-251 (1993).

Henderson, J.(S).Y., Benson, M.L., and Findlay, I.M.: *Aboriginal Tenure in the Constitution of Canada*, Scarborough, Ontario: Carswell, 2000.

Henderson, J.(S).Y.: *The Mi'kmaw Concordat*, Halifax, Nova Scotia: Fernwood Publishing, 1997.

Kuhnlein, H.V. and Turner, N.J.: *Traditional Plant Foods of Canadian Indigenous Peoples: Nutrition, Botany, and Use*, Philadelphia: Gordon and Breach, 1991.

Lewis, H.T. and Ferguson, T.A.: "Yards, Corridors, and Mosaics: How to Burn a Boreal Forest," *Human Ecology* 16(1): 57-77 (1988).

McCutcheon, A.R., Ellis, S.M., Hancock, R.E. and G. H. Towers, G.H.: "Antibiotic Screening of Medicinal Plants of the British Columbian Native Peoples," *Journal of Ethnopharmacology* 37(3): 213-223 (1992).

Morauta, L., Pernetta, J. and Heaney, W. (eds.): *Traditional Conservation in Papua New Guinea: Implications for Today*, Boroko, Papua New Guinea: Institute of Applied Social and Economic Research, 1980.

Robertson, R.E.: "The Right to Food—Canada's Broken Covenant," *1989-1990 Canadian Human Rights Year Book* 185-216 (1990);

(Royal Commission), Royal Commission on Seals and the Sealing Industry in Canada, *Seals and Sealing in Canada; Report of the Royal Commission*, Ottawa: Minister of Supply & Services, volume 2, 1986.

(Royal Commission), Royal Commission on Aboriginal Peoples, *Final Report of the Royal Commission on Aboriginal Peoples*, Ottawa: Minister of Supply and Services, 1996.

Sponsel, L.E.: "Amazon Ecology and Adaptation," *Annual Review of Anthropology* 15: 67-97 (1986).

Tennant, P.: *Aboriginal Peoples and Politics: The Indian Land Question in British Columbia, 1849-1989*, Vancouver: University of British Columbia Press, 1990.

Turner, N.J: *Plants in British Columbia Indian Technology*, Victoria: Royal British Columbia Museum, 1979, revised edition, *Plant Technology of First Peoples in British Columbia*, Vancouver: University of British Columbia Press, 1998.

(UNDP), United Nations Development Programme: *Conserving Indigenous Knowledge: Integrating two systems of innovation; An independent study by the Rural Advancement Foundation International*, New York: United Nations, 1994.

Vecsey, C.: "American Indian Environmental Religions," in Charles Vecsey and Robert W. Venables (eds.), *American Indian Environments; Ecological Issues in American Indian History*, Syracuse, NY: Syracuse University Press, 1980.

Vennum, Jr., T.: *Wild Rice and the Ojibway People*, St. Paul: Minnesota Historical Society Press, 1988.

Wenzel, G.W.: *Animal rights, Human Rights: Ecology, Economy and Ideology in the Canadian Arctic*, London: Pinter Publishers, 1991.

Wilbert, W. and Haiek, G.: "Phytochemical Screening of a Warao Pharmacopoeia Employed to Treat Gastrointestinal Disorders," *Journal of Ethnopharmacology* 34(1): 7-11 (1991).

Williams, M.: *Americans and their Forests; A Historical Geography*, Cambridge: Cambridge University Press, 1989.

CHAPTER 4

Globalization, Intellectual Property and Indigenous Peoples[1]

Erica-Irene Daes

Indigenous peoples today stand at the crossroads of globalization. In many ways, indigenous peoples challenge the fundamental assumptions of globalization. They do not accept the assumption that humanity will benefit from the construction of a world culture of consumerism. Indigenous peoples are acutely aware, from their own tragic experience over the past five hundred years that consumer societies grow and prosper at the expense of other peoples and of the environment. Indigenous peoples realize that a culture of consumerism is fundamentally dependent upon "eating other people's future", as the great Bengali philosopher Tagore once put it. In fact, most of the indigenous peoples I meet are opposed to the phrase "sustainable development", which they regard as a code word for the illusory goal of *continuous growth of human consumption.* We must not forget that the United Nations Conference on Environment and Development – the Earth Summit in 1992 – was unable to agree on any significant transfer of wealth from the North to the South, because such a transfer would require higher prices and a reduction in levels of consumption among the rich countries. Instead, the Earth Summit promised to boost growth and consumption in the South, without taming consumption patterns in the North. Biosphere reserves, and the lands set aside for indigenous peoples, have been opened to mining and logging – in particular in Latin America and Asia.

We seem to have learned nothing from the human and ecological tragedies caused by the misguided development policies of the 1960s and 1970s. Large scale development projects such as hydro-electric dams, transmigration programs, and the so-called "Green Revolution" have not just displaced millions of people, levelled rainforests, emptied rivers and exterminated more of the world's biological diversity. These projects also set ethnic and social conflicts into motion that may haunt us for generations yet to come.

The very existence of the world indigenous movement is a *product of globalization,* especially in the field of information technology: air travel, telephone, and now the Internet have helped to link indigenous peoples together

---

[1] This lecture by Erica-Irene Daes was given at a seminar on the occasion of her appointment as a Doctor *honoris causa* at the University of Tromsø in March 2003.

worldwide, to increase the visibility of indigenous peoples, and to amplify indigenous peoples' collective voices. In Canada, there is an Aboriginal Peoples' Television Network; in Guyana indigenous peoples have mapped their ancestral territories using remote sensing satellite technology. Indigenous peoples worldwide are using the globalization of a communication of ideas to combat the globalization of reckless consumption.

The international lawyers share a heavy historical responsibility for managing the next stage of globalization better than we managed previous stages of the process. In particular, I believe that we must continue to insist that the rules of the international market place are not only procedurally neutral but also *substantively fair.*

If it is true that the world is rapidly becoming a global village, then we have more reason and responsibility than ever to treat other with respect and reciprocity.

Indigenous Cultures and Globalization

As I have already argued, the globalization of trade and communications presents opportunities as well as challenges for indigenous peoples – as indeed it does for all of us. Thus, globalization is creating two potentially opposing forces: the global marketing of goods and the global marketing of ideas. Indigenous peoples are rich in ideas and stories; it has always been their principal form of capital.

In this connection, I must re-emphasize that the optimistic forecast is entirely dependent on growing public access to communications technologies – access that is equitable and affordable by all. Communications channels must be supported and protected, as global public utilities, or else the balance of global power will shift back again to the countries, companies and individuals with the greatest stocks of money and ammunition.

Globalization presents us with a profound contradiction, however. It is creating a global market for the dissemination of fresh ideas and new voices, while making it easier for one voice to drown out all the others. It is providing each of us with fingertip access to the whole range of human cultural diversity while, at the same time, it is dissolving all cultures into a single supermarket with standard brands. It is making it possible for even the smallest society to earn a livelihood by selling its ideas, rather than selling its lands or forests. But it is also threatening the confidentiality of indigenous peoples' most private and sacred knowledge.

Currently there is a debate within the international community regarding the so-called "digital divide". Developing countries, as well as impoverished regions and minorities within industrialized countries, have argued that access to the Internet has become a basic necessity that should be accessible and affordable to all. They reason that access to the Internet can boost the educational and skill levels of their populations – and that a lack of access to the Internet is a greater competitive disadvantage for countries that already suffer severe poverty and indebtedness. I would like to suggest that, for indigenous peoples, the major problem of the future would not be gaining access to the Internet, but keeping their most private and sacred knowledge out of the Internet.

Anyone who has been following the legal battle over free distribution of recorded music over the Internet – *the Napster case* – is aware that the globalization of communication has made it far easier than ever for indigenous peoples' sacred and special knowledge to be appropriated illicitly. At the touch of a finger, volumes of confidential material can be placed irreversibly in the global public domain – the global commons – where it can then be transformed and commercially exploited by others.

The Search for a New Legal Paradigm

There is another kind of initiative gaining support in the international community, which in my opinion is equally wrong-headed. It is an attempt to create, through diplomatic negotiations, a new category of intellectual property. Work on this approach is proceeding under the auspices of the parties to the United Nations Convention on Biological Diversity, and (separately) under the auspices of the United Nations Food and Agriculture Organization, in connection with revising the International Undertaking on Plant Genetic Resources.

This approach was attempted once before, nearly thirty years ago. I refer to the 1971 amendment to the Bern Convention on copyright, which authorized states to adopt *sui generis measures* for the protection of national "folklore", and to the model legislation on folklore subsequently prepared by the World Intellectual Property Organization (WIPO) and UNESCO. Many scholars have already criticized specific elements of the model law, such as its definition of "folklore", as well as its general orientation of regarding folklore as property of the state, rather than of peoples or communities. It is not my intention here to discuss the technical merits or demerits of the model law, but to draw attention to the fact that it has become, *de facto,* a strictly regional instrument. As the distinguished Professor Paul Kuruk of Ghana has written in the American University Law Review, already two years ago, laws for the protection of national folklore are almost exclusively found in Africa – and African states are frustrated, because it is nearly impossible for them to enforce such laws in the industrialized countries where most of the commercial producers and consumers of folklore actually live.

The Convention on Biological Diversity was a crucial step for the protection of intellectual property. It recognizes the need to "respect, preserve and maintain", the ecological knowledge of indigenous peoples and local communities, and to ensure that the benefits of commercial applications are shared equitably. The Convention has been almost universally ratified, which enhances its importance as a legal foundation for future elaboration. In this connection, I should like to observe that if the Parties to the Convention and the International Undertaking are seriously concerned for the protection of indigenous ecological and genetic knowledge, they should reflect carefully on the fate of the model folklore provisions. Let us assume, for the sake of argument, that WIPO, the Food and Agriculture Organization (FAO) and other United Nations agencies eventually succeed in adopting a universal definition of indigenous knowledge: they agree that states should adopt national laws for the protection of indigenous knowledge, and confirm that national laws for the *sui generis* protection of indigenous knowledge are compatible with the Trade-Related Aspects of

Intellectual Property's Agreement (TRIPs Agreement).[2] What would be the consequences for indigenous peoples? First of all, indigenous peoples would need to convince their national governments to draft and adopt national legislation. That will take some years; at present, such laws exist (to the best of my knowledge) in Costa Rica, Peru, and the Philippines, although it is gratifying that the Andean Pact countries as a whole are committed to such legislation.

But ninety five per cent (95%) of the world's indigenous peoples live in the developing countries, and legislation enacted by these countries is insufficient, in itself, to prevent the piracy of indigenous knowledge by researchers and corporations in industrialized countries.

The real issue is not the problem of defining indigenous cultural and intellectual property, nor of agreeing that the heritage of indigenous peoples should, in principle, be protected by law, like other property. The real issue is *enforcement,* where disputes routinely cross international frontiers, and generally involve parties with vastly different levels of power, in terms of both information and finance. From a practical viewpoint, these are very serious problems, which the international community has duly failed to address until now.

But let me return for a moment to the model folklore provisions. As I indicated a moment ago, the model law regards folklore as *state* property, not as indigenous people's property. Not only does this mean that indigenous peoples must rely on state officials to prevent infringements, and to receive their fair share of any royalties or compensation; it also means that that the state determines, through legislation, the standards and procedures under which indigenous peoples may use, learn and teach their own intellectual heritage. The same state-centered philosophy characterizes the aforesaid Convention on Biological Diversity and the proposed revisions of the International Undertaking. In fact, many State parties to the Convention have adopted access and benefit-sharing laws that are very similar to the model folklore provisions, insofar as the State retains the authority to grant research, access and the use of licenses, all of which affect indigenous peoples and their ancestral territories.

---

[2]   The TRIPs Agreement is Annex IC of the Marrakesh Agreement Establishing the World Trade Organization, signed in Marrakesh, Morocco on 15 April 1994.

I find this approach difficult and worrisome. In my opinion, efforts by states and intergovernmental bodies to define indigenous peoples rights and responsibilities in their own heritage are *contrary to the principle of indigenous self-determination.*[3]

It has been my honor, in my capacity as Special Rapporteur of the Sub-Commission on Promotion and Protection of Human Rights, to elaborate a United Nations study on the Protection of the Heritage of Indigenous People, which has already been published, translated into all of the official United Nations languages, and disseminated all over the world. On the basis of this study, I drafted a set of Principles and Guidelines for the Protection of the Heritage of Indigenous Peoples. My principles and guidelines emphasize, *inter alia*, the authority of indigenous peoples themselves to license or veto research. The same principles and guidelines also affirm the applicability of *customary law, as the ultimate determinant of rights and responsibilities in relation to indigenous cultural and intellectual property.*

The above-mentioned set of guidelines and principles were supplemented and revised by a seminar organized in Geneva from 28 February to 1 March 2000. Two very distinguished Professors, Marie Batista and Sigrified Wiessner, with a deep knowledge of indigenous issues, and in particular of their aspirations and rights concerning the protection of indigenous intellectual and cultural heritage, were chairing two drafting groups of the seminar, one working on the principles and the other on guidelines. The relevant report of the seminar was duly submitted to the aforesaid Sub-Commission. The Sub-Commission, after proper consideration, adopted it unanimously and transmitted it to the Commission for Human Rights for further action,[4] where it is still pending.

WIPO has also organized an important seminar on the Protection of Intellectual Property of Indigenous Peoples, in 1998,[5] and has meanwhile undertaken a study of customary intellectual property laws, which I believe reflects a more promising direction for future international discussion and action than attempts to negotiate universal substantive standards.

Two Challenges for the United Nations System

Let me to return again to the issue of *enforcement*, which I believe merits the particular attention of international lawyers who anticipate representing the in-

---

[3] In connection with the principle/right of self-determination for indigenous peoples, see among many others Daes 2000b.

[4] The Sub-Commission on the Promotion and Protection of Human Rights, 52nd session, document: E/CN.4/SUB.2/DEC/2000/107, (accessed on 10 April 2003 at: http://www.unhcr.ch/huridocda/huridoca.nsf/FramePage/Docs%2052SubCom?OpenDocument&Start=1&Count=15&Expand=2).

[5] Roundtable on Intellectual Property and Indigenous Peoples, Geneva, 23 and 24 July 1998 (accessed on 10 April 2003 at: http://www.wipo.org/eng/meetings/1998/indip/).

terest of indigenous communities. So far, our collective efforts to advance the rights and interests of indigenous peoples have focused on a standard setting in the field of public international law. We have appealed to the community of states to respect and protect the indigenous nations and peoples who live within their borders. In the fields of cultural protection and bio-piracy, however, the key actors are *not states,* but private entities, such as universities, museums and business corporations – and they are generally headquartered in countries other than the countries where their activities adversely impact indigenous peoples.

Meanwhile, the underlying consensus-based and state-centered legal para- digm of the United Nations system is gradually yielding to a new paradigm, represented in different ways by the World Trade Organization and the Interna- tional Criminal Court.

In some states, there have been a number of interesting cases since the 1970s involving trans-boundary tort liability. Recent decisions have not only dealt with classic human rights issues, such as torture and forced labor, but also with the destructive mining of indigenous peoples' territories. The defendants are individuals and corporations – precisely the kinds of non-state actors that the International Criminal Tribunal should, but generally cannot, realistically prosecute.

In the final analysis, then, the fate of international law will depend on the growth of competent, consistent and effective national court systems – a culture of international judicial courage and neutrality, in an international political en- vironment of clear respect for the law.

What does all this have to do with the intellectual property of indigenous peoples? I submit that we need more than a strong international consensus that indigenous peoples are the owners of their own intellectual and cultural heri- tage. Indeed, continued efforts to define and codify the nature of indigenous peoples' intellectual property rights would be counter-productive and incom- patible with these peoples' right to self-determination. The crucial missing ele- ments – the challenges to which I believe we should direct our creative energy as lawyers or human rights defenders or as indigenous peoples representatives – are firstly, strengthening the trans-boundary jurisdiction of national courts, to enforce private international law and secondly, establishing international respect for the customary intellectual property laws of indigenous peoples, as a matter of choice of laws.

References

Daes, E-I (Special Rapporteur): Protection of the heritage of indigenous peoples. Final report, 1995 (Document: Sub-Commission on Prevention of Discrimination and Protection of Minorities, 47th session, E/CN.4/Sub.2/1995/26, annex).

Daes, E-I: *Protection of the Heritage of Indigenous People.* New York: Human Rights Study Series, No. 10, 1997.

Daes, E-I (Chairperson-Rapporteur): Report of the seminar on the draft principles and guidlines for the protection of the heritage of indigenous people, 2000 (Document: Sub-Commission on Prevention of Discrimination and Protection of Minorities, 47th session, E/CN.4/Sub.2/2000/26).

Daes, E-I: "The Spirit and Letter of Right to Self-Determination of Indigenous Peoples: Reflections on the Making of the United Nations Draft Declaration", in: Aikio, P. and Scheinin, M. (eds.): *Operationalizing the Rights of Indigenous Peoples to Self-Determination.* Turku/Åbo: Institute for Human Rights, Åbo Akademi University, 2000,b.

Kuruk, P: "Protecting Folklore under Modern Intellectual Property Regimes: A Reappraisal of the Tensions between Individual and Communal Rights in Africa and the United States" in *The American University Law Review*, 1999.

CHAPTER 5

The Challenge of Indigenism:
The Struggle for Sami Land Rights and Self-Government in Norway 1960- 1990[1]

Henry Minde

Place: the middle of nowhere, many miles outside the town of Alta, 15 January 1981. The phrases "D-Day" and "duel at daybreak" tell of a drama hanging in the air that has been building for a long time. A hundred or so international journalists in Alta are filing reports about an extraordinary atmosphere of insanity and madness. Gathered round the TV news programme, Dagsrevyen, *watched by 60% of the Norwegian population on a regular basis, the nation witnesses the largest assembly of uniformed police in Norwegian history. On this particular day the security forces have been clearing the camp at Stilla. Over the past few days this has been overrun by "river-rescuers" from all over the country, and by "Sami activists" and "Sami sympathisers" from far and near. The evening's TV ends with a programme called "På sparket" [Off the Record]. The subject-matter today is: "Does Norway support its indigenous people? When power plant construction turns into minority conflict."*

* * *

The Alta affair, which on one level was about damming the Alta river as part of a gigantic hydro-electric power project in the Sami heartlands, changed the status of the Norwegian Sami, past, present and future. It led to the disintegration of the old political power structure in Norway, as it related to the Sami, which I shall discuss analytically as a political 'domain'[2] in general terms. It contributed to a number of political changes affecting the Sami and led to a change of the institutional landscape, which in turn affected the Sami. The Alta affair also contributed to various issues being placed on the political agenda. Even today, twenty years later, the question of Sami rights has not been fully resolved in Norway. At the same time, it is clear that the Alta affair and the developments

---

[1] This paper is a revised and shortened version of the one presented in Bjørn Bjerkli and Per Selle (eds.): *Samer makt og demokrati*, Gyldendal Akademisk, 2003 (Minde 2003,a). In this version I have reduced the number of references to Scandinavian source material.

[2] The Norwegian word used in this context is *segment*.

that followed could only have happened as a combination of several processes, some of which took place in the midst of sizeable community conflicts that were caused by the Alta affair. One important circumstance was the growth of the international indigenous peoples' movement.

In this chapter, I shall sketch the background before the dramatic Alta affair took place, what it led to, and how it changed Norwegian politics and the power structure relating to the Sami. There is no doubt that the change in Norwegian politics with respect to the Sami was provoked by the Alta affair, but as an event itself Alta affair cannot fully explain of the developments that have taken place within the Sami political power structure since that time. Here, the international discourse concerning indigenous peoples' legal position in a global context has played an important role.

The Sami Political Domain

From the middle of the nineteenth century, Norwegian politics relating to the country's minority groups in Nordkalotten,[3] the Sami and the Kven,[4] took the form of a consistent policy of assimilation, the so-called "norwegianization". It is said that behind this policy of assimilation "was a combination of the complete enterprise and thought process" (Eriksen and Niemi 1981 : 61). This policy was introduced in the cultural sector "with the school as a battlefield and the teachers as the frontline soldiers" (Niemi 1997 : 268). Language became a goal and a symbol by which 'norwegianization' would stand or fall. Many sectors of society were drawn in, in addition to schools. The institutional co-ordination of the different sectors came to be defined as a characteristic of this policy during the twentieth century. It was created behind closed doors and implemented by central and local government bodies working together (Eriksen and Niemi 1981).

There is no doubt that the efforts made by the state to persuade the Sami and the Kven to discard their language, change their attitude with respect to their fundamental values and get rid of their whole Sami identity have been considerable, prolonged and single-minded. Assimilation was, to a certain extent, supported by existing racism on an everyday basis, but the governmental policy certainly contributed in its own right to a massive downgrading of those exposed to it. The vastly different levels of power between the state administration, which carried out the policy, and the minority groups, who were the recipi-

---

[3]   *Nordkalotten* is the widely-used Norwegian equivalent of the lesser-known geographical term in English, northern Fennoscandia, encompassing the northernmost regions of Norway (Nordland, Troms and Finnmark), Sweden (Norrbotten) and Finland (Lapland).

[4]   The *Kven* is the Norwegian name for the Finnish settlers in Northern Norway and their descendants. Originating from the area around the Gulf of Bothnia, they began to settle in Finnmark from the Late Middle Ages. A regular migration took place from early eighteenth century to the two northernmost regions in Norway, Troms and Finnmark.

ents and clients, led to long periods of apathy and powerlessness. This resulted in remarkably little social unrest throughout the entire period of modernization and norwegianization in the north (Minde 2002,b).

The policy of norwegianization was continued inspite of a change of government in 1935, when *Det norske Arbeiderparti* [the Norwegian Labour Party] came to power (Eriksen and Niemi 1981 : 279 ff). After the Second World War, the Kven question was quickly brushed under the carpet in government policy terms. The policy of assimilation with only minor changes dominated for many years. True, a new government, formed by Labour Party and led by the Prime Minister Einar Gerhardsen, had sought to re-organize minority policies that affected the Sami. This happened in connection with the so-called *'Samekomiteen'* [the Sami Committee], which submitted its recommendation in 1959. This recommendation was taken up for consideration by the Parliament in 1963. This committee and the following political process were strong indicators that a new policy on minorities was evolving. The international human rights debate during the post-war period had stimulated new ideas. But in the light of strong opposition from the ethnic Norwegian and Sami population in the Sami heartlands, the national authorities showed little inclination to implement the proposals launched by the Sami Committee (Minde 1985 : 422 ff).

The continuation of the old assimilation policy was due to a special power structure that was strengthened unintentionally by the Sami Committee. The policy had the character of a 'domain', as it was described, in analytical terms, in a governmental research project about the power structure (1973-1982). This term refers to a power structure relating to certain matters in Norwegian society, a structure that develops over time and consists of distinct networks that are specifically linked to politicians, bureaucrats and lobbying organizations, and which are also surrounded by media personalities. It is important to note that such domains can build up defences around their own political environment, and that, over time, they can develop their own standards that take more account of particular interests within their own domain than of overall national interests. If this happens, administrative and political crises arise that can lead to dramatic changes to the system of governance (Egeberg, Olsen and Sætren 1978 : 122-124). The political domain that developed after the Second World War with respect to Sami matters consisted of the following:[5]

(1) The Ministry of Agriculture, which had a co-ordinating role, of sorts, in the Sami question. The historical background to this was that the interests of reindeeer herding often conflicted with those of agriculture.There was therefore a tradition for the Ministry to interpret Sami rights in a consistently narrow fashion. It was averse to new kinds of ideas and Sami political demands. This proved fatal for any broader development. An example of this may be seen in

---

[5] For a more detailed account, see Minde 2003,a.

the fact that at a large international conference in Kautokeino in the summer of 1978, organized by the United Nations, the Secretary of State Ole K. Sara (born 1936), who was himself a Sami, took the opportunity to criticize *Norske Samers Riksforbund* [the Norwegian Sami State Alliance], the largest Sami organization. There dearly was a mutual lack of trust and respect between the government and Sami organizations during the 1970s.

(2) Before the Labour Party became the most influential party at the national level, the local branch of the party in Finnmark had been opposed to norwegianization. The old scepticism towards the policy of norwegianization still existed during the first years after the war, but the debate about the Sami committee's recommendations c.1960 formed a cross-roads in the Finnmark Labour Party's attitude towards the Sami question. From then on the regional party was dominated by a faction who were sceptical of the Sami. Welfare ideology and the everyday economical concerns of the people also became crucial for many of the Sami voters. The controlling role of the middleman adopted by local Labour politicians, regardless of their ethnic origins, made it difficult for the central authorities to get precise descriptions of the situation concerning the Sami, until the Alta affair.

(3) One of the proposals of the Sami Committee that actually was carried out was to establish a new state organization, *Norsk Sameråd* [the Norwegian Sami Council], in 1964. The idea was that the Norwegian Sami Council should be a broad-based Sami political organization, which would help to strengthen "Sami self-recognition as an ethnic group". For many reasons these expectations were not fulfilled. So it was no surprise that the Norwegian Sami Council steered an extremely careful political course with regard to the authorities. This was evident when, for example, the Council voted at an early stage in favour of the construction of the Alta hydro-electric project.

(4) *Norsk rikskringkasting* [the Norwegian State Broadcasting Company, usually referred to as NRK] was deliberately used by the Norwegian authorities in the work of norwegianization in the period between the wars. This also continued to a certain extent after the Second World War, right up until the 1960s. Fostervoll, the Head of Broadcasting, who had earlier been Minister of Religion and Education, opposed and deferred demands from Sami for greater air time for programmes in Sami. At his departure in 1962 he maintained happily that the broadcasts had "stabilized themselves".

The Sami political sector that established itself after the Second World War kept watch on the old assimilation policy regarding the Sami. The power structure established boundaries around who could legitimately take part and who was excluded. This made room for a small minority of politicians and 'experts' who spoke *on behalf of* the Sami. The most extreme manifestation of the measures that were decided upon at a central level was the political surveillance of Sami organisations, which extended from the 1950s until at least 1983-84

(Berg og Eriksen 1998:226 ff). The accusation that ethnopolitical work was an 'Un-Norwegian Activity' hung in the air and Sami organizations became more circumspect during the era of the Cold War.

By the early 1970s, a multicultural approach seems to have permeated Norwegian minority policy with regard to the new immigrant culture (Tjelmeland 2003). In the field of Sami politics, similar thoughts and enterprises met with opposition for much longer. We have already seen that the policy towards the Sami was burdened by a long tradition of assimilation. This was ingrained in people's thinking, as well as in institutional systems. Such a tradition was not easy to reverse overnight. Perhaps even more importantly, unlike those of immigrants, the indigenous people's rights included questions of territorial possession and ownership and the right to use land and water.[6] As we have seen, the colonial inheritance was such that the time was not yet right for major and enduring change in the minority policy, as it related to the Sami. Before that could happen, the Sami organisations had to undergo a complete metamorphosis in the eyes of the authorities and the public: from being a pressure group for the disadvantaged to becoming a mouthpiece for international human rights.

Sami Internationalism: Solidarity or Self Interest?

Almost no examples seem to exist before the Second World War of the Sami comparing their own situation with that of other indigenous peoples (Minde 1996: 228 ff). The first sign of a new anchoring of identity is found in the journal *Samefolket* [The Sami People] in 1963, when an editorial article with the title "The Sami are the Indians of Sweden" was printed. But it was only in about 1970 that this perspective broadened. In the first place, there was a more general focus on "colonized people", in the neo-Marxist jargon of that time. One example of this was the collection of articles called *Nordisk nykolonialisme. Samiske problem i dag* [Nordic neocolonialism. Sami problems today] (Homme 1969), which contained contributions from members of Sami organizations and eminent social scientists. There was a constant flow of books from abroad that made a strong impression. The background to, and ideology of, 'Red Power' in the United States became known in Scandinavia with Vine Delorias book *Custer died for your sins* (1969, published in Sweden in 1971). The way in which the Prairie Indians lost their lands, their livelihoods, and often their lives, in the space of one short generation, was brought to life in Dee Brown's *Bury my heart at Wounded Knee* (1971, published in Norway in 1974).

---

6   Within the debate on multiculturalism a distinction was often made between immigrant and indigenous minorities on this basis, see Will Kymlicka 1995: 22 ff., 63 ff. Social anthropologist Robert Paine (1999) has maintained, in a commentary on Kymlicka, that this distinction is of such overriding importance that the theories of 'multiculturalism' do not apply to policy concerning indigenous peoples.

A Pan-Sami Strengthening

This change of attitude towards the Sami as an indigenous people reflected the changing ideological climate that took place in the youth culture of the western world, especially in university environs. The young Sami generation was caught up in this development, through the general effort to improve the schooling system that was undertaken by the Nordic welfare states. An increasing number of young Sami people began to study at the old universities in the south throughout the 1960s and 1970s, in Norway as well as Sweden and Finland. A new generation of Sami politicians were inspired by ideas of equality and the right of self-determination, such as those set down in declarations of human rights and conventions, and those expressed in conflicts in the Third World and the Fourth World (by First Nation peoples).

Changes during the 1970s in the international engagement of the Sami people can only be understood when seen in the context of the general re-evaluation of Sami culture that was also occuring at the same time. The Sami language was no longer "a dying language", but a "mother tongue". *Joik*, which had earlier been characterized as a "horrible drunken commotion", was now accepted as "folk music" and later as "music under the stars".[7] From being perceived as "immigrants", the Sami people now had a strong claim to have come into existence as a group of people in their own right in Nordkalotten. The Sami's past came under the heading of not only "ethnography" but also "history", like that of the Norwegians. Viewed as a whole, this supported the radical Sami cultural flowering, which was disputed among the Sami themselves, but which was extended considerably throughout the 1970s, in cultural and institutional terms (cf. Drivenes and Jernsletten 1994: 267 ff).

New Sami organizations were incorporated or started up within the framework of the *Nordisk sameråd* [Nordic Sami Council][8] which from 1956 onwards was elected by conferences. The Council began to arrange conferences about the question of Sami rights, published copious conference reports and minutes of meetings, and managed to get Sami matters placed on the Nordic Council's agenda[9] (Hill & Nickul 1969; Jernsletten 2002).

---

[7]   *Joik* (in plural *joiker*) a traditional mode of Sami singing that is believed to be one of the oldest forms of music in Europe. Rather than singing about a person or place, the *joiker* (singer) attempts to sing the essence of a subject.

[8]   Nordic Sami Council was a non-governmental organization consisting of Sami organisations in the Nordic countries. After the fall of the Iron Curtan, the Russian Sami organisations were included at the Sami conference in 1992 and accordingly the organisation changed its name simply to Sami Council. The net adress is (accessed on 20 April 2003): http://www.saamicouncil.net/

[9]   Nordic Council was formed in 1952 as a forum for co-operation between the Nordic parlaments and governments. The net adress is (accessed on 20 April 2003): http://valhalla.norden.org/eng/info_uk/index.html

The conferences arranged at three-year intervals by the Nordic Sami Council gradually developed into workshops concerning Sami political matters, which were used as a forum for launching ethno-political statements that emphasized to the Nordic states that the Sami were "one people with their own area of residence, one common language and their own structure of culture and society", as it was termed in a cultural political programme that was adopted at the Sami conference in 1971. Its central demand was "that we be acknowledged as an ethnic group and be given support and influence in questions that concern us. We wish to have a Sami democracy. We wish to have this right to self-rule acknowledged to us collectively and to be placed on a level with others" (*Sámiid kulturpolitii'ka*, 1974). This rhetoric resembled language used by Native American leaders.

The next Sami conference, in 1974, adopted a declaration of rights and resource management, amongst other things. It is worth noting that instead of referring to the Sami as an ethnic minority, it was now fundamentally accepted that the Sami were an indigenous people: "the region inhabited by the Sami today has been inhabited and used by them, long before it was inhabited or used by other people. As an indigenous people, the Sami therefore have the right to these Sami heartlands, on the grounds of use since time immemorial" (the eighth Sami conference, 1974). At the same time, it should be noted that these rights were demanded at the 1974 conference according to traditional Nordic legal procedure (established custom and tradition/use since time immemorial), and not in the way that indigenous people's organizations were later to ask on behalf of their members, namely the demand for "irrevocable and inborn rights which are due to us in our capacity as Aboriginals" (World Council, 1978).

What had happened between 1971 and 1974 to explain the shift in the Sami's ethno-political focus? And what was it that further shaped the background, so that the pan-Sami NGO, Nordic Sami Council, came to take part in the preparations for a joint organization for the indigenous peoples of the world?

"We have the same problems and should address them together internationally"

This message dominated the front page of the largest daily newspaper in the Nordic countries at that time, *Dagens Nyheter*, on 11 June 1972. This came about because the Canadian Indian leader, George Manuel, undertook a journey north to the Sami town of Rensjön, in the Kiruna municipality, whilst he was taking part in the UN's first environmental conference in Stockholm, as a Canadian delegate. The journey to *Sápmi*[10] was first and foremost a means to attract

---

[10] *Sápmi* is the Sami word for the area of northern Scandinavia where the majority of the Sami population is based.

the attention of the media and convey his message about international solidarity between the indigenous peoples of the world. But more important than the media attention was the contact that was established between Manuel's staff and the Sami organizations. At the environmental conference Manuel met with Aslak Nils Sara (1934-1996), who was then working in the newly-established Norwegian Department of the Environment. Sara has himself related how his meeting with Manuel was one of the most important inspirations for his later international involvement in this issue (Sara 1995: 58).

The conference for Arctic peoples that took place in Copenhagen in 1973 (cf. Jull in Chapter 2 of this book) was a preliminary interlude in the Sami's international focus. The conference was held at the initiative of individual rep-

The Sami are also indians

resentatives from Indian and Inuit organizations north of the sixtieth parallel in Canada. Because IWGIA[11] undertook to arrange the conference in collabora-tion with the Greenlandic organizers, the Sami organizations were invited along as well. About fifteen Sami representatives took part, all of them men. Many of them would later assume distinguished positions in the Sami political world. The conference delegates committed themselves in ceremonious terms to the creation of a joint organization "to further our joint and collective interests". The subsequent conferences were nevertheless limited to and based on the language and culture of the Inuit: in other words, this conference must be seen as a forerunner of the series of circumpolar Inuit conferences that were first ar-ranged in 1977.

The Sami representatives were experienced a strong sence of Arctic broth-erhood when they heard the young Indian leader, James Wah-Shee, who acted as a powerful intermediary. His opening speech was quoted *in extenso* in the Sami newspaper *Ságat* (14.12.1973). The speech calls attention to the power of indigenous people to safeguard nature and manage resources in freedom, and to respect their family and the land. The Sami at the conference are said to have undergone an experience that gave them the inspiration and belief to continue working in collaboration with other indigenous peoples (Valkaepää 1979, p.110).

The preparations for the foundation of the World Council of Indigenous Peoples (WCIP) were carried out to a great extent by the staff around George Manuel in the National Indian Brotherhood (NIB).[12] It was by means of this network that organizations and institutions were selected and given the chance to send representatives to the preliminary meetings. Sara was selected from the Nordic Sami Council to represent the Sami.

Encountering representatives of other indigenous peoples obviously created great enthusiasm amongst the representatives of all the Sami organizations (Minde 2000: 31 ff). But the respect for, and perceived legitimacy of these organizations was very low within the Norwegian political structure concerned with Sami matters (Minde 1985: 427 ff). The capacity for effective political

---

[11] IWGIA stands for *International Work Group for Indigenous Affairs*. The organization was founded in 1968 by anthropologists and has its administrative base in Copenhagen. The Net address is (accessed on 20 April 2003): http://www.iwgia.org/sw619.asp

[12] NIB was founded in 1969 and was an organization for all the Canadian Indians who lived within the Indian local communities and came under the administration of the Canadian state (the so-called 'status Indians'). The political and administrative structure of NIB underwent a major restructuring in 1982, with the aim of becoming more representative of and responsible for their local communities. With this in mind, the organization's name changed to its current title of Assembly of First Nations (AFN). Their Net address is (accessed on 20 April 2003): http://www.afn.ca/

activity for the Sami organizations was correspondingly rather limited[13] and the active Sami politicians found themselves walking a tightrope. This situation was reflected by three important questions, which had to be addressed: the question of the definition of indigenous people; prioritizing the level of action; and the choice of the level of conflict as far as the authorities were concerned.

In the first place, the question was raised amongst indigenous peoples as to *whether the Sami were an indigenous people*. I shall limit myself here to considering how the question was handled by the Sami in the process of founding the WCIP. A formalization of the international collaborative work of indigenous peoples demanded clarification about who should be permitted to participate. At the meeting in Guyana in 1974 three criteria were agreed upon, which would be used as a basis for the invitations.[14] In order for an indigenous group to be accepted, it was stipulated that:

- it should comprise a people living in a land with a population consisting of different ethnic and racial groups
- they should be the descendants of the original group of people who lived on the land
- they do not have control over the leadership and administration of the lands they live in

The American Oglala Sioux-Indian, Sam Deloria, who proposed this definition at the meeting, remarked that on reflection it was extremely broad. He noted that it was difficult to make the definition any narrower without shutting

---

[13] The first nation-wide organization (an NGO) was founded by and for the Sami in Sweden and Norway just after the Second World War. *Norske Reindriftssamers Landsforbund* (NRL) [The Sami Reindeer Herders' Association in Norway] was founded in 1947/48. Membership in the organization was reserved to active reindeer herders. The most important Sami organization in Sweden, *Svenska Samernas Riksförbund* (SSR) [The Swedish Sami Association], was established in 1950. The association was to consist of a union of Sami communities and associations (and later reindeer grazing districts). Its work was to cover four important sectors: the economic, social, administrative and cultural sectors with special regard to continued existence of reindeer husbandry. In 1968 a handful of local associations founded *Norske Samers Riksforbund* (NSR) [the National Association of Norwegian Sami]. The main objects were to assert the rights of the Sami peoples and to endeavour to improve the position of the Sami population socially, culturally and economically. Around 1980 the organization consisted of 25 local organizations. As a reaction to the radicalisation of the Sami movement around 1970 some "moderates" who had their nucleus in Finmark Labour Party formed *Samenes Landsforbund* (SLF) [the National Association of the Sami]. The organisation stressed that they should have respect and esteem for Norwegian authorities. Accordingly they rejected all actions in connection with the Alta affair. When the authorities changed the policy towards the Samis, the organization deleted the statement about respect and esteem and objected to the new policy.

[14] The following account is built on "International preparatory meeting of the Indigenous Peoples' Conference", Minutes from meetings hold on 8 and 9 April 1974.

out groups of people whom one would wish to include. Those he had in mind were expressly the indigenous peoples who were citizens of the Scandinavian welfare states. Deloria was concerned that it should not be taken as read that "indigenous people" felt themselves, by definition, to be under-represented and unhappy with the state government. Quite the reverse: he claimed that it was necessary to include groups of indigenous peoples of this kind because they could be held up as examples to the others. Although Deloria's proposal was carried by the interim committee and ratified at the foundation meeting that was held at Port Alberni on the Canadian West Coast, in October 1975, the question of the Sami's status became an acute problem at the meeting. The delegates from Latin America, who had themselves had experience of land colonization, and the surveillance and infiltration of organizations were suspicious. As far as they could tell, the Sami were white European people who had no reason to be there (Valkeapää 1979: 114). There were two circumstances which turned the situation to the Sami's advantage. The first was that the leader of the IWGIA, Helge Kleivan, spoke up. He outlined the history of the Sami people in Spanish, in such a way that it was accepted that they were "White Indians". Secondly, they were thoroughly convinced that the Sami were genuine indigenous people when the artists made their appearance, especially when Ailohaš (Nils-Aslak Valkeapää)[15] began with his modern *joiker*. In this way, and well before the Alta affair, the Sami people passed a test that resulted in them being credited with the status of indigenous people on an international scale.[16]

Secondly, the participation of the Sami in WCIP stimulated a debate about how the international work should be prioritized. At the national meeting of the *Svenske Samers Riksforbunds* (SSR) [Swedish Sami State Alliance] in 1977, three different attitudes to the question were crystallized:[17]

- The "Internationalists", who did not perceive any conflict in committing themselves on both a Nordic and an international scale. Aside from a sense of solidarity, they felt compelled to put forward arguments that also worked in favour of the Sami, such as that agreement would lend strength, that WCIP was a weapon in the struggle to promote the Sami cause, and that WCIP was a natural extension of the organizational history of the Sami.
- The "Nordic camp" who, for the moment, wanted to prioritize the Nordic collaborative work. They sought more information and reasonable debate about WCIP involvement. Furthermore, they worried that international con-

---

[15] Nils-Aslak Valkeapää (1943-2001) won the Nordic prize for Literature for his poetical work and was also an internationally recognized artist and performer. He used Ailohaš as his professional name.

[16] Here I am building upon an interview with Aslak Nils Sara (08.10.1995) and personal clarification from Ole Henrik Magga (June 2001); both took part in the meeting at Port Alberni.

[17] Minutes of 1977: 48–72 og Appendix 4. Re. About SSR: see footnote no. 13.

ferences would go over the head of ordinary people and they felt that the internationalists were "floating off into the wide blue yonder".
• The "Anti-Internationalists", a minority in the debate, who did not perceive this question to be a matter of priority, rather a matter of principle. In addition to the arguments used by the Nordic camp, they were worried above all that WCIP membership would lead to reprisals on the part of the Nordic states, because the Sami would be thought to be supporting an extremist group.

Publicly, there was no comprehensive discussion in advance before their affiliation the Sami to WCIP. Perhaps more surprisingly, no debate of the principles was triggered when membership of WCIP was approved at the Nordic Sami Council's conference at Enare in 1976. The immediate enthusiasm seemd to carry the whole of the organized Sami movement into this collaborative work, without any need to discuss the matter in any great depth.

Thirdly, in spite of the Alta affair, the Sami leadership maintained a moderate level of conflict towards the Norwegian authorities. Indigenous peoples' organizations in the USA and Canada made conscious use of the international indigenous peoples' network to put pressure on their own authorities. The Sami organizations focused their demands initially on cultural matters, in preference to land and water rights. When, for example, the question arose of tabling a resolution about the Alta affair at the WCIP general assembly in Canberra in 1981, some of the Sami were sceptical about this, because "when you look at everything as a whole, Alta seems like a little branch in the Brazilian jungle".[18] And we shall see below that the Sami leadership took part in the international fire-fighting exercise after the Alta affair. Why this moderation on the part of the Sami, compared with the indigenous peoples on the North American continent?

• The Nordic states had strong ideological objections against getting involved in affirmative action concerning cultural minorities; not, as in the USA, on procedural-liberalistic grounds, but on the grounds of social democratic ideals of equality. This is why, for a very long time, the demand from the Sami movement consisted only of a sustained call to be recognized as a people – the 'politics of recognition'.[19]
• The process of cultural assimilation had been going on for longer among the Sami than among the North American Indians. The ethno-political mobiliza-

---

[18]   Leif Halonen (born 1944) in the Norwegian newspaper *VG*, 25.04.1981.

[19]   Concerning the context that these concepts form part of, see the influential book by philosopher and political scientist Charles Taylor, *Multiculturalism : examining the politics of recognition* (Taylor 1994) and the debate that has followed in its wake, cf. *Theory, Culture*

tion was much more vulnerable among the Sami. In other words, the Sami leadership had to be prepared to encounter strong political condemnation and sanctions from both Norwegian and Sami quarters. As a result, they ran the risk of losing support among both existing and potential members.

The indigenous peoples' movement started to work in alliance with the growing and strengthening environmental movement. It should be noted that this was an ambiguous alliance, in terms of the indigenous peoples' own agenda (see Manuel and Posluns 1974). On the one hand the indigenous peoples' movement was in danger of being caught in the role of "the noble savage": comparing their own culture with fragile plants in need of protection was an appeal to paternalistic attitudes in the western world.[20] On the other hand, the alliance formed the basis for a co-ordinated policy that in many places resulted in indigenous people being given stronger political influence, improvements to their legal status and a redistribution of society's goods in their favour. The Alta affair in Norway is a good example of this.

The Alta Affair as Indigenous Peoples' Issue

The affiliation of the Sami and the Norwegian state's international involvement in the minorities question became an important factor in the radical changes that took place in Norwegian politics of the minorities, in the wake of the Alta affair. In this section I shall be concerned with the main features of this affiliation until the Alta affair and will look at the consequences this had in the Norwegian political domain concerned with Sami issues.

None of the Nordic states treated the Sami as a people affected by the conventions of international law, until the Alta affair. When the Nordic states judged whether the Sami were eligible under the International Labour Organisation's Convention No. 107 of 1957 on Indigenous and Tribal Populations, this was rejected, amongst other reasons, on the grounds that the Sami were well integrated in the general life of the community. And when the Norwegian authorities ratified the UN covenants on civil and political rights and economic, social and cultural rights with the later and much-discussed joint Article 27, the

---

& Society 2001, nos. 2–3, a publication of articles about the "multicultural" debate. The most relevant question for us in this debate is the contention that the 'politics of recognition' among marginalized groups during the 1980s and 1990s switched its focus from *distribution* (welfare politics) to *identity* (the politics of symbolism). Since this is probably a correct observation, I would maintain that the international politics of the indigenous peoples forms an exception to this – and that the opposition it has encountered has been all the stronger as a result of this.

[20] For a more detailed analysis of the conflicting relationship in practice between indigenous and environmental organizations, as regards particularly to Latin America, see Brysk (2000: 228-37).

relationship of this to the Sami was not raised at all.[21] The idea that the Sami were an indigenous people in a modern sense, according to international law, was quite unfamiliar to both the Norwegian authorities and the vast majority of the Sami, until the Alta affair.[22]

The Sami's work developing an indigenous people's network, through the Nordic Sami Council and WCIP, contributed to the fact that the authorities' attitude to this question began to shift. We see this most clearly in Norway. The international law section of the Foreign Office led the way, and the first sign of this became apparent in 1975. The department referred, amongst other things, to the weak economy that was documented in connection with work on an action plan for inner Finnmark when they answered an enquiry in connection with the preparation of the Cobo Report about discrimination against indigenous peoples.[23] The Government made contributions to WCIP from the time of the Kiruna conference in 1977 onwards. And when Thorvald Stoltenberg, then Secretary of State,[24] delivered Norway's main contribution to the UN conference against racism in 1978, he linked the expression "indigenous people" directly to the Sami ethnic group, and the Norwegian delegation were the driving force behind getting the matter of indigenous people raised in one of the working groups; it was even promoted as a point in its own right in the programme of action resulting from the conference.[25] During the Alta affair, this helped to

---

[21] The covenants were adopted by the UN General Assembly on 16 December 1966 and entered into force 23 March 1976. Norway ratified these covenants 13 September 1972, but they were not included into the Norwegian internal law system until a parliamentary resolution 21 May 1999.

[22] On the other hand, at times there had been a widespread understanding that the Sami, in archaeological and historical terms, were the Nordic countries' indigenous people (*'urvånere'*, *'urbefolkning'* etc.). Concerning this debate amongst archaeologists, see Hesjedal 2000, and among historians and researchers of legal and Sami matters, see Pedersen 2001: 371 ff; Hansen and Niemi 2001; and Niemi 2002. In the meantime the debate became much more acute during the Alta affair, especially after Einar Høgetvedt's individual public report, *Vern av urbefolkninger* [In defence of indigenous peoples], *NOU* 1980: 53. For example, a qualified majority of people attending the Norwegian Archaeological Society's meeting in 1981 accepted "that the historical criteria for the categorization of the Sami minority in Norway as an indigenous people are fulfilled", see *Aftenposten* 26.02.1981, *"Arkeologer i hissig debatt om samene"* [Archaeologists in intense Sami debate].

[23] In 1972 the UN commissioned an investigation concerning discrimination against indigenous people, the so-called "Cobo-rapporten", printed in a series of revised versions between 1975 and 1986. The final document has the following UN reference: UN.Doc.E/CN.4/Sub.2/1986/7/Add.4. For background information concerning the Cobo report, see Minde 2001: 111 ff.

[24] Later he became Defense Minister (1979-81) and Foreign Minister (1987-89 and 1990-93) in Labour governments.

[25] The question had not been placed on the agenda "in case the Norwegian delegation did not support it", as Aslak Nils Sara, a member of the Norwegian delegation declared to *Nordlys* 07.11.1978.

emphasize the disparity between what was said internationally and what was done on a national scale. It is worth noting that just a few months before the Parliament approved the development of the hydro-electric power project in Alta (November 1978), Norway succeeded in mustering support, at the 1978 conference, to give indigenous peoples "the right to maintain their traditional livelihood and way of life" and "the right not to have their land, land rights or nature resources taken away from them".[26] Later, the Department of Foreign Affairs would use this work in the international fire-fighting exercise that took place after the Alta affair.

Once the public became aware that this process could influence the ensuing treatment of the Alta affair, the question was discussed exhaustively. Sami organizations and some parliamentary parties raised demands that Norway should immediately ratify the ILO Convention 107. The matter was revived even more thoroughly when a public report on the whole matter was issued in the autumn of 1980. It concluded that the Sami people came under the definition in the treaty, and that Norway fulfilled most of the minimum requirements set to meet the terms of the treaty, apart from the section on land and water (NOU 1980: 53).[27] This reservation helped to strengthen the impression that the Alta affair had changed in character.

"The Sami's legitimate rights"[28]

The Alta affair developed in several stages: from being a matter of power development, to a local community matter, to an environmental concern, to a matter relating to Sami rights, before ending up as an indigenous peoples' issue.[29] The decision to construct the Alta/Kautokeino dam was voted in by a large majority in the Parliament on 30 November 1978. The majority consisted of most of the representatives from the two largest parties: the Labour Party and the Conservative Party. In parliamentary terms, these parties formed a clear majority in their own right. If the resolution were to be overturned, it would be as a result of one of these parties executing a complete volte-face. And since the matter was decided in Parliament, it was the Labour government that bore the entire responsibility for carrying through the resolution. The Alta affair went through

---

[26] Later cited by UD special advisor Knut Sverre: "Statement at the seminar in Kautokeino, 26 February 1981 about possible Norwegian ratification of the ILO Convention 107 concerning the protection of indigenous peoples", Document no. 90 in the archive of the *Samerettsutvalget* [Sami Legal Commission].

[27] About this report *NOU* 1980:53, see footnote no. 22.

[28] This expression was used by Prime Minister Odvar Nordli when he justified the government delaying construction work at a press conference (*"Derfor firte regjeringen"* [Why the government gave way], *Arbeiderbladet* 16.10.1979).

[29] An overall depiction of the conflicts around the Alta development is given in Øystein Dalland's book *Demningen* (1989), cf. also Brantenberg 1991.

many crises during the years that followed, culminating in the police dismantling the Sami camp and getting rid of the chain-gang in Stilla.

The Alta affair became particularly bitter within the Labour Party because
it activated two important lines of conflict in the party: the conflict between
"power socialists"[30] and environmentalists, and that between the centre and the
periphery in Norwegian minority policy (Nyhamar 1990: 323). At this time, the
political milieu in Finnmark – where Alta is located –still consisted of strong
adherents to the heavy-handed norwegianization ideology from the period between the wars. They used Labour's ideology of equality for all it was worth:
equality was defined as the complete homogenization of language and culture.
The idea of demanding positive discrimination, to give minority cultures the
chance to develop, was seen as old-fashioned and reactionary. Many probably
also owed their allegiance to the powerful socialist camp at this time, but even
if this didn't influence their feelings, they used the same arguments to shore up
their position against "the Sami activists" (Minde 1985: 431 ff).

The Sami people were also, naturally enough, strongly influenced by the
Norwegian state's 120-year-old policy (Eidheim 1971: 50–67; Faaberg 1984:
79 ff; Minde 2003b). Many had tried to become "good Norwegian citizens"
and had endeavoured to be more Norwegian than the ethnic Norwegians. It
was an important aim to give their children a better education than the one they
themselves had had, and there were many who were proud to have children
who went to university. There was absolute bewilderment when the children
who were part of the 1968 generation came home and announced that they had
joined not only the NSR (the established Sami organization) but also the radical
Sami group, ČSV.[31] Some parents felt betrayed, and their bitterness intensified
when such "delusions" were supported by so-called "friends of the Sami" from
the south of Norway, who had scarcely ever set foot inside a *gamme* [Sami
dwelling made of peat] or a *lavvo* [Sami tent]. But unlike the "friends of the
Sami", the Sami young generation could not be deterred so easily (cf. Stordahl
1996: 78–100).

We know that during the hunger strike of 1979 Prime Minister Oddvar Nordli turned to his advisors and asked them to provide documentation about what
Norwegian Sami politics actually consisted of. The only thing the civil servants
could provide was to dust down the government's parliamentary report on the

---

[30] A typical expression in media and political jargon, describing people within the Norwegian
Labour Party who supported electrical development and heavy industry.

[31] *ČSV* was a Sami network that existed in the early 1970s, on the same lines as 'Black Power'
and 'Red Power'. The word did not denote any formal organization, but came to stand for a
symbol of the Sami movement, those who wanted to change the circumstances of the down-
trodden, and especially for those who were in favour of a taking a confrontational stance in
minority politics. The letters 'Č', 'S' and 'V' are the most used in the Sami language (see
Stordahl 1996: 87 ff).

Sami Committee's proposal, dated 1962-63. The Prime Minister and his government's policy over the next few days was closer to the Sami Committee's fundamental viewpoints than the prevailing counsel of the departments. The Prime Minister justified the halt in construction, after a one-week hunger strike in front of the Parliament building, saying that notice must be taken of "the Sami's legitimate rights". Until then, the government and Parliament had refused to take up the question of Sami rights. Whatever the government had meant by this expression, it was immediately taken up in deadly earnest. "The word has been uttered. And there it stands. It is binding for both the Prime Minister and his Minister of Justice", wrote law historian Gudmund Sandvik.[32] The political map had to be redrawn: from one day to the next, what had been characterized as "extremist" became now, with the Prime Minister's blessing, "moderation". The established Sami organizations, NSR and NRL, suddenly discovered that the authorities were asking their advice and listening to what they had to say. Nevertheless, the authorities did not follow the advice they were given – this was especially true later on in the process, when the construction work was set in train once more, in Alta, in January 1981.[33]

The Domain: the End of an Era

What were the consequences in the political domain that were concerned with Sami issues? As we have seen, the Sami were internationally legitimated as an indigenous people by the international indigenous peoples' organization WCIP. During the Alta affair this helped to bolster the fighting spirit within Sami organizations, and this new status also activated external support. Officials in the Norwegian Foreign Office reacted with alarm to reports of Norway's falling reputation in the area of human rights. This made an impression in governmental and ministry circles. The dramatic turn of events in the Alta affair caught the political power structure by surprise and had immediate consequences for the Sami political power structure:[34]

---

[32] *"Samenes legitime rettigheter"* [The Sami's legitimate rights], *Arbeiderbladet* 19.10.1979.

[33] In the programme *Timen er din* [Take Your Time], broadcast on NRK P2 (25.12.1989), Ole Henrik Magga (born 1947), then President of the Sami Parliament, was asked what had been the most disappointing experience during the Alta actions. Magga then picked out the resumption of construction work in the autumn of 1981 and described the tacit agreement NSR had obtained in meetings with the government: "I remember I stood there doing the washing up and I couldn't believe my ears when I heard on the radio someone boasting on behalf of the government that it was all happening, and of course nobody had been told about it (...) It was a slap in the face, because we'd sat in a meeting where we could have kicked up quite fuss and made things difficult for the government. We didn't do that, and it was a conscious decision." In 2002 Magga was elected as the first Chair-person of the UN's Permanent Forum on Indigenous Issues.

[34] For a more detailed description, see Minde 2003,a.

(1) The Ministry of Agriculture's legitimacy as a co-ordinating body within the departmental system was undermined from within the government. By January 1980, the reindeer herding office had already been relieved of its co-ordinating responsibilities in matters relating to the Sami. This role was taken over by a newly-established office (later a division) for Sami matters in the Ministry of Municipal and Labour Affairs.

(2) It became obvious that the Labour Party channels simply could not provide the necessary insight into this field. So, at the same time as Prime Minister Nordli signalled a provisional retreat during the hunger strike, he introduced a series of consultations and hearings with Sami organizations and institutions. The Finnmark Labour Party's role of intermediary in matters relating to the Sami was consequently abolished, under strong protest. It was maintained in these quarters that the Sami actions "were a set-up by professional activists";[35] it was implicitly understood that the Sami were irresponsible children who didn't know what was good for them, and that the sympathy the activists had encountered "(was) based on nothing more than picture postcards",[36] i.e. that opinion had been led astray by the media coverage of the event. Their legitimacy in the question of Sami matters was based on knowing 'these losers' [i.e. Sami politicians] of old: they themselves were the real Sami experts, who knew how to handle the Sami.[37] A hard line of local supporters of the development and opponents of the Sami incited growing opposition to the Sami claims. It also became gradually obvious that this opposition was supported by the central party office, but that a more pro-Sami attitude was gaining ground at regional level. In the years that followed, this became evident during important choices of direction in the years before Parliament decided to establish a *directly*-elected Sami Parliament (1987) and add a new paragraph concerning the Sami to the Constitution of Norway (1988). Both decisions were a result of the Sami Legal Commission's part-proposal, submitted in the spring of 1984. The so-called "Sami political revival meeting" of the Finnmark regional council in autumn 1985 was watched with the greatest attention, when this body considered the Sami Legal Commission's proposal. The decision here was regarded as an indicator for the later handling of this issue, since it concerned the largest Sami region, where ethnic antagonism was traditionally at its strongest (Minde 1985). The fact that a majority of the Labour group provided a clear majority for the proposal within the regional council as a whole was therefore described

---

[35] Editorial article in *Finnmarken*, 13.12.1979.

[36] Editorial article in *Finnmark Dagblad*, 18.10.1979.

[37] Cf. letters and resolutions that were sent at the height of the Alta affair to the central authorities by the district administrative offices, municipalities and branches of the Norwegian Labour Party in Finnmark. These are printed as enclosures in St. meld. nr. 61 (1979-1980). See in addition the newspaper report of the regional society's annual general meeting, *Finnmark Dagblad* 03.03.1980.

as "historic". It also gave the green light to the paragraph concerning the Sami in the Constitution, and a directly-elected Sami Parliament. Former Secretary of State Ole K. Sara opened the debate with a statement that incorporated an acknowledgment on the party's behalf, as well as his own: "the Sami Legal Commission's proposal has been the basis of a change of attitude by the people in our region". He also set this in historical relief, saying that "previous regional council debates about the Sami question have always been about money, but this is something quite different."[38] So it became clear that the supporters of norwegianization won the struggle concerning the Alta development, but they lost control over Sami politics. The decision of the Finnmark regional council in 1985 and the subsequent parliamentary decision must be seen as a new social contract between the state and the Sami people.[39]

(3) At the same time as the Labour government (under Nordli) handed over the responsibility for the co-ordination of Sami affairs to the Ministry of Municipal and Labour Affairs, it set in train an exhaustive re-organization of Norwegian Sami Council. Amongst other things, the Norwegian Sami Council was greatly expanded, in order to include members of Sami municipalities and organizations, and the Norwegian Sami Council was permitted to elect its own leader and deputy leader. After this reorganization, the Norwegian Sami Council elected the NSR veteran and vice-president of the WCIP, Aslak Nils Sara, to act as chair person until 1989. The Norwegian Sami Council became a driving force behind the new reforms that took place during the 1980s.

(4) The handling of the Alta affair by the Norwegian State Broadcasting Corporation (NRK) should be mentioned in this context. NRK's coverage of events showed more goodwill towards environmental, and particularly Sami, activists than large sections of the political élite and the northern Norwegian left-wing press might have wished.

But the activists promoted their message, first and foremost, because of the nature of its *content*. "Street theatre" alone was no use, especially since the established élite used every weapon in the media armoury to adhere to their definition of what the affair was "really" about, namely development and power projects, saying that the Sami interests amounted to autumn grazing pastures for 21 reindeer (sic). In other words, the Sami hunger-strike in front of the *Stortinget* [Parliament building], in connection with the Alta affair, would never have got the media coverage it did receive, had it not been for the fact that the authorities' handling of, and general attitude to, this matter cemented

---

[38] The matter got extensive coverage in the regional newspaper *Nordlys* 07.12.1985 and in *Finnmark Dagblad* both before (04.12.1985) and after (06.12.1985) the regional council meeting (reports and editorials).

[39] The political process after the second report from the Sami Rights Commission submitted in 1997 about *the Natural Resources of the Sami Culture* (NOU 1997:4) may tear this contract to pieces (cf. Minde 2001:122-25).

and strengthened the very picture that the activists sought to present of them.[40] Before the action took place, it was discovered that the work on the access to the construction site had started without the necessary legal authority. When the government's lawyer defended the authorities' course of action in a much-publicized article in *Aftenposten* (10.10.1979), he revealed unintentionally how little notice had been taken of Sami interests, and he used the excuse that "this hasn't been demanded of the reindeer herders either". This simply added fuel to the fire. From his lookout post in Akersgata [the Fleet Street of Oslo], *Dagbladet* columnist Arne Skouen penned this dogma concerning the Alta affair:

> the more we read about the way the Alta development is being handled, the more clearly we understand that we are sacrifices for the worst of all forms of oppression: that which has developed into such a mechanical tradition that no-one reacts any longer. (*"Ytring"* [Expression], *Dagbladet* 12.10.1979).

At the same time, Hans Normann Dahl, in his daily cartoon, had depicted the Alta affair in an international legal perspective, which was reinforced over time as the affair later developed. The cartoon illustrated a double standard in Norwegian minorities policy: it was fine to talk about indigenous people far away, but not the ones in your own backyard (*"Krokodilletårer"* [Crocodile Tears], *Dagbladet* 11.10.1979).

To sum up, the Sami and environmentalist groups succeeded during the Alta struggle in mobilizing support for their claims and arguments through the coverage they got in the media. A prominent part of the political establishment, as well as the public opinion in general, began to reflect on the historic and present structure of power between the Sami and the state. In particular, how the old domain, comprised of the institutional quartet, formed a unique set of power relations. In the analytical terms of Giddens (1984:41-45) this may be depicted as follows: When the distinct structure of power came to the forefront of the public debate, the consciousness of the Sami-state relation was transformed from one that was tacitly practical to a discursive form of consciousness. In the public opinion, then, the minority policy of the old domain was suddenly exposed as being contrary to prevalent international and national attitudes. Consequently, the Sami organizations and the Norwegian state were both confronted with the same crucial political challenge: how should the Sami policy be accommodated to take into account the development in the 1970s and 1980s of human rights concerning indigenous peoples?

---

[40] I refer here to Robert Paine's detailed analysis as to why the hunger-strike outside the Norwegian Parliament building in 1979 gained the public's trust (Paine 1985).

- Poor indians

Oil on Troubled Waters

The state's demonstration of power, especially the mustering of 600 policemen in Stilla in January 1981, aroused international attention. Norwegian self-perception as foremost defender of human rights was hanging in the balance. The Sami's status as an indigenous people was raised in *Nordisk Råd* [the Nordic Parliamentary Council]. The Norwegian Sami policy was strongly criticized by the indigenous peoples' foremost international organizations, the World Council of Indigenous Peoples (WCIP) and the International Indian Treaty Council. A series of NGOs sent protest statements, both publically and through more diplomatic channels (Minde 2002: 114 ff). In the human rights committee in 1982-83, for the first time, Norway was given a thorough interrogation about the position of the Sami people (cf. Opsahl 1984).

Norwegian and Sami Initiatives

In this situation the Foreign Office very quietly took some important initiatives in co-operation with the Sami organizations and the re-organized Norwegian Sami Council. The first initiative was to set up a group of Nordic civil servants who would "promote the interests of the indigenous peoples". The first meeting of the group took place in December 1979. Observers from Canada and Australia took part in later meetings. Here, amongst other matters, the support of WCIP and IWGIA was co-ordinated. It was this latter group that was behind

95

the next initiative. A proposal in the Cobo Report, to set up a working group to address the question of indigenous people, was brought forward. The proposal was advocated at the UN Human Rights Commission in March 1981, but at the first round of talks it was moved down to a lower level in the UN system, to the Sub-Commission on Human Rights. In order to resolve matters relating to indigenous peoples, it was very important that the Foreign Office succeeded, in the same year, in its campaign to get the researcher Asbjørn Eide elected to the Sub-Commission. Together with Thorvald Stoltenberg and Aslak Nils Sara in the state delegation, he had brought forward the question of indigenous peoples at the racism conference in 1978, and later in 1981, together with Greek expert Erica-Irene Daes. Eide proposed to set up a working group to address the indigenous peoples' issue (WGIP). The proposal was rushed through the UN system and WGIP met for the first time on 9 August 1982 in Geneva. WGIP was to follow up this development by collecting information about the conditions in which indigenous peoples were living, and it was to begin the work of developing new standards for the rights of indigenous peoples.[41] A final initiative – and the most important one – was the active role played by Norway when the question of revising the disputed ILO Convention 107 was raised. This question had been taken up within the internal system of the ILO before Norway, as we have seen, could fulfil the process of ratification.

Because of the integration objectives of the old indigenous peoples' convention from 1957, the ILO administration in Geneva was strongly condemned by the indigenous peoples' representatives at the first meeting of the WGIP. Lee Swepston, the head of administration, who had previously carried out research into the indigenous peoples' situation in Latin America, acknowledged the criticism and proposed to the ILO committee that the matter should be opened up for revision. Meanwhile it was obvious that this proposal would not have been accomplished if it had not been for the lobbying activity carried out in Geneva since 1984 by Leif Dunfjeld (born 1943), ostensibly on behalf of WCIP but in reality on behalf of the Nordic Sami Council as well. But the Sami contribution for getting this process of revision launched wasn't over yet. It should be mentioned briefly that in the meetings at the ILO's working conferences in 1988 and 1989, which were concerned with the rough drafts of the new convention, Leif Dunfjeld represented the Nordic Sami Council, Leif Halonen was nominated to the working party delegation, and Aslak Nils Sara joined the government delegation as an adviser (in his capacity as leader of the Norwegian Sami Council). The sources available show that this network of Sami representatives played an important role.

---

[41]   This note is compiled from reports from government committee meetings, reports from the WCIP meeting in Canberra in 1981 and reports from the Norwegian delegation in Geneva, in the *Utenriksdepartements* (Foreign Office) archive, series 26 8/54, bd. 9.

Drafting a New ILO Convention (No. 169)

The interpretation of Land Rights Articles 14 and 15 (NOU 1997: 5:31 ff.) has been a key point in the debate about the new ILO's Convention No. 169 from 1989. The articles are concerned with ownership and/or rights of use. This was an area of the law where Norway obviously did not fulfil the demands in order to be able to ratify the old convention. The crucial question was (and is) whether these demands were altered or – more precisely – *awarded lower status* in the new, revised convention. In the parliamentary bill that preceded its ratification by Parliament in 1990, the Department of Justice has emphasized that strong rights of use satisfy the demands set by the new convention (St. prp. nr 102 (1989–90): 4 ff.).

I have shown earlier that during the crucial negotiations at the ILO working conference in 1989, the state delegation found themselves in a difficult voting situation when considerations concerning international legal standards and strong local interests parted company and developed into opposing attitudes (Minde 2002: 117 ff.). One of the most important aims for the delegation was to launch the proceedings in such a way that a new convention would take into account indigenous peoples' rights to the maintenance and development of these indigenous peoples' "own culture" and in the directives relating to the proceedings, the delegation was further instructed to "keep themselves oriented to the views of the representatives of indigenous peoples' groups that are in line with policy, especially from a Sami point of view".[42]

The other main objective was that the new convention could not proceed any further with regard to land rights than could be ratified by Norway. According to the directive, this presupposed that "we do not wish to have to agree to a convention that enjoins acknowledgment of ownership rights to traditional territories". But to lower the threshold with regard to land rights was at odds with the principal objective of the indigenous peoples' caucus groups; and during the course of the proceedings this became a mandatory requirement for their support. At the working conference in 1989 this claim was supported by members of the workers' group, a fact that played an important role in the ILO's tripartite decision system.

If agreement wasn't reached at the 1989 conference, the process of revision would be ended, according to ILO regulations. When the negotiations had got stuck, a smaller group, encompassing the Norwegian state delegation, sat down to explore the possibility of a package deal. Partly as a result of Norway's attitude, the negotiations remained so entrenched that the different parties prepared themselves for a showdown. The indigenous peoples' groups drafted a press

---

[42] "Directive for the Norwegian state delegation to the ILO working conference for the revision of the ILO convention 107", Utenriksdepartementets (Foreign Office) archive, serie 26, 8/54, bd. 9.

statement whereby Norway would have to shoulder considerable responsibility if the process was unsuccessful:

> The employers are joined by several governments, including those of the Canada, India, United States, Argentina, Bolivia and the Nordic countries, who seek language in the revised Convention that effectively would make indigenous land ownership not a right but an option of the government. In particular, *language sought by the Nordic countries would allow governments to choose arrangements other than ownership in the form of vaguely stated rights of "use"* [author's emphasis].[43]

Since the Norwegian state delegation represented the Nordic states in the emergency group, Norway was on the verge of being left to negotiate conflicting pressures. Confronted by this fact, the delegation asked for time out to reflect upon what they should do. It has still not been made clear which political contacts were then approached, but we do know the outcome: a compromise was established. The delegation sent a report home as soon as this compromise had been reached and the convention adopted at the official meeting of the working conference:

> From the Norwegian side, a proposal was put forward, as you know, *to place rights of use on an equal footing with rights of ownership in Article 14*, which is the main issue concerning land rights. Although this proposal was presented as a strengthening of the convention, in that it offered protection to many kinds of rights, the proposal was interpreted by many as a weakness, and accordingly met with considerable opposition, particularly from the NGOs and members of the workers' group, but also from many of the governmental delegates. *The proposal was withdrawn after the working group delegates demanded this, as a condition of accepting the compromise package,* and after certain changes had been made to Article 14 to oblige Norway, Finland and Sweden [author's emphasis].[44]

Confronted by Parliament in 1990, the Ministry of Justice concluded that strong rights of use (for example reindeer pasturing rights) complied with the claims laid down by the convention concerning rights of ownership and possession (St.prp. 102 (1989-90):7). The so-called "International Rights Committee" (a sub-committee of the Sami Legal Commission) maintained in a report in 1997 that "this standpoint cannot be right" (NOU 1997:5:36). This assessment was based solely on a detailed study of the official ILO report from the working conference.

---

[43] Press release, 20 June 1998, Samerådets Arkiv, file "ILO".

[44] Fax dated 26 june 1989. Utenriksdepartementets (Foreign Office) archive, serie 26, 8/54, bd. 9.

The primary sources from the state delegation therefore confirm that the Ministry of Justice's ruling *was* in fact incorrect. This report reveals that in the first place the Norwegian proposal, put forward at the instructions of the State delegates, was not accepted as part of the compromise. Secondly, the delegation decided not to vote against the proposal for the new convention. Faced with the possibility of being blamed for a collapse in negotiations, the Norwegian delegation confined themselves to announcing their satisfaction with the result and following instructions concerning their specific reasons for voting in this way: that they did not consider the firm assurance of *land use* to be a violation of the requirement of *ownership*. But we can now conclude that this reservation has not proven to be the straw that saved the Ministry of Justice. The strong rights of use (e.g. reindeer pasturing rights) obviously *do not fulfil* the claims laid down by the convention concerning rights of ownership and possession. Notwithstanding this, the consequence of the Ministry of Justice's ruling – whether deliberate or not – was that the principal aspect of Norwegian foreign policy concerning indigenous people was frankly obscure.

The Norwegian policy at the time of the ILO negotiations, in 1988 and 1989, of a revised and new convention on indigenous people, must be understood not only in the light of the Alta affair but also in connection with the particular foreign policy in the 1980s, and with more universal processes of how the states redefine their preferences.

Norway stood out as a pioneering nation in the development of human rights, and placed great emphasis on maintaining international obligations. We have seen that the Alta affair contributed to Foreign Office taking upon itself an active and enterprising role in the indigenous peoples' issue, which had just been placed on the agenda within the UN system. Here, Norway was able to play its traditional role of bridge-builder in relations between weak groups in developing countries and rich western states. As mentioned by Johan Jørgen Holst just before he became Foreign Minister (1985:26), Norway wanted to "promote the cause of justice". In other words, it was not surprising that the Norwegian state delegation chose to vote for a package deal that won qualified support from the working conference.

In addition, Norway's conduct in Geneva in 1989 stands out as a good example of a process noted by various political scientists: through its participation in international fora and organizations, the state has become conditioned at various times to the acceptance of new norms, standards and concepts. This perspective has proven to be particularly fruitful in analyzing the expansion of human rights over the past few decades (Finnemore 1996; Risse and others 1999). The growth of the human rights issue and breakthough in this field may, paradoxically, be seen as one of the decisive factors in the cultural globalization that influenced and established boundaries for the national policy during the period that followed.

Conclusion

The expression "the silent revolution" has been used to characterize the changes that followed in the wake of the Alta affair. The Alta affair not only exposed the power structure: it is also a striking example of how strong, traditional political domains can fall at the feet of seemingly weak groups of people (the Sami make up barely more than one per cent of the Norwegian population, and throughout this period they were split politically with regard to the minority policy). The usual explanation for political crises is that they are the result of a conflict of interests. The outcome is then determined by the type and extent of resources available to all parties. An explanation of this kind is obviously unsuited to the reality of this situation. The theory advanced by the Norwegian historian Francis Sejersted is more applicable to an understanding of the developments in Norway after the environmental and Sami action in 1979 and 1981. Sejersted's premise is that those involved in politics are generally looking for a consensus. So the political system usually collapses, not because of a clash of interests, but because of problems of governance. It is not the crises in themselves that provoke the changes, "but rather the unintentional and unfortunate consequences of the policy that has been carried out" (Sejersted 1983, quotation on p. 69).

Within such a perspective, I shall summarize as follows: the political discourse that resulted from the environmental and Sami political action in the autumn of 1979 revealed a "cognitive dissonance" that had arisen with regard to Norwegian Sami policy. In the media, for a limited period, the Sami themselves got the chance to *speak on their own behalf* for the first time. Norwegian Sami policy found its way onto the political agenda, as did Sami politicians, such as NSR leader Ole Henrik Magga. People who were not normally concerned with Sami issues were now challenged to take sides in intense debates about (a) whether the Sami were "aboriginal", (b) whether the Norwegian Sami policy justified civil disobedience and (c) the relationship between law and justice. The debates were concerned with fundamental questions about the relationship between the state and the Sami people and revealed *unresolved problems of governance*. The Nordli government's immediate response after the Sami hunger strike in 1979 (e.g. a commission on the Sami rights issue) consisted of old proposals, dating either from the Sami Committee of 1959 or those issued later. The fact that the proposals had earlier been either directly rejected or very quietly put on ice demonstrated the defensive opposition to change and the paternalistic attitude of the Norwegian political domain concerned with Sami issues. Now a political crisis had arisen, where the existing political domain was defended only by the local media and the 'old guard' in the north. Elsewhere in the power structure, people were seized with doubt, bewilderment and the desire to distance themselves from the situation. The attacks against the authorities' Sami policy came from all political quarters and encompassed every level of power, exposing an underlying consensus concerning Norway's obligations in international law.

The state embarked on a learning and re-organizing process that ended once and for all the out-dated political domain concerning Sami issues. If one compares the Norwegian minority policy towards the Sami with that of Sweden and Finland in the same period (see Sillenpää 1994; Eriksson 1997), the differences become striking. There, the old centres of power in Sami politics have not been discredited in the way that they were in Norway during the Alta affair. The old attitudes in the north still have a strong influence in state politics, especially if the representatives from this region make up the balance of power in the national assemblies. This difference between the Nordic states is most apparent in the handling of the new ILO Convention 169. Norway's priority was to be *the first state* to ratify the convention. Neither Finland nor Sweden has yet done so.

Once the Alta affair had been defined by the media as both a Sami matter *and* an indigenous people's matter, the political rules of the game altered drastically. The authorities' handling of the Alta issue was no longer evaluated in connection with electrical power and modernization; rather with colonial legacy, the assimilation policy and the Norwegian self-image of playing a leading role in the development of international human rights. The questions raised by the Sami movement required political solutions that delved behind formalistic, liberal state theories and traditional analyses of power and democracy. The history, culture and politics of the indigenous peoples put indigenous politics outside the usual confines of interest groups, class and social movements, because the political claims are of a higher moral order and they seem to assert a higher priority for settlement, as mentioned recently by Geoffrey Stokes (2002:184) in his analysis of Aboriginal peoples' self-determination in Australia. After the Alta affair this was the fundamental problem, which required new political solutions in Norway as well.

References

Bergh, T. and Eriksen, K.E: *Den hemmelige krigen. Overvåking i Norge 1914–1997.* Vol. 2, Storhetstid og stormkast 1955–1997, Oslo: Cappelens Akademiske Forlag, 1998.

Brantenberg, T: "Norway: Constructing Indigenous Self-government in a Nation State: Samediggi – the Sami Parliament in Norway", in: Jull, P. and Robarts, S. (eds.): *The Challenge of Northern Regions.* Darwin: North Australian Research Unit: Darwin, 1991, pp. 66-128.

Brochmann, G. "Velferdsstat, integrasjon og majoritetens legitimitet", in: Brochmann, G., Borchrevink, T. and Rogstad, J. (eds.): *Sand i maskineriet. Makt og demokrati i det flerkulturelle Norge.* Oslo: Gyldendal Akademiske, 2002, pp. 27-55.

Brown, D: *Bury my Heart at Wounded Knee. An Indian History of the American West.* New York: Bantam Book, 1971.

Brysk, A: *From Tribal Village to Global Village.* Standford University Press, 2000.

Dalland, Ø: *Demningen. En Alta-saga.* Karasjok: Davvi media o.s, 1989.

Deloria, V: *Custer died for your Sins. An Indian Manifesto.* New York: Avon Books, 1969.

Drivenes, E.-A. and Jernsletten, R: "Det gjenstridige Nord-Norge. Religiøs, politisk og etnisk mobilisering 1850–1990", in: *Nordnorsk kulturhistorie,* vol. I, Oslo: Gyldendal Norsk Forlag, 1994, pp. 210-281.

Eidheim, H: *Aspects of the Lappish Minority Situation,* Oslo-Bergen-Tromsø: Universitetsforlaget, 1971.

Egeberg, M., Olsen, J.P. and Sætren, H: "Organisasjonssamfunnet og den segmenterte stat", in: Olsen, J. P. (ed.): *Politisk organisering,* Bergen-Oslo-Stavanger-Tromsø: Universitetsforlaget, 1978, pp. 115-142.

Eriksen, K. E. and Niemi, E: *Den finske fare. Sikkerhetsproblemer og minoritetspolitikk i nord 1860–1940.* Universitetsforlaget: Oslo-Bergen-Tromsø: Universitetsforlaget, 1981.

Eriksson, J: *Partition and Redemption. A Machiavellian Analysis of Sami and Basque Patriotism.* Umeå: Umeå University, Department of Political Science, 1997.

Finnemore, M: *National Interests in Internatioanl Society.* Ithaca-London: Cornell University Press, 1996.

Faaberg, A.B.: Norsk minoritetspolitikk. Trekk fra 1960- og '70-åras utvikling i samiske spørsmål. Unpublished hovedfagsoppgave in history, University in Oslo, 1984.

Giddens, A: *The Constitution of Society.* Cambridge: Polity Press, 1984.

Hansen, L.I. and Niemi, E: "Samisk forskning ved et tidsskifte: Jens Andreas Friis og lappologien – vitenskap og politikk", in: Seglen, E. (ed.): *Vitenskap, teknologi og samfunn.* Oslo: Cappelens Akademiske forlag, 1984, pp. 350-377.

Hesjedal, A: *Samisk forhistorie i norsk arkeologi 1900–2000,* Unpublished dr. art.-thesis, Tromsø: Institute of Archaeology, University in Tromsø, 2000.

Hill, R.G and Nicul, K (eds.): *The Lapp Today.* Oslo-Bergen-Tromsø: Universitetsforlaget, 1969.

Holst, J.J: "Om utenrikspolitikk og Norge", in: Holst, J.J. and Heradstveid, D. (eds.): *Norsk utenrikspolitikk.* Oslo: Tano, 1985, pp. 13-33.

Homme, L: *Nordisk nykolonialisme. Samiske problem i dag.* Oslo: Det Norske Samlaget, 1969.

Jernsletten, R: "The development of a Saami élite in Norden", in: Kristina Karppi and Johan Eriksson (eds.): *Conflict and Cooperation in the North,* Umeå: Skrifter från forskningsprogrammet KULTURGRÄNS NORR 38, 2002, pp. 147-112.

Kymlicka, W: *Multicultural Citizenship. A Liberal Theory of Minority Rights.* Oxford University Press, 1995.

Manuel, G. and Posluns, M: *The Fourth World: An Indian Reality,* Toronto, 1974.

Minde, H: "The Sami Movement, the Norwegian Labour Party and Sami Rights", in: *L'image de l'autre. Étrangers-Minoritaires-Marginaux. Sous la direction d'Hélène Ahrweiler.* 16e Congrès Internal des Sciences Historiques, Stuttgart, 1985, pp. 412-443.

Minde, H: "The Making of an International Movement of Indigenous Peoples", in: *Scandinavian Journal of History,* 1996: 3, pp. 221-246.

Minde, H: "Sami Land Rights In Norway: A Test Case for Indigenous Peoples", in: *International Journal on Minority and Group Rights,* 2001:2–3, pp. 107-125.

Minde, H: "Urfolksoffensiv, folkerettsfokus og styringskrise: Kampen for en ny samepolitikk 1960-1990", in: Bjerkli, B and Selle, P. (eds.): *Samer makt og demokrati,* Oslo: Gyldendal Akademisk, 2003,a, pp. 87-123.

Minde, H: "Assimilation of the Samis – Implementation and Consequences", in: *Acta Borealia*, 2003,b, (in press).

Niemi, E: "Kulturmøte, etnisitet og statlig intervensjon på Nordkalotten", in: Andersson, Rut Boström (ed.): *Den Nordiska mosaiken: språk- och kulturmöten i gammal tid och i våra dagar*. Humanistdagarna vid Uppsala universitet 1997, Uppsala, 1997, pp.261-272.

Niemi, E: "Kategorienes etikk og minoritetene i nord", in: *Samisk forskning og forskningsetikk*. Oslo: Den nasjonale forskningsetiske komité for samfunnsvitenskap og humaniora, 2002, pp. 22-44.

NOU 1980:53, *Vern av urbefolkninger*.

NOU 1984:18, *Om samenes rettsstilling*.

NOU 1997:5, *Urfolks landrettigheter etter folkerett og utenlandsk rett*.

Nyhamar, J: *Arbeiderbevegelsens historie i Norge. Nye utfordringer (1965–1990)*, vol. 6, Oslo: Tiden Norsk Forlag, 1990.

Opsahl, T: "Urbefolkningene i Menneskerettskomitéen", in: *Mennesker og Rettigheter*, 1984: 2, pp. 20-22.

Ot.prp. nr 33 (1986–87). *Om lov om Sametinget og andre samiske rettsforhold* (sameloven).

Ot.prp. nr 53 (2002-2003). *Finnmarksloven: Rettigheter i Finnmark Fylke.*

Paine, R: "Etnodrama and the 'Forth Worls': The Saami Action Group in Norway, 1979–81", in: Dyck, N (ed.): *Indigenous Peoples and the Nation-State*, St.John's, Newfoundland: Institute of Social and Econmic Research, Memorial University, 1985, pp. 190-235.

Paine, R: "Aboriginality, Multiculturalism, and Liberal Rights Philosophy", in: *Ethnos*, 1999: 3, pp. 325-349.

Pedersen, S: "Fra bruk av naturgoder etter samiske sedvaner til forbud mot jordsalg til ikke-norsktalende", in: *NOU* 2001: 34, *Samiske sedvaner og rettsoppfatninger*, pp. 289-381.

Protokoll från Svenska Samernas Riksförbunds Landsmötet i Arvidsjaur den 14–17 juni 1977.

Risse, T., Ropp, S.C. and Sikkink, K: *The Power of Human Rights. International Norms and Domestic Change*. Cambridge University Press, 1999.

Samernas åttonde konferens, Nordisk sameråd 1974.

Sámiid kulturpolitii'ka, Helset (Helsinki), 1974.

Sara, A.N: "Oppdagelsen av oss selv og verden", in: Brantenberg, T., Hansen, J and Minde, H: *Becoming Visible: Indigenous Politics and Self-Government*, Tromsø: Sámi Dutkamiid Guovddáš, 1995, pp. 57-60.

Sejersted, F: "Politikk som interessekamp eller styringsproblem", in: Berg, T.: *Deltakerdemokratiet*. Oslo: Universitetsforlaget, 1983, pp. 51-69.

Sillanpää, L: *Political and Administrative Responses to Sami Self-Determination*. Helsinki: Societas Scientiarum Fennica, 1994.

Stokes, G: "Australian Democracy and Indigenous Self-Determination, 1901-2001", in: G. Brennan, G and F. Castles, F. (eds.): *Australia Reshaped: Essays on Two Hundred Years of Institutional Transformation*. Melbourne: Cambridge University Press, 2002, pp. 181-219.

Stordahl, V: *Same i den moderne verden. Endring og kontinuitet i et samisk lokalsamfunn*. Karasjok: Davvi Girji, 1996.

St.prp.nr 102 (1989-90). Om den 76. internasjonale arbeidskonferanse i Genève 1989.

Taylor, C: *Multiculturalism : examining the politics of recognition*: Princeton University Press, 1994.

Tjelmeland, H: "The Norwegian Encounter with Pakistanis: Diversities and Paradoxes on the Road to Norway's Immigration stop", in: Ohliger, R (et.al., ed.): *European Encounters, Migrants, Migration and European Societies since 1945.* Asgate forlag, 2003, (in press).

Valkeapää, N-A: *Helsing frå Sameland.* Oslo: Pax forlag, 1979.

World Council of Indigenous Peoples Second General Assembly. Helset/Helsinki, 1978.

The Sea

CHAPTER 6

Culture Loss and Sense of Place in Resource Valuation: Economics, Anthropology and Indigenous Cultures

Robert Snyder, Daniel Williams and George Peterson[1]

I. Introduction

The Exxon-Valdez oil tanker ran aground on Bligh Reef outside the Valdez Arm of Prince William Sound, Alaska on March 24th 1989. Aside from attracting enormous media attention, this disaster focused a great deal of research and analysis on the ecological (Brown et al. 1993), political (Piper 1997), economic (Cohen 1993), and social (Jorgensen 1995; Gill and Picou 1997) impacts of the spill. With an eye toward likely litigation over damages, much of this research quickly centered on assessing the economic costs of the spill to affected industries and economies both local and global. Our aim in this chapter is to reflect on some of the particular difficulties associated with assessing the "culture losses" of indigenous peoples impacted by the spill. That such problems were encountered should not be surprising given the fact that economic impacts are generally assessed using concepts (e.g., cost, compensation, and property) designed to function within western economic and judicial systems.[2]

This chapter builds on disciplined and interdisciplinary perspectives on culture loss that have emerged during various attempts to assess natural resource damage. The term culture loss addresses two broad but interrelated categories of loss, loss of possession and loss of kinship or belonging (Kirsch 2001). In the former category culture loss includes the loss of possessions such as natural resources and customs such as livelihood practices for which one might claim rights or ownership. As such these losses imply value and property relations

---

[1] Robert Snyder is a doctoral student in Social anthropology at York University, Toronto, Ontario Canada. Daniel R. Williams is a Research Social Scientist, and George Peterson is a Research Economist, both with Rocky Mountain Research Station, USDA Forest Service, Fort Collins, Colorado. Send Correspondence regarding this paper to: Daniel R. Williams, Rocky Mountain Research Station, 2150A Centre Ave., Fort Collins, CO 80526 USA; e-mail: drwilliams@fs.fed.us.

[2] We use the phrase "western economic and judicial systems" loosely recognizing that it problematically reifies very diverse moral and ethical principles.

that are alienable or more or less amenable to economic compensation in some form. In the latter category, however, relationship to land or resource involves an intimate bond or sense of place, that take on the characteristics of kinship ties and belongingness, which are inalienable. Both possession and belonging, when applied to property, are grounded in the assumption that property is a manifestation of social relations (Rose 1994:227 cf Kirsch 2001:168). Simply put, property does not exist without people to make it meaningful. If the acquisition of property is a social manifestation then so is loss. For example many people possess land by rights given by the state and simultaneously through kinship or as members of a particular group. Thus, assessment and remuneration in cases of culture loss are also socially mediated. The possibility that disparate groups will need to resolve conflicts over resource damage increases as more people are connected across the globe by resource interdependencies.

Efforts to determine appropriate compensation for losses suffered by indigenous peoples practicing traditional subsistence lifestyles test the limits of current social science and institutional arrangements to identify and deliver an equitable solution to resource damages that result in culture loss. Our intention is to illuminate new spaces for dialogue between the various interest groups involved in assessing and mitigating these losses. We begin by highlighting some of the positive and negative outcomes of past attempts to engage this monumental task within economics and then anthropology. Throughout, we show that the beginnings of a solution may reside in the work being done around the issues of culture loss and sense of place. Concluding, we review how the natural resource valuation process has been tested and transformed by sustained challenges from indigenous and Western perspectives and suggest that an equitable solution may reside in an interdisciplinary synthesis of the knowledges at hand.

To give but one concrete illustration of what we mean by the challenges encountered in assessing resource damage and culture loss, one esteemed economist serving on an advisory panel organized after the oil spill suggested that the way to determine the value of damage suffered by a particular village was to estimate the cost of relocating that village to a similar undamaged site. At that point, one of the authors (Peterson)[3] objected noting that such an estimate would have to make the very untenable assumption that the two locations are substitutable. Further, such an estimate would have to ignore the value of what might be characterized as the sense of place that millennia of cultural development had created. The very concept of a culture -- its ways of life and subsistence practices, systems of meaning, social organization, and identity -- cannot, as modern economic concepts presume, easily be separated from its geographic

---

[3] Peterson represented the United States Department of Agriculture on the Economic Steering Committee for the Exxon-Valdez damage assessment.

location.[4] Because so much of what constitutes a culture is woven into spatial patterns and localized meanings, to move a culture would be tantamount to destroying it. Much of what is valuable to the culture is embedded in the place. Though this economist wasn't suggesting the village actually be moved, only that the value of its loss could be equated to the cost of relocating, the suggestion demonstrates that economic compensation would have little meaning to such a culture. Monetary compensation might allow villagers to enter into the western economy and purchase goods to replace those goods traditionally extracted from the local environment, but money could in no way compensate for the culture loss.[5] And in fact, money might well do additional harm to the culture by modifying social relationships that were not monetized previous to the oil spill.

A key point of departure to frame this inquiry is to recognize, at least in part, how modern society interprets its relationship to nature and how this interpretation is woven into its science of valuation and legal and economic institutions in comparison to traditional subsistence cultures. The concept of "sense of place" is increasingly being employed as both an academic and popular way to represent the idea that there are aspects of human relationships to nature that legal, political, and market institutions under-represent in economic and other social transactions (Kirsch, 2001; Torgerson, 1999). In particular we draw on this concept to characterize the idea that individuals and communities possess some "endowment" of natural, cultural, and economic goods. In modern market economies a large portion of this endowment can be accounted in monetary terms and calculated as net worth, thus making economic approaches to environmental valuation a reasonable, though still incomplete, method for assessing

---

[4]   Implicit in anthropology has been a conceptualization of the human world as a mosaic of separate cultures located in specific places or regions (Gupta and Ferguson 1997). Traditional cultures, even nomadic ones, have some territory that defines and contains subsistence practices and carries meaning and identity to its occupants. While some anthropologists have begun to criticize the idea that cultures are necessarily bounded by geographic territory (see Gupta and Ferguson 1997; Olwig and Hastrup 1997), it is also very much the case that de-territorialization of cultures is intensified by modernization and globalization (see Appadurai 1991 and Clifford 1992). Thus, many cultures are no longer as territorially bounded as they once were, but the process of disembedding cultural practices and social relations from place has profound implications for cultures that experience this transformation as the anthropologists cited above examine. Much the same can be said of any society undergoing modernization as evidenced by the large literature on the sociology of modernity (cf. Giddens 1991; Urry 2000).

[5]   The concept of culture loss is problematic within western property rights (Kirsch, 2001:168). If the government decides it needs someone's land to build a highway that landowner is only entitled to fair market value. One's sense of place tied to the family homestead is not generally recognized as a property right. But this is part of the problem; things of salient value in an indigenous culture may not be recognized as things of monetary value within western culture and legal systems.

damage. Still, as individuals, we recognize that much of what we own -- our property, possessions, natural gifts and talents, and our relationships to family and community -- is not entirely represented in such accounts. Possessions have sentimental value unique to their owner. And more to the point, nature, natural resources, and local place as repositories of memories, relationships and the daily routines have meaning and significance in our personal and collective lives that cannot be reduced adequately to monetary value.

In contrast, one way to characterize traditional subsistence societies is to note that much of their endowment is not circumscribed within market transactions or recognized as property rights. Thus, the difference of concern here between subsistence cultures and modern economies is a matter of the degree to which economic transactions account for the value of one's total endowment or "sense of place". Moreover, much of what constitutes a subsistence culture's natural endowment is linked to specific knowledge of place that allows it to effectively produce and distribute goods of both a subsistence and symbolic nature (Kirsch, 2001:175). In a subsistence society meaning and relevance of much of a culture's knowledge and practices are specific to geographic places, for example, the knowledge of the particular location and timing of harvestable plants and game. Similarly complex social relations are also spatially organized. Harvesting locations, for example, may be allocated to families or other social units in such a way as to maintain certain hierarchies of status and power and even familial ties and obligations. Take the culture out of its place and such knowledge and practice may lose meaning, and change and disrupt social organization.

II. What Monetary Valuation Misses
From a western economic perspective the key problem created by the Exxon-Valdez oil spill is assessing the monetary damage. But environmental resource damage assessment encounters serious obstacles when the question is damage to indigenous subsistence-based cultures, what Kirsch (2001) describes as "culture loss." Following a brief review of the economics of non-market valuation, this section identifies those obstacles and explains why we must seek out alternative legal theories and valuation methods.

A Brief Review of The Economics of Non-market Valuation
Economic value is the amount of money one is willing to trade for the thing in question.[6] In a market economy, equilibrium between supply and demand assigns monetary marginal market prices, which individual producers and con-

---

6   Although we generally think of economic value in terms of money, it need not be measured by a monetary metric. Money is simply a parameter of exchange in a monetary market economy that simplifies exchange relationships. In a barter economy specific exchange rates among goods and services define economic value.

sumers then decide whether to accept, based on the economic value to them. Market prices effectively measure economic value (are economically efficient) only for marginal transactions under perfect competition.

Even in the hypothetical perfect market, prices do not measure the economic value of non-marginal quantities, i.e., quantities large enough to change the market price. Market prices also fail to include the value of goods for which markets are imperfect or do not exist, such as goods that are non-rival and/or non-excludable in consumption (e.g., public goods) or are non-priced for other reasons, such as government policy or cultural tradition (Randall 1983), values not based on legal property rights, and derived values removed from the consumer's awareness and market exchange by ignorance and externality (Loomis et al. 1984; Peterson et al. 1987; Peterson et al. 1992).

The domain of things that fall into the non-priced account is large. For example, Rolston III (1981) and Driver et al. (1996) identify a complex spectrum of hard-to-define values that motivate human feelings and behaviors toward the natural environment. Many of the benefits and costs tied to the natural world, including the benefits of global biodiversity, forest health, wilderness, outdoor recreation, scenic beauty, and sense of place, are non-priced.

When measured and applied correctly, economic value answers important questions. Cost and revenue accounting helps individuals and private firms evaluate financial efficiency. Benefit-cost analysis (BCA) with non-market values included addresses the broader concept of economic efficiency as seen from the perspective of social welfare. Economic impact analysis addresses the equity objective by showing how an action distributes costs and benefits among people.

There are also many important questions that economic value cannot answer (Peterson and Brown 1999). Some of these questions lie outside the economic domain. Others may be within the theoretical boundaries, but the economic answers may be incomplete or biased because the state of the art is not perfect or because resources are insufficient to allow valid measurement.[7] The problems identified below arise because monetary economic valuation theories and methods presume that the value of all goods and services can be measured as a monetary exchange value, that is, that there is some amount of money that can substitute for the good or service in question.

Inability to Measure Some Values in Economic Terms

Valid and credible economic valuation of all the important non-market costs and benefits generally is not achievable for three reasons: (1) The monetary

---

[7]   This discussion of the limitations of economic value in capturing the value of biodiversity views the topic primarily from the microeconomic perspective (Henderson and Quandt 1980; Silberberg 1978). Other problems exist at the macroeconomic level (Daly and Cobb 1989; Daly 1980; and Korten 1992).

economic paradigm is not appropriate for some things; (2) where monetary economic valuation is appropriate, the state of the art is often inadequate; and (3) application of available methods to meet reasonable standards of quality is often too expensive. For these reasons, monetary economic analyses in situations where the non-market components are significant tend to be biased toward private goods with market prices. That bias is especially severe for subsistence and barter-based cultures where a substantial portion of an individual's total endowment or "net worth" is not easily measured in monetary terms. The bias is, of course, not a difference of kind, but a difference of degree.

Each of us, whether wheeling and dealing in a Western market economy or living a subsistence life style in a barter-based indigenous culture, values aspects of our environment, experiences, possessions, and associations with others that don't appear on ledgers and can't be converted to cash. Those of us in a market economy can, however, account for a substantial amount of what we consider to be our "net worth" as privately owned real estate, bank accounts, income, cash on hand, and personal property. We also have a lot of experience trading such things in markets. But, we also hold and enjoy sentimental and spiritual values, memories, feelings, and traditions associated with sense of place and personal associations, and other important aspects of quality of life that are difficult or impossible to measure in terms of money. The cultural difference occurs because when people in subsistence and barter-based cultures add up their net worth, a much smaller proportion appears in monetary accounts. Their interests in situations like natural resource damage assessment will therefore be represented poorly unless we can find more effective ways to involve them in the process.

Things for Which Money Cannot Compensate: To explain this point, we must differentiate among three types of economic value: the value a person assigns, the value the market assigns, and value assigned by institutional fiat. From the personal point of view, there may be things for which there are no acceptable substitutes that money can buy, for example, the value of the life of a loved one or the sentimental value of a home that has been in the family for generations but is now condemned by eminent domain.

The market generally does not recognize the portion of such values not defendable as legally defined property rights.[8] From the market point of view, there will be many substitutes for the loved one in the work force, so that aspect of the person will have a market value. The family home will also have a market price. These prices will generally fall short, however, of the value assigned

---

[8]   Kirsch (2001:172), however, cites the case of Eisenring v. Kansis Turnpike Authority in which the court held that where the usual means of assessing market value were lacking it was proper to assess the market value of a property by considering its intrinsic value and its value to the owners for their special purposes.

by an individual to whom the life or the house has unique personal value. Given free choice, the individual might not be willing to sell at any price.

Some economic values are assigned by institutional fiat, such as the value of an eye or of an arm, as specified by accident insurance contracts. These are economic values, but they do not necessarily compensate the victim for the full personal value of the loss. The individual might not be willing to sell the eye or the arm at any price, but the "price" assigned by the insurance convention is better than no compensation at all.

Likewise, money cannot compensate for the total value of critical factors that enable human life to exist, and it cannot compensate either for many religious, spiritual, cultural, political, and symbolic values (Driver et al. 1996). Even where money might compensate in theory, measurement of economic value might not be possible, because it requires people to be willing and able to see them in the context of exchange with money as the numeraire. Such a context may be impossible for people to conceive in some situations. Or, they may view the question as a violation of the values in question. For example, in a focus group conducted to test alternative ways to estimate willingness to accept compensation for the environmental damage caused by the Exxon-Valdez oil spill, a young women leaped to her feet and angrily shouted, "You mean to say I've been raped and you think there is some amount of money that will make me feel it didn't happen?" Subsistence and barter-based indigenous peoples might well shout the same lamentation.

Things for Which the State of the Art is Inadequate: The validity of non-market valuation methods, especially the contingent valuation (CV) method, has not yet been demonstrated sufficiently to satisfy many economists (Mitchell and Carson 1989; Cambridge Economics 1992; Arrow et al. 1993; Portney 1994), but CV is the only option available for monetary valuation of many environmental values.

Inability to measure the economic value of damage to subsistence users of natural resources in the case of the Exxon-Valdez oil spill demonstrates failure of the economic approach to valuation. From a Western economic perspective the indigenous peoples of Alaska who depend on natural resources for direct subsistence have made a life style choice that limits their monetary income. The damaged natural resources constitute a major portion of their total endowment. The appropriate measure in such a case is willingness to accept compensation (WTA), but the present state-of-the-art is not capable of valid measurement of WTA for non-priced environmental goods. In such cases, the only option, willingness to pay (WTP) to avoid the loss, severely underestimates economic value because what one is willing to pay is, of course, constrained by one's income or ability to pay. And because of cultural barriers, the individuals in question may not be willing or able to play the CV "game."

Consider, for example, an original painting by Renoir being sold at a public auction. You want to buy the painting but you are broke and have only five dollars in your pocket. Your bid of $5.00 evokes only laughter, and you go away in shame and disappointment as the wealthy high rollers bid huge sums of money for the painting you covet. As you leave, an official adds to your injury by saying, "You have insulted this establishment by implying that the value of that priceless art treasure is only $5.00!". On the other hand, assume that you already own the painting and have decided to sell it. Would you be willing to accept the $5.00 bid by the shabbily dressed person in the back of the room?

CV also requires people to visualize a thing as a commodity they would exchange for money in a market or in a political referendum. That requirement is a challenge for anyone when the thing is an environmental resource or sentimental value, but subsistence-based indigenous populations who have little or no experience either with money-based markets or with environmental resource referenda will have great difficulty even understanding the "game." If there are cultural barriers based on different styles of communication and negotiation, or if the subculture views the "establishment" with distrust, as is often the case, CV simply will not work. And, the very idea of exchanging traditional life style, sacred places, cultural symbols, and sense of place for money may be non sequitur. Again, the suggestion to measure the economic value of damage to a village affected by the oil spill as the cost of moving the village to an undamaged location with similar environmental characteristics is naive, because it fails to include the religious and cultural significance of attachment to place and knowledge of place resulting from hundreds and perhaps thousands of years of occupation. The new location would be an inferior substitute at best, and may be no substitute at all.[9] It is, perhaps, nothing but the lesser of two unacceptable evils. As explained by Hall (1966): "... People from different cultures not only speak different languages but, what is possibly more important, inhabit different sensory worlds."

When the Cost is too High: A basic principle of economics is that the cost of the analysis should not exceed the cost of being wrong. Many land management decisions simply do not justify the cost of rigorous monetary valuation of non-market factors. Meeting the standards prescribed by Arrow et al. (1993) in application of contingent valuation, for example, can be extremely expensive. Overcoming the obstacles described above is a major research challenge. The Federal Economic Steering Committee spent in excess of a million dollars de-

---

[9] This argument assumes, of course, that the villagers have rights to the values excluded by the cost of moving them to another location. If no such rights exist, the economist may have been correct in the eyes of the law, but the villagers' felt loss would be no less real (Kirsch 2001, Strathern 1999).

veloping a CV protocol for use with the general population.[10] It is probable that the indigenous subsistence-based population problem has no solution in the domain of traditional economic theory and method, but if there is a solution, finding it will require a very expensive research effort.

To their credit, the Economic Steering Committee recognized the inadequacy of the monetary economic approach and embarked upon an ethnographic solution. They convened a small task force of sociologists and anthropologists to attack the problem but an out-of-court settlement aborted the effort. The question remains, however, whether the need is to understand and more effectively represent the values held by indigenous peoples in the processes and institutions in which they are not able to participate effectively or to create new processes and institutions in which they can more effectively represent their own interests.

III. Anthropological Contributions

Anthropologists, like economists, ask how we can account for more of a group's total sense of place when valuing natural resource damage and culture loss. However, the ways that each discipline formulates questions of valuation and the methods used to answer the questions can be quite different. Anthropologists generally work to identify the complex ways that places are made meaningful within and between groups of people. Questions of where culture resides become highly contentious here. On the one hand anthropologists may argue that culture resides in the mind as Paul Bohannon did while testifying on behalf of Exxon in the Exxon Valdez hearings (Kirsch 2001:171). When used in testimony, the consequence of this conception of culture is that remuneration for lost cultural resources becomes a moot point. On the other hand anthropologists may argue that culture resides in material objects (see Weiner 1992), in which case compensation for damage to land, religious sites, etc. should be required. According to Kirsch (2001), the theoretical ambiguity surrounding the ways that culture functions in relation to place is to blame for some of the problems encountered in instances of culture loss due to natural resource damage.

Recent attempts by anthropologists to theorize the crossroads of culture and place in the context of resource valuation focus on the process of negotiation that takes place as networks of actors with varying degrees of power vie to protect their interests. Here, culture informs negotiation, creating a cultural politics of place, which is simultaneously material and ideological, thus steeped in power and history. In other words, places become meaningful to people because of the historically sedimented discourses and material practices that con-

---

[10]   The figure cited is approximate and based on memory, not hard facts, but the development of the CV protocol was a major and very expensive undertaking.

stitute the politics of a place (Moore 1998, Raffles 1999). The significance of power and discourse in shaping resource assessments is taken up below.

Anthropological contributions to the discussion of culture loss and resource assessment can be grouped along two trajectories, each aimed at contributing to a more holistic understanding of indigenous peoples' total endowment or sense of place. First, anthropologists emphasize the various interconnections between culture loss and natural resources. Second, anthropologists are increasingly interested in identifying the local and global players in the resource valuation process and the discourses that influence their choices.

Linking Culture Loss and Natural Resource Damage: Anthropologists draw on a variety of tools to learn about the relationship between subsistence based communities and the natural resources they manage. Joseph Jorgensen (1995) produced one of the most widely cited studies of the Exxon-Valdez oil spill utilizing a social indicator study to demonstrate the link between native people's and natural resources. Jorgenson worked in 30 villages near the communities affected by the Exxon-Valdez before, during, and after the oil spill. Conducting research to help the Alaskan and Federal government better understand the impacts of the Alaska Native Claims Settlement Act (ANCSA) of 1971, he asked questions about household economics, subsistence activities, social organization, ethics, and political activities.

Social indicator approaches are successful in so far as they can reveal significant relationships between people and their environment. For instance, Jorgensen (1995) demonstrated that the Exxon-Valdez oil spill caused job market fluctuations, changes in household visiting patterns, a greater reliance on monetary exchange, and changes in the variety of foods drawn on to subsist. These findings may sound obvious in light of such extensive natural resource damage. Nevertheless they are significant because they show that any natural resource valuation must include cultural values such as visiting patterns and consumption habits, highlighting the need to address culture loss.

Alternatively, the ethnographic method may be employed to assess the extent of culture loss. The ethnographic method combines interviewing techniques and observations (see Spradley 1979) to reveal a complex relationship between social and natural resource values (Dyer, 1993; Gill and Picou, 1997). Comparing transcriptions of interviews gathered in Cordova, Alaska, Dyer (1993) identifies four characteristics of the relationship between subsistence based peoples and natural resources: (1) Residents of subsistence-based cultures are linked strongly to their natural resource base by traditions that integrate them into the natural order; (2) to the extent that cultural activities may destroy renewable natural resources, subsistence based cultures manage their resources to maintain their sustainability; (3) because natural resources are utilized and renewable within bounded areas, they are viewed as limited and limiting in the variety they provide their human stewards; and (4) progress is resisted to the extent it threatens core cultural traditions and the natural resource base on which they are constructed. With each ethnographic inquiry more of a groups total sense of place is revealed and a new understanding of how natural resources and native cultures are enmeshed is produced.

Discourse and Power in Resource Damage Assessment: The links between natural resources and culture loss are further complicated when groups of people with different value systems attempt to value each others' natural resources or, more typically, when powerful interests value the resources of less powerful others. Following the Exxon-Valdez Oil spill social anthropologists set out to analyze the way that power and social relations shaped the outcome of the hearings for the various parties involved. Indigenous and non-indigenous boat owners, crew, accountants, lawyers and Exxon employees ended up in many conflicts as a consequence of this oil spill (Rodin et al. 1997). Each of these groups of actors is positioned differently in relation to power, in this case the most significant power being the ability and/or culturally determined acceptability of operating within "the rules of the game" as dictated by western economic and legal institutions.

The anecdote about using the cost of relocation as a valuation estimate described earlier demonstrates that the aftermath of the Exxon-Valdez oil spill led to an institutional recognition of a cultural divide between subsistence-based and western liberal economies. The challenge of learning how this divide is perpetuated remains. Language and unrefined practices of valuing culture loss are significant contributors to these miscommunications. For instance, "compensation" is a concept that works quite well for people who have a more complete understanding of the way the market values natural resources. In the Exxon-Valdez case, boat owners with western accounting practices could easily document monetary losses. Meanwhile, indigenous peoples often lacked adequate records of their losses (Rodin et al. 1997).

Current research on mining conflicts in New Guinea provides further evidence that anthropologists are attempting to learn more about indigenous peoples' sense of placein order to reveal the rules and consequences of the resource valuation game to all interested parties. For instance, through development work "the term compensation entered popular usage in the Mount Hagan area of the Western Highlands Province only in the last few years as local practices became more and more enmeshed with the regulations and practices of the State and as local practices themselves altered"(Strathern 1997:2). For Strathern, problems of indigenous resource valuation emerge in the uneven power relations between the State and localities, and the local resistance to encompassment by the State. These problems could be alleviated with more transparent rules of engagement.

The discourse of development provides interesting insights into the ways that States and or governments participate in the resource valuation relationships. States tend to monetize, bureaucratize, and politicize their relationships with indigenous others. This can be seen in development projects that perpetuate a need for indigenous others. For instance tourism is often promoted as *the* way of preserving "traditional" practices. The consequence is that indigenous peoples are left with few options other than performing their traditional songs, dances, etc. as the primary means of achieving modernity (Schein 2000). State led development plans in New Guinea tend to persist over time by redefining particular groups of people as "underdeveloped" or by promoting "preservation". By borrowing from these powerful discourses, the concept of compensation, for example, indigenous peoples can resist State domination of the valuation process.

An additional example of the power of discourse in the valuation process is highlighted by Burton (1997). Burton investigates the vocabulary of the New Guinea legal system and learns that the process of land valuation is vague to the point of being detrimental to indigenous peoples. For Burton, the question of "how much money?" is repositioned into a discussion of amelioration. Burton states, "there is an asymmetry of valuation in these matters: where there is a saleable or rentable value, the Valuer General has issued a valuation; where there is none, and no valuation has been issued, it is incorrect to assume a zero value and a consequently low level of liability for damage" (Burton 1997:128). Here, the inability of the legal system to value indigenous land creates opportunities for corporations to take advantage of indigenous resources.

Burton examines current methods of compensating indigenous people that often involve a "package of commodities, not one of them resembling the restricted exchange of tradition -- money, business advice, relocating housing, schools, clinics, roads" (Burton 1997:131). Furthermore he investigates the inalienability of land in indigenous exchange systems. As an alternative to the largely controversial methods currently in use, Burton suggests Incorporated Land Groups as "a step in the right direction, or perhaps inventing, ways of coping with individual rights within a group framework" (Burton 1997:132-133). Burton's greatest contribution to anthropological attempts to understand resource valuation and culture loss is that he goes beyond identifying the structural holes in the New Guinea legal system that allow corporations to take advantage of indigenous resources and suggests ways to fix the problems.

IV. Toward A Preliminary Synthesis

A number of substantial reasons have been presented that unpack why both economic and anthropological approaches to indigenous resource valuation have fallen short of a solution that is equitable to all parties. Current economic models for valuing resource and culture loss draw criticism because accepted domains of monetary valuation i.e. personal value, market value, and value by institutional fiat, often do not equate. The possibility of an equitable environmental resource damage assessment such as the Contingent Valuation model described above is further complicated by the high technology and implementation costs that accompany research into alternative remedies.

Anthropological approaches to resource valuation are equally problematic. Descriptive statistics constructed from ethnographic investigations can lead to the production of information that merely reconstructs what the investigators set out to find. More recently, the deconstruction of key concepts in natural resource valuation and culture loss discourse such as compensation, cultural loss, and the conception of culture (i.e., material vs. ideological) have done much to take apart what western institutions assume about the meaning systems employed by indigenous people. However, little effort has been made to amalgamate what anthropologists learn into a reasonable solution to the problem of resource damage valuation in contexts of culture loss.

Despite the disciplinary shortcomings outlined above, a synthesis of both economic and anthropological approaches could be of great utility for understanding more of the total sense of place endowment that makes natural resources a significant part of indigenous peoples' lives. Ideally, an understanding of economics equates with an understanding of the many western liberal capitalist assumptions that influence the questions we ask of people during the process of valuation research. Likewise, the ethnographic method employed by many anthropologists can help westerners interpret the system of meaning that makes up the "others" perspective on valuation of natural resources, and equally important, help indigenous peoples understand the assumptions built into the western legal and economic systems. When brought together, these disciplines recognize the crucial fact that resource management and resource damage assessment are currently embedded in western legal, political and economic institutions.

In the case of the Exxon-Valdez oil spill there is much evidence to suggest that the destruction of indigenous social fabric was the most serious outcome. In this situation, building community programs before the spill could effectively prepare both indigenous and western negotiators for the challenges of valuing culture loss in the context of resource destruction. Taking the concept of place as a starting point, we should begin to learn more about the ways that different attributes of social and natural endowments overlap in specific places. Furthermore, we should be asking what kinds of rights are required to secure indigenous peoples' relationships to places (Kirsch 2001). What arrangements of these endowments make people most resilient to property loss and culture loss? Can indigenous peoples and western economists negotiate resource valuation methods that include an appreciation for the culture loss that accompanies resource destruction? A dialogue across disciplines and between various interest groups may be the most productive starting point.

Identifying Actors, Interests and Ideologies: The Exxon-Valdez oil spill provides a particularly complex and telling tale of how different cultures' legal and political resolution mechanisms come together producing unexpected outcomes, bad and good, for many indigenous and western actors. The influences on each of these actors are multiple and contextual. Nevertheless, there are certain influences that guide legal and political institutions that may be generalizable. For western institutions these constraints might be time, overhead costs, and accounting methods. For indigenous peoples the influences that structure resource values and negotiation may be part of a formalized barter systems or laws built into belief systems and kinship structures. Each has their way of dealing with resource valuation and culture loss and when considered together could make cross-cultural attempts at assessing value more equitable. Identifying the actors and the influences or limitations on them will allow for a more precise understanding of what can be expected at the negotiation table. Such an inquiry would better educate social scientists about the power struggles and hierarchies that exist in established institutions, concurrently illuminating where and how various aspects of institutions either encourage the successful resolution of resource damage assessment or perpetuate miscommunications and conflict.

Learning the Right Questions to Ask: With the actors in the valuation process established, the next step towards better understanding culture loss in the context of resource damage is to identify the types of questions that each institution asks of itself and its members when attempting to resolve resource damage conflicts internally, and when actors from outside the community are involved. In brief this means a narrow institutional analysis of the decision-making processes that lead to resource damage resolution decisions. For instance, what influences shape a government agency's choice to ask a community a question about the value of their resources in a particular way? What assumptions and influences are buried in the choice to ask a question? One economist asked what the cost might be to relocate a community to an unspoiled piece of land. While this sounds out of line to many people there are a number of assumptions embedded in asking the question that need to be revealed so that better questions are asked in the future, questions that promote discussion rather than silence and frustration.

From the discussion of contributions to the discourse of resource valuation outlined above, it would seem that anthropologists are well equipped to identify the appropriate questions to be asking. The ethnographic method can provide nuanced interpretations of the decision-making processes that work best when resolving problems of resource valuation within a community. In turn, this information could be transformed into a set of questions that might help economic methodologists and legal theorists take a more centered position within the cultural divide, resulting in more culturally acceptable and productive questions during the valuation process.

References

Appadurai, A. (1991). Global Ethnoscapes: Notes and Queries for a Transnational Anthropology. In R. G. Fox (Ed.), *Recapturing Anthropology: Working in the Present*. Santa Fe: School of American Research Press.

Appadurai, A. (1995). The Production of Locality. In R. Fardon (Ed.), *Counterworks* (pp. 204-225). London Routledge.

Arrow, K. R., & al., e. (1993). Report of the NOAA Panel on Contingent Valuation. *Federal Register, 58*(10), 4602-4614.

Brown, E. D., & al., e. (1993). *Injury to Early Life History Stages of Pacific Herring in PRince William Sound After the Exxon Valdez Oil Spill*. Paper presented at the American Fisheries Society, Bethesda Maryland.

Burton, J. (1997). The Principles of Compensation in the Mining Industry. In S. Toft (Ed.), *Compensation for Resource Development in Papua New Guinea* (pp. 116-136). Port Moresby and Canberra: Law Reform Commission of Papua New Guinea and Resource Management in Asia and the Pacific, Research School of Pacific and Asian Studies, The Australian National University, The National Centre for Development Studies.

Cambridge Economics, I. (1992). *Contingent Valuation: A Critical Assessment*. Washington D.C.: Cambridge Economics.

Clifford, J. (1992). Traveling Cultures. In L. Grossberg & C. Nelson & P. Treichler (Eds.), *Cultural Studies*. New York: Routledge.

Cohen, M. (1993). Economic Impact of an Environmental Accident: A Time-Series Analysis of the Exxon Valdez Oil Spill in Southcentral Alaska. *Sociological Spectrum, 13*, 35-63.

Daly, H. E. (Ed.). (1980). *Economics, Ecology, Ethics: Essays towards a Steady-State Economy*. San Francisco: W.H. Freeman and Company.

Daly, H. E., & Cobb, J. B. (1980). *For the Common Good*. Boston: Beacon Press.

Driver, B. L., & al., e. (Eds.). (1996). *Nature and the Human Spirit: Towards an Expanded Land Management Ethic*. State College, PA: Venture Press.

Dyer, C. L. (1993). Tradition Loss as Secondary Disaster - Long-Term Cultural Impacts of the Exxon Valdez Oil-Spill. *Sociological Spectrum, 13*(1), 65-88.

Giddens, A. (1991). *Modernity and Self Identity: Self and Society in the Late Modern Age*. Stanford, CA: Stanford University Press.

Gill, D. A., & Picou, J. S. (1997). The Day the Water Died: Cultural Impacts of the Exxon Valdez Oil Spill. In D. A. Gill & M. J. Cohen (Eds.), *The Exxon Valdez Disaster*. Dubuque: Kendal Hunt.

Gupta, A., & Ferguson, J. (1997). Culture, Power, Place: Ethnography at the End of an Era. In A. Gupta & J. Ferguson (Eds.), *Culture, Power, Place: Explorations in Critical Anthropology* (pp. 1-32). Durham, NC: Duke University Press.

Hall, E. T. (1966). *The Hidden Dimension*. New York: Doubleday.

Henderson, J. M., & Quandt, R. E. (1980). *Microeconomic Theory: A Mathematical Approach*. New York: McGraw-Hill.

Jorgensen, J. G. (1995). *Social Indicator Study of Alaskan Coastal Villages VI.*: US Department of the Interior Alaska Outer Continental Shelf Study: Minerals Management Service 94-0064.

Kirsch, S. (2001). Lost Worlds: Environmental Disaster, "Culture Loss", and the Law. *Current Anthropology, 42*(2), 167-178.

Korten, D. C. (1992). A Deeper Look at Sustainable Development. *World Business Academy Perspectives, 6*(2), 25-36.

Loomis, J. B., & al., e. (1984). *A Field Guide to Wildlife Economic Analysis.* Paper presented at the Transactions of North American Wildlife and Natural Resources.

Mitchell, R. C., & Carson, R. T. (1989). *Using Surveys to Value Public Goods.* Washington D.C.: Resources for the Future, Inc.

Moore, D. S. (1998). Subaltern Struggles and the Politics of Place: Remapping Resistance in Zimbabwe's Eastern Highlands. *Cultural Anthropology, 13*(3), 344-381.

Olwig, K. F. (1997). Cultural Sites: Sustaining a Home in a Deteritorialized World. In K. F. Olwig & K. Hastrup (Eds.), *Siting culture: The shifting anthropological object* (pp. 17-38). London: Routledge.

Peterson, G. L., & al., e. (1987). *RM-138 An Improved Framework for Estimating RPA Values* (RM-138). Fort Collins, CO: USDA Forest Service, Rocky Mountain Forest and Range Experiment Station.

Peterson, G. L., & al., e. (1992). Pricing of Multiple Use Forest Values in Transition from Command Economy to the Market System. In N. E. Koch & N. A. Moiseev (Eds.), *Integrated Sustainable Multiple-Use Forest Management Under the Market System.* Copenhagen: Kandrup.

Peterson, G. L., & Brown, T. C. (1999). Trains are Pretty Good, but They Can't Take You to Australia... Yet. In C. S. Roper & A. Park (Eds.), *The Living Forest: Non-Market Benefits of Forestry.* London: The Stationary Office.

Picou, J. S., Gill, D. A., & and Cohen, M. J. (Eds.). (1997). *The Exxon Valdez Disaster: Readings of a Modern Social Problem.* Dubuque: Kendall/Hunt.

Piper, E. (1997). The Exxon Valdez Oil Spill: Government Settlement and Restoration Activities. In D. A. Gill & M. Cohen (Eds.), *The Exxon Valdez Disaster: Readings on a Modern Social Problem.* Dubuque, IO: Kendal/Hunt Publishing.

Portney, R. P. (1994). The Contingent Valuation Debate: Why Economists Should Care. *Journal of Economic Perspectives, 8,* 3-17.

Raffles, H. (1999). "Local Theory": Nature and the Making of Amazonian Place. *Cultural Anthropology, 14*(3), 323-360.

Randall, A. (1983). The Problem of Market Valuation. *Natural Resource Journal, 23,* 131-148.

Rodin, M., Downs, M., Peterson, J. S., & Russell, J. C. (1997). Community Impacts of the Exxon Valdez Oil Spill. In D. A. Gill & M. J. Cohen (Eds.), *The Exxon Valdez Disaster.* Dubuque: Kendal Hunt.

Rolston, H. I. (1981). Values in Nature. *Environmental Ethics, 3*(2), 113-128.

Schein, L. (2000). *Minority Rules: The Miao and the Feminine in China's Cultural Politics.* Durham: Duke.

Silberberg, E. (1978). *The Structure of Economics.* New York: McGraw Hill.

Spradley, J. P. (1979). *The Ethnographic Interview.* Fort Worth, TX: Holt Reinhart and Winston.

Strathern, A. (1997). Compensation: Or Moving Swiftly over Broken Ground. In S. Toft (Ed.), *Compensation for Resource Development in Papua New Guinea*. Port Moresby and Canberra: Law Reform Commission of Papua New Guinea (Monograph No.6) and Resource Management in Asia and the Pacific Research School of Asian Studies The Australian National University, and National Center for Development Studies The Australian National University.

Strathern, M. (1999). Potential Property: Intellectual Rights and Property in Persons, *Property Substance and Effect: Anthropological Essays on Persons and Things*. London: Anthlone Press.

Torgerson, D. (1999). Images of Place in Green Politics: The Cultural Mirror of Indigenous Traditions. In F. Fisher & M. Hajer (Eds.), *Living with Nature*. New York: Oxford University Press.

Urry, J. (2000). *Sociology Beyond Societies: Mobilities for the Twenty-First Century*. London: Routledge.

Weiner, A. (1992). *Inalienable Possessions: The Paradox of Keeping While Giving*. Berkeley: University of California Press.

CHAPTER 7

Maori Fishing Rights:
Coping With the Aboriginal Challenge [1]

Bjørn Hersoug

In 1984 Tom Te Weehi, a member of the Ngati Porou tribe *(iwi)* was gathering shellfish on Montunau Beach along the Canterbury coast (New Zealand). After being detected by a fisheries officer he was charged with breaching the rules for Amateur Fishing Regulations by being in possession of 46 undersized abalone. He resisted the charge, stating that he had obtained permission from the local guardian *(kaitiaki)* in advance. He was collecting the shellfish within the area traditionally controlled by his tribe and the catch was to be used for immediate consumption. In short he was, in his own view, only exercising a traditional right guaranteed by the Treaty of Waitangi of 1840 between Maori chiefs and the English Queen. The Court accepted his claim, finding that Te Weehi was exercising his right according to the Fisheries Act of 1983, where it is explicitly stated that "Nothing in this Act shall affect any Maori fishing right". Consequently, he had not committed an offence and the case was quashed (Kerins and McClurg 1996: 7).

In hindsight this was a lucky outcome, not only for Maori, but for the whole New Zealand fishing industry and not least the fledgling start of the new Quota Management System (QMS), being in its final stage of preparation. This was the first time that a general Maori fishing right was recognised by the Courts, supporting the view that customary fishing rights continued to exist until they were expressly taken away with the consent of the rights holders.

While New Zealand has been most famous in fishing circles for its quota management system, its handling of the Maori challenge deserves no less attention. In many ways it can be claimed that the solution to the "Maori problem" was an absolute precondition for the successful establishment of the ITQ-system. On the other hand, the QMS provided the "currency", making it possible to sort out the Maori *commercial* claims. Finally it can be argued that the provision of the separate sphere of *Maori customary fishing* is an innovative attempt at establishing the best of two worlds, keeping Maori in touch with the cultural roots of fishing while also participating in the modern commercial

---

[1] The article draws heavily on Hersoug (2002a). Much of the material used was provided through the generous co-operation of Sean Kerins, Treaty of Waitangi Fisheries Commission.

sector. Although we are still in the middle of a rapidly unfolding drama, we can draw some lessons from the New Zealand experience, regarding what is usually considered the complete incompatibility of aboriginal rights and the use of individual transferable quotas (ITQs) (Hooper and Lynch 1999). But first we have to give a short account of New Zealand's fishing industry, in order to provide a setting for the development of modern Maori fisheries.

New Zealand's Fishing Industry - Small, Exclusive and Export Oriented

New Zealand's exclusive Economic Zone (EEZ) is the fifth largest in the world, covering an area of 4,8 mill km^2 or more than 15 times the land area of the country. In spite of the large zone, productivity is limited with 2/3 of the area deeper than 1000 metres and only 5% shallower than 200 metres. Of approximately 1000 marine fish species in New Zealand waters 130 are fished commercially (only 43 species are considered commercially important). Species include shallow water finfishes and shellfish, pelagic as well as deep-water species. Only a small fraction of the commercially important species is based on shared stocks. The rest is exclusively within New Zealand's EEZ, making national management considerably easier than for most other fishing nations.

Within its quota management system (QMS) New Zealand has more than 180 separate fish stocks present in ten quota management areas, covering 43 species. This represents 85% of the total catch within the zone, with more stocks in line to be brought under the QMS. Some 117 species are still managed outside the QMS by a system of permits and input regulations. The industry is heavily concentrated, with approximately 80% of the total allocated quotas being controlled by ten companies. The remaining quotas are owned by approximately 2500 persons/companies, each commanding just a small fraction of the total quota for the particular species.[2] The three largest companies on the processing side (Sealord, Talleys and Sanfords) are also strongly vertically integrated, controlling quotas and owning vessels as well as retail outlets. Together they control around 50 % of the industry. The most important species, in terms of volume and value are given in table 1.

While the number of fishing boats have been steadily reduced over the last 15 years, there are still some 2 000 domestic vessels licensed, mainly connected to the inshore coastal fisheries. Only 71 are larger than 28 meters[3]. The number

---

[2]   Even with limitations on maximum quota ownership specified in the Fisheries Act 1996, it is hard to know the extent of effective concentration, as many of the larger operators also have controlling interests in smaller companies.

[3]   This figure contain all vessels required to be within the Vessel Monitoring System, that is all vessels larger than 28 meters and some vessels smaller than 28 meters fishing for orange roughy and scampi.

of foreign licensed vessels have been brought down to 11, while 80 are still foreign chartered.

The total number of fishermen is estimated to be 4 650, while the number of processing workers (including the aquaculture industry) is 5 870 (NZIER 2000).[4] The total direct, indirect and induced economic impact of the seafood industry is just over 1,7 billion $ of value added or about 1,8% of New Zealand's GDP. In spite of these moderate numbers, the importance of the fishing industry should not easily be discounted. First of all, with 90% of the total catch (including aquaculture) going to export markets, fish and fish products account for 5% of New Zealand's total export earnings, next only to diary, meat and forestry products.

Table 1: Volume and value of New Zealand's seafood export 1985-2000

Year	Quantity (1000 tonnes)	Value (mill NZ$)
1985	145,0	543
1986	158,2	657
1987	155,9	676
1988	209,9	722
1989	257,4	818
1990	210,7	744
1991	261,2	961
1992	292,8	1217
1993	305,8	1199
1994	289,6	1167
1995	322,2	1238
1996	328,4	1179
1997	338,0	1125
1998	350,4	1237
1999	322,8	1340
2000	279,2	1431

Source: Gaffney 1997, Statistics New Zealand and SeaFIC

Secondly, in certain areas employment from fishing, processing and aquaculture is the most important source of income, giving work to a large number of unskilled or semiskilled workers. Thirdly, fishing plays a central role also in terms of recreation and subsistence. This is acknowledged by the statutory recognition of customary Maori fishing, and by the large number of New Zea-

---

4   The numbers are calculated on basis of Full Time Equivalents (FTEs), which means that the actual number of participants is considerably higher.

landers participating in the recreational fisheries (anticipated to comprise 20% of the population), together with foreign tourists in the increasingly important game-fishing market. Finally, it is worth mentioning that the marine environment is considered to be an important part of New Zealand's "green image". This is supported by the fact that the size of New Zealand's EEZ grants the country a status of a marine "superpower", attracting considerable international interest in its management.

Besides for hoki, New Zealand's fisheries are based on a large number of small stocks. Total TAC for all species is estimated to be in the area of 5-600 000 tons annually, offering few possibilities of increasing domestic catches (Annala 1996). Further development will have to be obtained by fishing in international waters, by entering into joint ventures with other international fishing companies (presently Namibia, South Africa and Argentina) or by enhancing the value added element through further processing in New Zealand. In addition comes aquaculture, providing more than 30 000 tons (export volume 2000), mainly of farmed mussels, oysters and a small salmon growing sector. The aquaculture sector has increased rapidly over the last ten years and is generally considered to have the largest growth potential, provided that the conflicts over space can be solved. The most important export market is Japan (29% of total), followed by United States (20%) and Australia (11%).

Administratively the fisheries, including aquaculture, sort under the Ministry of Fisheries, established in 1995, after being split off from the ministry of Agriculture and Forestry (MAF). Altogether 274 staff are employed by the Ministry, the majority in Wellington, with regional offices in Nelson, Dunedin and Auckland in addition to nine local offices. More than half of the employed staff is occupied with fisheries compliance. Another 75 persons are engaged in the running of the QMS data system, working under contract with the Ministry. In addition comes personnel connected to other functions which have been out-sourced, like scientific investigations, mainly operated through the Crown owned National Institute of Water and Atmospheric Research (NIWA). The Ministry's 1999/2000 budget was in the order of NZ$ 64 mill, of which 25 mill (40%) is represented by registry and research services. Of the total Ministry spending NZ$ 34 mill is paid by the industry, recovered by cost recovery levies and transaction charges.

From having fisheries as a complete marginal industry prior to the 1978 extension to 200 miles EEZ (total export of NZ$ 25 mill in 1976), New Zealand has within 20 years managed to built a competitive export industry generating export income in the order of NZ$ 1,4 bill. In addition the home market generate approximately NZ$ 150 mill in fish sales annually. The key to this success story has generally been considered to be the introduction of the QMS in 1986, where ITQs figure prominently.

The Treaty of Waitangi (1840) – Establishing the Fishing Rights

Unlike many other former colonies New Zealand's aboriginal peoples were never conquered and forced under the jurisdiction of the coloniser. When Captain Hobson arrived at the Bay of Islands in January 1840 as representative of the English Crown, the idea was to make a voluntary agreement, whereby the original inhabitants were to operate under the protection of the English Crown, but without giving up their existing (collective) property rights. Article (2) of the Treaty of Waitangi, signed in 1840 by fifty chiefs (later 500) and representatives of the British Crown, read:

> "Her Majesty the Queen of England confirms and guarantees to the Chiefs and tribes of New Zealand and to the respective families and individuals thereof the full exclusive and undisturbed possession of their lands and estates, forests, fisheries and other properties which they may collectively or individually possess...so long as it is their wish and desire to retain the same in their possession..."(Orange 1987).[5]

Article (2) then went on to grant the Crown an exclusive right of pre-emption in respect of lands. In practice that meant that subsequent take-overs by the English, starting with Wakefield's famous New Zealand Company, were made by negotiated deals, although buying practices and prices paid may have been objectionable[6]. However, the English never bought any (marine) fishing rights, nor did Maori voluntarily cede any such rights. At that time English common law held that fish were nobody's property until caught, and furthermore, that only territorial waters ranging three nautical miles from the shore could be controlled by national governments, or in this case by the English Crown. Outside the territorial border was "mare librum" or in principle "open access" with regard to fisheries.

Maori tradition was completely different, being based on an intricate system of nested rights. Here extended families (*whanau*) controlled small streams, fishing grounds and shellfish beds in the immediate vicinity of their villages, sub-tribes (*hapu*) controlled larger rivers, shellfish beds and certain fishing grounds, while the tribe (*iwi*) incorporated the rights of its hapu and whanau. Major fishing expeditions and activities were undertaken at the iwi level (Kerins and McClurg 1996:3). Boundary markers were commonly used to demarcate both land and water areas, with fishing grounds being located through ma-

---

[5]   For obvious reasons the English version is quite different from the Maori, giving rise for substantial disagreements regarding interpretations of the Treaty (see Orange 1987).

[6]   After the land wars (1860-1872) English trading practices became less noble, with the eviction of Maori from large tracts of lands, especially in the Taranaki area. Nevertheless, most lands were taken over through sales and leases.

jor landmarks. Knowledge of *who controlled what* was known in minute detail and this knowledge together with knowledge of fish behaviour and catching techniques was handed down through generations.

Management was in many instances similar to modern day practices, with a local guardian regulating *when* fish could be harvested, *who* could harvest and with *what type* of gear. By using special area zoning *(tapu and makutu)* fishing could be further restrained, or to prevent fish from being taken out of season, the use of complete closure *(rahui)*. By the time British settlers came into contact with various Maori tribes they had a well developed social system, with rules and structures guiding their fisheries. The point should not be over-emphasised, however. Over and above iwi level there were few possibilities of solving conflicts (except struggle and internal warfare), and aggregated effects of resource use could not always be dealt with. On the other hand, the number of inhabitants was small and the catch technology relatively simple, although much more sophisticated than among their European competitors. Hence, pressure on the marine resources was moderate, tempered also by limited markets within reasonable distance.

This was soon to change, when English settlers started to utilise local shell-fish resources extensively, giving rise to the first Governmental Fisheries Regulations in 1877. Although it was explicitly stated that: "Nothing in this Act.... shall be deemed to repeal, alter, or affect any of the provisions of the Treaty of Waitangi, or to take away, annul or abridge any of the rights of the aboriginal natives to any fishery secured to them thereunder", Maori fishing rights were systematically undermined in subsequent laws and regulations. Through the Oyster Fisheries Act of 1892 Maori property rights were unilaterally constrained. Furthermore, all subsequent legislation (15 laws altogether) was based on the assumption that whatever type and level of the European commercial and later, recreational use, it would not interfere with Maori customary fishing. This attitude of formally keeping with the provisions of the Treaty of Waitangi, while paying little attention to the practicalities, was maintained right up to the Fisheries Act 1983, where again it was stated that: "Nothing in this Act shall affect any Maori fishing rights".

Having protested against their deteriorating marine rights for 140 years without much success, the early 1980s saw an upsurge in Maori grievances (Bess 2001: 27). Different tribes tried to protect their rivers, estuaries and in-shore fishing grounds from outside interference in the form of sewage disposal schemes, and power plants, as well as industrial processing plants discharging "degraded" water. According to Kerins and McClurg (1996: 7): "The claims were last ditch attempts by Maori to protect fisheries habitats from poor or inadequate planning processes which denied the recognition of Maori Treaty rights to traditional resources." By that time the Maori claims had an avenue for redress, namely the Waitangi Tribunal.

The Waitangi Tribunal – Rediscovering the Fishing Rights

By the early 1970s New Zealand had experienced a political swing to the left, giving a political opportunity for addressing Maori grievances? and more generally, figuring out how New Zealand should deal with two peoples within the framework of one nation. The establishment of the Waitangi Tribunal in 1975 under the Treaty of Waitangi Act was primarily to make recommendations to the Government on claims relating to the practical application of the Treaty and to determine whether certain (political) matters were inconsistent with the Treaty principles. Originally the Tribunal only had the powers to address issues from 1975 onwards, but in 1985 its mandate was widened to examine claims all the way back to 1840. Although most of the initial claims were land claims, fisheries claims multiplied over the years, giving the opportunity for large hearings and much publicity. In a country with a relatively strong environmental movement, protecting marine resources offered Maori tribes the moral "high ground". At last it was demonstrated that Maori rights referred to more than subsistence fisheries and the subsequent claim to certain fishing sites. Through extensive research the Tribunal claimed:

- The Treaty guarantee includes both the preservation of a right to fish and a protection of the place of fishing.
- The guarantee cannot be diminished if Maori fishing rights have in fact been subsumed into the current fishing regime without willing consent.
- The duty to protect is an active duty. It requires more than the recognition of a right.
- (Furthermore), the Crown must take all the necessary steps to assist Maori in their fishing to enable them to exercise that right (Waitangi Tribunal 1988: 218-220).

The Tribunal affirmed that the Treaty guaranteed to Maori: "The full, exclusive and undisturbed possession of their fisheries for as long as they wished to keep them" (Ibid: 220). "Fisheries" was here interpreted to mean the activity and business of fishing, the fish caught, the places where they fished and the property rights in fishing (Kerins and McClurg 1996: 8).

The claims and later the recommendations of the Tribunal came at the worst possible time, from the point of view of QMS proponents. After two years of struggle the QMS was to be launched in 1986, only to be dragged into a new debate over who possessed the original fishing rights. For how could the State (Crown) allocate permanent fishing rights (in terms of individual transferable quotas) when Maori, through the "constitutional" Treaty of Waitangi, were guaranteed all along "the full, exclusive and undisturbed possession" of their fisheries?

Treaty of Waitangi Fisheries Commission – Bridge Over Troubled Waters

With the expanded mandate for the Waitangi Tribunal from 1985 the course was set for collision with the introduction of the new QMS, where individual transferable quotas were going to be allocated to existing private operators in perpetuity. Some tribes, in particular the Muriwhenua tribes of the north, claimed pre-existing and un-extinguished property rights in the fisheries off their coast. Against this background the Waitangi Tribunal recommended the Minister of Fisheries stop the ITQ scheme until negotiations could be carried out with the affected tribes. At that time ITQ had been issued for 29 species, covering more than 80% of the commercial fisheries. Numerous tribes and Maori organisations had applied for an injunction, which was finally granted by the High Court in November 1987.

Fearing an endless litigation process, the Government of the day agreed with Maori parties to establish a joint working group to sort out how Maori fishing rights could be exercised in a modern context. In the end not much common ground could be found and each side produced its own report. While Maori started out claiming 100% of the fishing resources, they ended up proposing 50% as a compromise. The Crown offered 100% of the inshore fisheries quotas and only 12,5% of the deep sea fisheries (equivalent to the Maori proportion of the population). In order to proceed with the negotiations and not compromise the integrity of the fledgling QMS, Parliament passed the Maori Fisheries Act in 1989 as an interim arrangement, pending the settlement of the fisheries claims. The Act provided for the establishment of the Maori Fisheries Commission (MFC), which was to receive 10% of all existing quota within the QMS. Since quotas for 29 species already had been allocated, that meant that Government would have to buy back quota, based on the principle of willing buyer-willing seller. The plan was to buy 2,5% per year over four years, having the deal finalised by October 1992.[7] In addition MFC was granted NZ$10 mill in order to run the Commission and to set up a commercial arm, Aotearoa Fisheries Limited. The Commission used its profits from leasing out quotas to acquire further fisheries assets, companies as well as quotas. Equally important to this commercial arrangement was the guarantee that the Act provided in terms of securing areas of specific significance to Maori as "a source of food or for spiritual and cultural reasons". These areas, called *taiapure* in Maori, could

---

[7]   In practice it proved difficult and very expensive to acquire the 10% of total TACCs. In some cased MFC was therefore given cash to buy quotas for itself, but payment often fell short of actual market price, leaving MFC with a quota deficit by the end of 1992.

be claimed and after due consideration be acknowledged in official fisheries regulations.[8]

From a Maori perspective, both the commercial and non-commercial (customary) components of the interim settlement were unsatisfactory, and an increasing number of tribes continued to press their claims. The Government agreed that no further species should be brought into the QMS until an agreement was made or a resolution made by the court. With the prospect of more litigation the Government again proposed discussion between the parties, and a Fisheries Task Force was established in 1991 to advise the Minister of Fisheries on "appropriate legislative change and reform". The Fisheries Task Force produced two central documents, a public discussion paper (MAF 1991) and a report to the Ministry of Agriculture and Fisheries (MAF 1992). At that time New Zealand already had five years of experience with the QMS, giving the Fisheries Task Force the opportunity to assess its benefits and problems. Not only did the Fisheries Task Force find that the QMS "is a suitable foundation for the development of a consistent and comprehensive fisheries management regime" but they also concluded that: "The principles of the QMS do not appear fundamentally at odds with the Treaty of Waitangi. Indeed there appears to be scope to adapt the QMS as a means of providing effective recognition of Maori fishing rights secured by the Treaty" (MAF 1992).

Regarding traditional (customary) fisheries, the Fisheries Task Force saw a need to identify and clarify Maori rights, which extended beyond a mere share of the total allowable quota (TAC) but would also have to include real involvement in management as well. In its final report the Fisheries Task Force envisaged two components to the traditional fishing right; a harvesting right, which could be exercised in general fishing areas not excluding others, and a more exclusive right *(mahinga kaimoana),* which would be a small area (estuary, reef or coastline) where local tribes would be able to exclude all others from harvesting (Maori as well as non-Maori) (Kerins and McClurg 1996: 13).

"Now or never" – the 1992 Sealord Deal and Deed of Settlement

By early 1992 the prospect of an agreement appeared rather remote. Threats of litigation flourished, giving good times for lawyers but not for the fishing industry, and particularly not for the QMS, which was dependent on a stable regime and secure catching rights. In September 1992 it became clear that one of New Zealand's leading corporate companies wanted to sell its major fisheries subsidiary, Sealord Limited, the largest seafood company in the country. It appeared to Maori and Crown negotiators that this was a "now or never" opportunity – "acting on the rising tide". Within two weeks of active negotiations it

---

[8]   At present 13 Taiapure areas have been gazetted, although not all of them are operative, due to management difficulties.

was agreed that the Crown should pay NZ$ 150 mill in three annual tranches to fund a Maori take-over (50%), with Brierley Investments Limited taking over the other 50%. The Maori/ Brierley bid was successful and Maori interests now owned 23% of all ITQs within the QMS (Sealord commanding 26% of TACCs at the time).

In addition, the Settlement Act passed in September 1992 promised Maori 20% of quota for all new species brought into the QMS. The Act also promised regulations providing for customary fishing to be developed. Finally, Maori representatives were granted seats on fisheries statutory bodies, to reflect the special relationship between Maori and the Crown. In return Maori would have to accept the Deed of Settlement (Fisheries Claims) as a full and final settlement of all their claims relating to fisheries (not aquaculture!) and quit all their court proceedings. As could be expected, not all tribes agreed to the compromise. Iwi representing approximately 20% of all Maori did not accept the Deed of Settlement, claiming this was not a fulfilment of the original Treaty of Waitangi.

With the Settlement Act, the Maori Fisheries Commission was reconstituted as the Treaty of Waitangi Fisheries Commission (*Te Ohu Kai Moana*). The number of commissioners was increased from seven to thirteen and the staff increased to cope with the increased workload and the more complex role of the new Commission. The Commission was charged with a formidable challenge. According to the very detailed prescription of the legislation the Commission should facilitate two different allocation processes: one applicable to the assets granted to Maori before the settlement (the 10% of Total Allowable Commercial Catches (TACCs) within the QMS + cash) called pre-settlement assets (PRESA), and another dealing with the assets granted through the Sealord deal (shares + cash) and the 20% of new species, commonly referred to as the post-settlement assets (POSA).

While PRESA assets were to be allocated to the tribes after due consultation process, POSA would require a new Maori Fisheries Act, to replace the preliminary 1989 Act. Without going into the many details of the Act, it is important in order to understand the ensuing difficulties, to stress that PRESA from the beginning was meant to be exclusively for the tribes (*iwi*) involved in marine fisheries, while POSA was a pan-Maori settlement, meant to benefit all Maori. While some tribes were bitterly disappointed and others grudgingly accepted, it is not difficult to see that from an international perspective this was a favourable deal, probably the best deal ever made with any aboriginal people in terms of fisheries.

Everybody therefore expected a relatively short interim period while the allocation model was worked out followed by the final distribution of assets (PRESA) to the tribes. Ten years later the Commission is more alive than ever, having recently been re-appointed with a mandate running for at least two additional years. What happened? Before describing the difficulties of distribution, we shall take a brief look at the Treaty of Waitangi Fisheries Commission, which has established itself as a major player in New Zealand's fishing industry.

The Treaty of Waitangi Fisheries Commission – Between Commerce and Policy

When the Governor General approved the Maori Fisheries Act in 1989, it was designed to be an interim arrangement pending the settlement of the fisheries claims. To cater for the provisional assets a management structure was put in place, the Maori Fisheries Commission (MFC). At the same time, the MFC was obliged by the Act to establish a company, Aotearoa Fisheries, to act as the commercial arm of MFC, to which 50% of the quota received from the Crown would be transferred. The remaining 50% was to be leased annually, with preference given to Maori lessees.[9]

Over the next few years MFC manoeuvred skilfully, acquiring further fisheries assets, most notably Moana Pacific Limited, a relatively large fishing company involved with processing inshore species. In 1992, when the Settlement Act was passed, the MFC was renamed the Treaty of Waitangi Fisheries Commission or Te Ohu Kai Moana (TOKM), the number of commissioners increased from seven to thirteen and the staff extended. The first major task of TOKM was to develop a scheme for distribution of the pre-settlement assets. After years of meetings, consultation and research, an allocation model was put forward in mid 1997 (TOKM 1997). After further consultation it was edited slightly and finally put out for approval in late 1998. Complementary work by TOKM has provided guidelines for settling conflicts between tribes as well as developing specifications for appropriate governance structures (tribal organisations) in terms of establishing democratic, accountable and transparent structures. However, a large number of iwi were still not satisfied and in time of writing yet another allocation proposal has been produced and is now out for consultation (TOKM 2002).

The second major task of the Commission has been to look after the assets, that is, to develop quotas, shares and cash held in trust for the tribes. This policy has involved buying up additional processing companies and diverting into aquaculture.[10] Commission members participate in the boards of the acquired companies, and in the largest (Sealord Ltd.) the chairman has been the chairman of the Commission up to mid 2000.[11] TOKM has also bought additional

---

[9]   These Maori companies or organisations could then forward lease quotas to other interests, often ending up with the awkward situation that TOKM controlled quotas were used by competitors of TOKM held companies.

[10] The subsidiaries include Sealord Group, Moana Pacific Fisheries, Pacific Marine Farms, Prepared Foods Limited and Chathams Processing Group.

[11] In 2001 the other half of Sealord Group Limited was sold (from Brierly Invest) to Nissui, one of Japan's largest fishing and processing companies. The legal ownership of the Sealord

quotas when available for a reasonable price, partly in order to secure the efficient running of its "own" companies. The system is based on annual leases, where the lessees get a rebate compared to the ordinary leasing price of that particular quota. The total value of the rebate is, according to TOKM managers, roughly calculated at NZ$ 20 mill per year, which is an indirect contribution to the participating tribes. This has been instrumental in helping a number of tribes to set up their own fishing operations, and at present TOKM is assisting some 63 small-scale Maori companies.[12]

The third major area covered by TOKM has been the field of education, specifically geared towards the fishing industry, where more than 1300 scholarships have been granted since 1995. Students may obtain scholarships for a range of different types of education, from vocational training to research at PhD level. TOKM has also entered into a contractual relationship with SeaFIC's training division, supplying training courses for personnel already employed in the fishing industry. As a consequence of the long delayed process of allocating the assets, TOKM has increased the value of the assets considerably, from an estimated value of NZ$ 350 mill in 1992 to more than NZ$ 700 mill in 2002.

An unintended consequence of the delay has been the building of a very powerful player in the New Zealand fishing industry, which has competence in a number of fields, ranging from business management to customary fisheries. With 25 fulltime employees and a number of hired consultants TOKM participates in all major events relating to the industry and presents opinions and feedback on all major issues of government legislation. With a possible allocation of the assets in the relatively near future, TOKM will not be idle. The Commission will still be responsible for overseeing the phasing in of the remaining stocks into the QMS, where Maori are granted 20% according to the Act.[13] Even with these tasks solved, there will probably be need for an umbrella organisation, overseeing Maori interests. Not surprisingly, the present Commission has suggested a new, reorganised commission with a new mandate to take over as soon as the allocation issue has been solved (TOKM 2002).

Distribution More Difficult Than Production?

Through the Settlement Act of 1992 the Maori Fisheries Commission was left with a hot potato, the allocation of assets amongst Maori. No precedent

---

Group's quota interests was transferred to a corporate trustee, where all shares are owned by TOKM.

[12] Some claim that these companies would not have survived if they had to pay the full lease price. An alternative view is of course to say that these tribes should not have to pay a leasing price at all – being the rightful owners of the quotas from the start!

[13] In 2001 the Government decided to introduce 50 new species into the QMS from 2002 to 2004.

existed for this exercise and the task was not made easier by the expectation of near unanimity among Maori over a final solution. For six years the Commission consulted extensively, asking for submissions, evaluating different options, participating in numerous meetings with tribes and sub-tribes as well as individuals. Finally it came up with a solution for the distribution of PRESA (commercial quotas, shares and cash), aptly called the *Optimum Method for Allocation*.

Through the hearings of the Waitangi Tribunal two of the most active and influential tribal groupings (Muriwhenua and Ngai Tahu) presented extensive historic evidence about fishing activities on the continental shelf. The Tribunal found that iwi and hapu had exclusive rights to inshore fisheries and a smaller "development interest" in deep-water fisheries (TOKM 2000: 9). Consequently, fishing quotas were divided into deep water and inshore. The defining criterion has been the 300-metre depth contour, giving a fairly clear demarcation of inshore and offshore species. The inshore quotas held by TOKM should then be distributed to the tribes according to the length of coastline pertaining to their tribal area. If, for example, a tribe has 30% of the coastline in a management area for species x, this tribe is entitled to 30% of the inshore quota (held by TOKM) for that fish stock in that quota management area (QMA). If an iwi's coastline straddles two quota management areas, that iwi will receive inshore quota from the two QMAs.

Deep-water quotas were split into two parcels, with half the deep-water quotas being allocated according to coastline (as with inshore quota) while the other half should be allocated on a population basis. If an iwi makes up 10% of the affiliated Maori population of New Zealand, it should receive 10% of half the deep-water quota[14]. According to the Fisheries Commission: "This deep-water allocation method takes into account the Waitangi Tribunal finding that modern rights to the deep-water fisheries are to an extent developmental and that all Maori are entitled to share in that development" (TOKM 2000: 10).

A special case is made for the Chatham Islands, where the tribes' quota shares are actually based on what has been caught within a separate 200-mile zone over a specified number of years.[15] The Commission has also been aware of the organisational requirements on the receiving side, that is, among the tribal organisations. Each of the 78 tribes with an interest in marine fisheries have been asked to establish one (and only one!) organisation, able to show that it holds sufficient mandate from iwi members. Furthermore, this organisation

---

[14]   The affiliate population of each iwi is to be determined from 1996 census data.

[15]   A tricky question remaining is, however, that many tribes make claim to the same coastline, especially in the border zones between tribal areas (*rohe*). So far the Commission has urged the different tribes to seek voluntary agreement. If this is not successful, the Commission will facilitate dispute resolution. A publication setting out the Commission's dispute resolution procedures has been widely distributed (TOKM 1995).

has to be structured according to certain standard requirements, referring to the existence of a formal constitution, free and open elections and the provision of relevant information. Another basic requirement is the division between economic and political responsibilities.

The largest stake, the 60 000 tons of quota held in trust, was to be allocated as described above. The additional shares were to be distributed according to quota volume to each iwi. The remaining cash, approximately NZ$ 50 mill, was to be split with $ 40 mill distributed according to population size and $ 10 mill set aside for a development fund, targeting Maori living outside their tribal area, not having (or not wishing to have) close tribal links. The distribution of the POSA should be decided at a later stage, after having distributed the PRESA.

With this elaborate model the Commission could present the "optimal solution" to its owners, the tribes – take it or leave it! Of the 78 tribes (iwi) acknowledged by the Commission, 37 representing 50,6% of affiliated Maori, accepted the model without conditions. 17 rejected the model (representing 42,7% of affiliated Maori), while the rest were either undecided or would have to sort out organisational issues before they can decide on the distribution process. Although technically a majority, the result was not politically very convincing, especially since certain tribes withdrew their support on a later stage. Litigation now started from within, with a number of Maori organisations claiming that another model and other principles should have been applied. They challenged the whole concept of redistributing assets to tribes, but lost in the High Court. Nevertheless, the case was taken further to the Privy Council in London, one of the few remaining Commonwealth institutions, effectively blocking redistribution for another year. In July 2002 the Privy Council dismissed the appeals and thereby upheld the High Court ruling that: *the Commission by statute is required to allocate PRESA solely to iwi or organisations representative of iwi, and that iwi in this context means only traditional Maori tribes* (TOKM 2002).

But the fight continued. According to a prominent leader of one of the "rejecting" tribes:

"The Treaty tribes[16] are a bunch of bully boys who have controlled the Sealord settlement since its early beginning. The model that will finally be acceptable is the one having widespread support from Maori people (as opposed to the iwi leadership). The current manawhenua manamoana model has never been put to that test. The 35 Iwi that the Treaty Tribes claim are in support of their model are in fact those Maori leaders whom the Commission has managed to buy off and who have got fat at the expense of the majority of Maori people" (Northland Age 31 October 2000).

---

[16] An alliance of tribes originally having signed the Treaty of Waitangi in 1840.

Ten years of squabbling over allocation has also left the politicians in a delicate position. Originally the distribution issue was left to Maori because it was too complicated and too sensitive to handle in Parliament. Now representatives of the proposed model are urging the Government to pass legislation that may facilitate the deal, having recognised that leaving the issue to the courts may require years before any allocation can be made. This position is also supported by SeaFIC, the generic industry organisation for all New Zealand seafood producers. The present Government, just like the previous ones, is still hesitant, knowing that a political decision at this stage will immediately be challenged in court. The outgoing chairman of the Commission, Sir Tipene O'Regan has questioned the logic:

"To some extent, the Commission's detractors play to that curious Pakeha (white) mindset which demands unanimity of Maori whilst accepting huge differences within the power culture. This view has it that, for some reason, Maori should be the only cultural group in the history of mankind where every member must agree on key issues" (TOKM 2000: 7).

At present the Government is buying time, having replaced some of the commissioners including the chairman, with members thought to be more favourable towards urban Maori. They have been given two years to sort out a solution. After presenting four different models for allocation and consulting extensively with the various tribes, the reorganised commission came up with a new and more accommodating proposal. Without going into all the details, the main difference from the original proposal ("the optimal allocation") is that urban, non associated Maori have been given a better deal through the allocation of a substantial fund for social human resource development and that Maori commercial interests should be consolidated in a new company (Aotearoa Fisheries Ltd.) with limited transferability of shares. The new proposal also contain the provision of a new TOKM with only seven members, elected by an electoral college consisting of representatives from all the iwi in a particular region (TOKM 2002).

In the meantime the funds accumulate, while public trust deteriorates – ultimately threatening not only the fisheries agreement but possibly also future settlements.[17] In the present atmosphere of allegations and counter allegations, endless litigation and ten years deadlock, it is worthwhile to remember that the Commission was tasked with three distinct challenges: restoration of rights, compensation to rights holders and assistance to Maori wishing to enter the

---

[17] Seen from the perspective of the Treaty tribes (the tribes having agreed on the allocation principles) the delay deprives them of important development possibilities, with the loss calculated to NZ$ 1 mill per week! (see NZIER 2000).

business and activity of fishing. Without any precedents and operating in a climate of very divisive politics, *it had to be complicated.* This is even more so because the seemingly technical distribution process has raised a number of more profound issues such as:

- What is a tribe and sub-tribe (iwi and hapu)?
- What role can tribes possibly play in a modern capitalist society like New Zealand ?
- What is the link between the tribe and its members? (What about Maori who prefer new organisational forms?)
- What is the relationship between Maori politics and Maori economic development?

Before turning to these complex issues, I shall present the outcome of the other half of the 1992 agreement, namely the customary fisheries. Such a split between commercial and subsistence fisheries had never been experienced by Maori before it was introduced in 1892, and it was never accepted.[18] Maori argued that customary take was an integral part of their fisheries, along with more commercially orientated fisheries for barter or for sale. How did the two fisheries end up on different courses, with different procedures, different management and even different participants?

Customary Fishing Rights – Old Practices in a New Setting

The concept of customary fishing rights is a modern one, although the activities involved are age old. While the early colony regulations sought to split the customary (subsistence) fishery from the emerging (European) commercial fisheries, the customary rights were never specified, neither as a specific portion of the catch nor as a special management regime. That happened for the first time with the Fisheries Task Force giving advice to the Ministry of Agriculture and Fisheries in 1992. Here it was explicitly argued that Maori commercial fisheries could easily be integrated in the QMS, while the customary fishery could be established as a separate category, different also from the recreational fisheries. Section 10 of the Treaty of Waitangi (Fishery Claims) Settlement Act (1992) declared explicitly:

> "It is hereby declared that claims by Maori in respect of non-commercial fishing for species or classes of fish, aquatic life or seaweed that are subject to the Fisheries Act 1983
> a. Shall in accordance with the principles of the Treaty of Waitangi, continue to give rise to Treaty obligations on the Crown; and in pursuance thereto

---

[18] This split was introduced through the Oyster Fisheries Act in 1892.

b. The Minister....shall
  (i) Consult with tangata whenua (Maori tribes) about; and
  (ii) Develop policies to help recognise – Use and management practices of Maori in the exercise of non-commercial fishing rights."

The Minister was required to develop regulations for customary food gathering by Maori, and protection of important traditional fishing grounds, "to the extent that such food gathering is neither commercial in any way nor for pecuniary gain or trade" (ToWDSA 1992). As part of the process the then Ministry of Agriculture and Fisheries presented a background paper (MAF 1993) discussing issues for the development of customary fishing regulations. With the assistance of the Treaty of Waitangi Fisheries Commission these proposals were widely discussed and consulted upon. It was repeatedly stressed by Maori interests that the involvement in fisheries was not only to provide food but to transmit traditional knowledge from one generation to another. As pointed out by Kerins and McClurg (1996: 20): "This debate reinforced the fact that need is not a number."

The whole basis of traditional Maori management was exercising a right to decide *who should fish, where, when and how (gear type)*. Hence the challenge was to develop a customary regime within the modern regime, trying to match old management techniques with modern requirements. As could be expected, resistance to the project was encountered both from commercial interests (mainly non-Maori) as well as among recreational fishers, who feared a further reduction in their already insecure rights. Nevertheless, the process of consultation, drafting regulations, receiving submissions and drawing up the final regulations, slowly moved ahead, more or less with the same content for North Island and South Island, although the administrative procedure differed somewhat. In the case of the North Island regulations, the Ministry received more than 500 submissions, which were all considered and dealt with, before the final draft was accepted by the Minister in 1999.

New Zealand's Customary Fishing Regulations are based on certain underlying principles (Hooper and Lynch 1999: 6). The first refers to mandate, that is, the need to have mandated representatives responsible for fisheries in each area. The Customary Fisheries Regulations therefore oblige the tribes to appoint guardians (*Kaitiaki*) who will be responsible for managing customary fisheries within their areas. Disputes over who should be Kaitiaki have to be solved by the tribes themselves, with no role for the government or its administration. As soon as the guardians are appointed, their names are gazetted in the paper, and their activities actively underpinned by compliance officers, fulltime as well as honorary.[19]

---

[19] *Kaitiaki* are nominated by the tribes but appointed by the Minister. At present the biggest problem (in the North Island) is to get the kaitiaki nominated, due to tribal and intertribal

The second principle refers to the actual management of the fishery. The local guardians are supposed to specify:

- The date that species will be taken
- The person authorised to take the fish
- The species that may be taken
- Size limits of the species taken
- The methods by which each species may be taken
- The area(s) of the fishery
- The purpose for which the fish may be taken

The regulations also provide for the establishment of particular areas, known as *Mataitai Reserves* covering traditional fishing grounds. Within these areas no commercial activity may take place, while other users must comply with the special bylaws laid down by the guardians. It is, however, a rather complicated process to get such Mataitai Reserves formally accepted, and at the time of writing, only two have been approved.

The third principle refers to the generation of accurate information back to the Ministry on the actual removals from the fishery. Fishers must report their actual catches back to the Kaitiaki, who in turn must record the information and report back quarterly to the Ministry of Fisheries.

There is no provision in the Settlement Act 1992 for limiting the customary take in any fishery. In practice an allowance is made, based on traditional catch in previous years. As is consistent with the provisions of the Settlement Act, customary take has priority, even before commercial quotas are allocated. Some operators (commercial as well as recreational) claim the fisheries are unregulated (uncapped). According to Hooper and Lynch (1999: 7) that is not the case. The fisheries are limited by the *kaitiaki*, not the state, and in many cases these guardians are stricter regarding catch and catch limits than the traditional state regulations. When local over-fishing does occur, this is primarily due to poaching, although it is frequently claimed that the fishery is carried out under the authorisation of an old preliminary fisheries regulation (Regulation 27). At present there is considerable uncertainty as to what will be the outcome of customary Maori fisheries management. Pakeha fishers (of European descent) hope that Maori commercial interests will put pressure on excessive customary take, while customary Maori fishers are hoping for some commercial constraint.

The fourth and probably most important principle refers to accountability. Individual customary fishers are responsible to the local guardian, who in turn is responsible both to the tribe and to the Ministry. The State is ultimately re-

---

conflicts. In the South Island this work has been contracted to the development corporation of the largest tribe, Ngái Tahu.

sponsible for the overall sustainability of fisheries as well as for delivery according to the Treaty of Waitangi and all international treaty obligations.

Closing the Gap?[20]

So far this account of Maori resurgence has dealt exclusively with fisheries policy. The Maori revival should, however, not be perceived as something special or exclusive to fisheries. Just as the QMS revolution was part of a larger economic/management revolution, whereby neo-liberal models were introduced over a whole range of sectors and institutions, the establishment of Maori commercial and customary rights must be seen in a larger perspective. In the early 1950s there were few signs that tribes and sub-tribes (*iwi and hapu*) would emerge as the central agents of a new fisheries policy, or for that matter, agents of a new economic development.

According to Kawhuru (1989: xiii), as recently as the late 1950s, early 1960s, it was held in official circles that "tribe was an anachronism". By that time 40% of Maori had moved to urban areas and had started setting up new social structures and organisations, a clear indication that the existing tribal structures were not able to provide a decent living for the rapidly expanding Maori population.[21] In the late 1960s the assimilation policy was challenged by a new process of *ethnification* and *indiginisation* among Maori, parallel to similar movements among other indigenous peoples. In New Zealand these processes were intimately connected to cultural expressions, that is, to Maori language, customs and not least to school education. In the economic sphere the tribe as an important actor started to emerge in the early 1980s, when protests against sewage and industrial waste were channelled through tribal organisations. This development must be seen in a larger political context, starting with the establishment of the Waitangi Tribunal in 1975. The Tribunal was a first step in addressing Maori grievances with a mandate to advise the Government, but only on grievances from 1975 onwards.

With the mandate extended in 1985 to encompass grievances dating all the way back to 1840, the political significance of the Treaty increased. From then on Maori grievances, relating to land policy, and fisheries as well as educational

---

[20] Closing the gap between Maori and the white (Pakeha) majority has been a consistent theme within New Zealand politics over the last 20 years. More recent research has questioned the systematic validity of such a gap, measured by income, employment and other indicators of socio-economic standing (see Chapple 2000). In commercial fisheries there is little doubt that Maori for many years were discriminated against, and consequently had little participation in and influence on the management of the resources.

[21] As pointed out by Hooper, it was definitely both push and pull factors at work. The rapid economic expansion in the post-war period offered employment in the industry and service sectors, while extended educational opportunities also contributed to the rapid urbanisation of Maori. In 1945 25% of the Maori population was living in urban areas while in 1981 the figure had increased to 80% (Ministry of Maori Development 2000: 12).

policies, had a channel – which was far more efficient than the six Maori seats in Parliament. But this channel was of course not "neutral" in political and organisational terms. By using *judges*, hearing *claims* and having cases prepared by *lawyers* (and consultants) the Tribunal played an important part in what may be called the "juridification" process, that is the channelling of political grievances through the judicial apparatus. What had started out 15 years before as a cultural revival soon turned to a question of restoring rights – rights that originally were granted to Maori through the Treaty of Waitangi 145 years earlier. According to Rata (2000):

> "During the late 1980s and the early 1990s an explicit distinction emerged between Maori development and tribal (iwi) developments. The tribes saw themselves increasingly as the political, social and economic form of Maori organisation and strove to have this self-perception institutionalised in government policy."

Evidently, this process was driven from both sides: by the tribes themselves, who were setting up development organisations trying to influence government planning, policy and service delivery, and by the State, which had the notion that revitalised tribes could take over from heavy and expensive bureaucracies. Certain tribes had already set up development organisations to take care of the economic activities, while others had to constitute themselves as tribes in order to set up the economic structures. With the increasing expectations of delivery, every tribe wanted to be in the best possible position. This process of first organising the tribes and then setting up the economic organisations was largely assisted by the Treaty of Waitangi Fisheries Commission, which insisted on a uniform set of requirements for tribes to be eligible for the redistributed assets. In conclusion it is probably correct to say that this process of *re-tribalisation* partly drove and in turn partly was driven by the redistribution process.

The important outcome is that Maori fisheries development, both commercially and culturally, was seen as being channelled through and connected to the tribal structures, or what Rata (2000) has named "neo-tribal capitalism". The central point is that this solution was by no means self-evident. Other countries with strong tribal presence have chosen completely different solutions, such as Namibia and South Africa, where tribal affiliation is irrelevant to the question of whom should be given access rights in the fisheries. What then are the prospects of this neo-tribal capitalism? With Maori interests now controlling approximately 40% of the fishing sector (in economic terms), there is considerable interest in which direction the tribes may move.

One scenario is that Maori interests will prefer the suggested co-ordinating structure (), and will use the considerable profits acquired to buy additional quotas and processing facilities and gradually dominate more and more of the New Zealand fishing industry. This will take place not only through the proposed

Aotearoa Fisheries Limited, presently controlling approximately 25% of New Zealand's entire quota, but through decentralised commercial initiatives by the various iwis as well. Over time Maori companies will diversify their operations to other countries and the Sealord Group has already established subsidiaries, alliances and joint ventures in more than 20 countries. Assets in terms of shares and quotas will be kept within the Maori structure and only part of the proceeds will be used directly for social development, which will be directed through the tribal structures. The greatest direct benefits for the tribes involved will be the employment created in fishing, processing and gradually in aquaculture.

Another possible scenario is a gradual dispersion of part of the fisheries portfolio. Both quotas and shares are transferable and many tribes may prefer to cash in what they have been allocated. Some will be under considerable pressure to hand out the compensation, while others may prefer to invest in other sectors, like tourism or domestic trade. The fishing industry is difficult and fiercely competitive and there are no guarantees that the large number of small Maori controlled companies will survive in the longer run. If this is the case, it will be difficult to keep Maori assets together, even if limitations are placed on the transfer of shares to stop "cannibalisation" of existing companies. Having accepted ITQs as the going "currency" it is difficult to backtrack and impose severe limitations on transferability. Maori will still benefit, but more as owners of capital (having capitalised the resource rent) than as active entrepreneurs and participants in the fishing industry.

However, only the first scenario offers the possibility of co-ordinating the commercial and the customary fisheries, that is of bringing together what was split by the English legislation back in 1892 (the Oyster Act) and maintained through the Settlement Act of 1992. In this situation Maori interests will have to make tradeoffs between what should be caught in the customary sector versus what should be allowed in the commercial. Knowing that Maori interests already are heavily involved in aquaculture and furthermore, that all Maori enjoy recreational rights, just like any other New Zealander, it is easy to see that Maori hold the key to a harmonisation of different rights in the marine area (Hersoug 2002).

Maori fishing – coping with diversity

This article has been concentrating on Maori fishing rights, trying to show how the introduction of the QMS provoked a re-emergence of old fisheries claims, but also how the QMS provided the currency (the ITQs) to solve the Maori grievances in the commercial sector. On a global level this policy has been highly successful, even if the actual distribution of assets has met with unprecedented difficulties. With approximately 15% of the population, Maori interests now own 33% of the quota rights. With a solid capital base they are also in a position to buy more quotas whenever they are up for sale. Although the details of a future arrangement remain unclear, Maori will be a major player in the New Zealand fishing industry, especially if the quota rights and assets are professionally administered.

Even more challenging has been the question of creating a Maori customary fishing regime, a process that has taken nearly ten years. At present it is definitely too early to report on success or failure of this regime. Suffice to say that the arrangement is innovative and original, and permits all coastal Maori to maintain a traditional link to the fisheries, even in cases where they do not have any commercial interests. As a matter of right Maori customary fishing has priority (allowances are made *before* the allocation of Total Allowable Commercial Catches, underlining the significance of cultural traditions.[22] What is interesting in the case of New Zealand's fisheries management regime is the blending of an extremely competitive commercial sector with traditional fishing practices and a large recreational sector. New Zealand has definitely not found *the solution* to how such diverse interests can co-exist without major problems. That is part of the unfinished business after the introduction of the QMS, now being implemented through various co-management arrangements and tried institutionalised through Fisheries Plans. But New Zealand has tried a number of new and innovative approaches, from which there is a lot to be learnt, provided that the lessons are adapted and customised to local conditions. The most important lesson is probably summarised by the national historian Belich (2002: 487):

"New Zealand history suggests that Maori problems will never be solved except by Maori themselves, but they have to be given the necessary tools, which may include some cession of authority as well as resources. It is quite true that Maori have to pull themselves up by their own bootstraps. But this may require that they be given back some bootstraps first."

---

[22] At present the Minister has set aside an allocation in order to cover the customary Maori fishery, but so far there is little data and hence only a vague idea of quantities involved. Within the commercial and recreational part of the fishing industry many would prefer to see a fixed share also for Maori customary fisheries. TOKM has recommended allowances in the range of 10-20% of most (inshore) fish stocks. Other Maori leaders see the capping of Maori customary fisheries as threatening the content and spirit of the Agreement, which guarantees Maori the right to provide fish for their cultural and spiritual needs. The amount of fish needed will therefore of necessity vary, requiring other parts of the industry to adjust. The determination of customary take is therefore still unresolved, complicating the idea that various stakeholder-groups have fixed shares in the TACs, which can be used for negotiated deals.

Abbreviations:

EEZ . . . . Exclusive Economic Zone
ITQ . . . . Individual Transferable Quota
MAF . . . . Ministry of Agriculture and Fisheries
MFC . . . . Maori Fisheries Commission
NIWA . . . . National Institute of Water and Atmospheric Research
POSA . . . . Post-settlement Assets
PRESA . . . . . . Pre-settlement Assets
SeaFIC . . . . . . Seafood Industry Council
TAC . . . . Total Allowable Catch
TACC . . . . Total Allowable Commercial Catch
TOKM . . . . . . Te Ohu Kai Moana (Treaty of Waitangi Fisheries
              Commission)
QMA . . . . Quota Management Area
QMS . . . . Quota Management System

References

Annala, J. 1996: New Zealand's ITQ system: have the first eight years been a success or a failure? *Fish Biology and Fisheries* 6, pp. 43-62.

Belich, J. 2002: *Paradise reforged. A history of the New Zealanders.* Allen Lane/Penguin Press, Auckland.

Bess, R. 2001: New Zealand's indigenous people and their claims to fisheries resources. *Marine Policy.* Vol. 25 (2001), pp. 23-32.

Chapple, S. 2000: Maori socio-economic disparity. Paper for the Ministry of Social Policy, Wellington.

Gaffney, K.R. 1997: *Property based fisheries management: Lessons from New Zealand's Quota Management System.* Masters Thesis, Victoria University, Wellington.

Hersoug, B. 2002a: *Unfinished business. New Zealand's experience with rights-based fisheries-management.* Eburon, Delft, Netherlands.

Hersoug, B. 2002b: *Fishing in a sea of sharks. Reconstruction and development in the South African fishing industry.* Eburon, Delft, Netherlands.

Hooper, M. and T. Lynch 2000: Recognition of and Provision for Indigenous and Coastal Community Fishing Rights using Property Rights Instruments. In Shotton, R. (ed.): *Use of property rights in fisheries management.* FAO Fisheries Technical Paper 404/2. FAO, Rome.

Kawhuru, I.H. (ed.) 1989: *Waitangi, Maori and Pakeha Perspectives of the Treaty of Waitangi.* Oxford University Press, Oxford.

Kerins, S.P. and T. McClurg 1996: Maori Fisheries Rights. Unpublished draft. TOKM, Wellington.

MAF 1991: Fisheries Legislation Review. Public Discussion Paper. Fisheries Task Force, MAF, Wellington.

MAF 1992: Sustainable Fisheries. Fisheries Task Force, MAF, Wellington.

MAF 1993: Kaitiaki o Kaimoana Treaty of Waitangi (Fisheries Claims) Settlement Regulations. MAF, Wellington.

New Zealand Institute of Economic Research 2000: Allocating Fisheries Assets. Economic Costs of Delay. Report to Treaty Tribes Coalition, NZIER, Wellington.

Orange, C. 1987: *The Treaty of Waitangi*. Allen &Unwin, Wellington.

Rata, E. 2000: *A Political Economy of Neo-tribal Capitalism*. Lexington Books, Oxford.

TOKM 1995: Disputes Resolution Procedures. Treaty of Waitangi Fisheries Commission, Wellington.

TOKM 1997: Proposed Optimum Method for Allocation Consultation Document. Treaty of Waitangi Fisheries Commission, Wellington.

TOKM 2000: hui-a-tau report. Treaty of Waitangi Fisheries Commission, Wellington.

TOKM 2002: ahu whakamua. Report for Agreement. A report by the Treaty of Waitangi Fisheries Commission on the allocation of assets and distribution of benefits of the Fisheries Settlement. Treaty of Waitangi Fisheries Commission, Wellington.

ToWDSA 1992: Treaty of Waitangi Deed of Settlement Act

Waitangi Tribunal 1988: *Report of the Waitangi Tribunal on the Muriwhenua Fishing Claim* (Wai 22). Ministry of Justice, Wellington.

Waitangi Tribunal 1992: *The Fisheries Settlement Report*. Brooker and Friend Ltd., Wellington.

CHAPTER 8

The Coastal Sami: a 'Pariah Caste' of the Norwegian Fisheries? A Reflection on Ethnicity and Power in Norwegian Resource Management

Einar Eythórsson

Introduction

The sub-title of this article, "A Reflection on *Ethnicity and Power* in Norwegian Resource Management", may require some explanation. Why are ethnicity and power relevant to the discussion of fisheries resource management? More to the point, what kind of ethnicity, and what kind of power? The article is an attempt to use the concepts of *power*, *domination*, and *pariah* caste to analyse the mechanisms that have prevented the voice of a group of relatively numerous, small-scale fishermen in northern Norway, the coastal Sami, from being heard by Norwegian fisheries managers. It is also an attempt to interpret events that have recently caused the coastal Sami to be perceived as relevant stakeholders in the fisheries, within the same conceptual frame.

In the debate on various forms of user participation and co-management of common property resources (CPRs), the virtues of stakeholder involvement are often phrased in terms of an improved legitimacy of management régimes. Co-management may be defined as "an arrangement where responsibility for resource management is shared between the government and user groups" (Sen and Raakjær Nielsen 1996:406). In many cases, however, the concepts of 'user groups', 'stakeholder' and even 'fisherman' are applied without clear definitions, as if their content were obvious and uncontested. This problem has been addressed by Mikalsen and Jentoft (2001), who apply a classification developed by Mitchell et al (1997), where stakeholders are grouped according to three attributes: *legitimacy, power* and *urgency*. Stakeholders who possess all three attributes are classified as *definitive*, those who possess two out of the three are *expectant*, while those who possess only one (legitimacy, power or urgency) are *latent* stakeholders. The introduction of these concepts into the co-management debate may be helpful in the analysis of how certain groups have become defined as stakeholders, while the participation of others, for whom a great deal may also be 'at stake', in terms of the way resources are managed, is considered

149

irrelevant in the process of decision-making. It is not necessarily obvious which groups should qualify as involved parties in management. Resource management régimes are not only technical measures to preserve resources: they are also institutions for distributing rights and benefits. The institutions make the rules concerning distribution and these rules are based on a definition of who is entitled to the rights and benefits involved. Anyone who has the power to define who the stakeholders are is in a position to decide which groups should be consulted, and become otherwise involved in the management process.

As shown by Jentoft and Kristoffersen (1989), stakeholder involvement has been institutionalized within Norwegian fisheries management for more than a century, mostly through the involvement of the *Norges Fiskarlag* [Norwegian Fishermen's Union]. The union has been considered a legitimate representative of all fishermen, irrespective of scale and geography. Until recently it has been considered irrelevant to include other interest groups: the established system of stakeholder representation has been reluctant to involve groups who don't define their primary interests with reference to a national community of professional fishermen. This applies to local and regional interests, but even more to the coastal Sami as an ethnic minority. The idea of fishermen in Norwegian fisheries claiming the right to be heard as representatives of matters pertaining to the *coastal Sami* has been considered not merely irrelevant, but highly inappropriate.

This article considers not so much the fact that the coastal Sami have now become visible as stakeholders in Norwegian fisheries management, but more over the puzzling fact that they remained invisible for so long.

Coastal Sami as Stakeholders in Fisheries Management

The struggle for the acceptance of indigenous rights to use and participate in the management of CPRs, such as the marine fish resources in Norway, is basically a question of mobilizing political resources in order to change some of the key definitions of a management régime. In Norway's case, this means including a 'new' category of resource users, *the coastal Sami*, in the company of stakeholders in the fisheries.

As this category of stakeholders has previously been considered irrelevant to fisheries management, it is no wonder that the representation of a Sami identity among the fishermen created quite considerable scepticism. Some wondered if those who now presented themselves as coastal Sami were merely Norwegian fishermen who had redefined themselves opportunistically as coastal Sami, hoping that the increased focus on indigenous rights might bring them some extra benefits. The strong reluctance to include Sami fishermen as such in the group of stakeholders in the fisheries also makes one wonder why it was previously considered irrelevant.

During the 1990s, local spawning in the Northern Norwegian fjords attracted the interest of marine biologists in Tromsø, who were interested in what appeared to be a substantial number of sub-stocks of cod. The issue was addressed by a somewhat unorthodox research project, combining biological stock assessment with a survey of fishermen's local knowledge about these stocks. Whilst the project revealed a number of 'unknown' spawning sites for coastal cod, it also showed that these spawning sites have long been well known among local fishermen (Maurstad and Sundet 1998). If the existence of these sites had been kept as a local 'secret', this outcome would have been easier to explain. But it is well documented that there had been no secrecy about these sites. On the contrary, local fjord-fishermen (many of whom are coastal Sami) have struggled for almost a century for protective regulations to save local sub-stocks from destruction (Eythórsson 1993, Andersen 1997), but with only limited success. The puzzling fact is that while marine research during the 1990s 'discovered' the existence of apparently disparate sub-stocks of coastal cod, which regularly spawned in certain areas of the Northern Norwegian fjords, these stocks had been more or less well known for at least one hundred years.

This leads on to a discussion of the relational aspect of knowledge. How is the relevance and 'visibility' of knowledge dependent on the authority and position of the holders of knowledge? (Eythórsson 1998a). Does the relational aspect of fisheries knowledge have anything to do with the relations between ethnic groups on the coast of northern Norway (Eythórsson and Mathisen 1998)? What exactly constitutes the *relational aspect,* which apparently makes certain types of knowledge irrelevant and, moreover, renders the holders of such knowledge 'invisible' in fisheries arenas? What is more, the invisibility of the coastal Sami has not been confined to fisheries arenas: in spite of being in a numerical majority within the Sami people of Norway, they became increasingly invisible as a group in their own right during the era of modernization, particularly in the era after the second world war.

Bjørklund (1985) has documented the relatively sudden 'disappearance' of the coastal Sami from the census records during these years, when people who had classified themselves as Sami in the pre-war census classified themselves as Norwegians in the first post-war census. This happened under circumstances that were illustrated by the Norwegian anthropologist Harald Eidheim in his classic paper "When Ethnic Identity is a Social Stigma" (1971). Being a coastal Sami became associated with backwardness and the humiliating poverty of the past, while a Norwegian identity became associated with modernity and the new, prosperous Norway of the post-war era. Furthermore, the Norwegian nation state presented itself in ethnically homogenous terms, with almost no political or legal reference to the Sami minority group. According to organizational principles of the Norwegian welfare state, it was important for rural people to join nation-wide organizations, such as the Farmers' Union and the Fishermen's Union, in order to qualify for different types of benefits. By definition, these organizations were 'Norwegian', and their membership defined according to economic position and occupation. Asymmetrical power relations between ethnic groups may explain why the voice of the coastal Sami was apparently absent in the fisheries discourse in Norway during the post-war years, but this does not explain the nature of these relations. The forms of power involved in the processes that resulted in the 'disappearance' and a later 'reappearance' of the coastal Sami may be analysed by combining Foucault's concepts of power and domination with the work of the Norwegian anthropologist Harald Eidheim (1971). Eidheim's studies, which focus on ethnic identity among the coastal Sami in the 1960s, were inspired by Erving Goffman's *The presentation of Self in Everyday Life* (1959) and *Stigma* (1963). Eidheim's focus is on defining the situation in encounters between Sami and Norwegians, and between coastal Sami and Sami reindeer herders, as well as on the self-presentation of the coastal Sami in frontstage and backstage contexts. As pointed out by Engelstad (2001), Goffman did not present himself as a theorist of power, but his work can provide an important frame of reference to other theories of power and communication, including those of Foucault.

Power, Domination and 'Pariah Castes'

While institutions, stakeholder involvement and local knowledge have become household terms in the debate concerning the management of common property resources, the issues of power and domination have been focused on to a somewhat lesser extent. Power may be defined in different ways. The traditional approach to the study of power has been to look at resources and positions as the main sources of power. In recent decades, however, attention has been drawn to the communicative aspect of power, a development that has been largely inspired by the work of Foucault and Bourdieu. As a relational concept, power may only be studied as it becomes activated in some kind of social action, involving relations between two or more parties, or between the ruler and the subject. Foucault understands power relations to be the "means by which individuals try to conduct, to determine the behavior of others" (Simons 1995), and "a mode of action upon the actions of others". This understanding of power requires a relationship between two parties, and the possibility that the action of one party will be met by reaction by the other. Consequently, Foucault states "where there is power, there is resistance". In his lecture on "The Order of Discourse" (Foucault 1972), he outlines several dimensions of power in communication, as a set of procedures of exclusion, in the form of various types of prohibition concerning the content and performance of speech, and rules defining competent speakers (Engelstad 2001:17). Foucault's concept of discursive power may thus be useful for the purpose of analysing 'taboos' in the

Norwegian fisheries discourse, as well as the silencing of certain speakers who failed to adhere to the unwritten rules of the discourse.

According to Foucault, domination is, by contrast, different from power. Slavery, for instance, is not a power relation but a total domination, where there is no room for resistance.

In a majority/minority situation where the majority does not acknowledge the minority as a relevant subject, the minority may still have certain means to voice their reactions, provided that the minority acknowledges itself as a community. 'Low-caste' minorities often seek internal solidarity as a reaction to external domination and find ways to make themselves visible. Max Weber, writing about ethnic segregation and caste, says that status structures only become 'castes' in extreme circumstances,

> where there are underlying differences which are held to be 'ethnic'. The 'caste' is indeed, the normal form in which ethnic communities usually live side by side in a 'societalized' manner. These ethnic communities believe in blood relationship and exclude exogamous marriage and social intercourse. Such a caste situation is part of the phenomenon of 'pariah' peoples and is found all over the world. These people form communities, acquire specific occupational traditions of handicrafts or of other arts, and cultivate a belief in their ethnic community. (Weber 1948:189)

According to Fredrik Barth, pariah groups are usually associated with the breaking of basic taboos of the majority society. In Europe, groups such as executioners, horse-flesh dealers, collectors of night-soil and gypsies were rejected by the host population because of behaviour or characteristics that were positively condemned:

> Their identity imposed a definition on social situations which gave very little scope for interaction with persons in the majority population, and simultaneously as an imperative status represented an inescapable disability that prevented them from assuming the normal statuses involved in other definitions of the situation of interaction. (Barth 1969:31).

Like the concept of power, the concept of ethnic identity can be seen as purely relational: it is only relevant in relation to 'others'. In a social setting with no 'others' the concept is meaningless. In northern Norway, the ethnic identity of the coastal Sami is formed as relative to the Norwegian, the Finnish, and the inland Sami 'others'. As Barth (ibid:14) has pointed out, maintenance of ethnic boundaries is not necessarily a result of 'objective' cultural differences; the *ascription* of cultural features that signal the boundary may change over time, while the dichotomization between groups remains intact.

There is ample evidence from historical and ethnographic records to support the assertion that the Sami in Norway have for centuries been considered as a 'pariah people' by the Norwegian majority. In the old *Sagas* (written in the thirteenth century), accounts of encounters between Sami and Norwegians usually refer to the Sami's dark powers and their knowledge of sorcery, indicating an ascription of *taboo-breaking* characteristics. While this ascription has become less pronounced in modern times, the Sami, and particularly the coastal Sami stereotype of the early twentieth century, was associated with superstition and ignorance, and sometimes with rumours of taboo-breaking behaviour, such as feeding animals with human excrement.[1] However, as pariah people they were also recognisable as a subject people, exposed to the exercising of power on the part of the Norwegian authorities, and thus involved in certain power relations. This particular relationship with the majority population, as defined by the others as well as by themselves, formed their ethnic identity. The coastal Sami were not subject to the romantic image sometimes attached to the more exotic reindeer herders inland. Their mixed economy, with fishing and animal husbandry as main components, resembled the way of life of the Norwegian population in the coastal districts. A popular myth (without any roots in historical knowledge) was that they were a marginal and degenerated group, descending from reindeer herders who had lost their animals and moved to the coast, where they led a miserable life in poverty and ignorance.

A Mysterious 'Disappearance'?

By the turn of the nineteenth century, Sami intellectuals recognised the need to form a political organization that could voice Sami interests to the institutions of the emerging Norwegian nation state. The first Sami association was formed in 1903, but was discontinued in 1921, due to a lack of resources and difficulties in reaching the geographically scattered Sami communities. The leading figures of this first association were Isak Saba, the first Sami to become a Member of Parliament, and Anders Larsen, editor of the first Sami newspaper. They were both coastal Sami from the fjord districts, a fact which indicates that ethnopolitical mobilization, at this stage, was no less relevant among the coastal Sami than among the inland reindeer herders.

But when the second ethno-political mobilization among the Sami came about after the second world war, the coastal Sami had 'mysteriously' disappeared from the scene. In the Finnmark region and the northern part of the Troms region, the ongoing assimilation process was strongly reinforced by the war, as the Germans evacuated most of the population in this area in 1944, all the buildings were burned down and all infrastructures thoroughly destroyed. There was a common sentiment among young people who returned from 'exile'

---

[1] Unpublished records by *Norsk Etnologisk Gransking* from the Alta district.

in the more prosperous areas of Norway, that reconstruction was a chance to leave the old ways behind and re-establish the fjord communities as modern, Norwegian communities, without the stigma of economic and cultural backwardness. Anthropologist Robert Paine, who carried out fieldwork in a coastal Sami area in the early 1950s, described the attitudes among the younger generation: "They no doubt felt that Lappish[2] is a language of the past, associated with the 'backwardness' and isolation of the old days; they think of themselves as living in a new era and in a new Norway" (Paine 1957:xiii). Several authors have described the background for the apparently rapid change of identity from coastal Sami to Norwegian, from the 1940s to the 1960s (Eidheim 1971, Bjørklund 1985, Høgmo 1986). The stigma attached to the coastal Sami identity apparently left little room for 'resistance' to Norwegian domination. Rather than sticking to their position as a 'pariah caste' in Norwegian society, many coastal Sami gave in to the Norwegian assimilation policy. Sami identity could be played out 'backstage' in the fjord communities, but in 'frontstage' interaction, where representatives of the majority were present, presenting oneself as a Sami became a taboo. A man from a fjord community in Finnmark, who reached the age of sixteen in 1945, expressed mixed feelings about the attitudes in the post-war years in an interview in 1989:

"We were ashamed of our parents, who were so 'foolish' that they continued to speak Lappish. But sometimes I felt uneasy when people who surely knew Lappish suddenly insisted on answering in Norwegian. If you spoke to them in Lappish you were looked upon as an 'asshole'." (Eythórsson 1991:66).

Eidheim (1971) described his encounter with a coastal Sami community in the early sixties as a process where the Norwegian 'frontstage' identity was underlined early on in communication with the local people, while a Sami 'backstage' identity was gradually revealed as people took him into their confidence. As an outsider, paying a casual visit to the area, he would most likely notice no signs of ethnic diversity, still less of any ethnic border. Eidheim's interest in the Sami population was not welcomed:

my interests and questions annoyed most people in the community. Some young people avoided me for weeks when rumours about my interests spread through kitchen conversations; they took me for some sort of an unpleasant detective. Later on, people became more careless with the 'secret' that they habitually used Lappish in their daily life

---

[2]   *Lapp* and *Lappish* were still commonly used terms in the 1960s but, as they are considered negatively weighted terms, they have been replaced by *Sami* since the 1970s. However, old people in the coastal Sami areas may still refer to their native language as "Lappisk".

After a while, a few friends, notably from the older generation, started admitting their personal dilemmas of identity:

> This would often take the form of confessions: they were after all a kind of Lapp. Their parents and grandparents lived in turf huts, some of them as late as in the 1930s. Some people even wore Lappish costumes at that time, and Lappish footwear was in common use until World War II. They were bothered by not being fully proficient in Norwegian and by the spite and ridicule to which they were often exposed for this and other reasons in interactions with self-confident and arrogant Norwegians. They even had the suspicion that their low standard of living and the lack of industrial enterprises in the fjord might derive from their being an inferior race. 'The Lapps must be stupid' they said. Certainly they believed the average Norwegian to be of that opinion. In all details their miserable self-image was a reflection of the Lappish stigma as local Norwegians define it.(p 55)

Eidheim found that even if the ethnic border between coastal Sami and Norwegians was a kind of 'secret', which the coastal Sami carefully avoided making reference to in their encounters with Norwegians, the population on both sides was well aware of it. He illustrates this by the case of 'Per', a Lapp from the fjord community and a member of the township's school board. In spite of carefully avoiding any expression of his 'Sami-ness' in the public sphere, Per was readily recognised as a Sami by the other members of the school board. There appeared to be a kind of 'mutual understanding' on how to handle social confrontation between Norwegians and Sami in school board meetings: Per would acknowledge the superiority of the Norwegians and adopt a passive role:

> Per thinks that they know the nuances of suitable behaviour and effective action better than he himself, and objectively they have a fuller command of the code. They have the right identity, which makes them authorised initiators in the situation, while he is only some kind of a satellite. (ibid:59).

From the situation quoted above, Eidheim concluded that interaction in the public sphere took place within the statuses and institutions of the dominant Norwegian population. Even if the ethnic cleavage was definitely a premise in social confrontation, it was never mentioned:

> [I]t is an overruling axiom that the local population is made up of two ethnic categories, Lapps and Norwegians. Since the public presentation of a Lappish identity is not an alternative, it follows that in this sphere there is no institutionalised interaction in which a status 'Lapp' has accepted roles, i.e. Lapp and Norwegian are not complementary statuses. (ibid.)

In some respects, this form of self-repression, collectively denying one's ethnic identity, seems to resemble the case of homosexuals, which is often referred to by Foucault. Admitting one's coastal Sami background might be compared to admitting one's homosexuality in a society where homosexuality is a taboo. His point is that when members of a minority cease to acknowledge themselves as a distinct, collective subject, they lose the opportunity to relate to the majority. In which case, according to Foucault's understanding of power, there can be no power relations between the minority and the majority, since the minority has ceased to recognise its own existence as a relevant subject. This represents a shift, in his terms, from playing the role of a 'pariah-caste' in relation to the majority, to becoming 'invisible' subjects with no opportunity to relate to the majority. Superficially, this represented an escape from the role of a 'pariah caste', but the shift also eliminated the possibility of collective resistance to the majority power. In Foucault's terms, by denying their ethnic identity, the coastal Sami subordinated themselves to Norwegian *domination*.

Breaking the Taboo

Such a situation may explain to a certain extent why there were no references to the Sami background to local and regional politics at this time. The numerous letters and petitions to the fisheries authorities, sent by fjord fishermen in the coastal Sami districts in the 1950s and 1960s, are one example of this. The only case where I could find something that looks like a subtle reference to the situation of the coastal Sami was in a petition from a 'mass meeting' in Revsbotn in 1961. The petition gives a through description of how the Norwegian herring fleet, catching small herring fry, threatens the livelihood of local fishermen, and concludes as follows:

> We demand unanimously as Norwegian citizens and as members of Norwegian society that our livelihood from the cod fisheries in the fjords of Finnmark, as well as along the coast, should be protected by law. (Eythórsson and Mathisen 1998).

Such petitions often expressed frustration and disillusionment, and the experience of being ignored by the fisheries authorities and the Fishermen's Union. Andersen (2001) has described them as expressing the "collective anguish" of the coastal Sami fishermen, who found that the authorities systematically ignored their requests for protection of the fishing grounds in the fjords. In a public environment, such as the annual meetings of the Finnmark Fishermen's Union, efforts by the coastal Sami to voice their distress were effectively ignored by the Norwegian majority as inappropriate breaches of the code of interaction. The following quotes are taken from interviews with coastal Sami fishermen, who participated in annual meetings as representatives of local branches of the Fishermen's Union during the 1950s and 1960s:

"We used to sit in a separate row, the people from the fjords. But as soon as any of us spoke up, you could see that those 'big guys' became restless, they stared at the ceiling or out of the window, some started walking towards the door". ....[3]

"... I remember old Peder Benjaminsen from Laksefjord. Once, at the annual meeting of the Fishermen's Union, he came to the speakers' platform, to deliver a proposal on Danish seine restrictions for Laksefjord. The 'big guys', the Union leadership, were sitting on the front row, they were well aware of what Peder had on his mind. So they started telling jokes to each other, and laughed loudly, and when Peder had finished no-one in the room had heard a word of his speech..."[4]

In general, referring to oneself as a coastal Sami in fisheries debates was not only irrelevant, it was a *taboo* that it took considerable courage to break. Ragnar Nilsen, in his book "Fjord Fishermen and Resource Use in the North" (1998), has written about what he describes as "a coastal Sami revolt" in the Porsanger Fjord in 1983-84. Out of context, the 'revolt' may look like a rather insignificant act. Two leaders of local branches of the Fishermen's Union contacted the local leadership of a new Sami organization, *Samenes Landsforbund*[5] (SLF) [The National Sami Alliance], to seek support for a demand for local restrictions on the use of active fishing-gear in the fjord. The political platform of the SLF was based on loyalty to the Norwegian authorities; it had been established mainly as a reaction against the extensive grazing rights of Sami reindeer herders, and against the radical demands of Sami activists. The SLF found the fishermen's case interesting, however, and voiced strong sympathy for their demands. The case received some publicity, and within the Fishermen's Union there were strong negative reactions against the two fishermen who had brought an internal fisheries issue into an ethno-political arena.

By making their Sami background relevant in the fisheries political arena, the two Union leaders had broken a taboo. The Fishermen's Union's reaction was to exclude both of them for being disloyal to the Union, a form of reaction that had previously only been used against active Nazi collaborators at the end of the German occupation of Norway.

According to Nilsen, this event was a symbolic breakthrough, as it marked an end to the silencing of the coastal Sami:

We really faced a revolt and a liberation, as the coastal Sami issue was at last set free in a political and organizational context. The process which started from the

---

[3]   Interview with a fisherman in Revsbotn fjord 1992 (Eythórsson and Mathisen 1998).

[4]   Interview with a fisherman in Snefjord, 1996 (Eythórsson and Mathisen 1998)

[5]   Not to be confused with *Norske Samers Riksforbund* [The Norwegian Sami Association], which has a core membership among inland Sami and Sami academics.

demands for fisheries regulations in Porsanger took a course which made it possible to break through the barriers that had prevented coastal Sami identity from being voiced openly. The silence was eventually broken, for the first time since the war, the coastal Sami voice was heard. (Nilsen 1998:73).

The coastal Sami didn't experience an instant breakthrough after the 'revolt' in Porsanger Fjord. On the contrary, the fisheries authorities in the Finnmark region were even more restrictive in their attitude towards local fisheries regulations in the fjord areas during the years that followed (Eythórsson 1998b). The implementation of a vessel quota system in 1990 was a major setback for the coastal Sami, since almost none of the small-scale fishermen in the fjords fulfilled the criteria for receiving a vessel quota in the first allocation. However, a process where the coastal Sami eventually became visible and recognised as relevant stakeholders in the fisheries had been started. In 1990, the Ministry of Fisheries engaged a law professor, Carsten Smith, to write a report on the obligations of the Government towards the Sami, related to fisheries management, and in 1993 a special "Sami fisheries committee" was appointed by the Ministry. The Sami Parliament, established in 1989, has also become accepted as an organization that has a right to be consulted on fisheries issues. The power of the Sami Parliament is limited, but it has been heard on certain fisheries issues, such as more flexible criteria for quota allocation in Finnmark and the northern part of the Troms region.

Conclusion

How can the story about the coastal Sami contribute to a general discussion on stakeholder involvement in the management of common property resources? It is quite common for the exercise of power in management institutions to reflect certain political preferences, and these preferences tend to reflect the relative strength of the political parties and stakeholder organizations involved in decision-making within these institutions. In a democratic society, the power relations between those in a position to participate in a political dialogue, leading to management decisions, are more or less visible, and are open to scrutiny. However, these processes are not necessarily open to new participants. Outsiders, such as ethnic minorities and women in fishing communities, have often experienced an effective "silencing" by a compact community of insiders who consider their voices to be irrelevant. In the case of the Sami fjord fishermen, their specific interests could easily be ignored, as long as the coastal Sami had ceased to communicate their collective identity. Their story also illustrates the general dilemma of 'pariah peoples'. Assimilating into the majority community offers an opportunity to escape the 'pariah' role, but it also eliminates the possibility of engaging in relations with the majority and reacting collectively to the exercise of power. Discriminatory practices thus become 'invisible'. In

Foucault's terms, power relations were replaced by domination. The communicative aspect of power is illustrated by the 'discursive order', which ruled out any mention of ethnic identity by the coastal Sami in fisheries arenas. As Sami, they were subject to domination, while as fishermen and members of the Fishermen's Union, they were subject to power relations. As fishermen, they could voice resistance to power in a legitimate manner, provided that all utterances were kept within the communication channels of the Fishermen's Union. But, as indicated in the descriptions of encounters between Sami fishermen and the 'big guys' in the Fishermen's Union, the coastal Sami had the strong impression that their utterances were tolerated, but not taken much notice of. Apparently the Sami fishermen were not considered 'competent speakers' in the fisheries discourse, according to the Norwegian majority's definition of the situation. Consequently, attempts by the coastal Sami to communicate resistance through the Fishermen's Union may be characterised as 'quasi-communication', staged to conceal a situation of quite asymmetric power relation, or even concealed domination. The recent 'discovery' of local spawning sites for cod by fisheries scientists also illustrates the character of this quasi-communication. Despite the fjord-fishermen's continuing efforts to communicate the need for the protection of these sites, through Union channels for at least sixty years, it was nevertheless possible for the existence of the sites to be presented as a new discovery in the 1990s.

Reversing the process of domination involved breaking the taboo of coastal Sami identity, an emotionally painful operation for many people, especially those who felt that they had paid a high price for their assimilation into Norwegian society during the 1950s and 1960s. The harsh reaction from the Fishermen's Union to 'the coastal Sami revolt' indicates that taking the resistance of fjord fishermen out of the Union channels of communication and into an ethnopolitical arena was no small offence. The risk that such an act might eliminate the Union's control over political utterances by the coastal Sami, enabling them to enter into real communication with the Norwegian authorities, may explain the scale of the reaction.

Despite the Norwegian acceptance of a Sami voice on the fisheries arena over the last decade, little has been achieved in terms of real influence in decision-making concerning resource management issues. However, if it may be concluded that the situation of the coastal Sami has shifted from being subject to *domination* by the Norwegian majority to becoming subject to majority *power*, activated by power relations, then the change is significant. The taboo of coastal Sami identity has been broken, and they are able to relate collectively to the majority, hopefully without being identified with the 'pariah caste' image of the past. According to the classification of stakeholders applied by Mikalsen and Jentoft (2001), the coastal Sami have become *latent*, or even *expectant*, stakeholders in relation to Norwegian fisheries management, as the urgency, and to a certain degree, the legitimacy of their claims has become widely recognised. However, what still seems to be lacking is the third attribute, which would qualify them as definitive stakeholders: *power*.

Acknowledgements

Thanks to Ivar Bjørklund and Svanhild Andersen for useful comments on this article, and to Stein Roar Mathisen for various contributions to discussions and publications about the coastal Sami issue throughout the 1990s. The author, however, assumes complete responsibility for the views expressed in this article.

References

Andersen, Svanhild: *Ressurskamp og møter med offentlige instanser – noen utfordringer i en norsk og samisk utkant.* A Master thesis in Social Anthropology/Sami studies, University of Tromsø 1997.

Andersen, Svanhild 2001: Bruk og forvaltning av kystressursene i et samisk perspektiv. In: *Rapport fra Sametingets fiskeriseminar,* februar 2001.

Barth, Fredrik (ed): *Ethnic Groups and Boundaries. The Social Organization of Culture Difference.* Universitetsforlaget /Allen & Unwin, Bergen, Oslo /London 1969.

Bjørklund, Ivar: *Fjordfolket i Kvænangen.* Universitetsforlaget, Oslo 1985.

Eidheim, Harald: When Ethnic Identity is a Social Stigma. In: Eidheim, Harald: *Aspects of the Lappish Minority Situation.* Universitetsforlaget, Oslo 1971.

Engelstad, Fredrik: Theories of power in communication – a critical assessment. In: Engelstad, F., and J. Gripsrud (eds.): *Power, Aesthetics, Media.* Makt- og demokratiutredningen 1998-2003, Nr. 33. Oslo 2001.

Eythórsson, Einar: Ressurser, livsform og lokal kunnskap. En studie av et fjordsamfunn i Finnmark. Master thesis in Social Sciences, University of Tromsø 1991.

Eythórsson, Einar: Fjordfolket, fisken og forvaltningen. FDH-rapport 1993:12, Finnmark distriktshøgskole, Alta 1993.

Eythórsson, Einar (1998a): Voices of the Weak; Relational Aspects of Local Ecological Knowledge in the Fisheries. In: Jentoft, Svein (ed.): *Commons in a Cold Climate. Coastal Fisheries and Reindeer Pastoralism in North Norway: The Co-management Approach.* UNESCO / Parthenon Publishing Group. New York 1998.

Eythórsson, Einar (1998b): Det rådgivende utvalget for lokale reguleringer – erfaringer fra Finnmark. In: Sagdahl, Bjørn (ed.): *Fjordressurser og reguleringspolitikk. En utfordring for kystkommuner.* Kommuneforlaget, Oslo 1998.

Eythórsson, Einar and Stein R. Mathisen: Ethnicity and Epistemology – Changing Understandings of Coastal Sami Local Knowledge. In: Jentoft, Svein (ed.): *Commons in a Cold Climate. Coastal Fisheries and Reindeer Pastoralism in North Norway: The Co-management Approach.* UNESCO / Parthenon Publishing Group. New York 1998.

Foucault, Michel: The Archeology of Knowledge and The Discourse on Language. Pantheon, New York 1972.

Goffman, Ervin: *The Presentation of Self in Everyday Life.* Norwegian edition 1974. Dreyers Forlag, Oslo 1959.

Goffman, Ervin: *Stigma.* Penguin; Harmondsworth 1963.

Høgmo, Asle: Det tredje alternativ. Barns læring av identitetsforvaltning i samisk-norske samfunn preget av identitetsskifte. *Tidskrift for samfunnsforskning,* 27, pp 395-416 1986.

Jentoft, Svein and and Kristoffersen, Trond: Fisheries co-management: The case of the Lofoten fishery. *Human Organisation,* 48(4) 355-65 1989.

Maurstad, Anita and Jan H. Sundet: The invisible cod – fishermen's and scientists' knowledge. In: Jentoft, Svein (ed.): *Commons in a Cold Climate. Coastal Fisheries and Reindeer Pastoralism in North Norway: The Co-management Approach.* UNESCO / Parthenon Publishing Group. New York 1998.

Mikalsen Knut and Svein Jentoft: From user-groups to stakeholders? The public interest in fisheries management. *Marine Policy* 25 (2001) 281-292 2001.

Mitchell, R. K., Agle, B. R., Wood, D. J.: Toward a Theory of Stakeholder Identification and Salience: Defining the Principle of Who and What Really Counts. *The Academy of Management Review* 1997;22(4):853-86 1997.

Nilsen, Ragnar: *Fjordfiskere og ressursbruk i nord.* AdNotam Gyldendal. Oslo 1998.

Paine, Robert: *Coast Lapp Society I. A Study of a Neighbourhood i Revsbotn Fjord.* Tromsø Museum, Tromsø 1957.

Sen, Sevaly and Jesper Raakjær Nielsen: Fisheries co-management – a comparative analysis. *Marine Policy* Vol 20 no 5 pp 405-418 1996.

Simons, Jon: *Foucault and the political.* Routledge, London and New York 1995.

Weber, Max: *Essays in Sociology,* edited by H. H. Gerth and C. Wright Mills. Routledge, London 1948 (1991).

CHAPTER 9

From Norwegianization to Coastal Sami Uprising

Ragnar Nilsen

Theme and Focus

The question raised here is, what has happened and what is happening with regard to the management of what might be called the most important nature resource for the Norwegian Sami, namely marine fish resources? The integration of the Norwegian national state has not only led to the assimilation of the Sami indigenous people in the northern part of Norway: it has also caused Sami nature resources to become subject to the Norwegian administration system. So the Sami control over these and other communal resources is to a large extent dependent on Norwegian legislation and the Norwegian institutions in this region. Consequently, it is possible to view today's coastal Sami[1] fishing as the result of a complex interplay between the state policies in the north, including fishing policies, technical and economical developments in the fishing industry, and the Sami fishermen's own procedures to safeguard themselves, and their income and means of livelihood (Eythórsson 1998, Nilsen 1998).

Political mobilization and international organization on the part of the Sami and other indigenous peoples over the past two decades has led to changes in assimilation policy in the Nordic countries. The Nordic Sami have been acknowledged as an indigenous people, and their own Sami parliaments have been established in the three countries. The critical question concerning the rights of indigenous people to their own nature resources has, meanwhile, still not been clarified. This applies even in Norway, where the Sami's right to land and water has been in the process of being evaluated for over twenty years.

Important areas of activity, such as the fishing industry, watercourses and the use of land will be discussed, together with a brief examination of the more general state policies concerning the Sami community. The main emphasis will

---

[1] "Coastal Sami" here denotes people of Sami origin who live on the coast of northern Norway. The Sami are an ethnic minority in Norway who are both Norwegian citizens and Sami. From Ofoten (in northern Norway) northwards, people of Sami, Norwegian and Finnish origin live together in coastal and fjord communities. They make use of the same resources and have more or less the same type of economic adaptation. The Sami who live in coastal communities are known as both coastal Sami and sea Sami.

be on the developments within the fishing industry. I shall look at the effects of the fishing policies after the Second World War, and how the coastal Sami local community handled the challenges posed by this policy and economic development. The central issue here will be how assimilation and central political regulations worked against the feasibility of the sea Sami safeguarding their livelihood, and of their continued settlement in the traditional Sami fjord areas in northern Norway. But I shall also highlight the Sami counter-strategies against norwegianization and central government, with the Alta affair and the coastal Sami uprising during the 1980s as two important events.

A Blessing and a Curse

The Sami comprise a large section of the northern Norwegian coastal settlement from the Ofoten district northwards. The coastal Sami have been in the process of disappearing as a group of people in their own right in the course of the past century (Eidheim 1971, Bjørklund 1985, Høgmo 1986). In the Scandinavian welfare states, there has been a clearly stated policy of assimilating minority groups, including the Sami minority indigenous people in Finland, Sweden and Norway. The coastal Sami population has been hit so hard by the Norwegian state policy of norwegianization because, firstly, they have based themselves on the same kind of use of resources and the same means of livelihood as other coastal Norwegians. And secondly, the sea Sami have become integrated into the Norwegian welfare community over the course of many decades, and have taken part in the generally developing prosperity in Norwegian society. An especially important part of the Norwegian policy of distribution for the coastal population was the adoption of a law concerning unprocessed fish in 1938 (the Raw Fish Act). Through this arrangement, fishermen in Norway are assured of a large part of the fisheries' income. So on the one hand, integration into Norwegian society has created a pressure as far as giving up one's own identity is concerned. On the other hand, integration has assured the Sami of a welfare development in line with other Norwegian citizens.

Farming, seasonal fishing and the use of wilderness resources have been the basis of existence for the Sami, Norwegians and Kven in the fjords and in outer coastal areas. The inland Sami in Nordkalotten[2] have been able to base themselves in their self-defined ethnic identity, which is associated with domestic reindeer herding.[3] So the Sami have typically – but mistakenly – been identified solely with reindeer herding.

---

[2] *Nordkalotten* is the widely-used Norwegian equivalent of the lesser-known geographical term in English, northern Fennoscandia, encompassing the northernmost regions of Norway (Nordland, Troms and Finnmark), Sweden (Norrbotten) and Finland (Lapland). [Translator's note.]

[3] In Norway and Sweden, the Sami have sole right to carry out domestic reindeer herding. In Finland, people of both Finnish and Sami origin may pursue this way of earning a living.

The sometimes rich resources of nature have been both a blessing and a curse for the Sami indigenous people in the North.

An abundant supply of fish from the sea, lakes and rivers, together with wild, extensive wilderness pastures and water power have been a blessing, because these resources have provided a basis for life and periodic abundance in an otherwise meagre and hard existence. They have been a foundation for self-sufficiency in the traditional combined adaptations in households and *siida*[4] arrangements that are so typical of Sami culture. They have also been the foundation for export/import, through the sale of furs and dried fish, and gradually through the sale of salted fish, reindeer meat, fish filleting and fish breeding. Finally, the water power brings extra income to the scarce community funds in the Sami communities that have housed large water developments.

They say that the Kven from Tornedalen and Finnish Lappland called the sea "the blue field" when they arrived as immigrants in northern Norway. These Finnish immigrants came, leaving behind failed crops, hungry, using their farming background to label these fertile ocean "meadows".

There is easy access to rich fishing resources right in along the coast, especially north of Vestfjorden. The big northern fish stocks periodically come in to the coast and the fjords in connection with spawning and food migration. The most important example is the fishing in Lofoten, where the grown skrei [the Norwegian name for mature cod] come from the Barents Sea and in towards the coast, down towards Vestfjorden, in the aftermath of winter, to spawn. Here the Sami, Norwegians and Kven have been able to make use of the coming of the fish with small boats and simple equipment for hundreds of years. Cod has always been a subsistence food, and it has been dried and been a central export article in this country since the Middle Ages. On the whole, cod also seems to have been the Norwegian Sami's single most important resource.[5] This applies to its importance as an export article and to the extent of the harvest, and thus the number of people of Sami origin who have been engaged in cod fishing. Cod has therefore been at least as important for the Sami as have reindeer.

The rich nature resources in the North have also been a curse, however, because they have been a source of attraction for outsiders. Traders and investors have come to make use of supplies of furs, fish, water power and minerals. Until the beginning of the twentieth century, this led to an exploitation of the

---

[4] A *siida* is a bilateral kin system, i.e. one in which the transmission of property rights or descent occurs equally through both the male and female lines. [Translator's note.]

[5] Non-nomadic Sami who have settled along the coasts and in the fjord areas have made up the greater part of the Sami population in Norway. For them, the marine resources, and especially the rich fish resources in coastal waters, have obviously been the most important. From Stuoranjarga in Ofoten, Henry Minde shows that fishing was as important for the Sami as for the Norwegian population in that part of Ofoten around the turn of the last century (Minde 2000, p.76). Ivar Bjørklund describes fish as the backbone of the Sami communities in the North Troms region during this period (Bjørklund 1985, p. 200)

local population, which was evident in the contrast between ostentatious wealth on the part of the merchants, on the one hand, and the fisher-farmer families' poverty on the other hand. Since the Second World War, expansive capitalistic fishing enterprise has led to the undermining of marine ecology, with its consequent effect on the fishing population. Both the local population and the natural ecology have been sacrificed to the heedlessness that often results when outside interests harvest local natural resources.

Generally, natural resources and their use appear to be critically important for the Sami population in the North. In this respect, the Sami's fate is shared with that of other indigenous peoples, and people who exist on the fringes of industrialized society all over the world. The rich natural resources in many districts in the region are important from both a material and a cultural point of view. Materially speaking, they continue to comprise a large part of the local population's livelihood and revenue. Because people of ethnic minority and inhabitants of other peripheral regions are influenced to only a limited extent by industrial and service development, there is a strong dependence upon primary goods and direct resource harvesting. Culturally speaking, the use of natural resources offers a sense of belonging and identity; reindeer herding by the inland Sami is a striking example of this. It appears that fjord fishing has a comparable symbolic effect for the coastal Sami during the 1980s and 1990s (Eythórsson 1999: 29).

Development, Identity and Power

A power perspective is relevant here. The local people's control over their own resources is important for their strategic position and influence, from both a national and a global point of view. This involves having the freedom to make use of fish stocks and reindeer pastures, which offer a material power basis. It also involves a process of categorization: in people's minds, resources, land and ownership are combined in a way that emphasizes their own identity and distinctiveness. Again, Sami reindeer herding is the most eloquent example, the reindeer being the essential symbol of Sami-ness. This empowerment process partly explains why indigenous peoples' rights must concern themselves to such an extent with the management of natural resources and why, therefore, the claim that is expressed in the wishes of the Sami and other indigenous peoples is the desire for land and water rights in their traditional areas of residence.

In a development context, the dependence of indigenous peoples on natural resources has been portrayed as a problem. In industrialized societies, a dependency on natural resources and primary goods has been regarded as an expression of backwardness and peripheral status. For a long time, industrialization was defined as a necessary development in the prevailing (that is to say, Western) global development paradigm. And the description of backwardness has been perceived as an additional burden for indigenous peoples, who have adhered to the use of natural resources. Within the prevailing Western development perspective, the coastal Sami's characteristically small-scale means of enterprise are something that must of necessity disappear as a result of these technical and economical developments.

The control of indigenous people and others over natural resources is also concerned with regulations and administrative rules, and therefore with public policy. In the Scandinavian welfare states, at any rate, the use of natural resources has been underpinned by regulation, by means of legislation and state or state-allied organizations. The background to this is that natural resources, such as fish, water power, woods and minerals, have been seen as communal resources, i.e. goods that should be managed in the community's best interests. An awareness of profit, an awareness of the importance of natural resources for national development and – gradually – an awareness of the need to protect the environment have all been behind the state's involvement in the management of natural resources in the Nordic countries (Nilsen 2002).

Even today, in Norway, Sweden, Finland and Russia, the harvesting and simple processing of rich natural resources make up a large part of the economic activity and export income in the northern regions. Thus, the rich natural resources in these lands are often to be found in the traditional Sami regions, i.e. in northern Norway, in Norrland, in Lapland and on the Kola peninsula.

Consequently, there is every reason to regard means of income and activities based on natural resources as potentially important elements in modern and post-modern economies and societies. And it is important to discuss development in the Sami regions in this development perspective as well, with regard to how the nature resources should be managed, to ensure that objectives are equal, the profit is fair, and a sense of identity and ownership are developed in these areas.

Social and Political Marginalizing

The marginalization of the coastal Sami population in northern Norway continued after the Second World War. Expressions of Sami identity through the use of language or by other means became stigmatized in Norwegian or norwegianized parts of northern Norway (Eidheim 1971). This active stigmatizing or denigration of the Sami created a day-to-day racism, particularly in the centres of population that flourished in northern Norway after the war. The state policy was characterized by the objectives of assimilation. The ambition was that the Sami should become so-called fully-fledged Norwegian citizens. This was perceived as necessary, so that the Sami could take part in the economic and social development that characterized the creation of the Norwegian welfare state. Teaching in schools using the Sami language was not permitted until well into the 1960s (Gaski 1994). The existence of Sami culture and a Sami civil society were perceived either as a problem or as non-existent, in terms of the self-conscious national strategies of the ruling *Arbeiderpartiets* [Labour Party] élite administration (Minde 1980). Much of the background to this was clearly that Sami culture and Sami means of enterprise were seen as backward and outside the prevailing trains of thought that were being developed in central areas of power.

The fact of being Sami was not reckoned to be a legitimate basis for interaction, in political and organizational terms. Norwegian citizens of Sami origin were not able to put forward demands and wishes as Sami people. The message was that working within and with the Norwegian community should be undertaken using the Norwegian language, and within the boundaries of Norwegian cultural standards.

Einar Eythórsson and Svanhild Andersen show how fishing within the Sami environment over several decades led to claims for the stronger regulation of the fjord and spawning areas, to prevent over-fishing (Eythórsson 1993, Andersen 1999). Like other coast fishermen, the Sami approached the authorities with repeated requests that the use of active equipment, such as trawl nets, purse seines and shrimp nets, should be prohibited in fjords, as well as in areas inhabited by young fish, and in spawning areas. The Sami and Norwegian coastal fishermen achieved only limited success in these claims. The most striking aspect of Eythórsson's findings, meanwhile, is that these claims were not formulated with reference to the fishermen's Sami background. Nor was this the case with regard to the claims that emanated from the most characteristically Sami coastal and fjord areas. He finds only one example where reference is made to the Sami in all the claims he has examined, and even this was made in an indirect fashion. Coastal Sami fishermen did not submit claims *qua* Sami until the early 1980s. A coastal Sami uprising, which started in 1983, led to the Sami people in the fjord areas and along the coast emerging in public as a group in their own right.

The areas where the Sami lived on the coast have traditionally been most strongly congregated around the fjord areas. In Tysfjord and Skånland, and in the fjords of North Troms and Finnmark, the Sami residential areas have made up the majority of the population in many rural and fjord communities. People of Sami origin also make up a significant population element in many of the outer coastal settlements and, gradually, in the growing population centres in that part of the country. On the coast, on the other hand, the Sami have constituted a minority, and a more open discrimination existed here during the first decades after the war than was the case in the fjord areas (Eidheim, ibid.).

This is why the fjord areas in the North stand out as the most important area of permanent settlement for the hard-pressed coastal Sami population during the period after the Second World War.

In the fjord areas, it seems that local co-existence has been based on a reciprocal understanding that many people are of Sami origin. Here a kind of implicit or unspoken agreement clearly held sway, that the question of Sami origin should not predominate, at least not openly, during the hardest period of assimilation after the war.

Socially, and from the point of view of their identity, the coastal Sami were weakened as a group by the norwegianization policy and social discrimination during the first decades after the war. They continued to live in the fjord areas, where they often comprised the majority of the local population, but without the means to put forward their interests as an ethnic group, i.e. as Sami or coastal Sami. An important part of their background was seen as irrelevant, or as a weakness that should not be stressed, and was therefore glossed over in their daily life.

In addition, the coastal Sami became marginalized as far as the rich local resources in the sea were concerned. Being of Sami or indigenous origin did not result in any special privileges concerning access to resources in the region of Norway inhabited by the ethnic group. Local or ethnic origin has been irrelevant in the matter of access on the basis of resources. Access regulations and other matters remain independent of ethnic and geographically-based ownership. In fishing, there has been a universal system of rights. All Norwegian citizens have the same access to the rich fishing resources along the coasts, regardless of which part of the country they live in, and regardless of their ethnic background. Admittedly, right of access has been variable, according to other criteria, such as boat size and type of equipment. But even these differentiations, which do determine the right of access, have been based on universal national criteria. Fishermen from southern Norway, using hand lines, have the same right of access as the local population in Porsanger in Finnmark to fish for cod in the Porsanger fjord. And trawlers and purse seine boats from different regions harvest the abundantly rich fishing resources beyond the coastal waters in the north.

Here we can see the contrast with other national fishing régimes. In Canada and the USA, it is evident that local ownership often generates fishing systems in the region, which in practice offer prior claim on the resources for local people (Berkes 1987, Acheson 1988). In Canada, indigenous people claim their right to fishing resources from pre-existing agreements (Davies and Jentoft 2001). A high court decision from 1999 grants the Mi'kmaq people in eastern Canada a right of access that is based on this kind of ethnic and treaty-based agreement. In New Zealand (Hersoug 2002), and in Greenland, we can see how the Maori and Inuit have gained control over extensive fishing resources as a result of their indigenous status. So, in these instances, residential and ethnic considerations determine special access to communal natural resources, and local and regional management systems are sometimes developed on a lower geographical level, to ensure that responsibility and influence are shared between the fishermen and fishing companies, where resource harvesting is concerned. As a result, we can clearly see a greater awareness concerning the special situation of the indigenous peoples than is the case in the Norwegian state political system.

In Norway, the system has been almost the opposite of this. It has not been legitimate to claim resource access on the basis of ethnic status or geographical ownership. So proximity does not secure rights in the Norwegian fishing system. And the system is centralized. National political and bureaucratic bodies make the decisions and implement the policies, in collaboration with the leaders of strong national interest organizations, such as *Norges Fiskarlag* [Norway's Fishermen's Union] and *Landsorganisasjonen* [the Labour Union], which organize the people on the larger sea fishing boats and workers in the fishing industries (Nilsen 2002). If coastal Sami and other coastal fishermen want to be assured of preferred claims to nearby fishing resources or local participation in administration, then they have to press their case through the "iron triangle" of politicians, bureaucrats and interest organizations in the Norwegian fishing sector. In addition, coastal fishermen and Sami fishermen have yet to achieve a breakthrough for a claim concerning the strengthening of small-scale and seasonal fishing catches. This would represent a break with the prevailing interpretations of the power élite in the Norwegian fishing sector, where seasonal catches and fish caught near the coast in smaller boats are defined as old-fashioned and barely sustainable.

The Undermining of Sami Fishing

Till about 1960, the sea Sami, like their Norwegian neighbours, were in the completely predominating category of fishermen-farmers, i.e. they operated as "peasant households", as categorized by Eric Wolf (Wolf 1966). The husband fished locally and seasonally, and was away for large parts of the year, while the wife was occupied with farming on a modest scale, i.e. a small-holding with one or two cows and some sheep, and looked after the young and the old. The man might also be a road worker in the summer, and the woman might work in the fishing industry during the seasons. So this was a many-sided, low-capital occupational combination, characterized by the requirements of the season in different areas of activity, and based on a blend of cash revenue and self-sufficiency, specifically as described by Ottar Brox (Brox 1966). Small-holdings of this kind aimed to achieve a reasonable income and security, rather than a single-minded maximization of profit, or ambition to expand.

In spite of low cash revenues and small investments, this means of livelihood provided an acceptable standard of living for established families, compared with the alternatives during this period: local paid work, long-distance commuting, or moving to the town. The background to the surplus and viability attached to a fishing and farming occupation lay in the combination of access to rich resources in the sea, good conditions for self-sufficiency, and in the institutional terms and conditions, among them the Raw Fish Act. And the background for the viability lay in the flexibility, in the ability to "turn themselves around", and in making use of the possibilities that were to hand at any given moment when it was a question of assuring income and an increase in subsistence.

The fisheries policy has had an ambiguous effect on Sami interests in coastal fishing. On the one hand, there are rules securing fish incomes, and regulations about the partitioning of the sea. These assure the fishermen of a considerable share in fishing profits and they partly ensure conservation in fjords and areas in proximity to the coast against the use of the active and non-selective gear that are used by the larger boats. Besides this, there was free fishing, until 1990, for the coastal fleet, who used selective equipment, in other words the smaller and medium-sized boats that fish with hooking gear and seine nets. On the other hand, there have been openings for trawling operations, as a result of the controversial changes to the laws concerning trawling in 1951. And the foreign trawlers continued their unregulated fishing outside the four-mile limit right up until the introduction of the two hundred-mile economic zone in 1977. In addition, the public authorities prioritized the larger trawlers and fish-processing factories in the allocation of state support to the fishing industries.

In agriculture, the state land use management encouraged single purpose use, by means of investment support and production support offered to individuals or families who concentrated on specialized farming management. But here, again, the specialization investments from the authorities in this sector did not produce the desired results. Studies of fjord settlements in the Troms and Finnmark regions in the fifties and sixties (Lillevoll 1982, Bjørklund 1985, Nilsen 1997) show why this is so. Fjord farms in the Sami areas responded to the state sector's initiatives by going over to new forms of occupational combinations. The authorities' support of the development of farm management stimulated an expansion of livestock, so that small-holding families went from having, for example, two cows to five, and began to send milk to the dairy. Accordingly, there was a change from farming on a self-sufficiency basis to small-scale commercial farming during this period. It was still the women who retained the responsibility for farm management. The problem was that it became much too difficult for the women to cope with commercial farm management on their own for most of the year, while their husbands were away during the seasonal fishing as crew members on the local fishing smacks. In addition, the long-distance fishing system was modified during this period, specifically because of the trawlers' hunting of young fish out at sea.

In this situation, the men changed over from fishing to building and construction work, with periodic long-distance commuting. This meant that they could be at home to help the women with the farming management more easily than if they had continued with fishing further afield. And so we can see a changeover to new types of occupational combinations, because of the new conditions in agriculture, reduced fishing access, and consequent alterations in small-scale farming.The traditional long-distance fishing, based on medium-sized coastal fishing boats from the fjord settlements, was pretty well liquidated during this period, because of the farms' total adaptation to the new, external conditions. Even though some of the men continued to fish using their own small boats, or were taken on as crew members on bigger boats from elsewhere, the reorganizations meant that the number of fishermen in the northern fjord settlements was greatly reduced during this period. Previously, practically all the men worked as fishermen for the greater part of their lives. After the reorganization, fishing had been reduced to one means of livelihood among many for men in the fjord settlements, which had a traditionally strong Sami population, in the Troms and Finnmark regions. Sami fishing communities have been maintained to this day in some settlements in these fjord areas. And the Sami language is still used in a few such places. But they are few in number and consist of fishermen with smaller-sized boats that harvest the local resources, and where individuals go out on shorter seasonal fishing trips beyond the fjord. In this way, Sami fishing has been marginalized, and revenue aside from fishing is still clearly a necessary provision to sustain the income and standard of living for fishing families in the fjord area.

The combination of many factors, at a local level and more generally, has therefore led to a greatly reduced participation in fishing in the coastal Sami areas. Firstly, we can see that over-fishing out at sea, and the use of active types of equipment in the fjords led to a reduction in the tonnage of fish near the coast and in the fjords. Secondly, an ongoing assimilation of and discrimination against the Sami, right up until around 1980, led to a weakened possibility of the Sami putting their own fishing interests forward. Thirdly, the authorities' support for specialized production investment appeared negative. Amongst other things, the single purpose investment, together with the weakened resource foundation, led to sea Sami farms taking on new occupational combinations that caused the liquidation of what had previously been the most important means of income for these farms, namely the fish in the sea. Finally, there is the matter of the general rationalization of fishing, which also concerns the coastal fleet. Taking everything into account, these factors and the relationship between them led to the number of fishermen in the coastal Sami areas being reduced, by the beginning of the 1980s, to a fraction of what it had been in the 1950s.

The interplay between the centralized state policy, the high-speed technical changes and the capitalizing of fishing has, however, contributed to putting the universal and top-down Norwegian systems under pressure. Within these national systems, some have come off better than others. As has been shown, the state-stimulated, capital-intensive mobile fishing with effective equipment undermined the resource foundation and basis of rights for many local fishing communities. On a national scale, there are certain kinds of fishing business clusters that are growing strong, by means of capitalist expansion and political strength. These units are in the process of taking over an increasing part of the national fishing resources. As a result, the basis for sea fishing is being undermined for fishermen and local communities, who are not characterized by the same capacity for expansion, and who cannot mobilize comparable strength to act on developments of the state fishing policy. This hits the northern Norwegian and sea Sami coastal fishermen particularly hard, since their work is based on the use of small boats, fishing locally and in proximity to the coast.

At the same time, the capital-influenced expansion and the displacement of the Sami fjord fishermen has laid the foundations for opposition to the centralized and universal development regulations. As we shall see, the marginalization of the population in the Sami fjord settlements has contributed to a general clash between the Sami minority population and the Norwegian national state.

Coastal Sami Uprising

The Sami are not giving up the harvesting of their most important natural resource without a fight. The emphasis on the Sami identity in the coastal districts, in the wake of the Alta conflict, will be shown to have found its way into the fishing political environment. The fishing industry issue became, in fact, a channel for what could be called a coastal Sami uprising in its own right, during the 1980s (Nilsen 1997).

The uprising started in certain coastal Sami settlements in the Porsangerfjord in Finnmark. Here there was still a functioning fishing environment of a Sami nature at the beginning of the 1980s, when the fishermen based themselves for the most part in local fjord fishing. The increasing Sami self-awareness and the emphasis on the Sami identity in everyday life and politics, during and after the Alta conflict in 1981, was an inspiration for two local leaders of the fishermen's union in the fjord area. They both spoke Sami, and one of them had experience from his work for a Sami organization. There were two Sami organizations in Porsangerfjord: a local branch of the established *Norske Samers Riksforbund* (NSR) [Norwegian Sami National Alliance], and a local branch of the newly-established *Samenes Landsforbund* (SLF) [Sami Country Alliance]. SLF was a moderate organization and had acquired a certain following, especially in the fjord districts.[6] The newspaper *Ságat* was a mouthpiece for this organization, and this was published in Porsanger.

---

[6] Terje Brantenberg has shown how the SLF has built itself up to a great extent by means of opposing the reindeer herding Sami (Brantenberg 1985). The organization has, on a general basis, gone against the idea that the Sami are an indigenous people who have special rights to natural resources and areas of land. In this respect, they disagree strongly with the other, larger Sami political organization in the 1980s and 1990s, *Norske Samer Riksforbund*. It is clear that this has weakened the Sami mobilization to ensure a basis of natural resources in their own areas.

The sea Sami in Porsanger and other places in northern Norway saw themselves as being pressurized from several quarters.[7] They were sceptical of Norwegian society as a whole, because of the heavy-handed assimilation policy.
But they were also sceptical of the inland Sami (or "super Sami", as they were
called locally), whom they associated with reindeer herding. They thought that
the reason why no proper quay or landing stage had been built for fishermen
in the extensive Porsangerfjord was because of a lack of public funding and
because of the claims from those concerned with reindeer management. They
thought that the reindeer herding Sami had received too many privileges and
too much power from the Norwegian authorities. Here, they were particularly
concerned that the reindeer herding Sami might hold back developments in the
fjord districts, on the grounds that local development projects encroached on
grazing lands for the reindeer. The coastal Sami, and the Kven and Norwegian
local populations in Porsanger, perceived claims relating to Sami land and water rights as claims from inland Sami, reindeer herding Sami and academics.
And they perceived these claims to be formulated in such a way that they were
also aimed against the sea Sami population. It is clear that the interpretation of
Sami rights claims by these coastal Sami has contributed to the coastal Sami being so hesitant about claiming rights as Sami people. They have claimed rights
as fjord residents who have wanted a stronger regulation of fishing in the fjord,
which they thought would be to the benefit of all those living in fjord areas,
regardless of their ethnic origin.

The people in Porsanger were most concerned about fishing in the fjord.
Like other fjord and coastal residents, they had been able to see for years how
the naturally rich fishing resources in the locality of their own fjord had been
reduced. There was an apprehension on the part of everyone in the fjord that
the reason for this was overfishing with active gear, especially the use of purse
seines and Danish seine nets. This type of fishing was carried out on boats from
outside the locality. So the frontlines here were clear and simple: the fjord population, of Sami origin, who were involved with small-scale fishing, with passive
and benign equipment, were ranked against those who were defined as being
involved in capital-based Norwegian fishing, from other areas, with equipment
that destroyed the small fry and "looted the fjord", as it was described locally.

The local fishermen in Porsanger had claimed extended conservation of the
fjord, to limit the damaging effects of the active equipment, for several decades.
And they had in fact managed to get the regulations changed to some extent,
for example the banning of active equipment from two of the side fjords in
Porsanger that were spawning fjords for the cod. But the continuing decline of

---

[7]   The local coastal Sami's attitudes and politics were expressed very well in the document
"Non-nomadic residents' rights in Sami coastal and fjord districts", which was published by
the Porsanger branch of the SLF in 1985.

the fishing stock showed that this was inadequate, according to the Fishermen's Union and the local population. Most of the claims for stronger fjord regulation had ended up in waste paper bins in Honningsvåg, as the local leaders of the fishermen's union put it. In other words, the claims were turned down by the leadership of the Finnmark branch of the Fishermen's Union and the Director of Fishing Industries in Finnmark.

In a situation such as this, the intense conflict over the development of the Alta-Kautokeino watercourse offered a timely possibility to the fjord population in Porsanger. The use of Sami identity by Alta activists in their mobilization, and the claim for stronger control over the management of natural resources for the indigenous people, were both important here. The Alta affair showed that it was legitimate to make use of both of them in the new political situation, and it demonstrated that ethnic identity could be a powerful piece of political equipment. The two Fishermen's Union officials made use of their Sami background or identity as a factor in the process of submitting their claim. And the claim submission had a Sami relevance, because it had been put forward by Sami organizations and Sami media. This was the beginning of a new era: now the Sami identity was being activated as part of a political mobilization in the public domain, by people who defined themselves as coastal Sami, and they were putting forward an important and controversial matter through Sami channels.

The novelty, therefore, was not in the content of the claims. These were concerned with regulation claims for fishing in the fjord that had been submitted innumerable times before. Nor were the claims especially radical, fundamentally. No claims were being made for exclusive local management rights for natural resources. No claims were being made with reference to the fact that the Sami should have the status of indigenous people. Finally, the claims were being put forward via a moderate Sami political organization, namely the SLF. What marked the beginning of a new era was that the coastal Sami had made political demands, after many decades of silence. Now, for the first time, this oppressed group was claiming rights on the basis of their own ethnic background. The coastal Sami had finally been set free in a political and organizational context.

Given this background, it is not surprising that the conflict became sizeable and very dramatic. The SLF and the newspaper *Ságat* used the regulated fjord fishing affair for all it was worth, with large print runs and harsh words from the leaders in the organization against the Norwegian fishing authorities and the Finnmark branch of the Fishermen's Union. And this caught on with the coastal Sami. The SLF increased its membership in the fjord by over two hundred in a short space of time. The two foremen of the Fishermen's Union were excluded from the Finnmark branch, on the flimsy pretext that they had both put forward a political claim relating to the fishing industry via an organization other than the Fishermen's Union. So the treatment of the two Fishermen's Union foremen must be seen as an illustration of how strongly the norwegianization line was still maintained in an organization of such importance as the Finnmark branch of the Fishermen's Union. The foremen took the Fishermen's Union to court to have their exclusion rescinded. Not surprisingly, the Fishermen's Union lost their case.

The scale and heatedness of this affair may best be understood as a result of giving an outlet to the cumulative discontent and feelings of injustice that the coastal Sami had experienced for a long time. This particular affair finally gave the Sami group the chance to step forward in the context of their ethnic background. The process of protest in Porsanger might be called an uprising and a liberation, in that it was at this point that the coastal Sami found their freedom in a political context. It was triggered by the fishing regulation claims in Porsanger, and made it possible to break through the barriers that had been an obstacle to any expression of the coastal Sami identity. The silence and suppression were finally broken. For the first time since the war, the coastal Sami had a voice of their own.

In a local perspective we can see that a Sami fishing settlement that had been marginalized, but which had nevertheless survived, became a basis, through the presentation of claims and through conflict, for rebellion against the state policy. One question then was how this would affect the central policy and fishing industry policy in the Norwegian society as a whole.

State Exclusion of Sami Fishermen

The coastal Sami rebellion based in Porsanger was stimulated by the political process that had got under way as a result of the conflict concerning the regulation of the Alta/Kautokeino watercourse. This in turn generated an innovatory expression of the sea Sami identity, with claims for better fishing industry regulation and greater local influence over such regulations. Today, we can see that the Alta affair and the associated actions led to a change of administration in the central Norwegian policy concerning Sami matters (Minde 2003), where the policy of assimilation was ended. But we can also see that the concrete changes that came out of this action, with respect to the central question of land and water rights, have amounted to very little. Changes in the content of assimilation policy relating to the Sami at the highest Norwegian level, and the establishment of a Sami Parliament, are the results over a period of two decades after the Sami rebellion. The question of rights has never been clarified, and the policy concerning important issues relating to the Sami society continues as before.

It seems that there are two reasons for the limited effect of the Alta/Kautokeino conflict and the coastal Sami protests, as far as the question of land and sea rights is concerned. After these conflicts in the early 1980s, no concrete changes in policy were formulated, but instead a long-drawn-out report process, which has still not been completed. One specific part of the report process was carried out by means of a departmental committee, which was supposed to assess the fishing policy relating to the Sami.[8] It seems as though an agreement was established between the Sami community and the Norwegian community, that changes in policy, which would affect the Sami community, should come about after the completion of the report process.

The developments within the fishing industries are clearly a good illustration here. Indeed, it might be maintained that the Norwegian fishing industry policy relating to the Sami has been developed in such a way that it has had even more harmful effects upon the Sami community since the Sami mobilization than was the case before.

Catching capacities in Norwegian fishing increased throughout the 1970s and 1980s. The public *Fiskarbanken* [Fishing Bank] and private banks invested in the sea fishing fleet, and Sami and Norwegian coastal fishermen "responded" by making their smaller and larger coastal fishing boats more efficient. The consequence was that the depletion of fishing stocks continued, and this led to a state settlement that formally excluded the majority of the coastal Sami fishermen from the resources that had clearly been of the greatest importance for the coastal Sami and their ancestors for hundreds of years.

In 1989, the Fisheries executive directorate took the drastic step of stopping cod fishing on 19 April with immediate effect in the middle of the most important season for cod fishing. When fishing was resumed again, special criteria concerning access to cod fishing were introduced. Until 1990, there had been free fishing with hook, net and line equipment for the coastal fleet. From 1990 onwards, only those who had caught a specific quantity of cod in one of the previous three years were given a guaranteed cod fishing quota. The fishermen who did not manage to satisfy this requirement came under the so-called competitive quota. Here, you could only fish as long as the total quotas for this group were not taken up, and in this way you risked being left with little or no income from cod fishing.

The way the criteria were set up had serious consequences. Firstly, exclusion from a fixed quota for those who had not been sufficiently active in the field to attain the fixed quota amount. Secondly, those who were to continue fishing by means of the guaranteed quota had to catch a stipulated tonnage of fish, which could not be achieved by means of local fjord fishing. In both instances, you ended up with the uncertainty of the competitive quota. Finally, there was a block on occupational combination. Those who earned too much in other occupations ceased to be eligible for the guaranteed quota.

The system was set up in such a way that the sea Sami were hit especially hard. Because of the reduction in basic resources, and the changes in fjord

---

[8]   *Det Samiske fiskeriutvalget* [The Sami Fisheries Committee] was set up by the Fisheries Department in 1993, at the request of the Sami Parliament. The proposals were submitted in 1997.

adaptations, many of them, as we have seen, had a considerably reduced stake in fishing. As a result of this process, they did not get a guaranteed quota. The livelihood of many of those who were still fishermen was based on local fishing, which was particularly susceptible to detrimental effect, because of ecological fluctuations, and had often been carried on in tandem with other means of livelihood.

Even the restricted fishing in the home fjords had to be abandoned by many of the Sami fishermen after 1990.

Paradoxically enough, it was the fact that they carried out such restricted fishing under the open-access fishing régime before 1990 that caused these fishermen to be excluded from getting a fixed quota under the new system. They were punished for having fished too little of a communal resource that was threatened with extinction. This shows the lack of logic within the system.[9]

Because of the uncertainty over the number of inhabitants with Sami background in the fjord areas and elsewhere, and because of inadequate fishing industry statistics, it is difficult to estimate how many fishermen have been excluded as a result of the new system. It seems, however, that the number of registered fishermen in the fjords has more than halved since 1990.[10] This clear reduction in the number of fishermen living in the traditional Sami fjord comes at a time of growth in fishing resources.

Reports Instead of Policies

In the 1990s, a new political situation had been established for the Sami in Norway. It was not possible to go back to the times before the protests in Alta and Porsanger, when the Sami had not been political activists on the basis of ethnic identity.

But the Norwegian national fishing industry was characterized by the same power structure as before. State fishing industry policy still took very little account of the fact that fishing was also an important means of livelihood for the Sami population along the coast.

In the first place, the basic resources became weaker again towards the end of the 1990s. The stakes concerning the catch, and especially catches of small-scale fish, in Russian and Norwegian fishing in the north, are excessive. As a

---

[9]   A consequence of the system was also that many small-boat fishermen fished more after the alterations than before, as Anita Maurstad shows in a study of fishermen of this kind in the Troms and Finnmark regions. Many small-boat fishermen obviously do not gamble on getting the greatest possible number of fish out of the sea as long as they fish freely, as the theory of the 'tragedy of commons' and the fishing bureaucracy expected they would. They fish as much as they think they need to, in order to achieve an acceptable income and have a good life. With these aims in mind it is, naturally enough, not in their interest to sit out at sea all year round, in order to earn the greatest possible income from fishing (Maurstad 2000)

[10]   Lillevoll, 1997, fig. 8.3.

result, there is not as great an overall profit from the fish as would have been achieved by means of more balanced and long-term sustainable fishing. Both the trawlers and the larger coastal fishing boats fish the cod, and other kinds of white fish, so hard that the total amount caught goes down and the coming of the fish along the coast and in the fjords is reduced. In addition, many local cod fishing stocks in the fjords have been depleted (Maurstad/Sundet 1998). It looks as though the depletion of local stocks may be blamed both on excessive local fishing and on the use of different kinds of nets. As far as these latter types of fishing tackle are concerned, it is first and foremost fishermen from elsewhere who have made use of them. At any rate, the depletion of local fishing stocks shows that the conservation measures that have been applied to the fjord areas, in order to ensure that fishing resources are sustained, are not working well enough. And this demonstrates the justification of the claims that lay behind the coastal Sami uprising.

Secondly, a centralizing of fishing rights into the hands of steadily fewer people is taking place in Norwegian fishing, and therefore also in Sami fishing. Although transferable quotas have not been formally introduced for the coastal fleet, an extensive trade in quota rights is nevertheless taking place, among the small-boat fishermen as well. This 'hidden' sale of fishing rights is a natural consequence of the vessel quota system. This has turned fishing rights into a unit of capital, since the right to fish is now divided up and has been allocated to each boat. When the boat is sold, the quota follows suit. So it is logical that the person who has been allocated this right sells it when the vessel is sold, even though this is not allowed. Through the sale of fishing rights, the capitalization of fishing takes place. The rights exchange hands for large sums of money on the market. And the logical consequence of that is that the fishing rights find their way into the hands of those who have the most capital, and by this means are shared between fewer people. The sale of quotas is becoming an especially big problem in fjord fishing, because this has been based on such a low capital input, and on such an uncertain type of fishing. As a result, it has become more difficult to carry on a type of fishing that will also cover the quota payments in Sami fishing and fjord fishing generally. Finally, it is becoming harder and harder to get into fishing, something which particularly affects young people in the Sami areas who want to fish using their own boat.

Thirdly, an even more extreme change in the direction of large-scale operations in Norwegian fishing industry policy took place during the 1990s. The newly-established *Statens nærings- og distriktsutviklingsfond* (SND) [state business and district development fund] has invested systematically in building up larger fishing concerns that would own many trawlers. Support was given to larger filleting plants, such as Røkkes Norwegian Seafood and West Fish, which are major fishing enterprises located in cities in southern Norway. The result of this is that an increasing proportion of what were previously communal resources in the north are now controlled by these southern Norwegian concerns. The industry is chained to an unfortunate method of fishing, where small-scale fish are caught in the trawl-fishing. Such fish could instead have been allowed to grow and spawn, thus finding their way to coastal waters as full-sized and sexually mature fish. Here, they could have been caught with the selective fishing gear used by the Sami and Norwegian coastal fishermen in fjords and fishing stations, i.e. hooking equipment and seine nets.

After the reorganization of Sami policy, this kind of issue in fishing industry policy does not pass unnoticed in Sami quarters. In contrast to earlier occasions, the Sami general public at the beginning of the 1990s was aware of the situation, became activated, and was able to protest against initiatives in Norwegian society which they perceived as encroachments of their rights. After protests on the Sami side against the vessel quota system in 1990, the Fisheries Department issued its own report about Sami fishing. Carsten Smith, who at that time was the leader of the Sami rights report, was in charge of the report. He concluded that the Norwegian state was obliged, both by the Norwegian constitution and by indigenous people's rights, to guarantee the material basis of the coastal Sami culture. According to Smith, this meant that the Norwegian State could not introduce changes to the regulations that weakened these material interests. He observed that this possibly might also mean that the State should set up initiatives that discriminated positively in the Sami's favour. In other words, initiatives that would compensate for the negative effects of the vessel quota system in the Sami areas (Smith 1990).

After the Smith report, a Sami fisheries commission was established by the Fisheries Department, at the request of the Sami Parliament. This commission was to come up with concrete recommendations that would amend the negative effects which the vessel quota system had had for the Sami fishermen. It is reasonable to see this work of reporting on the Sami position within the fishing industry as a result of the Sami uprising, and the need for consideration on the part of the authorities after the redefining of central Sami policy. But little of tangible worth has emerged from the reporting process.

The most tangible thing to come out of the Smith proposals and the work of the Sami fisheries commission was that small-boat fishing in the North-Troms and Finnmark regions became somewhat more free than in the rest of the country, and it has been a bit easier to pursue a combination of activities in this area. Both requests for free fishing for smaller boats and the proposal of an individual fishing zone for the Sami area were turned down by the Fisheries Department. Not even a trial project for a Sami fishing zone in the Lyngen fjord has seen the light of day (Holm et al 1997, Jentoft 1998 109-112).

Thus, as a result, the Norwegian fishing policy proceeds, broadly speaking, much as before, even in the Sami fjord areas. And thus it is clearly demonstrated that the coastal Sami mobilization of claims for local fishing regulations in the northern fjord areas have not reached fruition at the start of the twenty-first century. The coastal Samis have not managed to push through their claims to the centralized Norwegian power structure in the fishing business.

Both the Alta affair and the sea Sami uprising initiated in Porsanger have led to an increasing Sami consciousness that the Sami, as a people, have become activated politically in a way that is quite different from before. And they have contributed to the fact that the central Norwegian policy concerning the Sami has progressed from assimilation to formal acknowledgement, partly because the Sami have activated the international legal system with regard to indigenous peoples' rights. But the two mobilizations did not lead to an acknowledgement of the tangible claims that lay behind the Alta affair and the sea Sami uprising based in Porsanger.

Sami Fishing Policies

The power élite in the Norwegian fisheries domain has perpetuated a fishing policy that has obvious negative effects for the coastal Sami, in spite of the Alta affair and the sea Sami uprising, and in spite of the special reporting process. At the same time, it appears that the Sami society during the 1980s and 1990s managed, meanwhile, to build up measures that aimed to strengthen the situation of the small-scale fishermen in the fjords of northern Norway. This process is the result of the Sami society obtaining greater influence over parts of the public policy relating to *Sápmi*.[11] In 1982 a Sami development fund was established in the Communal and Works Department of that time, at the initiative of the *Norsk Sameråd* [Norwegian Sami Council]. This arrangement was placed under the authority of the newly-established Sami Parliament in 1959, and was significantly enlarged. Thus, a support system has been established that has helped fishermen in the Sami areas with subsidies for the purchase of boats and the development of landing stages and minor quays.

There is a connection between the maintenance of fishing environment and the systems set in place by the Sami development fund. Where the fund has invested in building up the infrastructure, and has supported the fishermen economically, and has done so since the 1980s, it appears that the fishing settlements have been able to be maintained to date, and some of them have even grown. This may be seen most clearly in some of the smaller coastal Sami fishing stations or fishing villages in some fjords in Finnmark. Here, the Sami development fund, partly also with contributions from the municipalities themselves, have initiated the subsidized purchase of boats and fishing equipment, as well as the means to build up landing stages and smaller quays, so that the fjord fishermen can deliver their catch locally.

---

[11] *Sápmi* is the Sami word for the area of northern Scandinavia where the majority of the Sami population is based. [Translator's note.]

These examples show that there are grounds for a continuation of small-scale fishing based in the fjord areas of northern Norway; areas that have stood out as important anchoring settlements for the coastal Sami population. The contention of those in power in the fishing industries – *Norges Fiskarlag* [Norway's Fishing Union], the fisheries politicians and the Fisheries Department – that only the year-round fishing carried out in the larger boats can survive and ensure recruitment into the modern fishing industry, seems to have been invalidated by fishing activities in Finnmark fjords.

Thus, there are grounds for a provisional claim that, from the Sami point of view, it has in fact been possible to ensure the protection of certain fjord areas from unfortunate effects of the Norwegian fishing policy. Sami politicians and administrators seem to have managed the difficult job of formulating elements of an independent fishing policy for the Sami region, and they have managed to ensure that the content of this policy has contributed to maintaining or shaping fishing activity and the fishing settlements in some parts of the Sami-dominated fjords in Finnmark and Nord-Troms.

The subsidy of boat purchase is obviously necessary, because the vessel quota system in the Norwegian fishing policy means that boat purchase, even in coastal fishing, requires an individual to pay for quota rights. And this becomes extremely difficult to achieve, given the low financial resources of fjord fishing. The subsidy of fishing infrastructure is necessary in the same way, because there may be too few fish in the fjords to justify building quaysides, breakwaters and landing stages. The background to this is that the Norwegian support system for the development of harbours and the fishing industry favours larger construction, or that the income from small-scale fishing in the fjords is too limited to pay off the interest on the necessary investments. So the discrimination or differentiation that have been the result of quota systems, and state support or bank support for larger fishing boats are also to be found in the support for harbour and landing stage development, which discriminates against small-scale economy. It is here that support from the Sami-controlled financial systems is necessary, to counteract the continuing state discrimination against Sami methods of working and local communities. And, as we have seen, it looks as though the Sami system actually functions in such a way as to combat the ongoing Norwegian discrimination against Sami methods of working, and small-scale methods of working, in the fjords and local communities where this system has taken effect.

So here there seem to be grounds to launch a preliminary optimistic conclusion. A policy exists, developed by the Sami themselves, within the fishing field of activity, that does not simply represent a break with the Norwegian policy. It also appears to succeed in sustaining an independence and a freedom from the ongoing oppression of Norwegian custom and practice, which affects important aspects of the Sami community. This discrimination may be seen as a continuation of the earlier policy of assimilation, albeit by other means than those that were in use until the late 1980s. But in spite of this, through autonomous coastal Sami administrative measures, the Porsanger fishermen and the coastal Sami uprising have achieved a step in the right direction.

Acknowledgements

Thanks are due to Terje Brantenberg for his thorough commentary of provisional drafts of this article.

References

Acheson, James: *The Lobster Gangs of Maine*. University Press of New England, Hanover 1988.

Andersen, Svanhild: Samiske fjordfiskere og offentlige myndigheter – et eksempel fra Vest-Finnmark. In: Bjørklund, Ivar (ed.): *Norsk ressursforvaltning og samiske rettighetsforhold. Om statlig styring, allmenningens tragedie og lokale sedvaner i Sápmi*. Ad Notam Gyldendal, Oslo 1999.

Berkes, Firket: Common-Property Resources and Cree Indian Fisheries in Subarctic Canada. In: MacCay, Bonny and Acheson, James (eds.): *The Question of the Commons. The Culture and Ecology of Communal Resources*. The University of Arizona Press, Tucson 1987.

Bjørklund, Ivar: *Fjordfolket i Kvenangen*. Universitetsforlaget. Oslo 1985.

Brantenberg, Odd Terje: The Alta –Kautokeino Conflict, Sami Reindeer Herding and Etnopolitics. In: Brøsted, Jens et al (eds.): *Native Power. The Quest for Autonomy and Nationhood of Indigenous Peoples*. Universitetsforlaget, Oslo 1985.

Brox, Ottar: Hva skjer i Nord-Norge? Pax forlag, Oslo 1966.

Davies, Antony and Jentoft, Svein: The Challenge and Promise of Indigenous Peoples Fishing Rights – from Dependency to Agency. *Marine Policy* 25, 223-237 2001.

Eidheim, Harald: When Etnic Identity is Social Stima. In: Eidheim, Harald (ed.): *Aspects of the Lappish Minority Situation*. Universitetsforlaget, Oslo 1971.

Eythorsson, Einar: Fjordfolket, fisken og forvaltningen. FDH-rapport 1993:12. Finnmark Distriktshøgskole, Alta 1993.

Eythorsson, Einar 1998: Voices of the Weak - Relational Aspects of Local Ecological Knowledge in the Fisheries. In: Jentoft, Svein (ed.): *Commons in Cold Climate. Coastal Fishing and Reindeer Pastoralism in North Norway: The Co-management Approach*. UNESCO / Parthenon Publishing Group, New York.

Eythorsson, Einar: Hvem skal forvalte ressursene? Forvaltning og rettigheter i fjordområdene i Nord-Norge. In: Bjørklund, Ivar: *Norsk ressursforvaltning og samiske rettighetsforhold. Om statlig styring, allmenningens tragedie og lokale sedvaner i Sápmi*. Ad Notam Gyldendal, Oslo 1999.

Gaski, Harald: Fornorskingspolitikk og språkundertrykking. In: Drivenes, Einar –Arne et al.: *Nordnorsk kulturhistorie 2. Det mangfoldige folket*. Gyldendal, Oslo 1994.

Hersough, Bjørn: Unfinished Business. *New Zealand Experience with Rights-based Fishing Management*. Eburon, Delft 2002.

Holm, Peter et al.: "Creating Alternative Natures: Coastal Cod as Fact and Artefacts. In: Symes, David: *Northern Waters. Management Issues and Practice*. Fishing News Books, Oxford 1998.

Høgmo, Asle: Det tredje alternativ. Barns læring av identitetsforvaltning i samisk-norske samfunn preget av identitetsskifte. *Tidskrift for samfunnsforskning,* 27, pp. 395-416 1986.

Innstilling fra Samisk fiskeriutvalg, 1997. Fiskeridepartmentet

Jentoft, Svein: *Allmenningens komedie. Medforvaltning i fiskeri og reindrift.* Ad Notam Gyldendal, Oslo 1998.

Lillevoll, Tor Arne: Yrkeskombinasjoner i deltidsjordbruket. Hovedfagsoppgave. Faculty of Social Science. University of Tromsø 1982.

Lillevoll, Tor Arne: Open commons for Coastal Sami Areas? In: Jentoft, Svein (ed.): *Commons in Cold Climate. Coastal Fishing and Reindeer Pastoralism in North Norway: The Co-management Approach.* UNESCO /Parthenon Publishing Group, New York 1998.

Maurstad, Anita: To fish or not to fish - small-scale fishing and changing regulations of the cod fishery in North Norway. *Human Organization* Vol. 59 (2000) No. 1 pp. 37-47.

Minde, Henry: Samebevegelsen, det norske arbeiderparti og samiske rettigheter. I: Thuen, Trond (red.): *Samene - urbefolkning og minoritet.* Universitetsforlaget, Tromsø 1980.

Minde, Henry: Diktning og historie om samene på Stuoranjarga. Skoddebergprosjektet *Diedut no 4* 2000.

Nilsen, Ragnar: The Coastal Survivors – Industrialization, Local Adaptations and Resource Management in the North Norwegian Fisheries. In: Jentoft, Svein (ed.): *Commons in Cold Climate. Coastal Fishing and Reindeer Pastoralism in North Norway: The Co-management Approach.* UNESCO /Parthenon Publishing Group. New York 1998.

Nilsen, Ragnar: *Fjordfiskere og ressursbruk i nord.* Ad Notam, Gyldendal. Oslo 1997.

Nilsen, Ragnar: Makt og motmakt på kysten. *Makt og demokratiutredningen.* Rapport nr 45. Oslo 2002.

Porsanger SLF: Fastboendes rettigheter i samiske kyst og fjordstrøk, Porsanger 1985.

Smith, Carsten: Om samenes rett til naturressurser - særlig ved fiskerireguleringer. In: *Lov og rett,* pp. 507-534 1990.

Wolf, Eric: *Peasants.* Prentice – Hall, New Jersey 1966.

CHAPTER 10

The Challenge and the Promise of Indigenous Peoples' Fishing Rights: From Dependency to Agency*

Anthony Davis and Svein Jentoft

Introduction

Contemporary fisheries management systems throughout the globe funda-mentally embody and express nation state proprietorial claims and regulatory authority respecting territorial coastal waters and, since 1977, the 200 mile Economic Management Zone (EMZ). Many nation-states have increased their exercise of proprietorial claim and authority over the last 30 years or so through development and implementation of fisheries management systems that, in es-sence, determine, allocate and regulate access to and participation in fisheries through devices such as licenses and quotas. These management systems treat access and participation as regulated 'privileges' defined and allocated by the state proprietor to fishers and fishing companies. In short, fisheries management for the nation state proprietor has become, in essence, the practice of defining and regulating the allocation of privileges. Many fishers have come to comply with and to work within this practice in so far as their conditions of access and economic advantage have been benefited through receipt of regulated license and/or quota 'privileges'. Notably, the expansion of and refinements in nation state proprietorship are co-terminus with the over exploitation of marine en-vironments as well as the collapse or near collapse of key marine resources (Apostle et.al. 1998, Davis 1996, Davis and Bailey 1996, Jentoft 1993, Hol-lingsworth (ed.) 2000, Hutchings 2000, McGoodwin 1990)

* Support for this research and collaboration has been provided by Anthony Davis' Professor II appointment within the Institute of Planning and Community Studies, University of Tromsø, as well as through research grants from the Social Science and Humanities Research Council of Canada (grant #s # 820-98-1028 and 833-99-1012). We would also like to thank the reviewers and Dr. Alida Bundy for their helpful suggestions.

Lately, the nation-states' proprietorial claims and regulatory authority are being challenged by the legal and political recognition that some indigenous peoples have particular 'rights' respecting access to and participation in fisheries (Bugge 1998, Rio Declaration, Agenda 21 - 1992). For many indigenous peoples, the recognition of fishing rights represents an affirmation of their unique political status within the nation-state as well as a material opportunity that they can mobilise to improve their commonly abysmal employment, income and social conditions (cf. Asch 1984, Bjørklund 1999, Dewees 1997, Indian and Eskimo Association of Canada 1972, Jull 1993, Sharp 1997, Stevens (ed.) 1997, Svensson (ed.) 1999, Waitangi Tribunal 1988, Wiber and Kennedy 2001). For non-aboriginal fishers and state fisheries managers, affirmation and expression of aboriginal commercial fishing rights raises many concerns. These concerns range from the ways and means to accommodate new entrants, through the implications of increased fishing pressure on usually diminished resources, to the impact of indigenous participation on incomes and the economic values of fishing enterprises, particularly the market values of allocated license and quota privileges.

Indeed, many non-indigenous fishers often greet the news of aboriginal fishing entitlements with howls of protest, demonstrations, threats, and predictions of dire outcomes. This certainly was the case in Eastern Canada following the recent Supreme Court of Canada 'Marshall' ruling (September 17th, 1999) which affirmed that Atlantic Canada's indigenous peoples hold a commercial fisheries treaty right, and in North Norway following the proposal by the Saami Parliament, at least as originally expressed, for the creation of a «Saami fisheries zone». Since September 1999, the Canadian government's Department of Fisheries and Oceans (DFO) has been scrambling to develop an effective management response to the 'Marshall' ruling, thus far without much success. In Norway, fisheries authorities have expressed both reluctance and opposition to the idea of a special assigned zone with certain rights and privileges reserved for fishers of Saami origin.

The difficulties in accommodating indigenous fishing rights within fisheries management systems predicated on nation-state proprietorship and regulation of 'privileges' are legion. In this essay, we examine a number of these difficulties through a comparative case study of developments associated with Eastern Canada's Mi'kmaq First Nation and Norway's Saami. Of particular interest to us are the implications of aboriginal fishing rights for the nation-states' proprietorial claim as the fisheries management authority and as the final arbitrator respecting access to and participation in fisheries. As Sharp has observed respecting the Maori indigenous claims experiences in New Zealand, «The fundamental issues between Maori and the Crown and Maori and Pakenha...are issues of agency...and the issues at stake were precisely [original] as to who had the right to act, and in acting to wield authority and to dispose of resources» (Sharp 1997:293). Indeed, much of nation states' struggles with indigenous peoples' rights is the failure to recognise and to accommodate indigenous peoples' desire to employ their rights with regard to self-defined prerogatives and needs, i.e., to act as self-directing agents. All too commonly states approach indigenous peoples and their entitlements with the mindsets and institutional tools of paternalistic providers, expecting 'their' indigenous peoples to be content with and appeased through receiving state-mediated 'largesse'. For their part, aboriginal peoples pursue entitlements as the legal-institutional means through which they can affirm identity, establish political-legal status, and achieve agency in relations with the nation state and non-aboriginal peoples. These qualities reside at the heart of the Mi'kmaq and Saami experiences discussed here.

We also think that the establishment of aboriginal fishing rights represents an opportunity for non-aboriginal coastal zone fishers and fishing communities to assess and to recast, in partnership with indigenous peoples, coastal zone fisheries management. Such an alliance may even enable non-aboriginal small boat, community-based, fishers to re-establish and affirm their access and participation entitlements in this age of state determined and managed privileges to fish. As Stevens argues, «Indigenous peoples can be powerful allies in conservation efforts» (1997:3). Further, we suspect indigenous-non-indigenous alliances will be critical in the further development of local agency in fisheries and coastal zone management.

The essay opens with a review of key moments in the development of Mi'kmaq and Saami fishing entitlements. This is followed by a discussion of the implications of these entitlements for fisheries management systems predicated on the notion that the nation-state is the unquestioned proprietor. Here we specifically explore the implications of aboriginal fishing entitlements for Norwegian and Canadian fisheries management systems. The essay closes with a discussion of the opportunities represented in aboriginal fishing rights for rethinking and recasting fisheries management, particularly within and for small boat, coastal zone and community settings.

Mi'kmaq and Saami Fishing Rights

A. The Mi'kmaq Case

My community has suffered from extreme unemployment for a very long time. The Marshall decision and the associated access to the commercial fishery has [sic] offered us hope. We share this fishery and we are concerned about its future. But never forget that we have a treaty right that we will not compromise for the sake of greed...(Chief Deborah Robinson, Acadia Mi'kmaq band, February 17, 2001)[1]

---

[1] 'Call to cancel licenses frustrates band', The Chronicle-Herald, February 17, 2001, p.A6.

On September 17, 1999 the Supreme Court of Canada issued a judgement that has shaken the very foundations of Canadian commercial fisheries and the fisheries management system. The Court ruled that Donald Marshall Jr., a status Mi'kmaq First Nations aboriginal, held a treaty right to engage in commercial fishing (*R. v. Marshall* 1999). Previous Supreme Court judgements have affirmed First Nations treaty rights to fish for subsistence and ceremonial purposes (*R. v. Sparrow 1990, R. v. Badger 1996*).[2] Unlike these, the 'Marshall' ruling raises fundamental questions respecting the legal authority and management entitlement of the state to regulate, within the existing fisheries management system, First Nations' participation in commercial fisheries.[3]

In August 1993, a couple of Canada's Department of Fisheries and Oceans (DFO) fisheries officers apprehended and arrested Donald Marshall Jr. for fishing eels without a license.[4] Marshall protested that he was simply exercising his treaty right to fish for a living. This event began a six year process by the Mi'kmaq First Nation of seeking legal judgement on provisions within their treaties. Of particular importance to them was receipt of a judgement respecting whether or not their treaties entitled them to fish commercially. After wending its way through the Canadian justice system, the case was finally presented before the Canadian Supreme Court, the nation's final legal arbitrators. On September 17, 1999 the Supreme Court issued a judgement affirming that

---

[2]   These decisions can be viewed in their entirety by following the links at http://www.lexum.umontreal.ca/csc-scc/en/index

[3]   On November 17, 1999 the Supreme Court of Canada, in denying a request by the West Nova Fishermen's Coalition for a stay of the Marshall judgement pending a rehearing of the case, availed itself of the opportunity to issue what is now referred to as the 'clarification' respecting the Marshall ruling. This represented a rather extraordinary and unprecedented intervention by the Court in what had become, following the original decision, an on-the-ground conflict between the federal government, non-aboriginal fishers and aboriginal leadership and fishers respecting fisheries management authority and the rules framing aboriginal participation in the commercial fisheries, particularly the high value small boat lobster fisheries. Notably, the Court's clarification emphatically and repeatedly underscored the judgement that the Crown bears the responsibility for justifying its' regulatory system respecting aboriginal participation. In the absence of appropriate justification, the simple imposition of an existing regulatory system would represent an infringement on and impediment to the ability of aboriginals to exercise their treaty rights (cf. R. v. Marshall at paras. 14, 15,18, 19, 21, 22, 26). Notably, this stipulation essentially has been ignored by government and non-native leadership. All have simply insisted that aboriginal participation in the commercial fisheries occur within the existing regulatory system. Contrary to this position, indigenous leaders argue that, in the absence of justifications, their treaty rights are not subject to exercise within the existing management systems. They insist that aboriginal people will develop their own regulatory systems, and that their prerogative to do so is rooted in their treaty rights and their associated rights of self-governance as independent nations. It is worth noting that the legal status of the Court's so-called 'clarification', relative to that of the original judgement, is at the moment unclear. Further litigation will most likely be required to sort this matter out.

[4]   The Mi'kmaq peoples occupied most of the Maritime Canadian woodlands at the time of European contact. They were hunters-gatherers with a mode of existence well tuned to avail-

provisions within the *1760-61 Treaties of Peace and Friendship*[5], negotiated between leaders of the Mi'kmaq, Maliseet, Passamaquoddy First Nations and representatives of Imperial Britain, provided these First Nations peoples with the right to fish for commercial purposes, i.e., to catch and sell marine resources in order to make a living. Donald Marshall Jr. was acquitted on all charges, and his people achieved legal affirmation of yet another critical treaty-based right.

It needs to be noted that for many Canadian First Nations peoples treaties are the foundation and the embodiment of their nationhood as well as the formal basis for their unique political and social position within the Canadian confederation. For them, the treaties concretely represent and acknowledge the 'fact' of their nationhood and of their identity as distinct peoples (Asch 1984,

---

able resource opportunities. Commonly, the Mi'kmaq spent the winter in extended family/kin groups while gathering into much larger social collectives during the late spring-early fall period. These gatherings formed on the coasts and estuaries. At this time, the Mi'kmaq sustained themselves through intensive use of the, then, abundant marine resources.

[5] Only the English, among all of the European Imperial powers contesting for a piece of the Americas, developed the policy and practice of negotiating and signing treaties with various First Nations peoples. It would be an error of mammoth scale to assume that this 'innovation' arose as a consequence of some sort of early 18th century English moral enlightenment and concern for aboriginal peoples' human condition. Notably, the English pursued this as a policy mainly in British North America and New Zealand, places where indigenous peoples posed considerable resistance to Imperial aims. This was not their practice, for example, when dealing with the aboriginal peoples of the West Indies, Australia, and Sub-Saharan Africa. In fact, early in their North American adventures the English more or less followed the European script of using aboriginal peoples when advantageous; but, as often as not, attempting to remove them from the picture through the application of systematic terror and genocide. Of course, aboriginal peoples tended to resist this; and, since they were still at this time a military force of consequence, the English and their New English colonists found themselves mired in a cycle of costly and destabilizing 'Indian Wars'. This situation was further confounded for the English by their more or less continual military conflict with the French and their First Nations allies. By the mid-17th century, the Imperial French had well-established and settled colonies in 'Acadia' (the Eastern Canadian Maritime Provinces) and in the area of the St. Lawrence River Valley (Quebec). The Imperial French never negotiated formal agreements with aboriginal peoples. Their approach was to develop trade and military alliances while introducing the 'humanizing' benefits of Catholicism and French culture. By the early 18th century, the Mi'kmaq were long-standing allies and trading partners of the Imperial French throughout Acadia. These First Nations peoples had generally adopted Catholicism and were often inter-married with French settlers. But, with French settlements still small in scale and widely dispersed, the Mi'kmaq remained in 'de facto' possession of the land and were still a force with which to be reckoned as the 18th century English-French Imperial struggles intensified. The Treaties of Peace and Friendship are examples of a tactical innovation developed by the 18th century Imperial British, initially in the 13 Colonies, as an efficient and effective means for militarily neutralizing Eastern North American Native Peoples in the context of their on-going imperial struggles with the French for possession of the continent and control of trade. Treaties were also considered by the English as an effective means for opening up land for colonisation and settlement. Beginning with the surrender of Acadia by the French to the English in 1711, an entire series of these treaties were negotiated and signed between the Mi'kmaq and the English. Re-engagement of English-French

The Indian and Eskimo Association of Canada 1972, Wiber and Kennedy 2001). Critically, in defining and concretising their nationhood, treaties for First Nations assure that they will not and cannot be treated simply as an ethnic community within a multiethnic Canada. This is recognised explicitly through the entrenched statements respecting First Nations peoples and their rights that are to be found within the Canadian Constitution (1982). First Nations insist that the leadership and elders negotiating treaty terms and conditions were primarily concerned that these qualities be entrenched and affirmed for their peoples. It is also held that the elders and leaders were also concerned that their nations' and peoples' interests be protected and advanced through explicit rights and privileges entrenched within treaties that specified each signatories responsibilities, obligations and benefits. In return, First Nations surrendered legal claim to vast territories that were then made available for European colonisation. A basic consequence for them was agreement to alter their way of life and culture while also accepting settlement on reservations.

Notably, the federal government has a history of suppressing, violating, ignoring and minimising treaty rights. In fact, until recently the Canadian Government had legally prohibited First Nations from mounting court challenges respecting treaties and treaty rights. None the less, a series of cases through the last 30 to 40 years as well as changes in the judiciary's moral, social and legal interpretative context have resulted in treaty right clarifications and affirmations, including 'modernisation' of interpretations with respect to the contemporary meaning of benefits, obligations and rights. Notably, the process of legal affirmation is one that First Nations have been forced to pursue by federal and provincial government resistance to and violations of treaty rights. The Marshall case was yet another moment in this track record. The federal government consistently refused to discuss, let alone negotiate, with the Mi'kmaq respecting Mi'kmaq claims of a treaty right permitting their participation in the commercial fisheries. This intransigence left the Mi'kmaq with no alternative but to mount the court challenge. Until very recently the federal policy respecting First Nations has been to foster social assimilation, to remove treaty rights where and when possible, and to 'modernise native peoples' through measures such as forced participation in residential school education. Further, the federal Indian Act, first passed into law in the mid-1870s, specifies the terms and conditions whereby Natives qualify for 'status' under the terms of treaties (Government of Canada 1985).[6] This was accomplished without any consultation or

---

hostilities often drew in the Mi'kmaq, thereby nullifying any existing treaty agreements. In the closing years of the English-French imperial struggles, the Mi'kmaq negotiated and signed, with the English, the final Peace and Friendship treaties. Provisions within these 1760 and 1761 treaties were the basis of the Mi'kmaq appeal to the Supreme Court of Canada and the Court's 'Marshall' decision. Jurisdiction over and responsibility for all 'Indian Affairs', including treaty terms and conditions, were transferred through the British North American Act (1867) from the British Crown to the newly constituted Canadian federal government.

engagement with First Nations. In short, the federal government has fostered a deeply deterministic 'patron' relation with Canada's First Nations wherein the government directs and controlls practically every core aspect of 'status' aboriginal existence.

Over the last 30 years or so Canada's First Nations have been in a struggle with the federal government to transform the basic character of this relationship. Increasingly First Nations have militated for the room within the Canadian confederation to direct their own affairs; that is, to claim agency. Litigation has been a key element in this process, employed as the means to clarify and affirm, within Canadian jurisprudence, the scope and obligations of their treaty rights. In the case of Donald Marshall Jr., the Supreme Court of Canada was asked to overturn his lower court illegal fishing conviction on the basis that provisions in the 1760-61 'Treaties of Peace and Friendship' assured a Mi'kmaq treaty right to engage in fishing for commercial purposes. In a 5 to 2 judgement, the Supreme Court ruled:

> This appeal should be allowed because nothing less would uphold the honour and the integrity of the Crown in its dealings with the Mi'kmaq people to secure their peace and friendship, as best the content of these treaty promises can now be ascertained...The trade arrangement must be interpreted in a manner that gives meaning and substance to the oral promises made by the Crown during the treaty negotiations. The promise of access to «necessaries» through trade in wildlife was the key point...(Marshall 1999:2).

Having affirmed the Mi'kmaq's treaty right to trade (sell) wildlife (including fish), the Court provided the following specification.

> The accused's treaty rights are limited to securing «necessaries» (which should be construed in the modern context as equivalent to a moderate livelihood), and do not extend to open-ended accumulation of wealth...What is contemplated is not a right to trade generally for economic gain, but rather a right to trade for necessaries (Marshall 1999:3).

In the Court's judgement, the Mi'kmaq right to participate in capturing wildlife for the purposes of trade is explicitly limited to the economic outcome of

---

6   Through narrowing the terms of qualification as well as through active assimilationist campaigns, the federal government has created an immense disenfranchised population, the so-called 'non-status' Indian. These persons currently have no rights and receive no special consideration with respect to existing treaties. These peoples have come to constitute the core of displaced Natives within the Canadian urban landscape, disproportionately marginalized, impoverished with many left with little else but the despair of substance abuse, criminality and the sex trade.

satisfying livelihood needs. The treaty right does not provide for participation in the commercial exploitation of wildlife on a scale that would enable wealth accumulation. Notably, the Court did not provide any direction respecting how to distinguish wealth accumulation from livelihood intended commercial activity. But, the Court is clear that the moderate livelihood limit provides the basis for regulating Mi'kmaq commercial exploitation.

> The treaty right is a regulated right and can be contained by regulation within its proper limits. Catch limits that could reasonably be expected to provide a moderate livelihood for individual Mi'kmaq families at present-day standards can be established by regulation and enforced without violating the treaty right. Such regulations would accommodate the treaty right and would not constitute an infringement…(Marshall, 1999:3).

While clear on the fact that the right can be regulated, the judgement notes explicitly that existing regulatory approaches such as the Canadian fisheries management system should not be simply assumed as the framework within which the right can be limited and expressed.

> The accused caught and sold eels to support himself and his wife. His treaty right to fish and trade for sustenance was exercisable only at the absolute discretion of the Minister [Minister of the Crown, Department of Fisheries and Oceans]. Accordingly, the close [sic] season and the imposition of a discretionary licensing system would, if enforced, interfere with the accused's treaty right to fish for trading purposes, and the ban on sales would, if enforced, infringe his right to trade for sustenance. In absence of any justification of the regulatory provision, the accused is entitled to an acquittal (Marshall, 1999:3).

In the Court's opinion, the right is to be regulated through some unspecified mechanism of establishing a material basis for the determination of a moderate livelihood. Existing fisheries regulations are clearly characterized, in themselves, as an interference with and infringement on the Mi'kmaq's treaty right.

Critically, the Court identified the right as a collective, not individual, right. That is, the ruling provides a right under treaty for the entire Mi'kmaq people.[7] The Court counselled the federal government and the Mi'kmaq to enter into negotiations that would specify the terms and conditions within which the right would be exercised consistent with the moderate livelihood provision (Marshall

---

[7]   Non-status Mi'kmaq leadership, arguing that since the Treaties of Peace and Friendship were signed over 100 years before development of the Indian Act, insist that non-status Mi'kmaq now also have the treaty right to a moderate livelihood from commercial fishing (Chronicle-Herald 1999b). Both the federal government and status Mi'kmaq leadership have resisted this interpretation.

1999, para 22, 23). Needless to say, these attributes of the ruling have challenged the jurisdictional and regulatory authority, as applied to the Mi'kmaq, of the entire Canadian government fisheries management system.

Confrontations, inflammatory accusations, and some on-the-water conflict have characterized developments since the September 1999 judgement. In light of the ensuing events, apparently DFO was entirely unprepared for Marshall's acquittal and the affirmation of the treaty right. Much to the dismay of many non-aboriginal harvesters, Mi'kmaq immediately made plans to begin fishing commercially, targeting the lucrative lobster fishery. Several boats set traps in a variety of Maritime Canada locations. Non-aboriginals threatened direct action to stop what was now being framed as a frontal assault on the conservation of sustainable lobster stocks and the basis of their livelihoods (Chronicle-Herald 2000c, Globe and Mail 1999d, 1999f).[8] DFO fisheries and Royal Canadian Mounted Police officers were engaged in keeping the sides separated as well as in seizing boats and gear, charging Mi'kmaq for fishing out of season and without licenses, and arresting non-aboriginals for destroying Mi'kmaq fishing gear (Chronicle-Herald 1999a, Globe and Mail 1999b,1999g,1999h, 2000a, 2000b).

In an attempt to impose order on the situation, DFO developed a strategy of negotiating one year, interim arrangements with individual Mi'kmaq bands, committing $150 million (Cdn.) to the process. In return for signing on, the bands were promised a specified number of licenses and equipped fishing boats, as well as other benefits such as access to fisheries-related training and education. In return for receiving these 'benefits' the Mi'kmaq bands were required to abide by the existing management system's rules and procedures. Although 30 of the 34 Maritime Canadian Mi'kmaq bands are reported to have signed interim arrangements covering the year 2000, on-the-water conflicts, boat and trap seizures, and illegal fishing charges garnered national and international attention with respect to the fishing activities of a couple of non-signatory bands, especially the Burnt Church band in New Brunswick and the Indian Brook band in Nova Scotia. Their leadership insisted that the Marshall decision enabled them to implement their own fisheries management system and that signing onto the interim arrangements might legally compromise the Mi'kmaq treaty right. For instance, Chief Reg Maloney of Indian Brook has asserted that the deals are little more than «...another flood of money drowning our treaty rights»(Chronicle-Herald 2001b:A4).

---

[8] Notably, the scale of Mi'kmaq participation in this fishery, in terms of both the number of traps being fished and the quantities of lobster landed, have amounted to well under 5% of all current non-aboriginal lobster fishing effort, i.e., thousands of traps as compared with hundreds of thousands of traps and thousands of kilograms of lobster as compared with hundreds of thousands of kilograms.

With the interim agreements set to expire in March 2001 coupled with the approach of the spring lobster season, the federal government through DFO is reported to have dedicated as much as $500 million (Cdn) to support the development of 3 to 5 year longer term agreements with Mi'kmaq bands. As with the earlier agreement strategy, the explicit goal is to enable increased aboriginal participation within the commercial fisheries through license and quota buybacks, boat and equipment purchases, and training. Once again, the Mi'kmaq in order to participate in these 'benefits' are required to abide by and to work within the existing fisheries management system. There is no denying that these resources are very seductive for generally resource poor Mi'kmaq bands. However, their leadership currently is taking a united position arguing that they want the federal government to negotiate fishing access with respect to a general agreement covering all Mi'kmaq bands, one that is an aspect of a broad-based renegotiation of treaty rights (Chronicle Herald 2001c). Mi'kmaq leadership is also concerned that participation in longer term fisheries only agreements will establish legal precedents compromising to the future interpretations of treaty rights and entitlements. As Chief Lawrence Paul has stated «We've been clear that the fishing agreements must not be viewed as defining treaty rights, but we are very worried Ottawa does not see it the same way...There's not even a mention of co-management»(Sunday Herald 2001:A4).

Many non-Mi'kmaq fishers continue to experience these developments with dismay and concern. While seemingly pleased with the federal government's strategy of framing Mi'kmaq participation within the existing management system, the particular practice of accomplishing this through buying existing licenses and quotas from non-aboriginals and redistributing these to Mi'kmaq bands is increasing viewed as unfair and destructive (Chronicle-Herald 2001e, 2001f, 2001g). In its urgency to purchase licenses and quota for redistribution to the Mi'kmaq, DFO is reported to be offering grossly inflated prices, in the mid hundreds of thousands of dollars (Cdn), that are benefiting individual sellers but that are distorting local market values to the extent that accessing licenses and quotas is now well beyond the financial means of most non-aboriginals. Further, only the license or quota holders are benefiting from the buy-backs. Crew working on the effected boats are reported to be receiving little, if any, compensation or benefit. They are left without their livelihood, unless they can find a situation aboard one of the diminishing number of non-aboriginal boats (Chronicle-Herald 2000a, Globe and Mail 1999e). While hopefully unintended by DFO, outcomes such as these have the potential to fuel social divisiveness and conflict within non-aboriginal coastal communities and families, let alone between Mi'kmaq and non-aboriginal fishers. As a consequence, it now appears that on-the-ground oppositional positions within the non-aboriginal fishing community are hardening and that the short-term prospects for Mi'kmaq and non-indigenous dialogue and alliances are rapidly diminishing (Chronicle-Herald 2001a, Globe and Mail 2001).

The Saami Case

The Saami Parliament proposed the foundation of a fisheries policy zone in Saami settlement areas. This is done in order to maintain and restore long-established rights in fisheries for the coastal Saami population. (Saami President Sven-Roald Nystø at the Saami Parliament fisheries seminar, Karasjok, February 21, 2001.)

Unlike the Mi'kmaq the Saami are not in a position to argue their case with reference to a special treaty. The legal issues involving the Saami relation to Norwegian state have evolved gradually and are still in process. When Saami claims have been pursued legally with respect to fisheries rights, the reference has been to international law pertaining to ethnic and indigenous rights much more so than to Norwegian law. 1990, which in many ways was a turning point in Norwegian fisheries, brought the Saami interests in fisheries management on to the public agenda as never before, beginning a process with which we have yet to see the end.

In that year the coastal and fjord cod fishery also became subject, within Norwegian fisheries policicies, to individual quota management. The open access principle for that particular fishery, which was an important factor in the original Norwegian settlement and development of North Norway, was abolished. 1990 was a year of crisis. Never before had the TAC (Total Allowable Catch) been set so low. Indeed, the situation looked extremely gloomy. But there had been warning signals. In the previous year, 1989, the cod fishery was ordered stopped as early as April 18. The Fisheries Director concluded that this should not happen again. «Never more April 18!», he proclaimed. Until that time, the cod fisheries had been managed by means of a so-called maximum quota, where the regulation specifies that no more than 85 percent of the TAC could be harvested before September 1. By mid-April, however, this limit had already been reached, hence, the closure. This crisis was felt particularly by small-boat fishers in the northern fjords as their traditional cod fishery season had not even started by April 18. The Fisheries Director responded quickly. The year after he introduced the vessel quota system.

In 1990 no one questioned the need for strict and drastic harvesting regulations. Nevertheless, the way the quota system was designed created immediate controversy, and from one quarter the criticism was especially harsh. The newly established Saami Parliament claimed both that the quota system neglected Saami interests[9] and that it was also in conflict with international

---

[9] The coastal Saami of Norway are a part of the Saami people, as a result of the historical processes, living in four countries - Norway, Sweden, Finland and Russia. The great majority of Saami live in Northern Norway and in the county of Finnmark (literally «the land of Finns -which is an old name for Saami). Besides reindeer pastoralism, small-scale fishing is the traditional occupation. More than 80 percent are employed in other more «modern» industries

law on minorities and indigenous peoples' rights. There is little doubt that this protest took the Norwegian government by surprise and that the protest could neither be overlooked or simply dismissed. Implicit in Norwegian fisheries legislation is the principle that a fisher is a fisher regardless of ethnic origin. Saami interests and rights are not mentioned in any Norwegian law pertaining to the fishery, and the rights of Saami were until then rarely an issue in the fisheries management discourse. A demand for special treatment and protection of Saami fishers on the grounds that they were indigenous peoples was at that time unprecedented.

The Saami Parliament claimed that the 1990 vessel quota system discriminated against traditional Saami fisheries adaptations. Further, the Parliament regarded the system as utterly unfair in so far as small boats with non-mobile technologies, which could not by any means be held responsible for the fisheries crisis, would be hardest hit in the regulatory system. The system divided fishers into two groups, depending on their historical fishing track record, as a way of determining their dependency on the cod fishery. One group, those who could document a certain activity level in the fisheries, obtained a guaranteed vessel quota while those who could not, primarily those with small boats and those combining fisheries with other employment activities such as small-scale farming, ended up on a competitive quota. This situated the latter with a less secure position within the commercial fisheries, while also providing them with much reduced fisheries-sourced income and earnings potential (Jentoft and Karlsen 1997).

Most Saami fishers could not fulfil the strict requirements to obtain a vessel quota. Not only did they fish on a small scale basis, they also often combined fishing with other occupations, such as farming. The Saami Parliament referred in its formal complaint to the Fisheries Ministry to what occurred in two typical fisheries dependent Saami communes in Finnmark. In one, none of the 90 registered fishers obtained a vessel-quota, in the other only one out of 70 had success. Those that did not receive a quota and thus had no guaranteed privilege to fish, were placed under the so-called maximum quota system. This quota was a far less profitable deal. In addition, and perhaps the most critical point from a Saami perspective, they achieved no guaranteed assurance to participate in the commercial fisheries, as the fishery could be stopped at any time regardless of whether fishers had been able to catch their share. In practice, this development further removed Saami fishers participatory privileges and rights in a fishery on

---

and occupations. No one knows the exact number of Saami, let alone of the coastal Saami. Their population has been estimated as somewhere between 50-100 000 persons, the majority living along the coast and fjords. The Saami Parliament was opened in 1987 in Karasjok, Finnmark. It has representation from all Saami groups in Norway. Vis-a-vis the Norwegian government, it has basically an advisory status (for more on Saami fisheries, see Jentoft (ed.) 1998).

which they could claim a long-standing dependency, despite the fact that fishing was rarely a full-time, all year activity as is more typical among Norwegian fishers residing on the outer coast. The Saami argument has only gained weight as the vessel-quota system over the years has led to a de facto transferable/tradeable system. When the vessels are sold the quota follows them, thus considerably inflating the price of buying into participation. By not qualifying for a vessel quota in the first place, Saami fishers were also in practice excluded from engaging in and benefiting from the profit-making attributes of the tradeable quota system.

In 1990, The Saami Parliament asked for more than marginal adjustments in the quota system. It also demanded a full clarification of Saami legal rights in fisheries. The Fisheries Ministry responded by assigning a law professor at the University of Oslo, Carsten Smith, to the task of examining Saami legal rights. Smith filed his report in the summer of 1990 (cf. Smith, 1990). This report has contributed considerably to the subsequent debates and reforms, and his main conclusions must therefor be presented here in some detail.

Smith began by discussing the UN declaration of civil and political rights, paragraph 27, concerning minority populations. He concluded that the Saami clearly can be defined as a minority population under this declaration, and that their indigenous culture must be protected. Importantly, he stressed that the «material foundation» for Saami way of life must be included in the concept of culture. Hence, their traditional industries must be protected, in addition to their communities, language and art forms. Notably, this argument had already been accepted by the Norwegian Parliament. This is evident in the addition of a new paragraph on Saami rights to the Constitution (paragraph 110a) which states that: «It rests with the Government to arrange the conditions so that the Saami people may ensure and develop their Language, their Culture and their Social Life.» Adding greater specificity, Smith contended that, even though fishing is not a unique Saami industry as is the case with reindeer pastoralism, fishing is nevertheless a traditional Saami occupation. Therefore it followed that the government has a legal duty to make sure that Saami fisheries are sustained, and that Saami fisheries adaptations should not be eliminated as a consequence of management measures.

Smith also found support for this conclusion in the ILO (International Labour Organisation) convention no. 169 regarding indigenous peoples which Norway was first among nations to ratify.[10] He acknowledged that non-Saami Norwegian fishers may legitimately claim that the fishery is part of their culture and that they are dependent as well on the fishery for their livelihood. Despite this, he argued that the same legal obligations of the government vis-à-vis the

---

[10] Although quick in ratifying the ILO convention, Norway has been slow in making it national law. This has not yet happened, although the convention frequently serves as a reference in court rulings respecting the Saami. Notably, the other Nordic countries, Sweden and Finland, with Saami populations have yet to ratify. Canada has not yet ratified the ILO convention.

Saami do not apply to the rest of Norwegian fishers. Regulatory and management systems that ostensibly treat Norwegian and Saami fishers equally can not always be defended: If «positive discrimination», i.e. preferential treatment, of Saami fishers is necessary to sustain Saami fisheries, then the government must do it. Saami fishers must then be granted privileges that their Norwegian counterparts may not enjoy. For instance, if necessary the government must provide Saami fishers with a relatively higher quota than Norwegian fishers.» This, according to Smith, may even be essential in consideration of sustaining the critical state of Saami culture in coastal areas.

Of all Smith's statements, the one on positive discrimination has been the most controversial. Notably, he maintained that discrimination on an individual basis would neither be preferable nor realistic. Rather, positive discrimination should be based on residence so that Saami communities rather than Saami individuals should be the beneficiaries of special status and treatment. Notably, Norwegians and Finns (in Norway named kven) also residing in Saami dominated fishing communities would benefit from these measures. Smith assumed that this principle would be accepted more readily among non-indigenous fishers than systems of individually-referenced positive discrimination.

The Norwegian government implemented some of Carsten Smith's recommendations immediately. For instance, the Saami Parliament was promptly given a seat in the national Fisheries Regulatory Council. This body provides advice to the Ministry on matters of fisheries management. On the issue of positive discrimination, however, the general attitude was much less welcoming. As might be anticipated, the Saami Parliament received the Smith report with great enthusiasm, and asked for the introduction of what was termed a «Saami Fisheries Zone» in parts of North Norway. This approach was offered by the Saami as an effective means whereby the Smith proposal for positive discrimination could be actualised with respect to support for communities rather than individuals. In the statement (Issue 33/1992) the Saami Parliament explained,

> With the demand of a distinct fisheries zone, the meaning is a collective right to fish in a commons open for all who reside within a geographically demarcated area. Given the government regulations that are necessary to sustain the resource base, local areas should obtain more responsibility in the management of their own resources. In such management institutions we see it as important that the Saami people, through the Saami Parliament, should be represented in line with those political institutions in which the local populations otherwise are represented. (Our translation)

The Smith report and the Saami Parliament left questions unanswered. Although the basic principles were thoroughly discussed, the more detailed management implications needed further elaboration. The Saami Parliament and the Fisheries Ministry each appointed one committee tasked to examine these issues. The Saami committee (Storslett 1995) had its report ready in January 1995, and launched quite radical ideas. The committee described the Saami fisheries zone proposal enthusiastically. The committee strongly believed in the symbolic value of the zone, and that it would trigger greater interest for Saami issues in general. Among its specific recommendations, this committee proposed that within the zone the fishers should be guaranteed a fixed percentage of the Norwegian TAC; that all mobile gear should be banned from the zone; that the zone should extend four nautical miles from shore; and, that the zone should include the counties of Finnmark, North-Troms, and certain communes in Nordland. The committee was proposing that the Saami fisheries zone would encompass a substantial area of North Norway and Norwegian ocean territory.

The proposals of the government committee were, not surprisingly, far more cautious. The report was submitted in 1997, five years after the committee had been formed and tasked (Samisk fiskeriutvalg 1997). This report recognised that Saami interests in fisheries had lost ground partly due to the quota system. On the issue of the Saami fisheries zone, only a minority of the members indicated support for the concept while the majority claimed they found the idea to be too vague. Furthermore, the committee expressed the fear that a ban on mobile gear would in fact hurt several Saami fishing communities as some employed this kind of fishing technology.

Meanwhile another, but unrelated, committee tasked with the responsibility of examining Saami rights had been in operation for more than a decade. This committee also produced a report that contained some consideration of the fisheries issues (NOU 1997). The committee repeated what has been confirmed in several court cases. That is, on the ocean the principle of no-one's property reigns, even though it can be proven historically that in some areas Saami enjoyed the privilege of first use. It claimed that the no-one's property principle has wide support among Saami. This committee regarded the proposal to establish a Saami fisheries zone positively. Thus, it placed itself in between the two other committees that had been established explicitly for the purpose of examining the Saami fisheries issues. Of importance is what this committee did not mention. To begin with, it only discussed the notion of a fisheries zone without any explicit association of the word Saami in relation to the proposal. Further, this committee's report did not elaborate the issue of a Saami commons right, which was part of the Saami Parliament's and its fisheries committee's vision.

The Saami Parliament discussed these reports in March 1998, and launched the concept of a «Fisheries Policy Zone for Saami Areas». It also proposed that experiments respecting the development and effectiveness of local co-management systems be undertaken in some Saami fjords on a ten year basis, followed up by research. The Fisheries Ministry in a white paper on «Perspectives on the Development of the Norwegian Fishing Industry» (St.meld. nr. 51, 1977-98) responded to some of these recommendations. The language employed here was minimally cautious, if not intentionally vague. This simply reflected the controversial qualities in and sensitivities to the issue. In short, the Ministry acknowledged that local management systems may become required in the future, but it was not willing to support the principle of positive discrimination with respect to geographical areas and ethnic groups. Rather, it preferred to make adjustments in the current quota system for small vessels and for people who combine fishing with other income generating activities. Thus, in 2001, the zone issue is still pending. In the Saami Parliament's 1997 to 2001 action plan the idea is less prominent. Instead, it defines a process for a more gradual development. The plan identifies three fjords in North Norway - the Tana fjord, the Lyngen fjord, the Tysfjord – that should be chosen as sites for local fisheries management experiments. So far, concrete actions have been taken only in the Tana fjord. The government's position respecting these experiments is, according to Ms. Ellen M. Bergli, the Deputy Minister of Fisheries, that they are «not negative», but that the Ministry still, as the point of departure, holds that the management of fisheries must remain a national responsibility. As to the question of a Saami fisheries zone, the Deputy Minister recently expressed the following perspective,

> I am not ready today to give an answer to whether the Fisheries Ministry would work to establish a fisheries zone. But what I can say is that we in the ministry, and in the government, will examine whether a Saami fisheries zone is a suitable tool (February, 2001).

It is fair so say that the government here finds itself in a dilemma. To accommodate the demands of the Saami Parliament, the government would have to depart from what it regards as the founding principle of fisheries management in Norway, i.e., that fish are a national common property resource. The law makes no distinction between large migrating and small local stocks, the latter being of most importance to Saami fish harvesting. It is with reference to this basic principle that the Norwegian government has thus far based its insistence that the right to fish can not be based on or defined by geographical residence, ethnicity, or, by implication, indigenous entitlement. Court cases such as the one argued in Salten Herredsrett in 1994 (Maurstad, 1995), that have challenged this principle, i.e. that the state is the sole legally constituted proprietor and manager of the nation's fish resources, have yet to accomplish little more than affirmation of the Norwegian nation state's position.

Implications for Fisheries Management

The issue is here and they're [the federal government and non-aboriginal people] going to have to deal with it. We're not here to take over the country or to take away from other people's livelihood. We're here to make sure our kids in the future will have something better to live on...I don't think government knows how to deal with native issues...(Donald Marshall Jr., Chronicle Herald, 2000b:A1-2).

The pursuit, emergence and affirmation of indigenous peoples' rights claims for participation in commercial fisheries have the transformative potential to turn entire fisheries management systems inside out and upside down. This potential largely explains the response to date of government agencies and of many non-aboriginals in both Norway and Canada. While there may be sympathy for the Saami and Mi'kmaq peoples and their concerns, in both settings governments fear the consequences for the fisheries management system as a whole of acknowledging and engaging with indigenous rights. As it is, the tasks and challenges of fisheries management are already complex, and many features of these management systems reflect the character of being a house of cards – uncertain and vulnerable to catastrophic collapse. Consequently, the over-riding Norwegian and Canadian governmental approaches have been to presume that indigenous peoples' fisheries entitlements must be somehow reconciled to and accommodated within the existing fisheries management systems. For example, the Canadian Minister of Fisheries and Oceans has proclaimed repeatedly since the Marshall decision that «...I, as the minister, have the authority to make sure that we are fully responsible and we operate in a consistent [manner (*original*)] towards conservation» (Globe and Mail 1999b: A3); and «As Minister of Fisheries and Oceans, I can regulate the fishery and I will regulate the fishery...Clearly there is a treaty right, but the court decision said that the right can be regulated...»(Globe and Mail 1999c: A3). The Marshall decision and subsequent events represent a direct challenge to the management authority and system of DFO and its Minister. A similar challenge confronts the Norwegian Fisheries Ministry and Minister with respect to the recognition of Saami fishing entitlements.

In both Norway and Canada one of the key areas of difficulty is rooted in the insistence by governments and many non-aboriginal fishers that indigenous participation be framed by the existing rules, regulations, licensing and quota privileges. For instance, the DFO's primary and initial goal is maintenance of the existing fisheries management system by containing Mi'kmaq participation within the limits realised through the purchase of licenses and quota from non-natives, transferring said licenses to the Mi'kmaq, and compelling the Mi'kmaq to abide by and work within the management system. This process is justified on the basis of resource conservation, implying that the core purpose of the ex-

---

[11]   Arguably, DFO would be hard-pressed to prove the assertion that the existing fisheries management system is dedicated to resource conservation. To begin with, DFO fisheries management policies have been directly intended to facilitate the accumulation of wealth for specific fishing effort, that is, the capital intensive, non-selective harvesting mid-shore

isting system is management for the purpose of resource sustainability[11]. But, in the absence of the requisite justifications, DFO's purpose is, first, to define and to contain the Mi'kmaq treaty right within a 'privilege' allocation and regulation management system. Certainly from the perspective of aboriginal peoples, this approach is akin to trying to force a round object into a square hole with the likely outcome being considerable damage to entitlements, self-determination, and economic benefits. Critically here, DFO's strategy is to redistribute to the Mi'kmaq privilege management devices or tools, licenses and quotas, that arise directly from and embody the nation states' proprietorship claim respecting access and participation in fisheries. Certainly this strategy is intended to minimally limit Mi'kmaq agency, and embodies the Canadian state's apparent inability to approach and negotiate with the Mi'kmaq as partners, rather than as clients. An example of this is seen in the state's refusal to recognise, let alone discuss, the self-management systems developed by several Mi'kmaq bands. This refusal has precipitated and deepened several of the confrontations and conflicts that where featured during the early days of responses to the Marshall decision (Ward and Augustine 2000a, 2000b).

Further, the current fisheries management tools were designed with the purpose in mind of limiting the numbers of persons fishing as well as the scale of targeted fishing effort or fishing power (e.g., trap limits, quotas, sector licenses and so on). Consequently, the management tools are defined as privileges allocated either to individual persons or to individual enterprises. Apparently DFO considers each Mi'kmaq band as the equivalent of a fishing enterprise that may hold and work with a number of licenses and\or a resource quota, leaving the issue of allocation dynamics a matter of intra-band preferences and decisions. Individual and enterprise license and quota holders are required to follow the appropriate rules and regulations when fishing. So, a Mi'kmaq band allocated 5 Class 'A' commercial lobster licenses for any particular zone would be permitted to fish the maximum numbers of traps permitted per license within that zone, and no more. Additionally, the Mi'kmaq may be permitted to employ only five boats when fishing the allocated licenses. Obviously this approach

---

and offshore corporate fisheries - the so-called 'economic' fisheries. Resource collapse and the groundfish moratorium are the consequence of this intention. There is little evidence that would convincingly prove that current fisheries management has moved away from this intention. For instance, DFO marine science co-organisers of the 1999 ICES Symposium (Montpellier) invited a senior executive of a major Canadian fishing corporation to take the place of a Canadian government fisheries manager and to represent Canada on a final day international panel discussion of fisheries management policy. Certainly this transposition embodies the commonality of DFO fisheries management goals and worldviews with those of wealth accumulation fishing. Indeed, DFO would seem to be at risk of contravening the substance and spirit of the Court's judgement should they compel the Mi'kmaq to express their treaty right within the existing 'privilege' allocation and regulation system, a system seemingly dedicated to assisting in wealth accumulation processes.

reflects neither the substance of the treaty right nor particular Mi'kmaq interests and concerns with respect to the exercise of their treaty right.

The Supreme Court's ruling explicitly states that the Crown can regulate the Mi'kmaq treaty right and place limits upon Mi'kmaq commercial fishing. But, the ruling is equally clear in stating that these regulations must be framed with reference to enabling the Mi'kmaq people access to a moderate livelihood. As earlier shown, the design of the existing fisheries management system is explicitly characterized by the Court ruling as an infringement on and an impediment to the exercise of the treaty right, unless otherwise justified. Further, the treaty right is clearly specified as a collective, not an individual, right. Consequently, the Mi'kmaq are left with the prerogative to determine the ways and means whereby their people will exercise the right with reference to the moderate livelihood provision. Yet, the Canadian state has continued to insist that Mi'kmaq participation only occur within the existing management system, with virtually no attempt to provide the requisite justification for this or to demonstrate how this will assure the Mi'kmaq access to a moderate livelihood.

In Norway, Smith's report to the Ministry acknowledged the governments' authority to manage the Saami fishery, as conservation of stocks would also be in the interest of the Saami. However, he stated that the government, in accordance with international law, has an obligation to create the conditions necessary to maintain fishing as a Saami way of life even if it would require special privileges (positive discrimination). This applies regardless of the fact that the relations between the Norwegian state and the Saami people are not embodied in and specified through a negotiated treaty, as in the case of Eastern Canada's indigenous peoples. The inclusion of the Saami paragraph in the Norwegian constitution has occurred only recently. It is a confirmation of the Norwegian government's duty and responsibility - in this case the Fisheries Ministry - to protect «the material base» of Saami culture.

Another key aspect of the Canadian Supreme Court's ruling and the acceptance of Smith's conclusion is pertinent to both governments' strategy of shoehorning the Mi'kmaq and the Saami into the existing management system. For example, by insisting that Saami interests should be articulated within the frames of the existing management system, the government continues to demonstrate that it is not prepared to engage in radical changes either in its relations with the Saami or respecting the place of the Saami within Norwegian fisheries. For instance, Saami representation in the Regulatory Council, one consequence of Smith's recommendations, is a minor change. Another representative at the table does not challenge the system as such (cf. Davis and MacInnes 1996). Likewise, relaxing some of the rules for the small boat fleet does not provoke anyone or threaten the integrity of the fisheries management system. Arguably, by asserting that Saami interests be framed according to the rules and principles of the prevailing management system the state implicitly rejects the concepts of a Saami Fisheries Zone and Saami agency. Obviously, the Norwegian government fears the consequences. Not only does it have to address a complex legal matter. The fear is also that a more radical accommodation and solution would spread to include others. Perhaps non-indigenous fishers would militate for similar claims and treatment. However, the government now finds itself in a difficult position, not unlike a vice. It would in any case have to demonstrate that the existing management system and the changes it can accept are able to satisfy the requirement of sustaining the material base and hence the culture of the Saami. If unable to satisfy this condition, the Norwegian government would not be fulfilling the obligations that are specified within international law and the Norwegian constitution. On this basis the Norwegian government may be subject to litigation processes similar to those in the Canadian setting and the Mi'kmaq case. It has been argued by another prominent Norwegian law professor that the language of the Saami paragraph in the Norwegian Constitution is rather vague and that this may weaken the Saami position if the issue should ever be brought to court (Smith 1986). Since then (1994), Norway has made the UN Convention on Political and Social Rights become national law. Here, the paragraphs of the convention have simply been copied. They do not refer, however, to indigenous peoples specifically but the convention does certainly also apply to them. International law regarding indigenous peoples has developed in recent years. For instance, the Declaration on Biological Diversity and the Convention on Elimination of all Forms of Racial Discrimination both have paragraphs that are referring to the resource rights of indigenous peoples. Most countries, including Norway and Canada have ratified these conventions. Now at the drafting stage within the United Nations' system N system, the Declaration on Indigenous Peoples, goes very far in explicitly stating the rights of indigenous peoples with respect to coastal waters and marine resources.[12]

A critical attribute underscoring non-aboriginal concerns is, to put it bluntly, the effect aboriginal entry and participation on both their catches\incomes and the market value of their fishing licenses and quotas. Willingly or not, many Canadian and Norwegian non-aboriginal small boat fishers have complied with the development of the existing 'privilege' allocation fisheries management system, at least in so far as it has provided them with substantial economic ben-

---

[12]   They read: «Indigenous peoples have the right to own, develop, control and use the lands and territories, including the total environment of the lands, air, waters, coastal seas, sea-ice, flora, fauna and the resources which they have traditionally owned or otherwise occupied or used. This includes the right to the full recognition of their laws., traditions and customs, land- tenure and institutions for the development and management of resources, and the right to effective measures by States to prevent any interference with, alienation of or encroachment upon these rights (Article 26). Indigenous peoples have the right to the restitution of the lands, territories and resources which they have traditionally owned or otherwise occupied or used, and which have been confiscated, occupied, used or damaged without their free and informed consent...» (Article 27.) (Gayim 1994).

efits. This is actually one of the most disturbing qualities of small boat fishing and coastal community experience with the fisheries management system and its agents. When first introduced, most licensing systems were not understood by many fishers to be a hard-edged regulatory and access limiting management device. In some instances, licenses were presented as simply a necessary way to account for the numbers and characteristics of fishers and fishing effort. Further, most fishers never understood that agreement to obtain licenses was, in fact, agreement with the notion of participation as a 'privilege' allocated to them by the nation-state. For the vast majority of small boat, coastal zone fishers, fishing is more than an occupation. It is a way of life that embodies their families' and communities' generations-deep engagement with making a living from the sea. It is what they are and what they do. Of course, few would have ever thought, at least until recently, of fishing in terms of either 'rights' or 'privileges'. Your people fished and you fished, likely on the same grounds, out of the same harbours, and in the same fisheries. It requires systems of imposed external regulations, limitations, and livelihood threats for such people to begin thinking about who they are and what they do in terms of such dry and lifeless legalisms such as 'rights' and 'privileges'.

However, the definition and affirmation of aboriginal peoples participation as a 'right' has had the effect of compelling some non-native fishers to begin thinking about their rights, or rather the formal absence of same. If they accomplish little else, decisions such as Marshall and proposals such as the Saami Fishing Zone have provided many non-aboriginals with the reason to recognise and to challenge the notion that their access and participation is as a consequence of 'privileges' allocated to them and regulated for them by the nation-state. For example, in many coastal and fjord districts Norwegian Saami and non-Saami live in the same communities, and fish side by side for the same species with similar technologies. When the rights issue was brought to the fore as a consequence of the 1990 quota system and the subsequent response by the Saami Parliament, many non-indigenous fishers started to ask themselves what their rights are, and not only in relation to the Saami but also vis-à-vis large scale fishing. Although «positive discrimination» on a community basis may put intra-communal tensions at rest, inter-communal or -district conflicts may arise. A Saami Fisheries Zone would not solve this issue; but, would raise the issues to a higher geographical and administrative level of consideration. Collective rights for those that reside within such a zone are not necessarily less controversial than a management system based on individual rights, as demonstrated in a meeting of the local branch of the Norwegian Fisher's Union in Finnmark. Here it was argued that the proposal for such a zone was to be re- garded as a form of unacceptable «reverse race discrimination». Consequently, they dismissed the whole idea that their commune should be included within a Saami fisheries zone.

Conclusions

Accommodating Mi'Kmaq and Saami commercial fishing rights within the existing management system, in a manner consistent with the terms of the Canadian Supreme Court ruling and the demands of the Saami Parliament and in a manner acceptable to all parties involved, including non-indigenous people, would appear for the moment to be out of reach. Certainly the Norwegian and Canadian governments and their fisheries managers have yet to come to grips with the fact that 'their' indigenous peoples will not accept anything less than self-determinant agency in relations with government and access to and use of resources. One must not forget the urgency of the matter. Indigenous peoples are under pressure from many sources. Smith, for instance, argues that coastal Saami culture finds itself in a «five to twelve» situation. Consequently, it is necessary to begin a new process as soon as possible, a process that will recast the very basis and substance of fisheries management as it prevails in the two countries. There is little direct evidence to suggest that the two governments are either capable of or interested in initiating an entirely new approach to fisheries management. What options are there to developing a process that both will successfully resolve the immediate indigenous and non-indigenous marine harvester conflict as well as put in place a fisheries management system dedicated to equitable access as well as fisheries ecological and livelihood sustainability?

There are several essential and promising starting points. In both countries, but more so in Canada than in Norway, fisher-organisations have begun exploring a community- and locality-based approach to fisheries management. That is, they are building experience, with their marine harvester memberships, in developing the ways and means to manage fisheries with respect to local concerns, practices, needs and preferences. Central to these initiatives is the principle of achieving long-term ecological and fisheries livelihood sustainability. These initiatives are realistically working through difficult problems such as coastal fishing boundaries, access rules, and distribution issues. Notably, there is no particularly Saami or Mi'kmaq quality in this approach, as it would generally benefit small-scale fishers and their communities. These initiatives are also consistent with Carsten Smith's proposals pertaining to the implementation of «positive discrimination» on a community rather than individual basis.

In many respects these organisations and their members are concerned about the same issues and outcomes as the Saami and the Mi'kmaq. That is, they want to participate in fisheries where they have some voice in their management and some assurance of access to a sustainable and reasonable livelihood. This is a common ground where indigenous and non-indigenous coastal zone small boat fishers can meet for the purpose of building a new fisheries management system. And, the situation is such that they, not the government and corporate interests, must initiate the processes in order to take advantage of and work with this common ground.

Allying with the indigenous peoples in developing entirely new approaches to the management of their fisheries would provide a golden opportunity for non-indigenous small-scale fishers to reassert a rights-based claim to their participation in the fisheries. On behalf of the nation as a whole, the Canadian and Norwegian State expresses its proprietorial claim respecting fisheries through its management system. The management system, in effect, allocates state authorised 'privileges' such as licenses and quotas. By accepting these practices as determinant access and participation criterion, marine harvesters are agreeing that they fish at the behest of the State, thereby enabling the State to assume the empowered role in the determination and imposition of fisheries management policies. So, a non-aboriginal small boat fisher alliance with indigenous peoples such as the Saami and Mi'kmaq would offer non-aboriginals the prospect of re-engaging a rights-based protection for their access to and participation in commercial fishing.

Would aboriginal peoples possessing widely recognised rights and in pursuit of agency be welcoming to developing alliances with non-aboriginal coastal zone fishers and communities? Both the Mi'kmaq and Saami have often expressed a willingness to work directly and co-operatively with local non-indigenous fishers. Since the Marshall decision there have been numerous meetings between Mi'kmaq and non-aboriginal fisheries leaders that are dedicated to working out understandings and co-operative relations. In Norway, the Saami Parliament, by reconceptualizing the Saami Fisheries Zone as a Fisheries Policy Zone for Saami Areas and by starting cautiously with initial experiments in selected fjord local management, is reaching out to non-indigenous fishers to become involved in a learning process intended to examine the feasibility of a decentralised management system in accordance with the Saami visions and the interest of small-scale coastal fishers in general. One key issue here is the extent to which local management, based on local common property rights, can work with respect to other privileged access based regimes. In Norway «everyone» can see that under the current management system which allocates privileges to individual boat owners in such a fashion that quotas are bought and sold, communities lose out and that access opportunities for Saami and non-Saami small-scale fishers alike have been dramatically reduced. Rooting rights within communities rather than with individuals might then benefit all small-scale fishers, not just Saami. The Saami solution to the management problem, although it may have scared the government, has inspired small-scale fishers and their organisations to start rethinking their positions and to be more innovative about fisheries management. But the framing of this discourse and the words employed are, however, crucial, as the language that was used in the local branch of the Fishers' Union demonstrated. Novel ideas, however well intended and innovative, do not always receive acclamation. Sometimes, a «non-ideal speech situation» - to express this in Habermasian - may distort communication in a way that conflict rather than consensus results.

It has been opined that allowing fish harvesters to manage fisheries is about as sensible as turning the hen house over to the fox, with harvesters lacking both the necessary knowledge about resources and the capability of reaching consensus. The scepticism of the two governments to devolution and localised management is justified in such presumptions. Of course this view offers a rather cynical, if not insulting and uninformed opinion of most fishers. It says that all fishers are alike in so far as they will selfishly and destructively compete with one and another to exploit marine resources until it is economically unfeasible to do so, usually at a point when targeted marine resourcse are thoroughly over-exploited and the ecosystem has been damaged. This view, one that underscores much of the present Norwegian and Canadian fisheries management systems, intentionally refuses to draw distinctions between fishers and fishing practices that are targeted on achieving livelihood goals and those that are employed in the interests of the corporate wealth accumulation agenda.

As the Eastern Canadian and North Norwegian cases indicate, indigenous and non-indigenous fishers are in a position to rewrite the basic principles of fisheries management systems so that they begin with the recognition and entrenchment of the distinction between livelihood and wealth accumulation fishing. The Canadian Supreme Court ruling clearly draws the livelihood – wealth accumulation distinction into focus as the basis of meaningful differences and determinations with respect to fishing activities and fisheries management. With this distinction in place it becomes possible to insist that fisheries be managed in the first instance on the basis of attaining and maintaining ecosystem integrity for the purpose of sustaining fisheries livelihoods and coastal communities. Once the livelihood and wealth accumulation distinction is in place, it becomes possible to develop substantial fisheries management policies and practices that would empower small-scale coastal fishers, regardless of ethnic or national origin, to assume direct roles and responsibilities in the co-operative management of their fisheries. Wealth accumulation fishing, now well proven as destructive and ecologically unsustainable, would only continue under direct state management. Further, its continuance would need to be contingent on the provision of proofs, following the precautionary principle, that accumulation fishing is neither destroying resources nor having any intervening or interfering effects on indigenous and non-indigenous coastal fishers' access to marine resources and sustainable livelihoods.

Certainly the legal recognition of indigenous rights respecting access to and participation in commercial fisheries is understood by aboriginal peoples as a critical step toward dismantling dependency and to achieving agency. Affirmation and expression of these rights offer indigenous peoples the possibility of further developing the social and economic basis for their ability to 'act' in their own interests. Furthering their capacity for agency is a critical step for aboriginal peoples. To begin with, agency empowers, and in so doing enhances identity and the concrete embodiment of 'nationhood'. Herein lies the promise of and the prospect for replacing the miseries created by dependency on the 'patron' state with an assured dignity rooted in the knowledge of and experience with self-directed livelihoods. Here also is found a common ground wherein an alliance of aboriginal and non-aboriginal small boat fishing peoples offers tremendous promise for achieving sustainable fisheries and fisheries livelihoods.

References

Apostle, Richard, Barret, Gene, Holm, Petter, Jentoft, Svein, Mazany, Leigh, McCay, Bonnie, and Mikalsen, Knut: *Community, State, and Market on the North Atlantic Rim. Challenges to Moderniy in the Fisheries*. Toronto: Toronto University Press 1998.

Asch, Michael: *Home and Native Land: Aboriginal Rights and the Canadian Constitution*. Toronto: Methuen Press, 1984.

Bjørklund, Ivar (ed.): *Norsk ressursforvaltning og samiske rettighetsforhol: Om statlig styring, allmenningens tragedie og lokale sedvaner i Sápmi*. Ad Notam Gyldendal, 1999.

Bugge, Hans Christan: 'Human Rights and Resource Management – An Overview'. Berge, Erling and Stenseth, Nils Christian (eds.), *Law and the Governance of Renewable Resources, Studies from Northern Europe and Africa*. Oakland: ICS Press, 1998, pp. 93-123.

Canada: The Indian Act. Ottawa: Government of Canada Printer, 1985

Chronicle-Herald: 'DFO crackdown 'just a mess'', October 22 1999, p. A4. (1999a)

Chronicle-Herald: 'Off-reserve natives threaten to sue feds', October 22 1999, p. A4. (1999b)

Chronicle-Herald: 2000a 'Fisherman suing over loss of job: West Pubnico man blames buy-back program', September 22 2000, p. A10. (2000a)

Chronicle-Herald: 'Marshall leads fishing rights march', September 29 2000, p. A1-2. (2000b)

Chronicle-Herald: 'Natives threat to Liverpool lobster stocks – fishermen', October 29 2000, p. A7. (2000c)

Chronicle-Herald: 'Pressure on for national fisheries plan', January 30 2001, p. A4. (2001a)

Chronicle-Herald: 'Chief unimpressed by aid offer', January 31 2001, p. A4. (2001b)

Chronicle-Herald: 'Treaty deals preferred – chiefs', February 1 2001, p. A4. (2001c)

Chronicle-Herald: 'Cancel Acadia band's licenses, lobstermen say', February 13 2001, p. A3. (2001d)

Chronicle-Herald: 'Give commercial fishermen more say – Liberal MP', February 13 2001, p. A3. (2001e)

Chronicle-Herald: 'Call to cancel lobster licenses frustrates band', February 17 2001, p. A6. (2001f)

Chronicle-Herald: 'Municipalities, fishing industry team up in suit against band', February 17 2001, p. A6. (2001g)

Coon Come, Chief Matthew: 'We have a dream too', Comment, *The Globe and Mail*, January 31 2001, p. A13.

Davis, Anthony: 'Barbed Wire and Bandwagons: A Comment on ITQ Fisheries Management.' Reviews in Fish Biology and Fisheries 6(1), 1996, pp. 97-109.

Davis, Anthony and Bailey, Conner: 'Common in Custom, Uncommon in Advantage: Common Property, Local Elites and Alternative Approaches to Fisheries Management. 'Society and Natural Resources, 9, 1996, pp. 252-265.

Davis, Anthony and MacInnes, Daniel: "'Representational Management or Management of Representation?' The Place of Fishers in Atlantic Canadian Fisheries Management". Fisheries Resource Utilization and Policy, Proceedings of the 1st World Congress of Fisheries, Theme 2, New Delhi: Oxford & IBH Publishing Co.Pvt.Ltd., 1996, pp. 317-333.

Dewees, Christopher: 'Fisheries for Profits: New Zealand Fishing Industry Changes for 'Pakeha' and Maori with Individual Transferable Quotas.' In Pálsson, Gísli and Pétursdttir, Gudrún (eds.): Social Implications of Quota Systems in Fisheries. Copehagen: Nordoci Council of Ministers. Tema Nord Fisheries, 1997, pp. 91-107.

Gayim, Eyassu: The UN Draft Declaration on Indigenous Peoples, Assessment of the Draft Prepared by the Working Group on Indigenous Populations. Rovaniemi: University of Lapland's Printing Services, 1994.

Globe and Mail: 'Ottawa seeking deal to limit native fishing', October 2 1999, p. A3. (1999a)

Globe and Mail: 'Violence escalates in conflict over fishery', October 6 1999, p.A3. (1999b)

Globe and Mail: 'Natives accuse Ottawa of issuing ultimatum', October 6 1999, p. A3. (1999c)

Globe and Mail: 'Lobster supply at risk: biologist', October 7 1999, p. A8. (1999d)

Globe and Mail: 'Opening of lobster fishery raises fears that value of licenses will plummet', October 7 1999, p. A8. (1999e)

Globe and Mail: 'Even experts can't agree on lobsters', October 11 1999, p. A4. (1999f)

Globe and Mail: '25 charged in dispute over fishery', October 13 1999, p. A3. (1999g)

Globe and Mail: 'Fisheries seizes native lobster traps', October 23 1999, p. A6. (1999h)

Globe and Mail: 'Mi'kmaq chase fisheries vessels', September 26 2000, p. A7. (2000a)

Globe and Mail: 'Mi'kmaq take fisheries to court: Nova Scotia band wants injunction to stop federal officers from seizing lobster traps', October 8 2000, p. A5. (2000b)

Globe and Mail: 'Fear driving fishery strategy, AFN chief says', January 30 2001, p. A7.

Hollingsworth, C.E. (guest ed.): Ecosystem Effects of Fishing. ICES Journal of Marine Science, Symposium Edition, 2000. 57(3).

Hutchings, Jeffrey A.: 'Collapse and recovery of marine fishes', Nature, 406, 2000, pp. 882-885

Indian and Eskimo Association of Canada: Native Rights in Canada. Ottawa: Indian and Eskimo Association of Canada, 1972.

Jentoft, Svein: Dangling Lines: The Fisheries Crisis and the Future of Coastal Communities: The Norwegian Experience. St. John's: ISER Press, 1993.

Jentoft, Svein: Commons in a Cold Climate: Coastal Fisheries and Reindeer Pastoralism in North Norway: The Co-management Approach, Man and The Biosphere Series. Casterton Hall; The Parthenon Publishing Group, 1998.

Jentoft, Svein and Karlsen, Geir Runar: 'Saami Fisheries, Quota Management and the Rights Issue.' In Pálsson, Gísli and Pétursdóttir, Gudrun (eds.): Social Implications of Quota Systems in Fisheries. Copenhagen: Nordic Council of Ministers, Tema Nord Fisheries, 1997, pp. 14-65.

Jull, Peter: A Sea Change: Overseas Indigenous-Government Relations in the Coastal Zone. A Report to the Resource Assessment Commission, Commonwealth of Australia, Canberra, 1993.

Maurstad, Anita: Customs in Commons - Commons in Court. Paper presented at the Fifth Conference of the International Association for the Study of Common Property. Bodø: May 24-28 1995.

McGoodwin, James: *Crisis in the World's Fisheries: People, Problems and Policies*. Stanford: Stanford University Press, 1990.

NOU – Norges offentlige utredninger: *Naturgrunnlaget for samisk kultur*. Oslo: Statens forvaltningstjeneste, Staens trykning, 1997:4

Rio Declaration, Agenda 21: Report of the United Nations Conference on Environment and Development, Rio de Janeiro 3-14 June 1992. Agenda 21 A/Conf. 151/26.)

Samisk fiskeriutvalg: Instilling til Fiskeridepartementet. Oslo, 1997.

Sharp, Andrew: *Justice and the Maori* (2nd. ed.) Auckland: Oxford University Press, 1997.

Smith, Eivind: 'Om "samerettigheter" og rettsvern'. Tidsskrift for Rettsvitenskap, 3/1986, pp.338-364.

Stevens, Stan (ed.): *Conservation Through Cultural Survival: Indigenous Peoples and Protected Areas*. Washington D.C., Island Press 1997.

Storslett, Einar: *Samiske fiskerier mot år 2000*. Rapport fra prosjektet Handlingsplan for gjennomføring av samisk fiskerisone. Karasjok: Sametinget, 1995.

Sunday Herald: 'Paul warns talks no panacea', February 11 2001, p. A4.

Svensson, Tom G. (ed.): *On Customary Law and the Saami Rights Process in Norway*. Proceedings from a Conference at the University of Tromso, Senter for samiske studier, Skriftserie – Nr. 8, Tromso, Norway, 1999.

Waitangi Tribunal: *Report of the Waitangi Tribunal on the Muriwhenua Fishing Claim*. Department of Justice, Wellington, New Zealand, 1988.

'Future challenges for the Saami Parliament.' Talk manuscript. Saami Parliament fisheries seminar, Karasjok, February 21, 2001.

Ward, James and Augustine, Lloyd: Draft for the Esgenoopotitj First Nation (EFN) Fishery Act. (manuscript available at (http://www.web.net/nben/ffa/00/actF)). (2000a)

Ward, James and Augustine, Lloyd: Draft for EFN Management Plan. (manuscript available at (http://www.web.net/nben/ffa/00/actF)). (2000b)

Wiber, Melanie G. and Kennedy, Julia: 'Impossible Dreams: Reforming Fisheries Management in the Canadian Maritimes after the Marshall Decision' (forthcoming from *Law and Anthropology*) (2001)

The Land

CHAPTER 11

Encroaching Upon Indigenous Land: Nicaragua and the 'Dry Canal'

María Luisa Acosta[1]

Introduction

Like the majority of Latin American states, Nicaragua has traditionally sought to achieve a sense of homogeneity in its population. In consequence, indigenous peoples and ethnic communities have been largely ignored. In Nicaragua this started to change in 1983, when the Organization of American States' Inter-American Commission on Human Rights expressed support for the Miskito people's rights in a report presented to the Nicaraguan government (OAS, 1983). This happened in the aftermath of a fierce conflict between the Sandinista régime in power and the indigenous peoples of the Atlantic coast. In 1987, this resulted in a constitutional reform that led to the establishment of the two autonomous regions of the Atlantic coast – *La Región Autónoma Atlántico Norte* (RAAN) and *La Región Autónoma Atlántico Sur* (RAAS).

The reform gave Nicaragua the first and one of the most progressive indigenous rights' régimes in Latin America. However, despite the constitutional recognition of indigenous rights and the official creation of a régime of multiracial and regional autonomy, the state has not yet created the legal and administrative mechanisms that are necessary for their effective implementation.

The actual situation of Nicaragua's indigenous peoples is therefore not very different from the one that existed during the Somoza régime, which was in power until it was toppled by the Sandinist revolution in 1979. The Somoza government encouraged western peasant farmers to move to the Atlantic coast, where land was supposedly free and idle – but in reality was indigenous land. In the absence of any political resolve by subsequent régimes to implement and enforce the law that was enacted two decades ago, the encroachment of indigenous land by *mestizo* peasant settlers and others has continued to this day, despite vociferous opposition by the affected indigenous and ethnic communities. The case of the Dry Canal, which is the focus of this chapter, falls squarely within the old pattern.

---

[1] The author is a lawyer and attorney on behalf of the Monkey Point Community and the Rama People in the Dry Canal case.

Indigenous Land Rights

Culturally, there has always been a disparity between Nicaragua's Pacific and Atlantic regions. While the Spanish colonization evolved in the west, the east remained an area the conquerors could never even penetrate, much less colonize. Until 1894, when the Atlantic province was integrated into the Nicaraguan state, the indigenous (Miskito, Mayagna and Rama) and ethnic (Creole and Garifuna) peoples who lived here were under the political and economic influence of the British Empire. This set the stage for a dominant western political class, mostly made up of Catholic, Spanish-speaking *mestizos,* who basically regarded the Atlantic Coast as a natural resource reservoir of the state. However, despite the dominance of the western part and Spanish *mestizo* culture, the indigenous peoples of Nicaragua's Atlantic region have to this day preserved their traditional possession of land, their internal forms of organization, their view of the world and their place within it and, to a varying extent, their aboriginal languages.

Since 1905, some 185,000 hectares of indigenous land in the Atlantic region have been titled, representing approximately ten per cent of the land demanded and occupied by the indigenous communities (Roldán, 2002). The limited titling of indigenous land has reinforced the discriminatory practices that tend to dispossess the indigenous and ethnic communities of their traditional lands. Notably, Nicaragua has not titled land for the specific purpose of indigenous tenure. Rather, the titling of indigenous land was always meant to facilitate agrarian reform in favor of immigrating peasants – particularly in times of political campaign – and war veterans, to pacify the area; titling was also used to create national parks and natural reserves, and in the granting of logging concessions (Acosta, 1998). This has created the current situation, where, although any citizen may solicit a Civil District Judge to grant a provisional title for the land that they have occupied for one year, peasants farmers are subject to agrarian reform after three years of land occupation. And although the government alleges that the Office of Rural Titling (OTR) has the legal authority to designate land to the indigenous and ethnic communities, not one of them has obtained a single title for their traditional land over the past decade (Hales et.al.,1998). The few titles granted to indigenous peoples of the Atlantic Coast were awarded at the beginning of the twentieth century, as a result of the Harrison-Altamirano treaty between Nicaragua and Great Britain.

It should be stressed that the existence of a pertinent legal framework does not seem to be the problem in Nicaragua. Article 107 of the constitution of 1987 establishes that a special law must be created to regulate indigenous land. The article states:

The agrarian reform shall eliminate any form of exploitation of farmers, and of indigenous communities in this country. It will promote the forms of property compatible with the economic and social objectives of this nation, established in this constitution. The land property régime of indigenous communities shall be regulated according to the law of the matter.

Also, Article 31 of the Law of Agrarian Reform, which has been in force since 1981[2], acknowledges that:

The State may dispose of a quantity of land, as necessary, so that the Miskito, Sumo and Rama can work individually and collectively, so that they benefit from their natural resources, with the objective that their populations can improve their living standards, and also contribute to the social and economic development of the Nicaraguan nation.

In reality, however, this article has not provided the means for the indigenous peoples to secure effective guarantees from any of the government agencies in charge of applying these rules, such as the Ministry of Agricultural Development and Agrarian Reform (MIDINRA), the Nicaraguan Institute of Agrarian Reform (INRA) and the OTR. The state also manifests a lack of political will in failing to support the important initiative of self-demarcation carried out in the territories of Rio Wanky or Coco and Bocay, in the BOSAWAS[3] biosphere reserve (Howard, 1996). This initiative comprised a process of participation, inter-communal negotiations, documentation of traditional land use, the creation of management plans and the mapping of territories – maps that were validated by the Regional Council of the Northern Atlantic Region and also by the *Ministerio del Ambiente y los Recursos Naturales de Nicaragua* (MARENA) itself (Stock, et.al., 2000). Nevertheless, the central government refused to issue titles for these territories.

In the majority of indigenous land rights' cases, the state has imposed agrarian criteria that are designed to benefit farmers, thus disenfranchising indigenous peoples. For instance, the agrarian reform ignores the concept of collective land possession and the concept of territory held by indigenous peoples, which they apply to rivers, the sea and forests in an integral fashion. For the indigenous peoples, their native soil is forest land and does not serve any agricultural function.

By comparison, countries such as Brazil and Colombia have demarcated large tracts of land for indigenous peoples, based on criteria that respect their

---

[2]   Decree No. 782, of July 19. 1981, *Law of Agrarian Reform.*

[3]   The Biosphere Reserve of BOSAWAS has an extension of 2,042,536 hectares, approximately 14% of the nation's territory. In it live 14,000 Miskitos and 6,500 Mayagnas (Sumos).

view of the world and their place within it, and which are different to those applied in agrarian reform (CEREC, 1993). In contrast, Nicaragua has no clear
policy regarding communal land property rights for indigenous and ethnic
peoples. Consequently, and in stark contrast to the progressive language of the
constitution, there are no effective mechanisms to end the discrimination and
human rights violations that the encroachment of indigenous lands represents.
A sad illustration of this fact is the Dry Canal affair, to which I shall now turn.

The Dry Canal

Canal Interoceánico de Nicaragua (CINN) [Nicaraguan Inter-Oceanic Canal]
is a consortium formed by international investors and foreign port, shipping
and construction companies, in co-operation with the Nicaraguan government.
The plan of CINN is to build a 'Dry Canal', to transport ship containers from
coast to coast by rail. The project requires the construction of free zones and
new ports on the Atlantic coast (in Monkey Point community) and the Pacific
coast (in Pie Grande), as well as a 375 km railway and a fenced area 500 metres
wide along the track. This mega-project also includes the creation of a land port
(for the land deposit of containers) on each coast (PBDET, 1996).

In July 1999, President Arnoldo Alemàn introduced a bill to the National Assembly that contained the contract of concession already negotiated between his
government and CINN. The communities owning the land where the 'canal' was
intended had not been notified, consulted or taken into account in any of the prior
negotiations between the two parties. The leaders of the affected communities
– the multi-ethnic (Creole and Rama) Monkey Point and the indigenous Rama
communities in the Bluefields municipality – presented an Appeal for Legal
Protection to the Nicaraguan President and to the Attorney General who, by
law, was required to sign the contract. In their appeal the communities demanded to be informed and consulted about the project, and they insisted that a
negotiation process should be set in train, to allow them to state their position.

Monkey Point is located 47 km south of the city of Bluefields (see map).
The first Creoles arrived here more than a century ago and established their
homes next to the Rama inhabitants, with whom they have since lived as close
neighbors. The Rama people[4] are descendants of the Chibcha Tribes. Today
they speak Creole English, while some have preserved their Rama language

---

[4]   The Rama group decreased in population during the eighteenth century. Nevertheless, in
1774 R. Hodgson speaks of "a large tribe of Rama Indians", a number of whom had separated from the others, although they maintained their original customs and language. They
occupied the banks of the Indio River all the way to lands near Lake Nicaragua. Despite
this, by 1841 only 500 Rama were left in Punta Gorda and 80 in Rama Cay in the entire area
between the northern margin of the San Juan River and the southern edges of the Escondido
River, a distance of just over 100 km, […] Two ideas, in part, derive from the combination of
circumstances mentioned above. Firstly, the similarity of many aspects of the material life of

(Collete et.al.,1986). At present they live in the areas of the Coco, Punta de Aguila/Willing Cay, Cane Creek, although their main settlement is Rama Cay, located in the Bluefields Lagoon 15 km south of Bluefields (see map).

The incursions to carry out technical and pre-feasibility studies onsite, and the negotiations regarding the concessionary contracts between the company and the government, have all advanced without the consent or participation of either the Monkey Point community or the Rama people. At no stage during the process have the public officials involved considered the property rights of the communities and their constitutional right to continue enjoying their forests, hunting, fishing and small-scale agriculture, or any other of the autochthonous activities necessary for the very survival of these peoples in their traditional lands. The members of both communities survive on agriculture. They cultivate corn, rice, beans, coconut, breadfruit, bananas, plantains, pejibaye [a form of palm tree whose fruit is used as a substitute for maize], etc., for their own consumption. They hunt deer, armadillos and wild boar with guns, rifles, spears or arrows. In the rivers they fish for shad, moharra, snook, tarpon and drum, and they also fish off their cays and in the sea. In addition they cut timber, but only for their own use, for the construction of their homes and kayaks – their main means of transportation. The economy is oriented towards subsistence and depends exclusively on the communal land and the forest, where the railway will cut through. Infrastructure on this scale will undoubtedly alter the use of the land for these people. It will also, unavoidably, affect the biological diversity and the fragile ecosystems of these tropical forests, thus creating a negative impact on the environment inhabited by these communities.

The main settlement of Monkey Point is precisely the area where the construction of the deep-water port for the canal is planned. The rest of the site, where the canal infrastructure is planned, crosses, divides and isolates the land that the Rama people have always occupied and used. Even though the main settlement of the Rama people is Rama Cay, there are also scattered Rama settlements on the mainland, which will be seriously affected by an infrastructure of CINN's magnitude.

---

the Rama and other aborigine peoples, which reflect a particular adaptation to the geographic environment in which they are to live. Secondly, proven common traits with the other human groups: the extraordinary resistance of their life traditions. If there have been changes, the 'continuity' has been stronger [...] established sites, their sizes and distance from one to another, and other traits, pointed out in investigations from 1974, that date back at least three centuries. According to Romero, 1995: "The Rama were drastically affected by both conquests, the Spanish and the English, and they have suffered the largest loss in population and territory of any indigenous group of the Atlantic Coast. A study places the Rama population at around 1,400. They live south of Bluefields in a small island called Rama Cay and in dispersed settlements on dry land as far south as the bank of the Punta Gorda River, The survival of the Rama is seriously threatened."

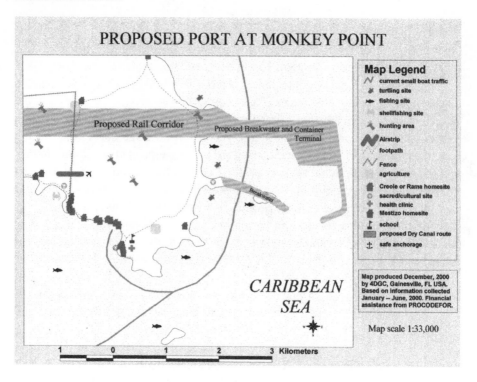

It is important to note that the relationship that the indigenous peoples have with their land is more than just economic and material: it also contains elements of spirituality, culture and religion. The Rama view of the world and their place within in it is not about dominating nature: rather, they attempt to inhabit it as an integrated and harmonic part. For the Rama, therefore, the loss of their territory brings a loss of identity, culture and the possibility of surviving as a distinct people (Yañez, 1998). The CINN mega-project has to be viewed in this perspective. Inevitably, the project will undermine the rights of these communities to their ancestral land and their opportunity to enjoy its fruits in both material and cultural terms.

Constitutional Provision

The actions and omissions claimed in the Appeal for Legal Protection constitute violations of a number of articles in the Political Constitution of Nicaragua. The combined effect of these articles should be to guarantee the indigenous and ethnic communities' property rights and land use, as well as their right to integrity and cultural survival. The wording of the articles cited below is clear enough:

> Art. 5. …The State recognizes the existence of the indigenous peoples, and that they enjoy the rights and duties consigned in the constitution, especially the ones to

maintain and develop their identity and culture, to have their own forms of social organization and to administrate their local affairs, akin to maintaining the communal forms of their land and the cultivation, use and enjoyment of the same, all in conformity to the law...

Art. 89.The State recognizes the communal forms of property of the lands of the communities of the Atlantic Coast. It equally recognizes the fruition, use and enjoyment of the waters and forests of their communal lands.

Article 36 of the State of Autonomy defines "communal property" as "constituted by the lands, waters and forests that have traditionally belonged to the communities of the Atlantic Coast". This article also takes indigenous land out of the commercial domain: it cannot be donated or sold. Nor can it be attached to a sequestration or to a mortgage. This article also states that indigenous land cannot under any circumstances be taken away or abandoned:

> Art. 180. The State guarantees these communities' enjoyment of their natural resources, the effectiveness of their forms of communal property and the free election of their authorities...

These articles of the constitution confirm the *sui generis* régime of communal indigenous land. They also recognize the property rights and management authority of indigenous peoples. Moreover, they confirm the government's commitment to secure these rights effectively. Article 90 of the constitution further underlines the cultural aspects of indigenous rights: the communities of the Atlantic Coast have the right to free expression and to the preservation of their languages, art and culture. It is claimed that the development of their culture and their values enrich the national culture.

Notably, Article 46 of Nicaragua's constitution also incorporates the principal international declarations, conventions and pacts on human rights within the national juridical order, with constitutional status. This implies that the state of Nicaragua has committed itself internationally to observing the right to property of the communal lands belonging to indigenous peoples, and their right not to be discriminated against for reasons of culture or race. Nicaragua has not ratified ILO Convention 169 regarding indigenous and tribal peoples, but has nonetheless participated in its elaboration.

The International Convention on Civil and Political Rights, with its constitutional status within the national juridical order, in conformity with Article 46 of the Constitution, has been applied explicitly to the Miskito and other indigenous peoples of the Atlantic coast of Nicaragua. The Nicaraguan government has also been exposed to pressure from the Organization of American States' (OAS) Inter-American Commission for Human Rights. OAS established that its affiliated states – of which Nicaragua is one – must respect and guarantee the cultural traditions of their indigenous communities with respect to their communal lands. OAS pronounced itself particularly in favour of indigenous peoples' ancestral rights over their lands, and their language and cultural rights, during the conflict with the Sandinista government in the 1980s. OAS required:

> ...special legal protection for the use of their language, the exercise of their religion, and, in general, matters linked to the preservation of their cultural identity. And attached to that, matters linked to the productive organization, which includes, among others, the problem of ancestral and communal lands (OAS, 1983: 78-79).

Consequently, there can scarcely be any doubt that both national and international law – which is referred to here only in part – would support the claims of the affected communities in the case of the Dry Canal. Despite this, the government seems to be fully committed to seeing the project through. This means, in essence, that the Nicaraguan state has given preferential treatment to a private, multinational consortium, at the expense of her indigenous and ethnic peoples. It may be argued, based on a solid legal foundation, that this constitutes open discrimination and a human rights violation.

A complicating factor, however, is that the Monkey Point community does not hold a written land title. Nonetheless, the community has traditionally exercised the right of temporary possession and land occupation, and has co-existed in harmony with the Rama people. Although the Rama people have fourteen royal titles, issued by the Mosquitian Titling Commission (Martínez et.al., 1995) these cover only a small fraction of the areas they have traditionally and historically possessed, and still use. In this instance, the property rights over ancestral and historic land do not rely on the state granting a written title, but on *sui generis* rights that are recognized in Nicaragua's Constitution (Articles 5, 89 and 180). The shared use by two or more ethnic communities or indigenous peoples of one common territory is a frequent form of land use on the Atlantic Coast of Nicaragua. The Creole and Rama populations are also united in their struggle against the CINN project.

Not only does the Dry Canal cut through indigenous communal land, it also intersects the legally protected Biosphere Reserve of south-eastern Nicaragua, which is part of the Atlantic Biological Corridor. The reserve is a responsibility that Nicaragua acquired from the World Bank, which assigned 7.1 million dollars in donations and 35 million dollars in projects complementary to this scheme. The corridor was established to protect the biodiversity and fragile ecosystems of Central America, such as the tropical rainforests of Nicaragua's southern Atlantic region. The Dry Canal will cut right through this area. Thus, there is an inconsistency between the conservationist objectives of the corridor that the state has committed itself to and its ambitions concerning the canal project. Nicaragua has also officially committed itself to adhering to the UN Convention on Biodiversity and to Agenda 21 on popular participation. Therefore, there can be no doubt that Nicaragua, besides its obligations expressed in Articles 60 and 102 of the Constitution, is required to strive to conserve biodiversity and respect the cultural practices and rights of indigenous peoples. What remains is to establish whether the government intends to fulfil these commitments in practice. So far there are few indications that the government intends to do so. The Dry Canal project is certainly a test case.

Request for the Suspension

The leaders of the affected communities who presented the Appeal for Legal Protection respectfully pleaded that Nicaragua's Honorable Supreme Court of Justice should order Dr. Arnoldo Alemán Lacayo and Julio Centeno Gomez to

1. Abstain from continuing a process that would grant a concession and its signing.
2. Initiate a process of dialogue with the ethnic community of Monkey Point and the Rama Indigenous Peoples, if CINN persists in developing its project on the lands of these communities.
3. Employ any other remedy that the Honorable Supreme Court of Justice determines as fair.

On 9 November 1999, the Court of Appeals of the South Atlantic Circumscription in Bluefields denied the Appeal on the following grounds:

> Considering, that the bills produced by any power of the State of the Republic of Nicaragua are processes in the making of the same, that is to say, no law has yet been created, this TRIBUNAL RESOLVES: To completely reject the Processing of this Appeal for being notoriously INADMISSIBLE, all in conformity to the Law of Appeals for Legal Protection in force, Law No. 49 and Law 205, The Law of reform to Articles 6 and 51 of the Law of Appeals for Legal Protection, number 2 of the cited Article 51, published in the journal "La Tribuna" on November 30th 1995.

The community leaders who had filed the appeal were not willing to give up as a result of this rejection. Instead, they re-introduced it as an Appeal of Deed or Complaint, directly before the Supreme Court of Justice of Nicaragua. Here the plaintiffs argued that the Court of Appeal erred in refusing the Appeal for Legal Protection. It took eleven months before the Supreme Court produced a ruling, stating that it would admit the Appeal presented against the President and the Attorney General. In doing so, the Supreme Court decided against the Court of Appeal. For the affected communities, this was clearly a small but important victory.

In January 2001, the claimants also promoted an Incident of Objection, Challenge or Implication against one magistrate member of the Supreme Court of Justice (Justice Guillermo Selva Argüello), demanding that he should be removed from any hearing of the case. Justice Selva was president of the National Assembly's Environment and Natural Resources Commission when the Bill for the approval of the CINN contract was introduced. He also took part in the legislative commission that passed the bill. He had also expressed an opinion in favor of the Dry Canal project in Parliament. When the claimants visited him in his office at the Environment and Natural Resources Commission of the National Assembly, in February 2000, Dr. Selva, then a member of the National Assembly, began by arguing that there are no indigenous peoples in Nicaragua and, besides, that the few who remain do not even pay taxes! He also expressed a firm opinion that the Dry Canal is economically very important for the nation and that it would not be stopped by a group of people. Dr. Selva concluded emphatically that the canal would be realized even if it meant changing the Constitution.[5] In January 2002 the Supreme Court passed judgment and dismissed the objection. A consequence of this decision the Supreme Court passed the Appeal to the Justice Department, so that the Court (which includes Magistrate Selva as one of its members) could hear the matter. Although the period of time granted by law for the Supreme Court to decide on appeals is 45 days, the Justice Department has not yet made a decision.

Civil Society Support

The Dry Canal affair has generated an interesting process of mobilization in the region as a whole. At the same time as embarking on the legal process, the affected communities sought public support, and a number of organizations and institutions have become involved as a result. The communities obtained technical assistance from the Committee of Non-Governmental organizations within the South Atlantic Autonomous Region. Support was also offered by the Center for Human, Citizens' and Autonomic Rights (CEDEHCA), the two universities of the region (Bluefields Indian and Caribbean University – BICU – and the University of the Autonomous Regions of the Nicaraguan Caribbean Coast – URACCAN), as well as the Institute for the Development of Democracy (IPADE), the Center for Investigations and Documentations of the Atlantic Coast (CIDCA), the Alexander Von Humboldt Center, The Center of Legal Assistance to Indigenous Peoples (CALPI) and the International Human Rights Law Group (Law Group). All this contributed to national and international attention and widespread media coverage.

To begin with, regional authorities ignored the Bill of Concession before the National Assembly, to say nothing of the matters it pertained to. Community leaders and the Support Commission therefore prepared radio programs and

---

5   "Indigenous people appeal against the Dry Canal." *The New Daily*, 17 February 2000; a report on the lobbying trip undertaken by the Monkey Point ethnical community and the Rama Indigenous People in Managua from 15 to 17 February 2000.

articles that were published in Nicaragua's major newspapers, opinion fora, etc., in order to inform regional authorities and the people on the coast about the project and the exclusion of which they had been made victim. When the Council and the Autonomous Regional Government of the RAAS and the Bluefields municipality realized that they had also been left out, they drafted resolutions demanding that representatives of the Regional Council and Government, the municipalities of Rama, Bluefields, Nueva Guinea, and representatives of the Monkey Point and Rama people should be included in a "Multi-Sectoral Commission" that the national government had organized to study and negotiate the CINN concession. The National Assembly accepted this and voted to include representatives of the Monkey Point Community and the Rama People as members of the Multi-Sectoral Commission. The inclusion of these representatives on the commission occurred only after intense lobbying, the presentation of an Appeal for Legal Protection and a Petition for Precautionary Measures before the Inter-American Commission for Human Rights of the Organization of American States (OAS) in 2000.[6] Although Parliament issued a decree, saying that the communities of Monkey Point and the Rama should be allowed to take part in the Multi-Sectoral Commission, but simultaneously giving the Ministry of Transportation and Infrastructure the power to grant the exploration concession to CINN "without further ado". In response to this, the communities presented an Action of Unconstitutionality against the President of the National Assembly and President of the Republic of Nicaragua. They also stepped forward to occupy their only seat among the seventeen public official members of the Multi-Sectoral Commission.[7]

The Multi-Sectoral Commission initiated meetings at the office of the Minister of Transportation and Infrastructure; in August 2001 these culminated with the signing of the Basic Regulations for the CINN project. The Basic Regulations regulate the terms of feasibility and final design, and thus also the conditions of the concession for the construction, operation and exploitation of the Dry Canal project. The participation of the communities of Monkey Point and the Rama in the Commission resulted in a consensus in Articles 18 and 28 of the Basic Regulations, expressed as follows:

---

[6] The ethnic community of Monkey Point and the Rama Indigenous People, in conjunction with their legal advisors from the Center of Legal Assistance for Indigenous Peoples (CALPI), and in coordination with the International Human Rights Law Group (IHRLG), presented on 11 May 2000, before the Inter-America Human Rights Commission (IHRC), a request for the adoption of urgent precautionary measures for the Communities of Monkey Point and the Rama People, in the hope of avoiding irreparable damage to the rights of these indigenous peoples, with respect to the violations of their rights in negotiations by CINN with the State relating to the law of concession concerning the Dry Canal. In September 2001, the IHRC presented a petition requesting information from the Nicaraguan chancellor about the evolution of the concessionary project for the Dry Canal, without the participation of the ethnic community of Monkey Point and the Rama Indigenous People, whose lands would be affected. The chancellor's office asked for a proroga-

Art. 18. In the case of the land property of the communities of the Autonomous Regions of the South Atlantic, due to their special status, the State is committed to facilitate the demarcation of the traditional communal lands of Monkey Point and the Rama People. For its part, CINN, within its capacities and criteria, is committed to not undermining the territorial aspirations of the communities affected. Such a demarcation of lands should be performed based on the historic rights of the communities and within the legal framework in force.

The human, constitutional and environmental rights of the Monkey Point and the Rama People shall be respected in the entire negotiation process between the communities, the State and CINN, in granting the concession, the construction period, final design, the beginning of the operations of the project and during the exploitation of the inter-oceanic railway of Nicaragua.

Thus, the State and CINN commit themselves to not undermining the access of the Monkey Point Community and the Rama People to their natural resources outside the area of the project, within the Rama territory, that are necessary for their subsistence as a people.

Art. 28. The State shall timeously design a plan for the relocation, socio-economic treatment and actions of repair and mitigation for the socio-environmental aspects directed to the areas and social sectors that are displaced and affected by the project, including the indigenous communities and ethnic groups, taking into account the special characteristics of these peoples and their relationship with their land, environment and the natural resources on which they depend.

The Basic Regulations also set the standards for the process and negotiation of future compensation that would be appropriate to the different parties affected by CINN's construction in the different jurisdictions and lands. However, another key part of the process established by the Ministry of Environment and Natural Resources (MARENA) is the reference terms for the environmental studies in connection with the Dry Canal project. Here, too, the representatives of Monkey Point and the Rama people plan to continue their active participation to prevent their natural resources from being affected.

---

tion to respond. At present, the communities are preparing a formal petition before the IHRC for the opening of a process of amicable solution between the State and the communities.

[7] The Multi-Sectoral Commission is presided over by the Minister of Transportation and Infrastructure (MTI) and is made up of delegates from the Ministries of The Environment and Natural Resources (MARENA), Foreign Relations, Development, Industry and Commerce (MIFIC); The Attorney General; The Nicaraguan Institute of Territorial Studies (INETER); also two members from the Transportation, Energy and Construction Commissions, who are representatives from the Environment and Natural Resources Commission, both of which form part of the National Assembly; The Regional Council of the Autonomous Region of the South Atlantic (RAAS); and one representative from the 28 mayors of the municipalities through which the project is supposed to pass, and the mayors of Tola and Bluefields.

The consensus expressed in these two articles is indeed remarkable. But as the indigenous people of Nicaragua know well, from experience, words on paper do not always make much of a difference. They are aware that process has barely begun. The work of the Multi-Sectoral Commission will culminate in a technical evaluation report of the studies presented by CINN, which are to be performed within three years. Once the studies have been concluded and approved, the commission will draft the final concession contract that will later be presented to the National Assembly for consideration. However, there is still a need to create a Multi-Sectoral Commission to study the proposals of another company interested in building the dry canal, the company *Servicio Intermodal de Transporte Global*, Sit/Global.[8]

Conclusion

It is important to emphasize that this is the first time that traditional indigenous community leaders have been permitted by law to participate in a governmental commission at such a high level, where all the other members are government representatives. This is setting a very important precedent in the state's recognition of the rights of the indigenous and ethnic communities. The Monkey Point Rama and Creole inhabitants, and the Rama of other communities, are now working on the documentation of their historic land claims. They are also working to achieve the demarcation of the same as a means of consolidating their rights. In pursuing their legal rights against the state in Nicaragua they have demonstrated extraordinary perseverance. Using the legal system in a country like Nicaragua, with its incipient rule of law tradition, where legal norms are most of the time merely desiderata, is a daring effort. It is also obvious that without the combined support of a number of organizations, and public backing, this case would have been lost. Here, perhaps, is a lesson for other indigenous peoples in their struggle for rights: you need to build coalitions with non-governmental organizations, universities and the media. Alone, the prospects of succeeding in making your claims heard are slim.

Despite the systematic discrimination against indigenous and ethnic communities in Nicaragua, the participation, even though limited, obtained by the ethnic community of Monkey Point and the Rama Indigenous People in the Multi-Sectoral Commission creates an important precedent, hope and expectancy, for them and for society as a whole in Nicaragua.

---

[8] The National Assembly, in issuing Decree AN No. 2879 on 28 March 2001, authorized the concession of exploration and establishing the conditions for the granting of a concession for the construction, operation and exploitation of an inter-oceanic railway in favor of Sit/Global. The decree also mandated that the communities of Monkey Point and the Rama People form part of the other Multi-Sectoral Commission, which will draft a technical evaluation of the studies presented by the company and will also draft the concession contract. This Decree does not contemplate the elaboration of basic regulations, as does the Decree AN No. 2878 issued for CINN. The commission has not yet started this work.

References

Acosta. Maria L.: *El Estado y la Tierra Indígena en las Regiones Autónomas: El Caso de la Comunidad Mayagna de Awas Tingni.* Indigenous Affairs. Working Group on Indigenous Affairs. IWGIA. No. 4. October- November-December 1998.

CEREC. *Reconocimiento y Demarcación de Territorios Indígenas en la Amazonia-La experiencia de los países de la región-* Serie Amerindia No. 4. Bogotá, Colombia 1993.

Charles R. Hales, Edmund T. Gordon and Galio Gurdian: *General Diagnosis of the Land Tenure in the Indigenous Communities of the Atlantic Coast of Nicaragua.* Central American and Caribbean Research Council (CACRC). Final Report (Consultation No. 084-96) : Austin, Texas; Bluefields and Puerto Cabezas, Nicaragua. Executive Report. Pages 28 and 29, 1998.

Collete, G. et al. *The Rama Language Survives.* In WANI: Magazine of the Nicaraguan Caribbean. Managua, Nicaragua, No. 4, June-September 1986.

Howard, Sarah: *Autonomía y Derechos Territoriales de los Sumos en BOSAWAS: El Caso de Sikilta* in WANI, magazine of the Nicaraguan Caribbean. No. 18. CIDCA-UCA. January-April, 1996.

Martínez, P. Et al. *Listado de Propiedades de las Comunidades Indígenas de las Regiones Autónomas,* IPADE, Managua, Nicaragua, 1995.

OAS: Report on Human Rights of a Nicaraguan Population Sector of Miskito Origin, OAS/Ser.L/V/II/.62 doc. 10 rev. 3, November 20th 1983.

PBDET. Reference Terms of the Inter-Oceanic Project of Ports and Railways of Nicaragua, for the presentation to the Government of Nicaragua, October 16th 1996. Page 1.

Roldán. Roque: *La Demarcación de Tierras en la Costa en el Contexto Latinoamericano* in WANI, journal of the Nicaraguan Caribbean. No.28. CIDCA-UCA. January-March, Pages 11 and 12, 2002.

Romero V., G. (1995). *The Societies in the Nicaraguan Atlantic Coast in the XVII and XVIII Centuries,* Cultural Promotion Fund, BANIC, Pages 270, 272, 1995.

Stock et al: *El activismo ecológico indígena en Nicaragua: Demarcación y Legalización de tierra Indígenas en BOSAWAS.* in WANI, magazine of the Nicaraguan Caribbean. No. 25. CIDCA-UCA, December 2000.

Yañez, C. *Nosotros y los Otros: Avances en la afirmación de los derechos de los pueblos indígenas amazónicos. Defense of the People.* Lima, Peru. August 1998.

CHAPTER 12

Sami Reindeer Management in Norway: Modernization Challenges and Conflicting Strategies. Reflections Upon the Co-management Alternative

Jan Åge Riseth

Introduction

On a general level, the title of this contribution reflects that modernization as a process, or number of processes, almost inevitably changes the basic conditions of people's lives and thus forces people to change their economic adaptation. Furthermore, it leads to the question: how should the pressure for change be met? Here, governmental authorities and indigenous groups and NGOs often choose different, and to some extent conflicting, strategies. Currently *co-management* is often considered to be a compromise between different conflicting strategies, as well as a solution to governing problems (cf. Jentoft 1998 and Berkes 2002). I shall reflect upon the potential of this option, using experiences from modern Sami reindeer management in Norway as a basis.

The Sami are the indigenous people of northern and middle Fennoscandia,[1] who are now an ethnic minority in four nation-states: Norway, Sweden, Finland, and Russia. Reindeer have been an important source of livelihood since prehistoric times, and the reindeer industry is still considered important for the sustenance of Sami culture. Further reindeer management covers most of middle and northern Norway, as well as considerable parts of the three other countries mentioned.

From the last part of the nineteenth century, Sami reindeer management in the twin kingdom of Norway-Sweden was exposed to a government ideology of social Darwinism that claimed that the herders' needs should give way when they conflicted with those of advancing non-Sami agricultural settlers. The preparation of the Norwegian Act of Reindeer Herd Management of 1933, which remained in force until 1979, was in actual fact based upon the idea of reindeer pastoralism as a dying way of life. However, reindeer management proved very vital, though the governmental policy towards Sami culture was

---

[1] This geographical term encompasses the northernmost regions of Norway (Nordland, Troms and Finnmark), Sweden (Norrbotten) and Finland (Lapland). *Nordkalotten* is the widely-used Norwegian equivalent.

generally repressive right up until the 1960s. Moreover, changes in society during the last part of the twentieth century suggest that Sami reindeer management encountered a complex set of challenges. I shall focus on a few aspects of these challenges, and the strategies implemented by Sami and governmental parties, with a focus on co-management.

Modernization Challenges

During the period 1960-1990 reindeer management experienced major technological, economical and political changes. The production system changed from subsistence pastoralism to a motorized and market-oriented industry, moving away from a near-complete dependence on animal and human muscle power to a high degree of dependence on motorized vehicles. In addition, market integration involved specialization in meat production, as well as a high level of purchase of consumer goods and means of production. At the same time, the Sami society came under the 'protection' of the modern welfare state giving access to extended schooling, housing, health care and social security. Politically, the step was taken from a limited civil servant policy to integration into a co-management system, giving industry representatives considerable influence over public sector policy. In short, a traditional livelihood encountered modernity at a high speed. This became a serious challenge for Sami communities and resource management.

Some of the processes involved started about a century ago, but the most important changes took place during the final decades of the twentieth century. In the late 1950s, Ørnulv Vorren, currently Professor Emeritus in Ethnography at the University of Tromsø, made a great survey of reindeer nomadism in Finnmark (Vorren 1962). In a lecture after the publication he focused on the importance of these changes and development processes, as follows:

- more extensive management (reduced man/animal contact)
- change from subsistence towards a money-based economy
- sedentarization (gradual change towards fixed settlement)
- change from an integrated way of life towards an occupation (reduced contact between family and herd)
- increased use of modern technology (Vorren 1964)

He concluded with this statement:

> The old traditional form of reindeer management, and its whole economic pattern, is ruptured. The consequences should be taken, and a new system adapted to modern economy and life form should be advanced. (Vorren 1964) [my translation JÅR]

230

This quotation states that a *revolution in production form* is going on, and also advances the view that reindeer management should be somehow re-organized. Motorization, which was probably the most fundamental change, was at that time (1964) just underway. Before we discuss the effect of these changes, let us look at traditional reindeer management, in order to identify some basic dilemmas and how they have traditionally been solved.

Traditional Reindeer Management

Robert Paine (1964) stated that traditional Sami reindeer management builds on three basic production factors, *land, herd* and *personnel*, all requiring some degree of internal balance between them. (1) Land provides *seasonally* specified nutritious and behavioural requirements constituting an *annual cycle*. Ideal winter pastures, for example, are found in dry continental areas, open or woodland, with access to arboreal or ground lichens, the latter under light snowcover, while good summer pastures are located in nutritious mountain areas. (2) The herd consists of animals of the species *Rangifer tarandus*, having the specific characteristics (cf. Syroechkovskii, 1995) of *excellent physical condition* (making long migration routes possible), *rapid maturity,* and the *ability to feed on lichens*. (3) The personnel are members of an *indigenous people* with an *ancient culture*, with reindeer as a central element, who live in a *band-organized* and *acephalous society* (*siida*). These characteristics imply a number of challenges and dilemmas, of which a number are summed up in Table 1.

Table 1. Challenges and Dilemmas in Traditional Sami Reindeer Management.

ECOLOGICAL	CHALLENGE	DILEMMAS	**GOVERNING ELEMENTS**
LEVEL	To have *sufficient* and *productive* Land	Land *access* vs. Land *protection*	Property Rights – External and Internal
LAND	Herd control in a PRODUCTION SYSTEM	Intensive vs. Extensive Utilization (Beach 1981)	Two Domains: Herding and husbandry (Paine 1964)
HERD	To live off the Land (ECONOMY)	To stay in business (subsistence)	Individually: Income and Cost Societal: *Regulatory Principles* (Douglas 1980)

There is a double challenge concerning the land required for reindeer management: not only maintaining access to sufficient land all year round, but also keeping the land productive by avoiding over-grazing. The threats are thus both *external* and *internal*, and are connected to property rights systems. This means that those property rights which provide protection against encroachment by other industries, etc. are necessary, but they are not sufficient in themselves to secure the land required. They need to be accompanied by a system of internal rights and regulations, in order to ensure sustainability.

The herd is controlled by means of a production system, where the man-animal contact can be close (intensive utilization) or distant (extensive utilization). The distinction between the domains of herding and husbandry is also important (Paine 1964). *Herding* is the collective work with a *siida* group herd out in the wild, while *husbandry* is the household work with a single animal (calf marking, castration, slaughtering, etc.) to realize its production potential. The potential contradiction between individual and collective interests require overall societal devices as a system of checks and balances. In the traditional acephalous society, the regulatory principles may be specified as shown in Table 2 (cf. Riseth 2000):

Table 2. Regulatory Principles of the Sami Herding Society

Principle 1	The autonomy of the husbander; *isit*
Principle 2	The social bonds of the extensive kinship system; *maadtoe*
Principle 3	Partnership and *siida* solidarity
Principle 4	Dialogue and consensus
Principle 5	Responsibility towards the land and the spirits

Briefly, these principles may be explained as follows. One axiom of the culture is that all husbanders are their own masters (Paine 1970: 55). In addition, there is a network of mutual obligations through genetic and social kinship (Pehrson 1964, Kappfjell 1991). The solidarity between *siida* partners can often be stronger than the solidarity between siblings (Meløy 1997). Unanimity is preferred for collective choice decisions and much energy is invested in increasing support for decisions being taken (Riseth 2000). Coming to terms with the land is important (Oskal 1995) and supernatural beings can act if necessary: if the herders do not pay attention, the culture does (Nergård 1996). This means, for example, that if a herder has pitched camp for the night in the middle of a common migration route, traditional spirits will leave him restless during the night. Modern people would probably give a psychological explanation to this, but more importantly, the functioning of this mechanism is dependent on keeping intact the cultural belief in these supernatural beings.

As far as this traditional regulation system is concerned, it should be noted that the collective forces at group (*siida*) level do not seem particularly strong. However, *the historical record is that the internal system has been functioning well for centuries and that the problems faced by the herders have had external causes*. It is obvious that modernization has magnified both external and internal pressures.

Modernization Implications

In (2) above we pointed to motorization as a far-reaching process of change. The expanding use of herding technology, such as snowmobiles, from the mid-1960s, and all-terrain vehicles (ATVs) during the 1980s, had two major implications: (1) an enormous increase in the herders' potential for control, and (2) an explosion in monetary costs to cover the investment in and operation of the new technology. On the top of this came the costs of sedentarization and the whole range of civilization goods. For the herders, this led to a potential cost/income squeeze: how could the costs be covered? The obvious apparent answer was to increase the size of the herd. In other words, the *subsistence minimum* (cf. Beach, 1981) of reindeer management increased, creating the need for more land. We shall return to the resource adaptation implications of this in the section concerned with resource adaptation and strategies.

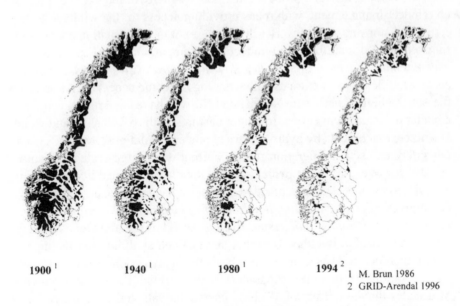

1900 [1]   1940 [1]   1980 [1]   1994 [2] 1 M. Brun 1986
                                                              2 GRID-Arendal 1996

Figure 1. Fragmention. Land area more than five kilometres from roads. Source: GRID-Arendal (1996) in Norwegian Reindeer Husbandry Administration *(1998).*

On the other hand, developments in society at large were making land more scarce as a resource. Land requirements for reindeer management are crucially very specific for each sub-season during the annual cycle, and the land use is rather extensive. Rutting areas and calving areas, for example, are each used for only a few weeks per year, but are both critically important for the annual increment and production. As a result of the repressive governmental policy mentioned in the introduction, *Sami property rights are weak, implying that reindeer management has had little protection against competing land-use.* During the twentieth century, modernization in the surrounding societies included encroachments that created *land fragmentation.* This is illustrated by the time series maps in Figure 1, which depict the gradual reduction of so-called "qualified wilderness areas" (an area more than five kilometres from any road) in Norway. This is a good indicator of land fragmentation during the last century. In addition to agricultural settlements, it includes railways, roads, mines, hydro-electrical power regulation, modern forestry and modern tourism development. The effects can be characterized as follows:

> The more the land is cut up and criss-crossed by the railway and road networks, and the more grazing lands are cut up into an uneven patchwork by the timber industry, the more difficult it becomes to stabilize the reindeer's movement, (Beach 1981: 52)

It is self-evident that this process must heavily increase the external pressure on reindeer management, with roads providing access to 'the wilderness' for a series of disturbing activities. Beach's main point in the quotation above is that fragmentation destabilizes the reindeer's movement. One implication is that *it becomes more and more difficult to follow the naturally given annual migration cycle.* Modifications or extra use of technology become necessary. As an example, several herder districts in Nordland in Norway have legal rights, codified in a bilateral pasture convention, to winter pastures in the Swedish inland woods. Due to encroachments by hydro-electrical power regulations, many rivers cannot safely be used as migration routes. Furthermore, large-scale clear-cutting forestry removes old forest, which was the source of arboreal lichens, making artificial forage necessary. In practice, migration has to be conducted by trucks, at a high extra cost. *The ultimate effect of fragmentation is marginalization of nature-based, including indigenous, livelihoods.* Thus the trend tends to be that either such types of livelihoods cannot be sustained at all, or the running costs reduce their potential as a subsistence basis for many people. A report from the United Nations development program (UNEP, 2001) indicates that in a number of decades the sum effect of all these encroachments and disturbances looks so serious that it may be difficult to continue reindeer management. Such a development has wide implications in a property rights perspective. Reindeer management has established rights of compensation for encroachments during the later part of the twentieth century. In other words, the formal property rights are clearly stronger than in previous times. However, as with other indigenous peoples, the Sami viewpoint is clear: money cannot compensate for the loss of land. The problem is that the long-term effect of encroachments and disturbances is undermining existing property rights. In an overall perspective, it seems clear that external resource pressures are intensifying the cost/income squeeze, as indicated, for modern Sami reindeer management. Thus, *the herders have to follow a two-front strategy; fighting both to keep the land and to survive economically* (cf. Table 1). Let us consider the role of co-management in more detail.

Conflicting Strategies and Co-Management

In spite of the repressive Norwegian national policy towards the Sami, there are indications (cf. Sara 1996) that Sami reindeer management during the era following the Second World War was, to a considerable extent, a *de facto* internally self-governing society, under a limited civil servant rule. In other words, the national state had limited ambitions in governing the herding society, though its ambitions in regulating the extent of the reindeer management were far-reaching. Furthermore, government influence within the herding society was limited in practice. As the general public policy towards the Sami changed during the 1960s and 1970s, the basis was created for a new national reindeer management policy in Norway. This was a result of negotiations between government and Sami parties. Let us have a brief look at some of the main strategy options available to these parties.

Generally, we might characterize the Sami's choice of strategy as *liberation v. subordination* and the government's choice of strategy as *top-down v. devolution*. It is obvious that the outcome of either strategy for both of the parties was also dependent on their counterpart's choice. The general experience is that top-down resource management by centralized government agencies does not work well, and that purely local-level management is often ineffective in a complex world of multiple stakeholders (Berkes, 1997). This general statement is particularly true in the case of acephalous societies experiencing a nation-state encounter, which is followed by attempts at state rule.

Co-management systems represent an alternative approach, and one that is more co-operative than central government. As Jentoft (1998:9) points out, co-management establishes organizational structures at the meso-level of society and builds on the capacity of local communities and user-groups to address collective problems. Co-management is based on two basic assumptions. First, local people must have a stake in conservation and management, and second, partnership between government agencies and local communities is essential (Berkes 1997:5). Defined more rigorously, *collaborative management*

235

(co-management) is "[a] partnership in which governmental agencies, local communities and resource users, non-governmental organizations and other stakeholders share, as appropriate to each context, the authority of a specific territory or a set of resources" (Borrini-Feyerabend, G. 1996, cited in Berkes 1997). A core attribute of co-management is that both the governmental bodies and the user-groups/NGOs have to *give up freedom to increase real control.* Governmental bodies have to consult their non-governmental counterparts before making decisions, while user-groups/NGOs have to limit their free opposition towards government (Riseth 1991). In other words, co-management implies a notion of certain costs and requirements in order to be successful. Ideally, the parties would come closer to each other and thus develop trust and common objectives, at least to some extent.

During the late 1970s a twin reform established reindeer management as a public policy sector based on co-management. The reform included an industry policy agreement and a new law. Thus, in 1976, the Ministry of Agriculture and the herders' NGO, the Sami Reindeer Herders Association (NRL), signed "*The Main Agreement for the Reindeer Industry*". The parties agreed upon the following explicit political objectives for Sami reindeer management: (1) production: optimizing meat production and sustaining the natural resource base; (2) income: securing an income for reindeer herding practitioners and a living standard at the same level as other occupational groups; (3) allocation: allocating total income in a way that would provide occupational security; (4) culture: developing reindeer management as a sustained basis for Sami culture (Landbruksdepartementet 1976).

The main agreement instigates negotiations on economic actions as a means to promote industrial development. *The main agreement is thus the formal constitutional basis of a new co-management system.* The concrete actions are decided in biennial short-term agreements, while the negotiations are conducted annually. *The reindeer management negotiations were established as a new collective choice arena from 1977.* The reindeer management agreement awarded relatively large sums of money to a society that had lived rather close to self-sufficiency. In 1980 the agreement encompassed ten million Norwegian kroner. This increased during the 1980s to reach a level of about eighty million kroner. Even allowing for the fact that a considerable portion of this sum was used for research, advisory services,[2] slaughtering firms, marketing, fence and corralling facilities, the amount of money transferred to families has nevertheless been quite considerable, affecting about two thousand people. So this money and the rules attached obviously had the potential of becoming a forceful factor in influencing the herders' resource adaptations.

---

[2]   Public agency professionals who provide guidance in new production methodology.

A special committee, established in 1960, developed a proposal (Reindrift-slovkomiteen 1967), but Sami property rights claims were controversial with regard to agriculture, which was used to having superior rights. It took a couple of decades before the new law was finally adopted (1978), after many changes, and set in force (1979). In an overall comparison, the main goal of the 1933 Act and its predecessors was clearly the regulation of reindeer herd management versus external interests, mainly agriculture, while the goal of the 1978 Act was to regulate the internal relationships of reindeer management. Looked at in a *de jure/de facto* perspective, we find that *while Sami reindeer herders in 1960 faced regulation by civil servants, with limited control and contact tasks, in the 1980s they faced collective choice arenas, participating as representatives in an integrated administrative and political governing system, as part of the total Norwegian state hierarchy.*

The implementation of the articles of the 1978 Act and the development of the agreement on reindeer management went on contemporaneously during the 1980s. Beyond the formal requirements of the agreement, a pattern of extended organization/government co-operation was established. *The most important policy decisions within the sector were in reality made jointly by the leading state officials and the herders' elected leaders.* Thus, during the 1980s, the reindeer herders managed to influence public sector policy considerably by means of their organization, NRL (Riseth 1991). The total institutional arrangement facing the Sami reindeer herders in Norway from the 1980s onwards thus includes three main elements: (1) the traditional, (2) the legally-based, and (3) the agreement-based. The total pattern of rules is thus rather complex. Based on Ostrom's principles for the design of institutions for common-pool resources (Ostrom 1990:90), this author (Riseth 2000) has focused on the creation of an *internal autonomous collective level* under the ultimate control of the re-source-users themselves as an important aspect for the successful governance of common-pool resources. During the 1980s we observed a rapprochement between industry and government. *The crucial point seems to be whether this rapprochement has received sufficient support at an internal collective level. If not, the new external rules would not have sufficient legitimacy, and would be in conflict with the traditional system.*

Despite the positive intentions of the introduction of co-management, the level of success was regionally diverse. Taking into consideration the different aspects of modernization and the requirement of an exact fit between the attributes of the physical world and the institutional system, we would generally expect a diversity of outcomes for different Sami regions, with their diversity of geography and history. This author has examined the different outcomes of the policy reform by means of a comparative study that selects high and low values in the dependent variables (Riseth 2000). The regions West Finnmark (denoted

'North') and Trøndelag/Hedmark (denoted 'South') have been compared, since they have experienced very distinct differences in performance.

Resource Adaptation and Strategies

The cost/income squeeze faced by herders (cf. the section on modernization implications) could in principle be met by two different strategies (Riseth 2000, Riseth and Vatn 1998). (1) The more obvious is to expand herd size. As long as there are ample pasture resources (and herd control is sufficient), this strategy is relatively unproblematic. Whenever resources are restricted, however, this results in competition between the herders. Since herding is a collective effort, this mainly will be a competition between different *siidas*. (2) The alternative strategy is to accept the pasture limitation and increase the productivity of the herd, based on herd restructuring: increasing the relative proportion of young (higher growth rate) and female (more births) animals, cf. Lenvik (1989). The two regions investigated seem to have chosen opposite strategy options, as indicated in Table 3. While the main strategy in the North seems to have been competitive herd expansion, in the South it seems to have been herd stabilization and an increase in productivity.

Table 3. Herd productivity measured as meat production per animal in the spring herd (1 April).[3]

		1976	1984	1987/88	1993/94
NORTH	West Finnmark	7.8 kg	8.9 kg	7.0 kg	8 kg
SOUTH	North Trøndelag	8.1 kg	10.5 kg	12.9 kg	14 kg
	SouthTrøndelag/Hedmark	12.5 kg	16.3 kg	14.8 kg	14 kg

Source: Kosmo, 1991:20 and Reindriftsforvaltningen, 1995:38.

The more general development of the North region illustrates this point. From the mid-1970s onwards, the lichen-rich winter and autumn pastures of Finnmarksvidda became increasingly severely overgrazed, due to a considerable growth in the total herd size (an increase of approx. 150% over fifteen years), reaching a historically new level in 1990 and then declining through the 1990s. The implications have included decreasing animal weight, a reduced offspring rate, increased predation, an emerging dependence upon artificial feeding, a

---

[3] 1 April is the equivalent of New Year's Day in the reindeer management year. Figures show herd numbers that have survived winter, but before calving takes place in May, i.e. the herd capital of the year counted on a generally accepted day.

reduced income, a slaughterhouse bankruptcy and, ultimately, increasing socio-economic problems during the 1990s and the turn of this century.

By contrast, Sami reindeer management in the South (North Trøndelag and South Trøndelag/Hedmark) has stabilized the herd size and has also managed to create high operating profits, due to the high productivity displayed in Table 3. This puzzle is analysed (Riseth 2000) by means of a broad approach, involving ecological as well as socio-economic factors. These factors include natural geography, and herder and government strategies, as well as the diversity in minority/majority relations. The outcome encompasses the fact that under technological change (motorization), ecological factors in the North clearly favour herd-expanding strategies, while those in the South support herd-stabilizing strategies. The most relevant ecological factors studied were (1) the relative seasonal pasture balance and (2) the landscape structure. In the case of the former, if winter pasture capacity is lower than summer pasture capacity (winter pasture limitation), this means that winter survival will tend to determine the herd size and the summer pasture can be utilized for production. This is ideal for the ecological adaptation of northern ungulates (Klein 1968). In the opposite case (summer pasture limitation), a relative excess of winter pastures can lead to overgrazing of lichen pastures (cf. enrichment paradox, Rosenzweig 1971). The access and abundance of this type of winter pasture determines the relative ease of out-of-season grazing. In a landscape with weak natural borders between season pastures (Ruong 1968), it is easier to graze autumn or winter lichen pastures out of season than is the case in a landscape with clear natural

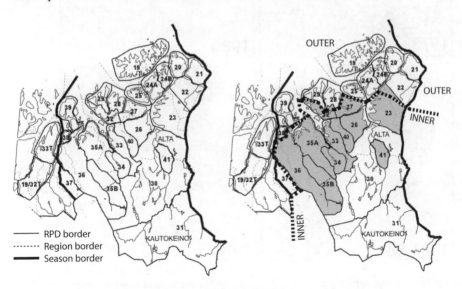

Figure 2. Panel A. Seasonal pastures (RPDs)

Panel B. Zonation of summer RPDs (inner v. outer)

borders. The grazing of lichen pastures not protected by snow-cover will lead to both the trampling and over-grazing of vulnerable, slow-growing plants. The combination of these two factors may thus reinforce the effects of each other in a destructive way.

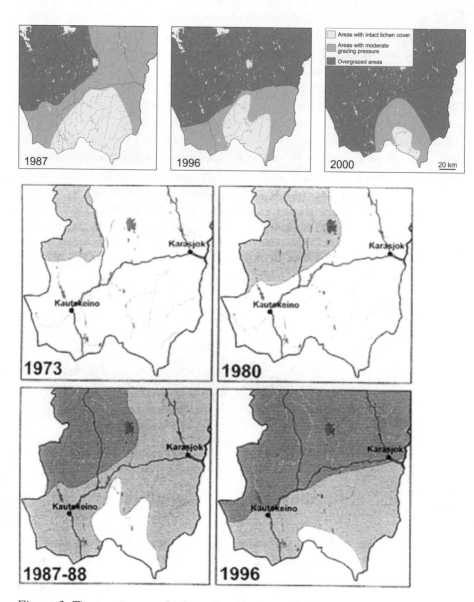

Figure 3. Time series panel of grazing impact on lichen pastures of Finnmarksvidda 1973-2000. Source: Johansen, B. & Karlsen, S.R. 1998 and 2002

In my analysis, I found that this was the case in the North as both the factors of (1) summer-pasture limitation and (2) a relatively open landscape, with weak natural borders between seasonal pastures, facilitated gradual out-of-season grazing from the mid-1970s and throughout the twentieth century. The core of my analysis of North land-use development is that *motorization in an open landscape gave* siida-*groups with insufficient summer pastures the opportunity of first using adjacent autumn pastures during the summer, and later using winter pastures during the autumn.* The physical organization of the pastures is shown in Figure 2a, whilst the zoning of summer reindeer pasture districts is shown in Figure 2b.

This easy access to winter pastures in the North has thus resulted in a rapid expansion in the practice of some herds utilizing the lichen pastures during the autumn and the winter. Overgrazing and subsequent deterioration of vulnerable lichen pastures in the North has been the negative result of these expanding strategies.

Time-series satellite images[4] *of the lichen pastures (Johansen and Karlsen 1998 and 2002), cf. Figure 3, and administration reports (Lappefogden i Vest-Finnmark 1972-79, Reindriftsagronomen i Vest-Finnmark 1980-1996) substantiate this pattern of development.*

The expansion of both herd size[5] *and winter pasture areas (cf. Riseth 2000: 177) is thus in the inner siidas,* adjacent to the fall pastures, those that have the greatest opportunity to take advantage of new possibilities. In South there has been no parallel to this type of development. Accordingly, we do not find a similar deterioration of lichen pastures as a result of out of season use of the vulnerable lichen pastures in the South.

Institutional Capabilities

How can we explain this from an institutional point of view? Recalling the regulatory principles of the Sami herding society (cf. Table 2), we note that dialogue and consensus (principle 4), and responsibility towards the land and spirits (principle 5), are the only powers working beyond *siida* level. That is, rather weak top-level institutions. Even though they were sufficient in older times, they have obviously not been strong enough to limit herd expansion in the North duirng the 1970s and 1980s. However, upon enquiry, I did not detect a marked difference between the traditional institutions of the North and South. This suggests that the institutional explanations seem to be connected with the co-management system and the basis for this system.

---

[4] including the neighbouring area of Karasjok.

[5] about 130% over ten years in the inner districts, contrasting with 38% in the outer districts (Riseth 2000:178)

It is crucial that the modern co-management institutions have not managed to limit expansion in the North, while this does seem to have been achieved in the South. From the socio-economic factors compared, the main finding is that a historically more extensive pressure from the expanding Norwegian farmer society led to organizational efforts from the early part of the twentieth century onwards. It seems as though this left herders in the South, and their leaders, better prepared for the changes from the 1960s onwards than their counterparts in the North, as it made them take the initiative to change their own situation. Thus herder pioneers, such as Anders Fjellheim at Røros, started to ask how they could improve the output of their herds. New attitudes caused them to make contact with agronomists and develop trust and co-operation with the advisory service during the 1970s and 1980s. Herders in the North did not, as far as is known, take this type of initiative during the same period. It is striking, however, that the public reindeer management policy in the early 1980s was based on an *apparent unity of objectives* (Riseth 1991), through the institutional system of co-management described above. If we reflect on the objectives of the main agreement (cf. the section concerning conflicting strategies and co-management), we may note that *three out of four objectives focus on production and income, whilst one focuses on culture.* The Ministry director responsible also emphasized that the authorities should consider the production objectives as the most important aspect of the agreement (Grue 1982). These facts may be clues to the *basic logic* (Sproule-Jones 1993) of the main agreement of reindeer management. The prevailing logic is thus a monocultural production optimalization, causing northern reindeer Sami to try to expand their herds to a level where the result is the "tragedy of commons" in inner Finnmark.

Furthermore, the legal system of the Herding Act of 1978 includes *a herd quota system* as an important part of the regulations. Though it is not directly expressed, the government clearly intended to use this as a basis for the agreement. Thus it seems that *the co-management system implemented is based on a specific bio-economic theory of production* (Lenvik 1989, Kosmo & Lenvik 1985). From what we have learnt above, we see that this theory has functioned well in the South. The reason also seems obvious: *professionals, who had gained most of their experience in the South, developed the theory at the request of herder leaders in the South* (Riseth 2000:169-172).

Moreover, data from the period itself does not support the idea that there existed an analysis of the North supporting the use of the same theory. One might speculate why there are no signs of a more regionalized policy in the late 1970s and the early 1980s. Elements of the answer are given by one of the main architects of the co-management system, Paul Fjellheim[6] (Fjellheim, 1987): the

---

[6]   A veterinarian from a prominent herder family in the South (brother of Anders Fjellheim, already mentioned), chairman and deputy chairman of the NRL over a number of crucial years, later an advisor for the NRL in annual agreement negotiations up until the 1990s.

conditions for co-management were still marginal in the 1970s, as parts of the ministry bureaucracy were still influenced by social Darwinist thought. In a broader perspective, we may consider this as an element of what North (1990: 14) calls the *path dependence of institutional change*. In other words, past events both provide opportunities and impose constraints for the future.

The demand for a modern production theory was thus very limited in the North. This author worked as a young advisory service worker in the North during the early 1980s. Subsequent reflection over my experiences with herders, who were seemingly interested, and carefully considered our suggestions concerning herd reduction and productivity increase, but ultimately continued as before, results in a hypothesis of *ambiguous strategies*[7] (cf. Riseth 2001). Such a hypothesis is also compatible with the Sami tradition of expressing agreement clearly, combined with a reluctance to express disagreement openly. The implementation of the herd quota system was dependent on decisions made by the regulation boards that were established under the 1978 Act. The majority of board members are herders. In the North, board members were reluctant to make decisions that imposed reductions in herd size. Furthermore, there are clear indications that groups of herders considered inefficient governing bodies to be an advantage as far as they were concerned (Karlstad, 1998). It also appears that the relative winners of the competition for pasturelands were among these groups. At a national level, the system of government was found to be inconsistent and goals were achieved to only a limited degree (Fjellheim 1986, Riseth 1991). I took part in a number of annual negotiation processes and it became clear that this was at least partly due to the fact that although the parties agreed formally with one another, they weighted aspects of the agreement differently. In concrete terms, governmental representatives in the early 1980s seem to have weighted governing possibilities, while the NGO seems to have weighted an increase in subsidies[8]. The problems were thus the result of the compromises made. Subsidies clearly promoted the Finnmark herd growth, since much of the money was used to avoid slaughtering animals (Kosmo & Lenvik, 1985). A great many inconsistencies were removed in the late 1980s. However, the herd growth had already come a long way by then.

Certainly, NRL was in a difficult position. At annual meetings, herders from the North openly criticized the leadership for being too close to the government. The organization percentage had always been low in North and high in South. In the late 1980s a competing NGO was founded as an *ad hoc* movement (cf. Paine 1994), but this vanished after a few years. In an overall perspective, it seems that many of the problems in the North are rooted in an insufficient

---

[7] In Sami language: *guoktelussat* (NOU 1995:6:201)

[8] The subsidy level started very low and recognition as an industry implied a comparison with agriculture, which had reached a relatively high level in the 1970s.

analysis of the situation. The responsibility for this should be shared between the governmental and the non-governmental organizations.

Analysis and Conclusion

What can we learn from this experience? The outcomes are mixed: we can cite both the success and the failure of co-management in Sami reindeer management in Norway. To analyse conditions of co-management in this case, we need to keep in mind the combined challenges and dilemmas connected to the production factors of land, herd and man (labour). It is obvious that where modern Sami reindeer management is concerned, the combination of strong external pressure on the land and weak external property rights causes a stress within the industry as a whole. Furthermore, modern technology has greatly improved herd control abilities, but it has also greatly increased production costs. The total effect of these processes is thus a double pressure on land and pasture resources: (1) an external pressure, caused by the disturbance, fragmentation and undermining of property rights, and (2) an internal pressure on herd expansion, to achieve increased income. The success of the co-management system will thus be dependent on the extent to which the system manages to handle these pressures simultaneously, constituting a double challenge.

It is clear that in our case the first challenge is not solved, while the second seems to be solved in the South, but clearly not in the North. In other words, the co-management system, as currently developed, cannot prevent the development of a pasture crisis in the North. Moreover, the situation in the South is not stable either: given the external pressure on the land it is, as the UNEP (2001) report indicates, only a question of time before this factor causes a pasture crisis as well. Success in terms of internal regulation is thus a necessary condition, but is not sufficient in itself for a long-term, stable co-management system. Considering that the situation in the North reduced external pressure and improved property rights, these factors probably contributed towards increasing trust towards governmental authorities, and thus improving the basis for co-operation on internal regulation.

Generally there seem to be a number of conditions for success. Both sides (or all important parties) should be mature enough (or prepared) to achieve real co-operation, i.e. to recognize that they have a problem that cannot be solved without involving their counterpart. The parties should then work hard to develop an analysis of a situation that is genuinely acknowledged. The challenge of path dependence should not be under-estimated. Furthermore, the long-term success of co-management systems is dependent on co-operation on a broad basis, on both the governmental and the indigenous side, creating a necessary trust through the recognition of indigenous rights, as applied in all parts and at all levels of the public system of governance. Indigenous NGOs should also work to broaden their level of representation and internal unity.

References

Beach, H.: Reindeer-Herd Management in Transition: The case of Tuorpon Saameby in Northern Sweden. *Uppsala studies in Cultural Anthropology*. 3.Uppsala: Acta Universitas Uppsalensis 1981.

Berkes, F.: Co- management.In: *The Common Property Resource Digest*, 43 1997.

Berkes, Fikret: "Cross-Scale Institutional Linkages: Perspectives from the Bottom Up." In *The Drama of the Commons*. E. Ostrom et al. Washington, DC: National Academy Press 2002.

Douglas, M.: *Edward Evans-Pritchard*. New York: Viking Press 1980.

Fjellheim, M.: Utvikling og problemer i reindriften-en reindriftspolitisk analyse. *Hovedoppgave* ved Institutt for Landbruksøkonomi, Ås-NLH 1986.

Fjellheim, P.: Historiske blikk. In: *NRL's Informasjon - Landsmøtet 1987, 25*. Tromsø: NRL 1987.

Grue, P.H.: Speech at the annual meeting of The State Agency of Reindeer Management. Informal notes (JÅR) 1982.

Jentoft, S.: Introduction. In: Jentoft, S (ed): *Commons in a cold climate. Coastal Fisheries and Reindeer Pastoralism in North Norway: The Co-Management Approach*. Paris:UNESCO/ Parthenon; 1-13 1998.

Johansen, B.E., and Karlsen, S.R.: *Endringer i lavdekket på Finnmarksvidda 1987-1996 basert på Landsat 5/TM data*. Tromsø: NORUT 1998.

Johansen, B. & Karlsen S.R.: Finnmarksvidda changes in lichen cover 1987-2000. Poster presentation at the 12th Nordic Conference on Reindeer Research. Extended abstract in Rangifer. Report No.6. 2002.

Kappfjell, T.: *Laahkoeh*. Kristiansund: Th.Blaasværs Forlag 1991.

Karlstad, S.: Institutional theory, Co-management and Sustainable development in Saami reindeer commons - Critical factors for a robust system of local management. In S. Jentoft (ed.) *Commons in A Cold Climate: Coastal Fisheries and Reindeer Pastoralism in North Norway: The Co-Management Approach*, 247-268. Paris and New York: UNESCO and Partheneon Publishers 1998.

Kosmo, A.: Mekanismer i reindriftens tilpasning. Kompendium for undervisning i reindrift ved Norges Landbrukshøgskole. *Rapport nr. 1:1991*. Alta: Reindriftsadministrasjonen 1991.

Kosmo, A. and Lenvik, D.: Ressurstilpasningen i reindriften. *Landbruksøkonomisk Forum*, 2/85: 23-27 1985.

Klein, D. R.: The introduction, increase and crash of reindeer on St. Matthew Island. *Journal of Wildlife Management*, 32:350-367 1968.

Landbruksdepartementet: St.prp.nr. 170 (1975-76) Om hovedavtale for reindriftsnæringen.Oslo.

Lappefogden i Vest-Finnmark, 1977-79. Årsmelding. Annual Periodical. Kautokeino1976.

Lenvik, D.: Utvalgsstrategi i reinflokken. *Norsk Landbruksforskning/ Norwegian Agricultural Research* Supplement no. 4, 11-25. Ås: Statens fagtjeneste for landbruket /Norwegian Agricultural Advisory Centre 1989.

Meløy, J. Aa.: Siida-systemet i reindrifta. Lecture. *Kurs i reindriftsrett*. Oslo: Juristenes utdanningssenter 1997.

Nergård, J.-I.: *The Psychology of Culture: Some sketches from the Saami world*. Ms. Tromsø: University of Tromsø 1996.

North, D.C.: *Institutions, Institutional change and economic perforance*. New York: Cambridge University Press 1990.

Norwegian Reindeer Husbandry Administration: Norwegian Reindeer Husbandry. Alta 1998.

Oskal, N.A.: Det rette, det gode og reinlykken. *Avhandling til dr.art.-graden i filosofi.* Universitetet i Tromsø 1995.

Ostrom, E.: *Governing the Commons. The Evolution of Institutions for Collective Actions.* Cambridge, USA: Cambridge University Press 1990.

Paine, R.: Herding and Husbandry. Two basic distinctions in the analysis of reindeer management. *Folk,* 6:83-88 1964.

Paine, R.: Lappish Decisions. Partnerships, Information Management, and Sanctions. A Nomadic Pastoral Adaptation, *Ethnology* 9(1):52-67), Pittsburg 1970.

Paine, R: *Herds of the Tundra. A Portrait of Saami Reindeer Pastoralism.* Washington and London: Smithsonian Institution Press 1994.

Pehrson, R.N.: The bilateral network of social relations in Kønkømæ Lapp Distrikt. *Samiske Samlinger* bd.VII, Norsk Folkemuseum.Oslo 1964.

Reindriftsagronomen i Vest-Finmark.1980-1996. *Årsmelding.* Annual Periodical. Kautokeino

Reindriftsforvaltningen, 1995. *Ressursregnskap for reindriftsnæringen,* Annual Periodical. Alta.

Reindriftslovkomiteen, 1967. *Innstilling fra Reindriftslovkomiteen.* Landbruksdepartementet.

Riseth, J.Å.: *Reindrift med framtid. Forvaltningslære,* Bd II: Myndigheter og organisasjoner. Alta/Guovdageaidnu: Reindriftsadministrasjonen / Samisk Utdanningsråd 1991.

Riseth, J.Å.: Sami Reindeer Management Under Technological Change 1960-1990: Implications for Common-Pool Resource Use Under Various Natural and Institutional Conditions. A Comparative Analysis of Regional Development Paths in West Finnmark, North Trøndelag, and South Trøndelag/Hedmark, Norway. *Dr. Scientarium Theses* 2000:1. ISSN 0802-3222. ISBN 82-575-0411-4. Ås: Department of Economics and Social Sciences, Agricultural University of Norway 2000.

Riseth, J.Å.: From excess to lack of winter pasture capacity- How can we explain the development of West Finnmark Reindeer Pasture Area, 1960-2000? (oral version in eng.) *Presentation at 11th Nordic Conference on Reindeer Research, Kaamanen, Finland, 18-20 Juni, 2001.* Abstract printed in *Rangifer Report No. 5, 2001.* Lecture (no. version) http://www.rangifer.no/ manus-riseth.html 2001

Riseth, J.Å. & Vatn, A.: "Adaptation Strategies under Technological Change. A Comparative study of Saami Reindeer Management Regions in Norway 1960-1990", pp. 61-83 in S. Jentoft (ed.) *Commons in cold climate: Coastal Fisheries and Reindeer Pastoralism in North Norway.* UNESCO/Parthenon Publishers 1998.

Rosenzweig, M. L.: Paradox of enrichment: destabilization of exploitation ecosystems in ecological time. *Science,* 171, 385-387 1971.

Ruong, I.: *Samerna i historien och nutiden.* Aldus Akademi. Stockholm: Bonnier Fakta 1982[1969].

Sara, M.N.: Boazu lea biekka buorri. En studie av reindriften i østre del av Kautokeino reinsogn på 1950-tallet. *Hovedoppgave.* Institutt for samfunnsvitenskap. Universitetet i Tromsø 1996.

Sproule-Jones, M.: *Governments at work: Canadian Parliamentary Federalism and Its Public Policy Effects.* Toronto: University of Toronto Press 1993.

Syrenochkovskii, E.E.; D. R. Klein, sc. ed.: *Wild Reindeer* [Translated from Russian] Smithsonian, Washington D.C. 1995[1986].

UNEP, 2001. C. Nellemann, L. Kullerud, I. Vistnes, B.C. Forbes, E. Husby, G.P. Kofinas, B.P. Kaltenborn, J. Rouaud, M. Magomedova, R. Bobiwash, C. Lambrechts, P.J. Schei, S. Tveitdal, O. Grøn, T.S. Larsen: GLOBIO. Global Methodology for Mapping Human Impacts on the Bioshere. The Arctic 2050 Sceanrio and Global Application. UNEP/DEWA/TR.01-3. ISBN: 92-807-2051-1 2001.

Vorren, Ø.: Finnmarksamenes Nomadisme. *Tromsø Musems Skrifter Vol.IX.* 2 volumes 1962.

Vorren, Ø.: *Innledning til et seminar 1964. Endringer i bosetning og reindriftsform i Finnmark. En foreløpig skisse.* Manuscript. Tromsø 1964.

CHAPTER 13

The Environmental Sustainability of the Property Rights Régimes in Inari: The Performance of Forest Government and Reindeer Herding Co-operatives

Jukka Nyyssönen

Introduction and Theoretical Framework

The case of Inari offers an opportunity to study the performance of two different property rights régimes, in a unique land ownership and ethnical setting. The land in Inari is owned almost exclusively by the state (93.7% of the land was state-owned in 1975[1]). It is managed by Forest Government of Finland (*Metsähallitus*) and its local representative, the District of Inari. As a state property régime, Forest Government has the right to determine the use and access regulations relating to land in Inari. Forest Government's land ownership is not "full ownership". The other régime utilizing the same land in Finnish Lapland is the Reindeer Herders' Association (*Paliskuntain yhdistys*). At a local level, reindeer herding is managed by the association's subordinate herding co-operatives (*paliskunnat*), which *resemble* common property régimes. However, this is only a resemblance, since a régime's claim to land is not one of private property for a group of co-owners. Co-operatives have rights of use concerning the land, and they lease small areas of land from Forest Government for herding infrastructure. The ethnical constellation is complex. The Sami are a minority in Inari, but the Sami reindeer herders are in a majority position in the herding co-operatives of Inari. Finns also have the right to practice reindeer herding. In addition, there are Sami loggers on the payroll of Forest Government. As is often the case with land ownership, the pattern of ownership is complex and natural resources are multi-functional. There are several layers of administrative control relating to land use. The entitlement rule applicable here is a rule of liability: reindeer herders have the right to intervene in the property, but they

---

[1]   Lapin Metsätalous, Lapin seutukaavaliiton julkaisu, Sarja A, No. 10, Rovaniemi, 1975, pp. 19-21.

are required to compensate the landowner.[2] This is done by means of pasture fees.

I shall study the success in maintaining environmental sustainability in resource management demonstrated by the property rights régimes, the District of Inari and the herding co-operatives in the rural district of Inari, Finland. This is measured by studying their success in maintaining the ecological basis of the livelihoods: has there been deforestation or overgrazing? How and why has the legitimacy of the régimes changed? This is done in the first, empirical part of the study. The second part of the study concentrates on the reasons for the success or failure of the performance. Was the state intervention successful? Was the régime constellation that was introduced successful? The performance of the régimes is studied by means of the analytical model provided by ecological economics studies in resource management sustainability. The aim is to study the success of the régimes in concrete terms, rather than at a purely notional level, through the analysis of the property rights régime constellation in Inari. Although I shall concentrate on the ecological viewpoint, I shall also make brief references to social legitimacy. I am leaving aside the question of economic sustainability, since the main concern of Forest Government was to launch and maintain the forestry project in Inari. The periods during which forestry in the district of Inari made a profit were, in fact, quite exceptional. The District viewed its task as being of a more social nature: it was a job provider more than an employer, and the resources were not utilized for long periods of time.

Property rights régimes are studied by a new branch of economics, that of ecological economics. In traditional economics, the prevailing object of study was economic efficiency; in ecological economics, economic efficiency is subsumed to become part of a larger problem of sustainability in the performance of a régime. The success of a régime is judged by the way it is able to combine a maximum flow of generated income, while maintaining its stock of assets (economic sustainability), as well as maintaining the integrity of its social and cultural systems, securing equity (social sustainability) and maintaining the stability of its biological and physical systems, at the same time as utilizing them economically (environmental sustainability). The environment's sustainability is kept at a satisfactory level by maintaining the ecosystem's dynamic ability to adapt to change, rather than by trying to conserve an ideal state of nature. Cultural sustainability can also be studied. In order to achieve sustainable performance, the tasks of a property rights régime must be well specified, and must be congruent with its environmental and social context. It needs to have the power to monitor its own area, as well as the tools to enforce processes of adaptation.

---

[2]   Hahn, Thomas: Property Rights, Ethics and Conflict Resolution, Foundations of the Sami Economy in Sweden, Acta Universitatis Agriculturae Sueciae Agraria 258, Uppsala, 2000, pp. 22, 25, 28, 88.

It must be capable of adjusting to both the ecological processes of change in the environment and the boundaries of governance. In order to function properly, the régime must have social, ecological and political legitimacy.[3]

Broadly speaking, since the collapse of the state-owned planned economy systems, private ownership has once again been viewed favorably in the field of economics, as well as in national economic thinking. The argument for poor efficiency in publicly-owned enterprises is that a company or régime with a clearly defined right of profit will perform better than those whose rights are diffused or uncertain. The "consensus" has been blurred in many respects,[4] and there is an extensive body of literature that concentrates on denying the assumed "tragedy of commons", a situation where natural resources with open access are plundered, in the absence of any real sense of responsibility for the resource. Garrett Hardin, who introduced the idea in 1968, saw private ownership as a necessity, in order to sustain environmental resources. In response, there is a growing new consensus about the advantages of common property régimes. Recommending the decentralization of resource management has become something of a slogan in the study of resource management in the Third World and areas inhabited by indigenous peoples. A third strand of thought in studies currently being undertaken examines the growing evidence that sustaining environmental resources is not dependent on the particular structure of the ownership. The management of the resource can fail or succeed, regardless of whether the resource is privately or commonly owned.[5]

---

[3] Bromley, Daniel, W.: Environment and Economy, Property Rights and Public Policy, Blackwell 1991, pp. 1-3, 22; Hahn 2000, pp. 5, 7; Hanna, Susan, Folke, Karl, and Mäler, Karl-Göran: Property Rights and Environmental Resources, Property Rights and the Environment, Social and Ecological Issues, Susan Hanna and Mohan Munasignhe (Eds.), The Beijer International Institute of Ecological Economics and World Bank 1995, p. 17-18, 22; Hanna, Susan and Munasinghe, Mohan: An Introduction to Property Rights and Environment, Property Rights and the Environment, Social and Ecological Issues, Susan Hanna and Mohan Munasignhe (Eds.), The Beijer International Institute of Ecological Economics and World Bank 1995, p. 4-5.

[4] The social efficiency viewpoint is studied with a critical view in, for example, Siedl, Christian: Poverty Measurement: A survey, Welfare and Efficiency in Public Economics, Dieter Bös, Manfred Rose, Christian Siedl (Eds.), Springer Verlag 1980, pp. 135-138; Concerning the strong belief in private property rights, see, for example, Hartley, Keith and Ott, Attiat F.: Introduction, Privatization and Economic Efficiency, A Comparative Analysis of Developed and Developing Countries, Attiat F. Ott and Keith Hartley (Eds.), Edward Edgar Publishing 1993, pp. 1-8. The whole book is a manifestation of private ownership endorsement.

[5] Bjørklund, Ivar: Når ressursene blir allmenning – samisk ressursforvaltning mot det 21. århundre, Norsk ressursforvaltning og samiske rettighetsforhold, Om statlig styring, allmenningens tragedie og lokale sedvaner i Sápmi, Ivar Bjørklund (red.), Ad Notam 1999; Hansen, Jostein: Porsanger: Ressursforvaltning, livskarrierer, og kulturtradisjoner i et etnisk sammensatt område, Prosjektnotat nr. 4, nov. 1988: Sosiale og økonomiske konsekvenser av petroleumsvirksomheten for samiske bosettningsområder. Nordisk Samisk Institutt, passim;

Traditionally, "property rights" are viewed as a necessary condition for efficient market functioning. According to Daniel Bromley (1991), "property rights" are widely misunderstood. There is even greater disparity in the use and given meanings for the terms "commons" or "common property". Bromley sees "the tragedy of commons" as merely a political weapon. Common property resources do not exist as an unified entity. Bromley states that there are only natural resources, which are governed as common, state or private property. In addition, there are open access resources (*res nullius*), to which no-one claims recognized property rights.[6]

In this article, "property" is defined as a benefit (or income) stream, and accordingly "property rights" is defined as a claim to a benefit stream that is agreed by the state and protected through the assignment of duty to others, who may somehow interfere with the benefit stream. Property is a social relation that defines a property holder with respect to something of value, a triadic social relation involving (1) a benefit stream, (2) right holders and (3) duty bearers. A property rights régime (property rights holder) is a structure of rights and duties that characterizes the relationship between individuals with respect to a particular environmental resource. Property rights régimes have the authority to decide what is scarce, i.e. possibly worth protecting, and what is valuable, and therefore certainly worth protecting.[7] In this article, environmental sustainability involves securing the ecological basis of the recurrence of a natural resource, whilst utilizing it economically. The Sami refers to the reindeer herding Sami of Inari, unless otherwise stated.

The Formation of the Property Rights System in Inari

The Lapp village, or *siida*, system[8] traditionally consisted of autonomous territorial areas, over which each village claimed a right of usage. These areas, with more or less strictly-controlled borders, were owned by the *siida*. Subsistence

---

Case studies from the Third World include, for example, Pradhan, Ajay S., and Parks, Peter, J.: Environmental and Socioeconomic Linkages of Deforestation and Forest Land Use Change in Nepal Himalaya, Property Rights in a Social and Ecological Context, Case Studies and Design Applications, Susan Hanna and Mohan Munasinghe (Eds.), The Beijer International Institute of Ecological Economics and World Bank 1995, pp. 168-177.

[6] Bromley 1991, pp. 1-2.

[7] Bromley 1991, pp. 1-3, 22; Hahn 2000, p. 21.

[8] *Siida* is Northern Sami, and means a Lapp or reindeer village. It refers both to the area and the people living in the autonomous area of *siida*. As this is the most specific term relating to the governmental area, and covers both the livelihood and legal aspect of the area formation, I shall use the term in this article. It was the main feature in community organization in most of the Finnish Lapland until the end of the nineteenth century. Tanner, Väinö: Antropogeografiska studier inom Petsamo-området, I. Skolt-lapparna, Fennia 49, Societas Geographica Fenniae, Helsingfors 1929, pp. 86-87.

was based on a circulatory system, consisting of fishing, hunting and gathering. The *siida* system entered a phase of deep change in the sixteenth and seventeenth centuries, because of the influence of the crown and the resettlement, as well as internal changes within the Sami livelihood. Nomadic, extensive and, in some cases, expansive reindeer herding begin to dominate the Sami subsistence from approximately the 1650s onwards. The annual circulatory system also changed: summers were spent in the coastal areas by the Arctic Ocean, and winters in the forests and lichen-pastures. Consequently the area of the *siida* expanded. Although the crown tightened its grip on the areas owned by the Sami, Sami land-ownership was recognized by the state in the 1750s. There was a sophisticated resource management and judicial system in existence before the arrival of the Finnish settlers, who had increasingly begun to settle in the Lapp-marks.[9] Nomadic reindeer herding persisted in northern Lapland, but the southern Sami settled in permanent dwellings, and subsistence was based on agriculture. In the process, the Sami language vanished from the southern *siidas*, resulting in deep cultural change. The closure of the state borders (in 1852 between Norway and Finland, and in 1889 between Sweden and Finland) meant an end to the circulatory system. Expansive reindeer herding was practised in Finland and in Inari, in the remaining winter pastures. A more permanent settlement, and a livelihood based on many sources of subsistence, had become the rule by the late nineteenth century. Thus the crown, and later the modern state, found itself in a situation that was not based on *res nullius*, with regard to property rights and livelihood. Access to pastureland was regulated throughout this whole period. Pasture circulation became based on a balance of labour, reindeer and pastures. In practice, the herder regulated the size of the stock according the quality of pasture lands and the availability of a labour force.[10]

---

[9] Lapp-mark is a governmental term, meaning the area north of the Lapland border, where Finnish and Swedish settling was prohibited. The prohibition and the rights of hunting and fishing were given by Gustav Wasa in 1543, and they were strengthened again by Carl IX at the beginning of the seventeenth century. However, settlement was encouraged during the seventeenth century, in spite of the border, by means of legislation that offered settlers tax relief.

[10] Bjørklund, Ivar og Bratenberg, Terje: Samisk reindrift - norske inngrep, Om Altaelva, reindrift og samisk kultur, Universitetsforlaget AS 1981, 32-37; Bjørklund 1999, pp. 20-21; Hahn 2000, p. 92; Korpijaakko, Kaisa: Saamelaisten oikeusasemasta Ruotsi-Suomessa, Oikeushistoriallinen tutkimus Länsi-Pohjan Lapin maankäyttöoloista ja -oikeuksista ennen 1700-luvun puoliväliä, Lapin Korkeakoulun oikeustieteellisiä julkaisuja, Sarja A, 3, Mänttä 1989, pp. 538-556, 579-584; Lehtola, Veli-Pekka: Saamelaiset - Historia, yhteiskunta, taide, Kustannus-Puntsi 1997, pp. 23, 26-27, 30-32, 36-37; Paine, Robert: The Herds of the Tundra, A Portrait of Saami Reindeer Pastoralism, Smithsonian Institution Press 1994, pp. 14-17, 103-104.

The modern state had started to influence Inari by the end of the nineteenth century, when the Finnish local government system was introduced to the Sami areas. State ownership of land was established by means of the Forest Law (1886). The ownership of land outside the established estates, which had formerly been owned by the Siidas, was designated *res nullius*, and was thereafter regarded as state property. The ideological and scientific argument behind the establishment of the state ownership of land was a social Darwinist one: the nomadic Sami culture was stagnant, and the Sami had no conception of property rights relating to land. In addition, property rights institutions seem to have been feasible only for more advanced (i.e. majority) cultures. The Forest Law was based on ideas of ownership that followed the agricultural model and it guaranteed the right for people with no estate to seek land, in order to establish a leasehold on state-owned land. This right contributed to fixing a more permanent kind of Sami settlement. Another motivation for this law was to protect the northernmost forests of Finland from extensive fuel-wood harvesting and over-use. Reindeer herding was viewed as a harmful means of living. In southern Lapland this resulted in prohibiting access to pasture lands that had been "conquered" by agriculture.[11]

Forest Government took over the Sami area as a state property régime and state body responsible for the control of state-owned land. Forest Government claimed by definition the right to determine the regulations, and had a say in the practice of reindeer herding in Inari. The required permission for access to state property was established by means of fees for reindeer herding. The number of reindeers was monitored by means of a quota system.[12]

Reindeer herding management, based on a principle of reindeer herding co-operatives, came into existence in the late nineteenth century. The management system in Finland took account of the Finnish settlers' interests and forms of herding, unlike the systems in Sweden and Norway. The distribution of the areas was not based on any kin or *siida* system. The model was adopted from the Finnish local government system, with a chairman and self-governing bodies, which was responsible to the State. The Reindeer Herders' Association was established in 1926 as a national governing body for herders. Although the laws did not support the interests of nomadic reindeer herding, but instead juxtaposed it with a hostile agricultural system, the Sami strategy was to adjust to the system and integrate itself within it.[13] The Sami herders joined the govern-

---

[11] Hahn 2000, p. 96; Lehtola Teuvo, Kolmen kuninkaan maa, Inarin historia 1500-luvulta jälleenrakennusaikaan, Kustannus-Puntsi 1998, pp. 191-192; Lehtola, Veli-Pekka (Lehtola 2000a): Nickul, Rauhan mies, rauhan kansa, Kustannus-Puntsi , pp. 30, 33, 38, 40, 45.

[12] Bromley 1991, pp. 23, 25-26; Hanna, Folke and Mäler 1995, pp. 17-18, 29; Lehtola 1997, p. 42.

[13] Lehtola 1997, p. 42.

ing bodies at both a local and a regional/national level. The Sami are said to be under-represented in the national body, compared to Finnish reindeer herders.

The Phases of Forestry in Inari

In this section I shall look at the history of forestry in the established property rights situation in Inari. Was the intensifying forestry socially and environmentally sustainable, or not? Was there deforestation?

Due to a combination of natural resources and geographical factors, reindeer herding was the main source of subsistence in Inari at the beginning of the twentieth century. Reindeer herding was also the first attempt to adapt an organized livelihood to the subarctic environment. The main natural resources that Inari had to offer were reindeer pasture land and timber. The forests of southern Inari are unique frontier lands in two senses: they are the northernmost pine forests in Finland, and the outermost northwestern area of the taiga forest vegetation zone. The regeneration period is long, the growing season short and the stock of timber large. The timber-line ecosystem consists of a few species and is vulnerable to damage. Cattle-raising was practised and corn was grown occasionally, but with low-yield and mostly unsuccessful crops. The infrastructure was incomplete and the road network nearly non-existent, and hence the industry, aside from a few sawmill entrepreneurs later on, was of little significance. Given the pre-modern state of the distribution of livelihood, the introduction of forestry, together with public services in general, was one of the strongest factors in the modernization of Inari.[14] Consequently, and unlike the situation in southernmost Lapland, the threat of diminishing pasture lands came from forestry, not from agriculture.

The inter-war period denoted the first phase of forestry in Inari. Loggings were spread over large areas because only wood of timber quality was logged. The 1930s was marked by the blossoming of the rural district of Petsamo (an area to the east of Inari), and opportunities presented by expanding commerce and transport facilities. This involved the modernization of southern parts of Inari, in terms of infrastructure, but the actual economic results were weak: Inari was a gateway to the Arctic Ocean and remained a provider of raw materials. The loggings provided employment for both the Finnish and the Sami at that time. There are no signs of Sami resistance, although this may be due to a lack of sources. During the Second World War, Forest Government was occupied with providing wood for the German troops situated in Lapland. The war meant the introduction of a monetary economy and the burning of Lapland

---

14 Enare-Pasvik, Natur og folk i grenseland, Priroda i naselenue progranitshnoi oblasti, Inari-Paz, Inarijärvi-Paatsjoki, Yhteinen elävä erämaa, Manuscript by Kollstrøm, Rolf E. Sch., Makarova, Olga, Tynys, Tapio, Svanhovd miljøsenter 1996, p. 88; Nyyssönen, Jukka: Murtunut luja yhteisrintama, Inarin hoitoalue, saamelaiset ja metsäluonnon valloitus 1945-1982, Licentiate thesis, Finnish history, University of Jyväskylä, 2000, pp. 22-24.

by the retreating Germans. Due to the loss of Petsamo, the only log-floating route via Paatsjoki was lost, which brought a halt to the timber trade with Norway. The postwar period, during which the Sami area was rebuilt in a Finnish style, was a time of accelerated modernization and a diminished sense of Sami ethnicity. However, the full force of Finnish modernization was inhibited by two factors: an economic shortage, and consequent delay in the resettlement programme, and a recovery of reindeer herding, in spite of the aforementioned shortage. Forestry experienced a short-lived upswing in resettlement-loggings, but after the resettlement was finished a longer recession followed (See Figure 1).[15]

During the 1950s there was a weak, and therefore unsuccessful, effort to launch forestry in Inari. The effort was unsuccessful because of weaknesses in the infrastructure, such as the road network (which remained insufficient for another couple of decades), long distances to the manufacturing plants in Southern Lapland, and weak profitability. Although the effort was supported at presidential level (President Urho Kekkonen was a keen supporter of the industrialization of the peripheries of Finland), in industrial circles, and at a local as well as Sami level, the breakthrough of forestry was not achieved at this time. During the years 1952-1958 loggings increased steadily, but not in the way that

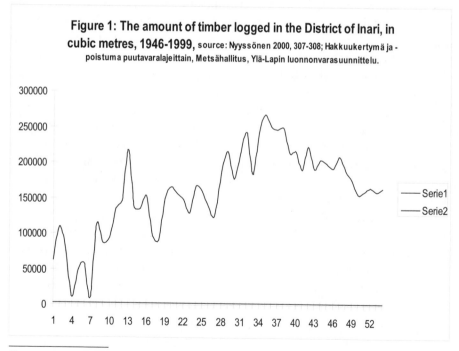

Figure 1: The amount of timber logged in the District of Inari, in cubic metres, 1946-1999, source: Nyyssönen 2000, 307-308; Hakkuukertymä ja - poistuma puutavaralajeittain, Metsähallitus, Ylä-Lapin luonnonvarasuunnittelu.

---

[15] Lehtola 1997, pp. 52-53; Nyyssönen 2000, pp. 22-39; Veijola, Pertti: Suomen metsänrajametsien käyttö ja suojelu, Metsäntutkimuslaitoksen tiedonantoja, The Finnish Forest Research Institute, Research Papers 692, Kolarin tutkimusasema 1998, pp. 83-84.

Forest Government officials wanted: timber was not mobilized on a large scale, and the means of forestry were unsatisfactorily light, both in terms of the machinery used and results achieved. The unemployment of forest workers was a problem throughout the 1950s.[16]

During the late 1950s, the first large-scale timber trade occurred when wood from Inari was exported to Central Europe and southern Lapland. This upswing, based on the manufacture of railway sleepers, was short-lived. The loggings were spread over large areas, but mainly near the few roads that existed. According to the Sami press, the legitimacy of the loggings was perceived to be high at this time. Forestry was welcomed and Forest Government was encouraged to intensify loggings in northern Lapland. The rare openings in the timber trade with Norway were welcomed and road construction works were seen as a problem only in the sense that there weren't any in progress in Inari. Even though there was Sami criticism of the allocation of profits from the usage of natural resources,[17] the economic modernization was not a problem as such. The emphasis on profit allocation indicates that the economic modernization was also perceived as a feasible strategy for the Sami. This further enhanced the perceived legitimacy of the loggings, and perhaps even the property rights situation.

As a property rights régime, the performance of Forest Government was marked by economic inefficiency but social efficiency, boosted by a high perception of its legitimacy – Forest Government was regarded as a potential employer and a source of modernization by the Sami community. Forest Government employed a small number of Sami workers. Environmental sustainability was evident only in the areas outside the logging zones that were preserved, or used exclusively as pasture lands. Environmental sustainability was achieved "incidentally". It was not on Forest Government's agenda, but infrastructural inadequacies prevented Forest Government from fulfilling its silvicultural plans, which at this time were extremely harsh and, when applied, mostly unsuccessful. The reason for these failures was that a means of efficient forestry that was suitable for southern forests had been introduced into the subarctic forests of Inari. The ecological damage sustained was not wide-spread.[18]

The period from the beginning of the 1960s to the present day was marked by consistent loggings (though on a periodic basis), a somewhat fluctuating amount of timber being logged and the consequent periodic unemployment of the loggers. The geographical distribution of the loggings expanded as a result,

---

[16] Nyyssönen 2000, pp. 51-67; Veijola 1998, p. 83.

[17] Nyyssönen 2000, pp. 68-73, 236-240; Veijola 1998, p. 84; Työttömyys Inarissa ja Utsjoella, Tunturisanomat No.2, 13.1.1950; Savottatoiminta vilkastunut Inarissa, Tunturisanomat No.4, 27.1.1951.

[18] Nyyssönen 2000, pp. 128-132.

mainly concentrated in the south-eastern parts of Inari. The final breakthrough of efficient forestry occurred in Inari in the mid-1970s, once the completion of the paper mill in Kemijärvi, in 1968, began to influence the timber trade. The amount of timber being logged increased, whereas the forestry methods were scaled down. In spite of this, the first voices of resistance were heard from the reindeer herding community. Demands for local democracy were met by entering into negotiations over the location of the loggings, from 1972 onwards. However, interest groups other than Forest Government officials had no real power in the planning of the loggings until the 1990s.[19] It may be seen that economic sustainability improved during this period, as the timber trade became more continuous. Social sustainability also improved during this period, since the recession in primary industry and changes in the structure of Finnish agriculture (which was directly connected to forestry, through agrarian forest-ownership) hit northernmost Lapland later than the agrarian areas of southern Finland, because of the late introduction of forestry in Inari. However, the perceived legitimacy of Forest Government by the Sami was beginning to crack.

Forest Government was a significant employer in Inari, even up to the late 1970s. An equity in the allocation of input into the local economy was achieved by employing the Sami. Environmental sustainability began to appear on the agenda, but in quite an ambivalent, negative sense. This was due to the numerous nature conservation projects that existed during this period. From Forest Government's point of view, conservation restricted the area reserved for loggings, which they considered to be ecologically sustainable. However, environmental sustainability was taken into consideration. For example, the mechanization of forestry was not completed, clear-cuttings were exceptional, and ploughing was not practised in its most extreme forms. Thus, by definition, forestry in Inari was not efficient. Deforestation was more evident in areas hit by brush fires. This applies only to the forests of Inari: the means of forestry were harsher and more harmful to reindeer herding in other parts of Lapland.[20]

The performance of Forest Government has been evaluated in different ways, and from different points of view. The environmentalists claim that even the lighter loggings are not suitable for the subarctic forests of Inari, where recurrence is easily damaged. The Sami emphasize the harm caused to reindeer herding. The interaction between lichen growth and loggings is something of an open question, but the harmful effect of forestry upon winter pasture lands, the condition of which is crucial for the success of reindeer herding, has been largely acknowledged. Winter grazing is hindered both by the freezing of the

---

[19]   Nyyssönen 2000, pp. 229-231, 282.

[20]   Compare Jernsletten, Johnny-Leo L. and Klokow, Konstantin: Sustainable Reindeer Husbandry, Centre for Saami Studies, University of Tromsø, Arctic Council 2000-2002, pp. 139-141; Nyyssönen 2000, pp. 177-191; Veijola 1998, pp. 87-90.

snow, due to a change in micro-climate at the logging sites, and also by logging waste.[21] Seen from the point of view of forestry officials, the picture is uncomplicated. In comparison with the unfortunate loggings in Southern Lapland in the 1950s, which were carried out by means of the most efficient forestry methods, the loggings in Inari stand out as a success in the history of forestry in Lapland. The forestry strategy in Finland and in Inari has been to secure the recurrence of the forests, thus securing the ecological and economical basis of the forestry and wood industries. Logging methods and silvicultural means have been adjusted to subarctic forests, so cases of deforestation are rare.[22] However, the perception of this strategy suffers from the lack of a larger perspective, i.e. beyond the sphere of forestry alone.

The Perception of the Forestry

The early manifestations of Sami resistance towards the forestry were expressed in the 1950s, during the first phase of Sami activism. The Sami activist front was not coherent, and the resistence was characterized by a lack of continuity. The early statements of resistance were aimed at the allocation of profits from the use of natural resources in the Sami heartlands. The issue was raised at the first Sami congress in 1953, and it was held on the agenda of the Nordic Sami Council, which was established in 1956. These statements form an exception in what was, to a great extent, a modernization-friendly Sami ideological environment in the 1950s. There was a short period of criticism in the Sami press in the end of the 1950s, which pointed out the need to examine relations between forestry and reindeer herding. In one of the most radical expressions of the Sami rights movement of the 1950s, the *Saamelaisasiain komitean mietintö 1952:12* [a report published by the Commission of the Sami Cause in 1952], forestry was viewed positively, as a potential for Sami employment. The main issues of the Sami activists were reindeer herding, media politics, education and language questions. During this period a common Sami ethnicity was built, which involved breaking away from the old, village-based identity. A more radical Sami ethnic movement emerged in the 1960s, which viewed the first

---

[21] Helle, Timo: Porolaidunnuksen vaikutus metsänrajametsien primaarisukkessioon, Metsänraja tutkimuksen kohteena, Turtkimuspäivä Ylläksellä 1994, Tapani Tasanen, Martti Varmola and Maarit Niemi (Eds.), Metsäntutkimuslaitoksen tiedonantoja 539, Jyväskylä 1995, passim.

[22] When compared to forestry in the USA, for example, Finnish forestry has been quite enlightened in its way of taking the entire ecosystem as a basis for its thinking. See for example Bakuzis, Egolfs, V.: Forestry Viewed in an Ecosystem Perspective, The Ecosystem Concept in Natural Resource Management, Edited by George M. van Dyne, second printing, New York University Press, 1971, p. 194; on the loggings in Inari and their suitability, see Kylmälä, Pauli: Avohakkuut, Rovaniemi 1973, pp. 37, 71. Pauli Kylmälä is a forest professional who wrote a pamphlet criticizing the loggings in Southern Lapland for being too harsh and for their poor recurrence results. However, he acknowledged that the loggings in Inari were suitable for the ecology of the forests. See also Nyyssönen 2000, pp. 277-281.

phase of the Sami activism as too sympathetic towards Finnish modernization. Accordingly, the demands radicalized. Demands concerning the recognition of Sami ownership of the old Lapp-marks were voiced, but the main emphasis was placed on legal and cultural issues. Following Ian Brownlie's analysis of the evolution of group rights claims, Sami resistance evolved during this period from calls for action, to maintain the cultural and linguistic identity, to land rights claims in the traditional territories. The claim of self-determination[23] was a later phenomenon in the Sami agenda.

The voices drawing attention to pasture land damages were absent in the 1950s, which may be an indication of the success of the property rights régimes in maintaining environmental sustainability; although the social sustainability was seen to be in crisis, the actual pasture land situation was not. The absence of protests may indicate only that there was no environmental frame of reference on which to build a resistance. The environmental movement and environmental issues were just beginning to appear in the Finnish media from the late 1960s onwards.[24] According to studies undertaken regarding the pasture lands during this period, the pasture land situation in Inari was good by comparison with southern parts of Lapland, but these positive results were exceptional. The majority of studies undertaken were quite consistent in pointing out the weakening of pasture land in Inari as well.[25]

The actual harm done to reindeer herding was observed and reported by the reindeer herders later, at the end of the 1970s, during the period of continuous logging. Similar observations were made by pasture land and forestry researchers, who came to almost identical conclusions concerning the harm to pasture lands and reindeer herding as a result of efficient forestry.[26] This was the first time the property rights situation had been questioned from the point of view of environmental sustainability. Later on in the 1980s, the course of Sami resistance began to follow that of Forest Government's loggings – Inari entered an era of ongoing forest disputes, mobilizing both the environmentalists and the Sami. To this day, Forest Government has emerged as a "winner": none of the cases taken to court were won by the Sami, and the loggings, supported by a strong local minority employed by Forest Government, were merely postponed

---

[23] Saamelaisasiain komitean mietintö 1952:12, pp. 44-45, 49, 55, 64-65; Brownlie, Ian: Treaties and Indigenous Peoples, The Robb Lectures, Ed. By F.M. Brookfield, Oxford University Press 1992, pp. 37-40; Hahn 2000, 114-115; Lehtola 1997, pp. 57-60, 62, 70; Lehtola, Veli-Pekka (Lehtola 2000b): Saamelaispolitiikan alkuvaiheet Suomessa, Faravid 24, Pohjois-Suomen historiallisen yhdistyksen vuosikirja, Acta Societatis historiae Finlandiae Septentrionalia, Oulun yliopiston historian laitos, Oulu 2000, passim; Nyyssönen 2000, 242-244.

[24] Myllyntaus, Timo: Suomalaisen ympäristöhistorian kehityslinjoja, Historiallinen Aikakauskirja 4/1991, p. 328.

[25] Nieminen, Mauri: Suomen porolaiduntutkimuksen historiaa, Poromies 4/1987, pp. 33-37.

[26] Nyyssönen 2000, p. 263.

or restricted in area. According to a large number of critics, the environmental sustainability of Forest Government's performance was low. The involvement of the environmentalist movements created problems in maintaining economic sustainability during this period. In addition, social sustainability reached a crisis in the late 1980s. The loggings in Kessi were postponed, due to a forest dispute in 1987-88, and members of the Skolt Sami community of the village of Nellim were under threat of unemployment. For the Skolt Sami of Nellim, forestry was an important source of extra income from the 1970s onwards. One must also bear in mind that the number of reindeer in Lapland was rising, reaching its peak in 1991.[27] This last-mentioned factor reflects the difficulties in applying property rights régime theories in conditions relating to a modernized indigenous people who have gained from the modernization, and whose livelihood is more or less committed to growth. The multiplicity of interest groups, with conflicting interests, also creates difficulties in the planning of a resource allocation.

The questioning of the property rights system on the part of the Sami has been motivated by both financial and, especially in the late 1980s, ideological factors: the Sami have begun to question the whole pattern of power and allocation of benefit streams in the Sami areas of the Nordic Countries.[28] Although the Sami movement has a strong national variety, it is a part of the global indigenous peoples' movement, and of the larger, international ethnic awakening and radicalization that motivated and provided modes of thought to the Sami resistance in Finland.[29]

The Performance of the Reindeer Herding Management

The widely-acknowledged notion that reindeer herding is the best-adjusted means of livelihood in the Sami region is quite new. Traditional Sami resource management has been criticized as wasteful, especially when it comes to the use of fuel wood at the turn of the nineteenth and twentieth centuries. This criticism was expressed by forest officials, who feared the lowering of the timber-line in northern Lapland. Karl Nickul criticized the *siida* system of the Skolt Sami for

---

[27] Nyyssönen, Jukka: Luonnonkansa metsätalouden ikeessä? Saamelaiset ja tehometsätalous, Luonnon ehdoilla vai ihmisen arvoilla? Polemiikkia metsänsuojelusta 1850-1990, Heikki Roiko-Jokela (toim.), Atena-Kustannus 1997, pp. 114-120; Nyyssönen 2000, p. 214; for information about the later forest disputes, especially the long-lasting dispute over the loggings near the Sami-village of Angeli, see Angelin hakkuut eivät uhkaa poromiesten oikeuksia, Helsingin Sanomat 17.12.1997 and Peurakairan hakkuukiista koskee koko Lapin paliskunnan aluetta, Lapin Kansa 14.12.1998.

[28] Compare Hahn 2000, p. 33.

[29] Lehtola, Veli-Pekka (Lehtola 2000c): Kansain välit - monikulttuurisuus ja saamelaishistoria, Beaivvi Mánát, Saamelaisten juuret ja nykyaika, Tietolipas 164, Irja Seurujärvi-Kari (toim.), Vammala 2000, p. 194; Minde, Henry: Samesaken som ble en urfolkssak, Ottar 4/2000, pp. 27-37.

its inability to control excessive deer-hunting in the nineteenth century. Nickul blamed the defects of the *siida* systems in curbing excessive hunting, although there were negotiations and feedback systems between the *siidas*.[30]

Reindeer numbers fluctuated throughout the period of inquiry. The number of reindeer was affected by the modernization itself: reindeer herding was capitalized and mechanized in this period, and the herders were tempted or, as they would argue, forced to increase their stocks because of the increased costs. Even though there has been a shift from "ecological to economical" reindeer herding (Jomppanen, Näkkäläjärvi 2000), the number of reindeer is still strongly affected by natural conditions. There have been many sudden declines in the number of reindeers due, for example, to snow conditions. The northern reindeer co-operatives, especially those of Inari, experienced a near-collapse in the number of reindeers between 1971 and 1980. This was due to a number of factors, most notably a dependency on just one source of nutrition (*Cladina Stellaris*). The pasture researchers also stressed the role of pasture sustainability, which had reached its limits. This was partly because of a change of pattern in pasture research, a shift from looking at relations between different means of living, to larger-scale, ecosystem-based research. In practice the pattern highlighted the role of an excessive number of reindeer in the pasture damage. After a significant rise in the number of reindeers, which reached a peak at the beginning of the 1990s (see Figure 2), the effects of the over-grazing became more evident in Inari, where pasture lands had traditionally been in better shape, compared to the situation elsewhere in the reindeer herding area of Finland. The pasture land damages, and damages to young forests in Inari, are the result of a multiplicity of factors, however; according to the scientists, the most important factor is the excessive number of reindeer. The sulphur emissions from the smelting furnaces of Nikel, an external influence from the Soviet Union/Russia, causing short-term stress in the forests of eastern parts of Inari, is a lesser cause of damage. Forestry itself is the third factor. How decisive is it?[31]

From the Sami point of view, the blame is assigned to the external influences. Loggings hinder winter grazing. The rise of snow scooter hours and winter feeding, and a consequent rise in costs, are also due to loggings and the diminished pasture lands. According to Marja Sinikka Semenoja, in those co-operatives where the loggings have been long-lasting and widely dispersed,

---

[30]   Lehtola 2000a, p. 52.

[31]   Enare-Pasvik 1996, pp. 86-89; Jomppanen, Tarmo ja Näkkäläjärvi, Klemetti: Poronhoitoon kohdistuvat paineet, Siiddastallan, Siidoista kyliin, Luontosidonnainen saamelaiskulttuuri ja sen muuttuminen, Jukka Pennanen, Klemetti Näkkäläjärvi (toim.), Inarin saamelaismuseon julkaisuja n:o 3, 2000, p. 86; Nyyssönen 2000, pp, 212, 215; Näkkäläjärvi, Klemetti: Porotalouden tuotto maksimoituu 1990-luvulla, Siiddastallan, Siidoista kyliin, Luontosidonnainen saamelaiskulttuuri ja sen muuttuminen, Jukka Pennanen, Klemetti Näkkäläjärvi (toim.), Inarin saamelaismuseon julkaisuja n:o 3, 2000, p. 83.

and the pastures diminished, the profit margins of the small reindeer owners have weakened. There has also been a rise in the number of reindeer: Semenoja blames a rise in costs for this, as well as a profitability crisis in small-scale reindeer ownership, which forces a herder to increase the stock.[32]

Semenoja stops here, and does not refer to the fact that the rise in reindeer numbers in itself diminishes the area of pasture land available, as well as the dry substance amount of lichen to reindeer, and worsens the overgrazing of

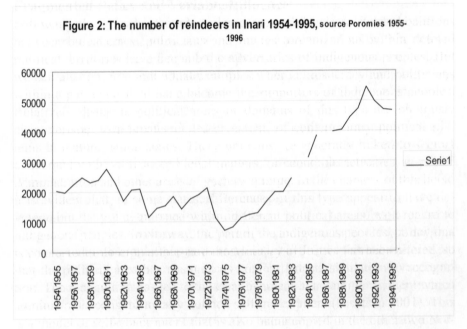

Figure 2: The number of reindeers in Inari 1954-1995, source Poromies 1955-1996

pasture lands. This viewpoint may be seen as one-sided. The rise in reindeer numbers and the diminished pasture lands as a result of forestry are two sides of the same coin, but all the same they worsen the pasture land situation in their own right, keeping the vicious circle moving ever faster.

The pasture land situation has also weakened in regions beyond the timberline, as well as those outside the areas that are reserved for forestry or areas of conservation. This is evident, for example, in areas north of Kessi and in the rural district of Ohcejohka, Utsjoki.[33] This may be because reindeers from exhausted pastures escape to the better pastures on the land belonging to other co-operatives[34], although the fences are quite efficient in checking this. The worsening situation has been acknowledged by the Sami, by Forest Govern-

---

[32] Semenoja, Marja Sinikka: Ensimmäinen kirje, Kirjeitä Kessistä, Puikko, Maire, Semenoja, Marja Sinikka, Tennilä, Esko-Juhani, Veijola, Pertti, Ed. by editorial staff, s.p., 1988, p. 38.

[33] Enare-Pasvik 1996, p. 88; Nyyssönen 2000, p. 215.

[34] Semenoja 1988, p. 38.

ment and by the scientists studying the condition of the pasture lands. The Sami themselves, while stressing the continuity of their closer relationship to nature and the harm caused by other livelihoods, admit that steps must be taken in order to improve the state of the pasture lands. One suggested method is to change the structure of ownership, with pension arrangements that would secure the continuity of reindeer herding.[35] The scientists have shown a greater readiness to stress the reindeer's role in complex interactions that cause damage to the pasture land, and are more keen to propose a reduction in the number of reindeer. In Inari, however, the improvement of pasture lands to encourage the growth of *Cladina Stellaris*, a lichen that is the main source for nutrition for reindeer during the winter, requires both a reduction in the number of reindeer and more careful planning in the use of the pasture lands,[36] a reference to the damage caused by Forest Government's loggings.

The Performance of the Régimes – From Co-Existence to Legitimacy Crisis

The most difficult task facing a property rights régime is to sustain the stock of ecosystem assets, while capturing the flow of the economic benefits thereof. In case of Inari, where the ecosystem resilience is quite weak, due to a long recurrence period, and in some cases also due to over-grazing, continuous wear and tear is evident in some areas.[37] I have outlined above the performance of the reindeer herding and forestry régimes, with regard to their environmental efficiency. It is evident that both régimes have to some extent failed in their performance. The failure to maintain the ecological basis of the livelihood is more evident in the case of reindeer herding, which did not manage to check the rise in reindeer numbers. Why was this? Why did the co-existence cease, and why were resources used unwisely?

Traditionally, the main reason for problems in the pasture land situation has been perceived as the reindeer herding itself. Until the 1940s, reindeer herding was viewed as a harmful and obsolete livelihood. After a change in ideological environment, from the 1960s onwards, the economic modernization and state intervention in reindeer-herding management and legislation were blamed for its problems. A lack of expertise and the hindering of the Sami from managing the pasture lands would have resulted in a deprivation of the resource and in

---

[35] Magga, Juhani: Poronhoidon tulevaisuuden näkymiä, Beaivvi Mánát, Saamelaisten juuret ja nykyaika, Tietolipas 164, Irja Seurujärvi-Kari (toim.), SKS 2000, pp. 168-169.

[36] Nieminen, Mauri: Pilaako poro luontoa? Beaivvi Mánát, Saamelaisten juuret ja nykyaika, Tietolipas 164, Irja Seurujärvi-Kari (toim.), SKS 2000, pp. 166-167.

[37] The ecosystem resilience here means the measure of perturbation that can be absorbed before an ecosystem shifts into another state. Systems are complex and self-organizing, permeated by uncertainties and discontinuities, and have several possible equilibrial states. There is no single possible equilibrium state. Hanna, Folke and Mäler 1995, p. 21.

a lowered, or non-existent, perception of the régime's legitimacy among the reindeer herders.[38] The former notion is obsolete, not to mention politically incorrect, and the latter grasps only the structural change, and presupposes colonialist intervention. It is sympathetic to the Sami herders, but in my view it oversimplifies the impulses and changes within the herding community after the intervention and establishment of the property rights régime configuration. Or, to be more precise, it perceives the changes only with regard to state intervention, implying that the Sami are mere reflectors or accommodators in the process. From a straightforwardly ecological point of view, the role of intensive grazing in weakening the pastures was a subject of intensive study and a known fact from the 1960s onwards.[39]

In the following section I shall analyse the reasons for the failure of the régimes by looking at the régime constellation. This provides an opportunity to examine the management structure and power relations, as well as the performance of both régimes. The components of the model used in this analysis, and the prerequisites of the environmentally sustainable management, are that (1) the tasks of the property rights régime must be well specified and be congruent with its environmental and social context, (2) the régime needs to have the power to monitor its area, as well as the tools to enforce adaptation processes, (3) the régime needs to be able to interact with the overall governing structure, and share similar interests, (4) the régime must to be capable of adjusting to both the ecosystem and the boundaries of governance, and (5) the régime's legitimacy needs to be accepted in social, ecological and political terms.[40]

In the case of Finland, blaming the intervention of the state for the failure of the system is justified, but only to an extent. The management structure was established along the lines of the Finnish model. After the state intervention, the rationale used in resource management was based on academic silvicultural knowledge, and the management did not utilize the local knowledge of the pasture lands. The connection between the two means of livelihood and the management régimes was marked by a twisted power structure, where indigenous knowledge was considered to be outdated and worthless. There was no exchange of opinion and no opportunity for feedback – the complaints of the reindeer herders were met with silence or disparagement, even in the 1960s. Forest Government has shown great difficulty in establishing a transparent participatory process based on an equal say in land use. In the era before the forest disputes there was no need to establish constructive conflict management.

---

[38] Bjørklund 1999, p. 23-27; Nyyssönen 2000, pp. 193-199.

[39] Nyyssönen 2000, p. 215.

[40] Hanna, Folke and Mäler 1995, pp. 17-18. The model is somewhat outdated in its use of the ecosystem concept. This does not, in my view, diminish the usability of the model, if and when the stress is laid on nature's ability to recover and change.

From the 1980s onwards, when the perceived legitimacy and social desirability of the property rights system collapsed in many parts of the Sami community, the lack of conflict management or possibilities for feedback were contributory reasons for a long series of dead-end disputes over land use. There was neither interaction nor any perception of legitimacy. An opportunity to utilize local, indigenous knowledge in resource management has been lost to this day.[41]

The absence of discussion concerning land-use, and the absence of the will to make contact and initiate discussion, are highlighted by the numerous disputes over the nature of conservation areas in the Sami heartlands during the entire post-war period. Here discussion was possible, because of a different hierarchy in the decision-making. Forest Government was not able to monopolize the negotiation process, as it did with negotiations about the loggings. The process was led by Ministry of Agriculture and Forestry, and later by the Finnish Ministry of the Environment. The Sami stake in the conservation cases was taken into account; the Sami mostly promoted nature conservation, since it provided protection for reindeer herding from other forms of land use.[42]

The root of this imbalance of power was that the groups with a stake in this resource were defined from a Finnish point of view. The Sami point of view was not taken into account. This led to a problem of poorly-defined boundaries: the two geographically inconsistent and overlapping property rights régimes made decisions that affected one another's ecosystem. The external pressure on the pasture lands, created by forestry, was made worse by the poor distribution of authority in the decision-making process.[43]

In terms of its role as a property rights régime, the construction of the reindeer-herding management was unsuccessful. In the first place, the decision-making rules of the régime were not consistent with the pattern of ownership. Reindeer-herding management combines a co-operative system in decision making, but a system of private ownership in relation to the commodity produced, and the commodity is produced on state-owned land. This inconsistency hinders efficient functioning and creates problems in decision-making and authority.[44] Secondly, reindeer herding management has a double task, and its tasks are not well specified: it looks after the interests of the herders, but it also checks that the quotas set by the Ministry of Agriculture and Forestry are not exceeded. These tasks contradict one another in times of low profitability, which are frequent in reindeer herding in Finland. Thirdly, and perhaps most crucially, the reindeer herders lack any means of excluding non-owners from their property, which renders their property rights only nominal, rather than having full com-

---

[41]   Hahn 2000, p. 72; Nyyssönen 2000, pp. 229-231, 282.

[42]   Enare-Pasvik 1996, p. 90; Nyyssönen 2000, pp. 255-257.

[43]   Hanna, Folke and Mäler 1995, pp. 19-20.

[44]   Hanna, Folke and Mäler 1995, p. 20.

mon property rights. The régime's inability to check the private profit-seeking of the herders, and the excessive number of reindeers, also implies a lack of internal authority on the part of the reindeer herders. However, this is a question that requires closer study. The adjustment of boundaries of governance was also unsuccessful: it neglected the age-old *siida* system and forced the herders to use the same land as another, more powerful property rights régime. The régime lacked the power to monitor and exert authority over other profit seekers. These are the institutional reasons for the depreciating adjustment of ecological boundaries.

One factor that persisted long after the establishment of the new régime constellation was the high legitimacy of the forestry and modernization projects among the Sami, which made the co-existence of the two livelihoods possible. The forestry project was welcomed and the reindeer herding was mechanized. Since the collapse of this perception of legitimacy, Sami strategies regarding both livelihoods have changed. There has been an increase in adjustment and defensive strategies, which are evident, for example, in an increase in livestock and the launching of several lawsuits. The problem is that both strategies have proven to be unsuccessful: the former has led to overgrazing and a need to decrease the number of reindeer, and the latter has resulted in lost lawsuits.

In the case of forestry, a long period of environmental sustainability, with its consequent legitimacy, was partly the unforeseen result of the lack of opportunity to make use of natural resources, and the utilization of lighter means of forestry. Recently, both livelihoods have lost their perceived legitimacy, or at least their credibility in the eyes of the public. There is strong evidence that this is not only a matter of image and reciprocal propaganda in an era of globalized environmental disputes, which has reached the old forests of Lapland: the Sami herders have to some extent lost the goodwill they enjoyed from the environmental movement, because of matters of systematic winter feeding and overgrazed pastures. The threat that Forest Government poses to reindeer herding is still acknowledged.

Analysing the situation with the aforementioned model, Forest Government failed in point 1, since its tasks were not congruent. Forest Government is responsible for both the loggings and nature preservation in Inari. It has also an indirect say in matters relating to reindeer herding, for example in leasing land for reindeer round-ups. It also failed in point 3, and *because of that*, in points 4 and 5. The adjusting mechanisms, for example situating the loggings away from winter pasture lands, were not utilized because of a lack of interaction. Consequently their perceived legitimacy collapsed. The reindeer-herding co-operative system failed in points 1 and 2, or at least, the failure was inbuilt in their administrative composition and power structure. The régime, with its ill-defined tasks, lacked power. The power structures in the régime configuration prevented the herders from interacting with Forest Government (interaction of this kind would have met the requirements of point 3). The failure in points 4 and 5 go hand in hand: the lack of internal authority might be the reason for the failure in environmental efficiency, since the régime's own adjusting mechanisms, for example checking the quotas, have proven to be inefficient[45]. The lack of power might be a more decisive factor in the case of the reindeer-herding management. The co-operatives have no means of keeping other profit-seekers off the pasture lands.

The legitimacy of the present property rights situation has been strongly questioned in many parts of the Sami community.[46] The ongoing work to reconstruct the property rights situation in the Sami area of Lapland has some positive indications for the Sami, though the situation concerning land ownership is not clear. Forest Government is still carrying on forestry in the remaining area reserved for economic use. The proposal concerning land ownership made by the Sami committee, led by the provincial governor of Lapland, Hannele Pokka, has not been accepted because of disagreements concerning the legitimacy of the Sami claim to collective land-ownership. The rejected proposal would have provided a means of progress in régime constellation and resource management. The proposal was based on the shared management of land, based on joint principles. The Northern Lapland District for Wilderness Management (formerly the District of Inari) would undergo some institutional changes, which have currently been frozen (as at November 2002); the new property rights régime would be called the District of the Sami home area, which would assume responsibility for directing the use of land. The new régime would still be linked constitutionally to Forest Government, but it would be governed by a board consisting of the Sami, Skolt-Sami and other interested parties, for example the rural districts of the Sami heartlands, and inhabitants of Finnish extraction. The Sami would also not be permitted to have exclusive rights of resource management. The proposal is marked by a traditional feature in the Finnish way of handling the Sami question, which has been one of avoiding conflict and extremism, and seeking compromise instead. The aim has been to secure both the minority rights of the Sami and the equality of all interested parties.[47]

The new, rejected Finnish institutional arrangement does not rise to the challenge of an adaptive management pattern, using measures such as institutional flexibility, learning and participation. (This would enable

---

[45]   In fact the quotas were adjusted upwards last time, in 1994. Poromies 2/1995.

[46]   Helander, Elina: Saamelainen maailmankuva ja luontosuhde, Beaivvi Mánát, Saamelaisten juuret ja nykyaika, Tietolipas 164, Irja Seurujärvi-Kari (toim.), SKS 2000, p. 179.

[47]   Tuulentie, Seija: Meidän vähemmistömme, Valtaväestön retoriikat saamelaisten oikeuksista käydyissä keskusteluissa, SKS:n toimituksia 807, 2001, pp. 267-268; Mulari, Risto: Valtio omistaa ja hallinnoi kunnes toisin todistetaan, Kiista Ylä-Lapin omistuksesta, Metsätalous-Forestry 1/2002.

unnecessarily institutional procedures to be checked by a continuous process of re-negotiation.) The Finnish model utilizes only the principles of transparency and local participation.[48] The process of re-designing the land ownership pattern has been relatively short, in a Nordic context, but a painful one for Finland. The search for compromises has been hindered by fears of a loss of assets, by quarrelling based on misinformation, and by an increased sense of dichotomy between the local communities. History has been harnessed to renounce the legitimacy of the Sami collective land ownership claim.[49]

A renewal of the management constellation has been prolonged because of an unusual ethnic constellation in Inari, as a result of which this case cannot be studied as a pure example of indigenous versus modern, Western means of livelihood. There is no united Sami reindeer-herding front, which is resisting the plundering of its natural resources. The current situation is that Forest Government has been more or less obliged to listen to demands, and change the property rights system, but the reluctance of the herders to take firm action to improve the pasture land situation is still evident at times.

Conclusions

The case of Inari is not a case of conservation-oriented traditional use substituted by state-run over-use.[50] This interpretation covers only the structure of the property rights situation: it does not say enough about the implications of the situation and its actual environmental consequences. Nor is this a case of the party that holds a right of use of state-owned land undermining the basis of its own subsistence. Inari represents an instance of the recent failure of two property rights régimes. Or, to be more precise, this case illustrates the failure of the régimes, handicapped by an unsuccessful property rights régime constellation. There are three associated reasons for the over-use: the problems originating from the régime constellation (state intervention/external influences), the performance of individual régimes (inefficiency), and the Sami strategy of dealing with external influences.

---

[48] Röling, Niels G., and Jiggings, Janice: The Ecological Knowledge System, Facilitating Sustainable Agriculture, Participatory learning and adaptive management in times of environmental uncertainty, N.G. Röling and M.A.E. Wagemakers, Cambridge University Press 1998, pp. 301-304.

[49] See two recent statements on the matter: Kitti, Jouni: Ketkä omistavat lapinkylien maat, Helsingin Sanomat 29.9.2002; Mulari Risto: Professorikaartin mustalla listalla, Metsätalous-Forestry 1/2002.

[50] Compare Jodha, Narpat, S.: Environmental Crisis and Unsustainability in Himalayas: Lessons from the Degredation Process, Property Rights in a Social and Ecological Context, Case Studies and Design Applications, Susan Hanna and Mohan Munasinghe (Eds.), The Beijer International Institute of Ecological Economics and World Bank 1995, p. 183.

The reindeer-herding management has been crippled by the lack of power in safeguarding its resources from outside intervention. This is due to the overall régime constellation in Inari. The herding management also suffered from an internal inability to prevent the unwise use of resources. The internal reasons for this are to be found in the inefficiencies of decision-making and incongruent dual responsibilities. Forest Government, the régime with both power and incongruent tasks, failed to sustain the public's perceived legitimacy of the forestry project. This is a problem in régime constellation, which was exacerbated by the negotiating attitude of Forest Government, as well as a lack of conflict management. This has been partly responsible for prolonging the crisis. The collapse of Forest Government's perceived legitimacy was partly due to the harm caused to the pasture lands. In other words, there were also weaknesses in the the régime's performance.

Environmental sustainability reached a crisis at the turn of the 1970s and 1980s, with an increasing number of reindeer and continuous loggings, both of which diminished the pasture lands. As discussed above, the state intervention and the established management structure form only part of the explanation for the problems both livelihoods have faced. However, it created the basis for forestry to dominate the pasture lands, and in doing so become the most harmful external influence on reindeer herding in Inari. The domination was not complete: for various economic, silvicultural and geographical reasons, there are large areas not used for forestry. Some of these areas suffer from overgrazing. For this reason, it is not sufficient to explain the difficulties of reindeer-herding as due to external influences alone. Reindeer herding has suffered from serious problems of profitability, which it has tried to solve by increasing the livestock. This Sami strategy has been proven to be unwise: the pastures are in some parts of Inari are exhausted and the extensive winter feeding is not always cost-efficient. This is a process that has been the hardest for the reindeer-herding management to revise, and where the failure of the régime has been most evident. The root cause of this over-use is to be found in the interaction between the three levels: externalities, Sami initiative (the unsuccessful response to the externality), and the dysfunction in the composition of the institution. The Sami tendency to blame forestry for its difficulties is partly a political strategy, partly a post-colonialist ideological slogan, partly a sign of genuine concern in the face of weakened pasture lands, and partly a legitimate concern about major disturbance in the winter pastures.

The ethno-political accusations of ecological deprivation, due to colonization, are more relevant in other parts of the Finnish Sami home areas, especially in the area of the herding co-operative of the Lappi in Sodankylä, where the water power projects destroyed pasture lands in the late 1960s. This area was one of the core areas for earlier Sami mobilization. Here the supporters of the common property régimes can muster a clear case of state-run over-use and colonialist plundering of the indigenous people. One must also bear in mind that there has been a decrease in the number of reindeers in Inari since 1991, which has been partly explained as an adjustment measure taken after the pasture land situation worsened.[51] However, the reduction in the number of reindeer has been relatively modest.

The environmental sustainability, i.e. the recurrence of the resource, is not fully explained by the nature of the land ownership. Nor is the environmental sustainability fully explained by management efficiency. Models are only models. One problem in applying property rights theories and management models, from the perspective of an environmental historian, is that the theories set an expectation of strict causality with regard to a complex ecological pattern concerning the recovery of the ecosystem. The recovery can be hindered by a lack of knowledge, or by a scarcity of resources, but the recovery of the resource is also dependent on various ecological factors with complicated connections, not just on the property rights system applied. The theories also tend to view the environment as either a management object or an externality. Ecologically-oriented historians might criticize the theorists' way of placing human beings outside nature, as its mere managers. In environmental history, the environment is shifted to the centre of focus, and indeed, by some historians, as a subject of history. The environment or, to be precise, nature, is not seen as a mere provider of livelihood, but also in the function of a tight-fisted provider of resources, which in turn places limits on human activity and requires humans to adjust, or even abandon, their plans[52].

In trying to find reasons for over-use and consider policy suggestions, it is necessary to pay greater attention to the ecological relations and consequences. A conflict management system, participation, information and planning are all needed, but in a modernized and growth-orientated environment the indigenous knowledge is not an automatic solution to the problem of the exhausting of resources. The demand for openness applies to both régimes: the reindeer-herding management must also be made more transparent.

---

[51] Jernsletten and Klokow 2002, pp. 132-133.

[52] See Myllyntaus, Timo: Environment in Understanding History, Encountering the Past in Nature, Essays in Environmental History, Edited by Timo Myllyntaus and Mikko Saikku, Helsinki University Press 1999, pp. 123-124.

References

Official publications:

Saamelaisasiain komitean mietintö 1952:12.

Literature:

Bakuzis, Egolfs, V. (1971): "Forestry Viewed in an Ecosystem Perspective", *The Ecosystem Concept in Natural Resource Management*, edited by George M. van Dyne, second printing, Academic Press, New York, pp. 189-258.

Bjørklund, Ivar (1999): "Når ressursene blir allmenning - samisk ressursforvaltning mot det 21. Århundre", *Norsk ressursforvaltning og samiske rettighetsforhold, Om statlig styring, allmenningens tragedie og lokale sedvaner i Sápmi*, Ivar Bjørklund (red.), Ad Notam, Gyldendal, pp. 15-28.

Bjørklund, Ivar og Bratenberg, Terje (1981): *Samisk reindrift - norske inngrep, Om Altaelva, reindrift og samisk kultur*, Universitetsforlaget AS, Tromsø.

Bromley, Daniel, W. (1991): *Environment and Economy, Property Rights and Public Policy*, Blackwell, Padstow.

Brownlie, Ian (1992): *Treaties and Indigenous Peoples*, The Robb Lectures, Ed. By F.M. Brookfield, Oxford University Press, Oxford.

Enare-Pasvik: Natur og folk i grenseland, Priroda i naselenue progranitshnoi oblasti, Inari-Paz, Inarijärvi-Paatsjoki, Yhteinen elävä erämaa: manuscript by Kollstrøm, Rolf E. Sch., Makarova, Olga, Tynys, Tapio, Svanhovd miljøsenter, Oslo, 1996.

Hahn, Thomas (2000): *Property Rights, Ethics and Conflict Resolution, Foundations of the Sami Economy in Sweden*, Acta Universitatis Agriculturae Sueciae Agraria 258, Uppsala.

Hanna, Susan, Folke, Karl, and Mäler, Karl-Göran (1995): "Property Rights and Environmental Resources", *Property Rights and the Environment, Social and Ecological Issues*, Susan Hanna and Mohan Munasignhe (eds.), The Beijer International Institute of Ecological Economics and World Bank, Washington, D.C, pp. 15-29.

Hanna, Susan and Munasinghe, Mohan (1995): "An Introduction to Property Rights and Environment", *Property Rights and the Environment, Social and Ecological Issues*, Susan Hanna and Mohan Munasignhe (eds.), The Beijer International Institute of Ecological Economics and World Bank, Washington, D.C, pp. 3-11.

Hansen, Jostein (1988): *Porsanger: Ressursforvaltning, livskarrierer, og kulturtradisjoner i et etnisk sammensatt område*, Prosjektnotat nr. 4: Sosiale og økonomiske konsekvenser av petroleumsvirksomheten for samiske bosettningsområder. Nordisk Samisk Institutt.

Hartley, Keith and Ott, Attiat F. (1993): "Introduction", *Privatization and Economic Efficiency, A Comparative Analysis of Developed and Developing Countries*, Attiat F. Ott and Keith Hartley (eds.), Edward Elgar Publishing, Ipswich, pp. 1-8.

Helander, Elina (2000): "Saamelainen maailmankuva ja luontosuhde", *Beaivvi Mánát, Saamelaisten juuret ja nykyaika*, Tietolipas 164, Irja Seurujärvi-Kari (ed.), SKS, Vammala, pp. 171-182.

Helle, Timo (1995): "Porolaidunnuksen vaikutus metsänrajametsien primaarisukkessioon", *Metsänraja tutkimuksen kohteena, Turtkimuspäivä Ylläksellä 1994*, Tapani Tasanen, Martti Varmola and Maarit Niemi (eds.), Metsäntutkimuslaitoksen tiedonantoja 539, Jyväskylä.

Jernsletten, Johnny-Leo L. and Klokow, Konstantin (2002): *Sustainable Reindeer Husbandry*, Centre for Saami Studies, University of Tromsø, Arctic Council, Gjøvik.

Jodha, Narpat S. (1995): "Environmental Crisis and Unsustainability in Himalayas: Lessons from the Degredation Process", *Property Rights in a Social and Ecological Context, Case Studies and Design Applications*, Susan Hanna and Mohan Munasinghe (eds.), The Beijer International Institute of Ecological Economics and World Bank, Washington, D.C, pp. 183-206.

Jomppanen, Tarmo ja Näkkäläjärvi, Klemetti (2000): "Poronhoitoon kohdistuvat paineet", *Siiddastallan, Siidoista kyliin, Luontosidonnainen saamelaiskulttuuri ja sen muuttuminen*, Jukka Pennanen, Klemetti Näkkäläjärvi (ed.), Pohjoinen, Jyväskylä, pp. 84-87.

Kitti, Jouni: "Ketkä omistavat lapinkylien maat", in *Helsingin Sanomat* 29.9.2002.

Korpijaakko, Kaisa (1989): *Saamelaisten oikeusasemasta Ruotsi-Suomessa, Oikeushistoriallinen tutkimus Länsi-Pohjan Lapin maankäyttöoloista ja -oikeuksista ennen 1700-luvun puoliväliä*, Lakimiesliiton kustannus, Mänttä.

Kylmälä, Pauli (1973): *Avohakkuut*, Rovaniemi.

Lapin metsätalous: Lapin seutukaavaliitto, Rovaniemi, 1975.

Lehtola, Teuvo (1998): *Kolmen kuninkaan maa, Inarin historia 1500-luvulta jälleenrakennusaikaan*, Kustannus-Puntsi, Jyväskylä.

Lehtola, Veli-Pekka (1997): *Saamelaiset - Historia, yhteiskunta, taide*, Kustannus-Puntsi, Jyväskylä.

Lehtola, Veli-Pekka (Lehtola 2000a): *Nickul, rauhan mies, rauhan kansa*, Kustannus-Puntsi, Jyväskylä.

Lehtola, Veli-Pekka (Lehtola 2000b): "Saamelaispolitiikan alkuvaiheet Suomessa", in *Faravid 24, Pohjois-Suomen historiallisen yhdistyksen vuosikirja, Acta Societatis historiae Finlandiae Septentrionalia*, Oulun yliopiston historian laitos, Oulu.

Lehtola, Veli-Pekka (Lehtola 2000c): "Kansain välit - monikulttuurisuus ja saamelaishistoria", *Beaivvi Mánát, Saamelaisten juuret ja nykyaika*, Tietolipas 164, Irja Seurujärvi-Kari (ed.), SKS, Vammala, pp. 185-196.

Magga, Juhani (2000): "Poronhoidon tulevaisuuden näkymiä", *Beaivvi Mánát, Saamelaisten juuret ja nykyaika*, Tietolipas 164, Irja Seurujärvi-Kari (ed.), SKS, Vammala, pp. 168-170.

Minde, Henry (2000): "Samesaken som ble en urfolkssak", in *Ottar* 4/2000, pp. 27-37.

Mulari, Risto (2002): "Professorikaartin mustalla listalla", in *Metsätalous-Forestry* 1/2002.

Mulari, Risto (2002): "Valtio omistaa ja hallinnoi kunnes toisin todistetaan, Kiista Ylä-Lapin omistuksesta", in *Metsätalous-Forestry* 1/2002.

Myllyntaus, Timo (1991): "Suomalaisen ympäristöhistorian kehityslinjoja", in *Historiallinen Aikakauskirja* 4/1991.

Myllyntaus, Timo (1999): "Environment in Understanding History", *Encountering the Past in Nature, Essays in Environmental History*, Edited by Timo Myllyntaus and Mikko Saikku, Helsinki University Press, Helsinki, pp. 121-138.

Nieminen, Mauri (1987): "Suomen porolaiduntutkimuksen historiaa", in *Poromies* 4/1987.

Nieminen, Mauri (2000): „Pilaako poro luontoa?" *Beaivvi Mánát, Saamelaisten juuret ja nykyaika*, Tietolipas 164, Irja Seurujärvi-Kari (ed.), SKS, Vammala, pp. 166-167.

Nyyssönen, Jukka (1997): „Luonnonkansa metsätalouden ikeessä? Saamelaiset ja tehometsätalous", *Luonnon ehdoilla vai ihmisen arvoilla? Polemiikkia metsänsuojelusta 1850-1990*, Heikki Roiko-Jokela (ed.), Atena-Kustannus, Jyväskylä, pp. 99-127.

Nyyssönen, Jukka (2000): *Murtunut luja yhteisrintama, Inarin hoitoalue, saamelaiset ja metsäluonnon valloitus 1945-1982*, Licentiate thesis, Finnish history, University of Jyväskylä.

Näkkäläjärvi, Klemetti (2000): „Porotalouden tuotto maksimoituu 1990-luvulla", *Siiddastallan, Siidoista kyliin, Luontosidonnainen saamelaiskulttuuri ja sen muuttuminen*, Jukka Pennanen, Klemetti Näkkäläjärvi (ed.), Pohjoinen, Jyväskylä, p. 83.

Paine, Robert (1994): *Herds of the Tundra, A Portrait of Saami Reindeer Pastoralism*, Smithsonian Institution Press, USA.

Pradhan, Ajay S., and Parks, Peter, J (1995): "Environmental and Socioeconomic Linkages of Deforestation and Forest Land Use Change in Nepal Himalaya", *Property Rights in a Social and Ecological Context, Case Studies and Design Applications*, Susan Hanna and Mohan Munasinghe (eds.), The Beijer International Institute of Ecological Economics and World Bank, Washington, D.C, pp. 167-180.

Röling, Niels G., and Jiggings, Janice (1998): "The Ecological Knowledge System", *Facilitating Sustainable Agriculture, Participatory learning and adaptive management in times of environmental uncertainty*, N.G. Röling and M.A.E. Wagemakers, Cambridge University Press, Cambridge.

Semenoja, Marja Sinikka (1988): "Ensimmäinen kirje", *Kirjeitä Kessistä*, Puikko, Maire, Semenoja, Marja Sinikka, Tennilä, Esko-Juhani, Veijola, Pertti, Ed. by editorial staff, s.p., pp. 26-45.

Siedl, Christian (1980): "Poverty Measurement: A Survey", *Welfare and Efficiency in Public Economics*, Dieter Bös, Manfred Rose, Christian Siedl (eds.), Springer Verlag, Berlin, pp. 71-147.

Tanner, Väinö (1929): "Antropogeografiska studier inom Petsamo-området, I. Skolt-lapparna", in *Fennia 49, Societas Geographica Fenniae*, Helsingfors.

Tuulentie, Seija (2001): *Meidän vähemmistömme, Valtaväestön retoriikat saamelaisten oikeuksista käydyissä keskusteluissa*, SKS, Helsinki.

Veijola, Pertti (1998): *Suomen metsänrajametsien käyttö ja suojelu, Metsäntutkimuslaitoksen tiedonantoja*, The Finnish Forest Research Institute, Research Papers 692, Kolarin tutkimusasema, Saarijärvi.

Newspaper articles:

Helsingin Sanomat 1997.

Lapin Kansa 1998.

Poromies 1955-1995.

Tunturisanomat 1950-1951.

CHAPTER 14

For and against the rights of the Sami people: The Argumentation of the Finnish Majority in the Debate on the Sami Rights

Seija Tuulentie

Introduction

During the last four decades indigenous minorities and other ethnic minorities have been fighting for the possibilities to preserve their own cultures. Indigenous Sami people have achieved a lot during these decades. In Finland these achievements concern mainly the fields of linguistic and cultural rights (Myntti 1997, 122-123). The right to use the Sami language with the authorities was legally confirmed at the beginning of 1992 and legislation on Sami cultural autonomy, which is based on three separate laws, came into effect at the beginning of 1996.

However, many issues that are important for the Sami minority remain unsolved. The most difficult of these issues is the question of land rights. In Finland, a comprehensive Sami Bill has been proposed three times (1952, 1973, and 1990), only to be left unrealized. The proposal in 1990 was especially radical in its suggestion that the state owned land in the Sami home region in Northern Lapland would be given to the communal ownership of the villages which would be established by the Sami. Since that proposal the rights of the Sami people have been strongly disputed in regional but also national publicity.

In the debate on minority legislation and minority rights, it is not only the minority identity that is at stake since it is a question of *relationship* between minority and majority. In addition, it is a question of power relationship, an interplay between what is defined as "normal" and what is seen as "different". In this article, I develop my idea of how the rhetoric of the nation state is used when discussing minority rights in a democratic Western state that has been regarded as relatively homogeneous but tolerant towards its national minorities.[1]

---

[1] Especially the situation of the Swedish-speaking minority in Finland has given the state a reputation as one that takes care of its minorities. Swedish is one of Finland's two official languages although only about 6 % of the inhabitants have Swedish as their mother tongue.

Fundamentally, the problem of minority rights is related to a concept of equality that is especially important from the point of view of citizenship in a nation state. Equality has been regarded as a basic value in Western democracies, and this universal ideal is often seen as incompatible with the claims of the specific rights for minorities. Thus, it is not easy to oppose the claims of an indigenous minority. I explore here the rhetorical strategies of those opposing and of those supporting the claims of the Sami.

The Significance of the Sami Minority for Finnish National Identity

The Sami are a tiny minority if we look only at the number of Sami people, about 7000 in Finland and from 50 000 to 100 000 in total. There are nevertheless at least four important features that make the case of the Sami especially interesting.

First, the Sami live in the territory of four nation states, Finland, Norway, Russia and Sweden, and they do not have a state of their own. The Sami themselves deny that they are aiming at the creation of "Samiland". However, in some contexts in Finland and in Scandinavian countries those representing the majority have considered the possibility of secession as a threat to existing nation states. For example, in the discussions on the legislation for the Sami cultural autonomy in Finnish parliament, Member of Parliament Osmo Kurola from Lapland expressed the fear that the approval of the proposal would lead to the establishment of the state called Samiland.[2]

Second, nomadism and other cultural features of the Sami place them in the category of what Rousseau called "noble savages". They become the representatives of something ancient that "we", civilised people, have lost in the process of civilisation but that "we" still crave for. Thus, Sami culture has not only symbolic value but it can be seen as an economic resource as well, especially for the tourism industry.

Third, the Sami are regarded as an indigenous minority who are said once to have inhabited all of Finland as well as the central parts of Scandinavia, and Karelia and the Kola Pensinsula in Russia. They are said to have been forced to withdraw towards the north by new settlers.[3] This forms a narrative of colonialism, and as a part of national identity it functions as a basis for collective bad consciousness.

---

[2] Kurola 19.4.1995. Textual data analysed in this article consists of the position statements by different organs and of parliamentary speeches. Position statements are available in the Ministry of Justice and in the Ministry of Internal Affairs. Parliamentary speeches are published in the series of Parliamentary documents and they are available also in Internet in address http://www.eduskunta.fi/thwfakta/vpasia/tsfram.htm. In footnotes these textual materials are expressed by giving the date in addition to the year.

[3] See for example Aikio 1985.

Fourth, it has been recognised in international law that indigenous peoples have a special status as the original holders of their traditional territories and that, at present, they are particularly vulnerable groups in need of special protection with regard to their territories, environment, livelihoods, cultures and languages.[4] When compared to another minority with special status in the constitution of Finland, the Roma people, the Sami have managed quite well. They have, as the Norwegian anthropologist Trond Thuen argues, gained national and even international attention.[5]

These features form a framework in which it is self-evident that the Sami culture is valuable and needs to be preserved and protected. However, when applying this principle into practice by legislation, opposing views arise. I argue that both as well the opposing views as those more favourable to the Sami claims are related to affirming, defining and validitating the national identity of the majority.

Thus, the concept of national identity is important in this context. The most crucial questions are, as Manuel Castells[6] argues, how, from what, by whom and for what our identities are constructed. Identities can be created by dominant institutions as a part of an identity project (which often occurs in nationalistic projects) but they become identities only when and if the social actors internalise them and take them as a part of their self-understanding. Thus, national identity is a narrative that tells what kind of community the nation state in question is. Although national cultures and identities are not coherent or essentialist, they are often presented as uniform and natural entities. Both the power of the state and multiple social practices are crucial when studying the construction of the national identity in its relation to minority questions.

In the relations between majority and minority groups in a nation state, the concept of power is of special importance. In most existing nation states, there is a majority of people sharing a certain comprehensive culture, mother-tongue, history and set of traditions, and these cultural features strongly constrain the action of the state. This kind of everyday nationalism, in contrast to "hot" or overt nationalism,[7] tends to ignore cultural factors and concomittantly to ignore, or at least to minimize, the existence of minority groups. Thus, there is always a threat of assimilationist aspirations. When assimilation succeeds, "the people" becomes linguistically and culturally homogeneous.[8]

---

[4]   Hannikainen 1991, 3.

[5]   Thuen 1995, xi.

[6]   Castells 1997, 6-7.

[7]   There are different kind of distinctions made on this basis. One is distinction between civic and ethnic nationalism (see discussion in Seymour, Couture & Nielsen 2000) and the other is between banal and hot nationalism made by Michael Billig (1995). My use of the dichotomy comes closer to that of Billig's, as I emphasise the meaning of common sense discourse to the national identity formation.

[8]   Seymour & al. 2000, 7.

277

In the modern world national identity has been a generalised identity and its framework, nationalism, has also been the framework for modern social consciousness.[9] As the Sami are claiming their rights, they are considered as struggling for the recognition of identity. However, my purpose is to show that in that debate the majority is also constructing its own identity. The difference between the two is that the identity of the majority is supported by an immense range of institutions and a huge body of resources. However, international community and generally accepted values work as a counterbalance for the indigenous minority.

Research Design and Methods

I have analysed 176 position statements given in relation to three legal proposals regarding the Sami rights in Finland and one hundred parliamentary speeches concerning legislation on Sami cultural autonomy in order to discover the rhetorical formations used for and against the claims of minority rights.[10]

The first legal proposal in my data was the proposed Sami bill of 1990 which was not adopted. The main object of this proposal was to restore to the Sami the land that nowadays belongs to the state. The second proposal was the Sami Language Act which was proposed in 1987 but it was not brought into operation until 1992. The third one was the proposal for the legislation on Sami cultural autonomy in 1994. These texts could be called political in nature, in the sense that they argue for or against the issue.

The contexts of my textual material are the legislation processes but the texts vary greatly in nature and in size. Most of the statements (115) are given by national or regional authorities but there are also many statements submitted by associations of local people or by private persons (61). The texts range from one page to over fifty pages and the style of the latter are sometimes very straightforward and informal. The statements by the authorities are, in contrast, formulated carefully and accurately, thus giving an objective and neutral impression.

Speeches in Parliament concerning legislation on cultural autonomy refer to national identity more directly than other texts. Speakers express clearly what

---

[9] Greenfeld 2000, 93-94.

[10] Government departments ask for position statements from different parties concerned after a legal proposal is published. In the case of legal proposals concerning the Sami, the parties included national, regional and local authorities, Sami organs, academic experts and different kinds of associations involved in the land use in the Sami region. In the case of the Sami Bill proposal in 1990, about half of the statements were given without request by local associations and private persons. After collecting the statements, ministries are supposed to send the proposal for parliamentary proceedings. This never happened in the case of the Sami Bill proposal of 1990, while the Sami Language Act and the legislation on Sami cultural autonomy were adopted. The question of Sami land rights is still unsolved, and, in 2001, a commission was appointed to clarify on what terms Finland can ratify the ILO Convention number 169 concerning indigenous and tribal peoples.

"we" as a nation should do and what "we" should not do. In the statements for the proposal, the legislation on Sami cultural autonomy was seen as a minor reform and it was not regarded as in anyway problematic. However, during the Parliamentary readings the issue became strongly contested. First it was left to await the next elections by 86 votes to 77. Then the next Parliament had to vote on the legal proposals, and the legislation was accepted by 159 votes to 20. Among the opponents were 5 of the 8 representatives from the province of Lapland.[11]

Attitudes towards the legislation have changed mainly because of the resistance movement among ethnically Finnish people in the Sami region. They have campaigned strongly against the legislation. They claim that they are as indigenous in the region as the Sami are. In their publications and statements, they called themselves Lapps and defined the Sami as a subcultural group of the Lapps.[12]

My methodological approach to these texts could be termed discourse analysis although I see discourse analysis more as a theoretical orientation than a concrete method in analysing texts. Most important is to see how linguistic practices construct social reality and justify some versions of it.

I carried out my concrete analysis by identifying the core rhetoric of the texts, especially those parts of the texts that present the basic argument and explicate the grounds for the argument. I have not done this by picking up specific terms defining national identity but by trying to follow the structures of argumentation so that the connection to the idea of the whole text is preserved. As Kenneth Burke has said, if you know a man has said "yes" you still do not know what was said unless you know the preceding actions and to what his word was addressed.[13]

Rhetorical analysis is an important device in studying how different versions of reality are made convincing, and how to make readers, listeners, or participants committed to them. Textual products can be seen as actions that change the world and that consist of many kinds of selections.

Important components of rhetoric are ethos, pathos and logos. Ethos can be understood in terms of self-presentation, the establishment of a viable identity as an actor, as Edmondson and Nullmeier put it.[14] Pathos is used for sensitising arguments' recipients, and logos refers to 'the argument itself'.[15] Chaim Perelman, in his new rhetoric, has emphasised the role of the audience.[16] The

---

[11] There are no Sami representatives in the Finnish Parliament, and all eight members of parliament from the Province of Lapland belong to the ethnic majority.

[12] For example publication Kiisa

[13] Gusfield 1989, 10.

[14] Edmondson & Nullmeier 1997, 224.

[15] Ibid. 226-227.

[16] Perelman 1982; Perelman & Olbrechts-Tyteca 1971.

question of the audience is not as simple as it might seem. The audience, as understood by Perelman, is not only the actual audience that is present but all those who the speaker wants to reach by his argumentation. Thus, for example the Members of Parliament are speaking more to the whole nation than to their co-representatives. This is an important point as the texts I analyse are directed towards a large public audience.[17]

In the field of the argument itself, the logos, the most important part for my analysis is the idea of general assumptions, loci,[18] which are part of the premises of argumentation. In every situation of argumentation there are some implicit assumptions that are not questioned. In general terms, the question is how commonsense knowledge is constructed in each society. However, values like truth, goodness, beauty and justice generally remain undisputed only as long as they are not applied to concrete situations. Conflict and contradiction will arise when these values are specified or applied.

These values could be seen as resources on which different lines of action could be based. In the case of the debate on Sami minority rights, the idea of the preservation and protection of Sami culture is a general value that nobody resists. However, when it comes to the realisation of this principle, confrontation is not long in coming.

Kenneth Burke's emphasis on the centrality of identification in rhetoric is central to the question of national identity. He claims that if people were not apart from one another, there would be no need for the rhetorician to proclaim their unity.[19] The counterpart of identification is division, and that is a threat to the national project.

Identification is explicit for example in the speech of a politician who, when addressing an audience of farmers, says "I was a farm boy myself" - or, in the case of the legislation on Sami cultural autonomy, when a Member of Parliament says that "We Finns know what it is like to belong to a minority."

Burke writes,

> Still, in pure identification there would be no strife. Likewise there would be no strife in absolute separateness. But put identification and division ambiguously together, so that you cannot know for certain where one ends and the other begins, and you have the characteristic invitation to rhetoric.[20]

---

[17] The statements collected from different parties and parliamentary readings are the two public phases in legislation process.

[18] Perelman uses the term locus and loci in the same meaning as Aristotle has used topos and topoi (see for example Edmondson & Nullmeier 1997, 228-229).

[19] Burke 1989, 182.

[20] Burke 1989, 184.

This describes well the situation in the discussion on the rights of a national minority, as ethnic relations have taken shape during hundreds of years and the boundaries between ethnic groups are not clear-cut.

In my analysis, both the state and its institutions as the voice of the ordinary people are present. I have distinguished four dimensions of national identity. These dimensions are constructed by applying studies of nationalism to my text material. I find that they represent the most important issues of the rhetoric of the nation when discussing the legal rights of an indigenous minority.

First, the *dimension of history*, and continuity at large, is related both to space and time. Spatial continuity refers to the national territories that are taken as eternal, natural and given. The most concrete expression of spatial continuity are maps. Closely related to spatial continuity and perhaps more profound is continuity in time, i.e. historical narratives of the nation. Past, present and future are tied together to create a coherent narrative of the nation that has its beginning in the ancient past and that will continue to exist eternally. This narrative creates meanings that help us to participate in the national destiny.[21] Time and space are connected in my textual material, especially in the context of the land rights of the Sami. The dispute about to whom the land belongs and what kind of possession rights the Sami should have touches the territorial continuity of the state.

The second dimension deals with the production of the nation as a "we" group in opposition to "the other". This *process of categorisation* is part of the power relations by which national coherence is produced. The minority might be described as an initiator of conflict and as a threat for national or regional consensus or as an integral part of "us" without any needs different from that of the majority.

Third, *the dimension of culture* is much referred to in minority rights debates. Differences or similarities in cultural patterns are used as an argument for or against the specific rights of the Sami. In everyday thinking as well as in some definitions in the social sciences, the concept of culture includes especially language, shared beliefs and values and habitual practices. Language becomes a crucial factor when discussing the boundary between Sami and Finnish cultures.

Fourth, *the institutional dimension* is extremely important when dealing with the status of the state. Legislation is part of the institution of the nation state, and the equality of the citizens is the state's foremost interest. Keeping order and gaining adequate knowledge about the people living within the territory are also important tasks for the state. The state intends that its citizens should internalize institutional practices and regard them as legitimate.

---

[21] Hall 1999, 48.

These four dimensions of the rhetoric on national identity have to some extent different contents in different regional fields. I have collected my preliminary ideas of these contents in the table 1:

	History	Processes of categorization	Culture	Institutions
Global and international level	*possibility of global future *territorial ar-range-ments	*universal human rights vs. particular group rights	*similarity/ difference	*international law *EU and other supra-states *role of the nation-states
State level	*the "official" history of the nation *future of the nation-state *governing the territory	*uniformity of the nation *status of the citizens	*national culture, national language *the question of multiculturalism	*legitimacy and legislation *institutional practices and maintenance of order
Local level	*history of the region * kinship and descent * mythical places	* equality of the denizens * threat of conflict	* local culture as part of the national culture	*self- government of the municipality and region *state authorities in the region

This table shows those thematic viewpoints on different regional levels that I find important in discussing minority rights in the context of national identity. In the next section, I analyse the statements given on the legislative proposals and the speeches given in the parliamentary proceedings in accordance with this framework. However, I do not explore systematically the levels presented in the table but I point out, rather, the connections and interaction between these levels.

Arguments on History and the Narrative of the Nation
The narrative of the nation, however accurate the facts it cites, embeds actors and events in the history of the nation whether or not they had any conception

of that nation[22] and the central actors are selected from a range of possibilities. For example, in the narrative of Finland's settlement, the Sami (or Lapps in that time) are seen simply as a group which has been peacefully assimilated into the majority population. What is counted as "settlement" here is in fact the expansion of Finnish farmers, not that of the nomads. Thus, the official history of Finland is explicitly the history of the Finnish nation.[23]

When discussing the claims of the Sami, it is often stated that the speakers should present *the historical facts*. Both those who oppose given legal proposals and those who defend them argue that guidelines for the present action can be found in the past. The quest for the historical facts is raised especially in relation to land ownership.

The basic argument of the defenders of Sami land rights is that the Sami previously had the ownership of the lands in Northern Finland but the state has one-sidedly claimed its ownership. Now the ownership of the land should be returned to the Sami.[24]

Opponents claim, however, that the state owns the land because of the declaration by the King Gustav Wasa in 1542. He declared that the unsettled wilderness belongs to God, the King and the Crown of Sweden. In addition, a further argument is that the situation has been unchanged for centuries.[25] Both of these traits of argumentation express a narrative based on historical facts.

But what is the nature of historical facts? Historical narrative can cite accurate facts and follow scientific practices accurately, and still be strongly partial in nature. Interpretations of historical facts are tied to present day and future expectations. The issue is, what kind of *questions* are possible in present discursive situation.

In the question of the Sami land rights the opposing view was weighted as more important as the view of the defenders, and the Sami Bill proposal was not adopted. The majority of the statements (73 of the total of 105) opposed the proposal.

The main starting point in the historical references of the opposing party was the existing situation. They argued that legislation has been carried on logically and the claims of the Sami have no historical legitimacy. This was based on the historical narrative of the nation and on the logical continuity of the events. This is how the National Board of Forestry puts it:

In 1542, Gustav Vasa declared that the unpopulated wilderness lands belonged to God, to the King and to the Swedish Crown. In 1683, the forest law declared public

---

[22] Calhoun 1997, 51.

[23] Tuulentie 2001, 81-93.

[24] Committee report Saamelaisasiain neuvottelukunta KM 1990:32.

[25] For example The National Board of Forestry, Statement for the Sami Bill proposal, 1991.

lands the private legal property of the Crown..The Forest Law that came into effect in 1886 was logically based on the above-mentioned regulations that date from the period of Swedish power.[26]

This opposing view was modified in the statements of those local residents of the Sami region that have been regarded ethnically as Finnish. Their version is what could be called the "local production of national identity"[27] or what I would call the local narrative of the nation. In that narrative, there are elements of descriptions by local amateur scientists, of national history and of local experiences. This forms an ontological narrative of "who we are".[28]

Narratives by "ordinary people" mix the local experiences and national history to argue for the existing situation and for the state administration over the land. However, the same kind of mixture of ethos, self-presentation, and logos, the argument itself,[29] is present in the narratives of the authorities and those experts who claim that their arguments are strictly based on historical facts. They underline their expertise to persuade the audience. For example, a statement by professor of public law, Pertti Eilavaara, begins by emphasizing in passive form that "in the statement the point of view is that of the researcher" and that "the expertness is independent of the preparation of the law proposal".[30] Thus, he presents himself as an expert who can evaluate the dispute objectively from outside.

This "logical" narrative of the nation was threatened by the Sami Bill proposal with the new interpretation of legal history. On the basis of research in legal history, especially by Doctor of Laws, Kaisa Korpijaakko, it was argued that the Sami had an ownership relation to the lands they inhabited in the 17th century.[31] This interpretation was accorded much publicity and it has gained a respectable status among Finnish authorities and intellectuals.

When rejecting the Sami claims, there are two important rhetorical formations in the argumentation concerning history. First, the indigeneity of the Sami

---

[26]   The National Board of Forestry, Statement for the Sami Bill proposal, 2.4.1991.

[27]   Thompson 2001, 29.

[28]   Margaret R. Somers (1994) has made a useful distinction between four kinds of narratives. First, social actors produce meaning in life by ontological narratives. These are used to define "who we are" and what we can do. The second types are public narratives which are called traditions. These narratives are attached to cultural and institutional formations instead of individuals. The two other forms of narratives are metanarratives through which we are attached to history, and conceptual narratives that produce generalisations where temporality and spatiality are not visible. Sociological concepts of actor and culture are examples of these conceptual narratives.

[29]   See Edmondson & Nullmeier 1997, 224-227.

[30]   Statement by Pertti Eilavaara, January 1991.

[31]   Korpijaakko 1989.

is questioned by the opponents. The term "indigenous people" refers to the idea of being the first settlers in the region. The Sami were nomads, and this gives the opponents the weapon claiming that the Sami population is actually not the indigenous population, and intending that the Finnish farmers have settled the territory. The territorial dimension is related to the nation state since the national borders were established fairly recently in northern Scandinavia and the Sami herd their reindeer in an area stretching from the region of present-day Finland to the region of Norway. Thus, the Sami can be regarded as newcomers from Norway.

Second, the Sami claims that are based on the restoring their land rights are rejected with an argument referring to progress. The idea of Sami administration in the North is condemned as a regrettable return to the hard times of the ancient past. That is a central point, for example, in the many statements by the municipality of Enontekiö and different associations in the northern region.

This kind of argumentation has a dual position with regard to time. In the question of aboriginity, the first are regarded as better in opposition to the newcomers. This is based on the idea that it is possible to trace the first ones and that they are more authentic than those coming later. Nevertheless, the idea of authenticity is related to the narrative of the nation, and it is seen as a valuable start but it is progress that makes it perfect. As Leerssen[32] puts it, history is represented as forward-moving in the centres; there society develops and changes. In contrast time stands still at the periphery. The periphery, as Lapland, is thus a kind of museum where we can see our origins.

For a minority and its defenders, the established narrative of the nation is extremely difficult to challenge, even if they have academic research on their side. This has become clear in the attempts to restore the land to the Sami in Finland. In spite of the research results, the defenders of the nationalistic version of history both on the local and on the state level have nevertheless to take into account the demands of international law. Thus, much of the argumentation is directed to the national audience that no great change is necessary in the future.

Emphasis on perceived historical facts in the debate also leads to the underestimation of the present-day political negotiations. Both parties think that the answer can be derived from the past, and thus, the process is not considered political in nature.

Arguments Regarding Different Categories of People
When dealing with the concept of identity, expressions of group formations are intrinsic to rhetoric. The "we" group always needs the "other" to exist. However, the categories are not fixed but are all the time produced in the processes

---

[32] Leerssen 1997, 4.

of categorization. Both ethnic categories and the category of the citizen are important in the construction of national identity.

The Sami and the Finns are categories that are used in many ways. On the local level, the process of categorization is bound to the tacit knowledge of who belongs to which group while on the state and legal level it is more important to explicitly categorize and classify people. The category of the Sami has turned out to be difficult for the legislators.

For a long time, the terms *Sami* and *Lapp* have been used as synonyms so that "Lapp" has been regarded as a name given by the majorities, i.e. outsiders, and "Sami" as the name used by the group itself. During the legislation processes in 1980s and 1990s, the use of these group names has, nevertheless, been unquestionable only in the context of language rights. Otherwise, when speaking of land rights or the cultural rights of the Sami, the terms have been challenged. As a solution to the legal management of the issue, in the Sami Bill proposal in 1990 "Lapp" was regarded as a term for property rights and "Sami" as a name of an ethnic group.

However, some of the local Finnish people in the Sami region claimed that ethnically and culturally the whole population in the Sami region should be regarded as a uniform group. Those Finnish speaking residents wanted to define the Sami as a linguistic subgroup of the larger one which they called the "Lapps". They claimed that all who had inhabit long enough (in some statements the time span was defined as 50 years) that northern region belonged to the group called the Lapps.[33]

This conclusion was adopted even by those members of Parliament who defended the legislation on Sami cultural autonomy. For example, MP Paavo Nikula stated that

> We know that there are actually three kinds of groups in Lapland. There are the Sami defined in this legislation; there are the Lapps who have been living here for centuries, too; and then there are the Laplanders - I hope this terminology is right - who have gone there by train and who have been living there for a very short time.[34]

The insecurity that he expresses in his speech by hoping that his categorisation "is right" reflects the situation of the Members of Parliament, as well as people at large, in Southern Finland. In spite of good will, they do not know much about the ethnic boundaries on the local level in Northern Finland.

---

[33] Kiisa-publication by the Association of Lapp Culture and Tradition, June 1995.

[34] Nikula 3.2.1995. In Finnish the term Lapp is lappalainen and the term Laplander is lappilainen.

The newly invented group of "Lapps" has founded an association of their own, and they have been paid attention in the media as an established party in the dispute.

The Sami Bill proposal in 1990 was quite radical with its proposal to restore all of the state-owned land in northernmost Lapland[35] to the Sami people. The challenge by the "Lapps" shows that even the most extreme claims by the minorities and their defenders do not remain unanswered although the concrete claims may be rejected. In the case of Finland, a considerable discussion on ethnic boundaries was aroused.

The processes of categorisation have crucial connections to power relations. One strategy in political argumentation is that of questioning the uniformity of a group. Subcategories of a group are used according to the context to justify or criticize claims.[36]

In the case of the Sami, it is easy to refer to linguistic subgroups since there are nine Sami languages. In Finland three different Sami languages are spoken. In addition, in the debate on Sami rights, opponents have drawn attention to the division between the Sami elite, i.e. the Sami politicians, and "the ordinary Sami", and to the division between the Sami living in the Sami region and those living in the towns, i.e. the "City-Sami".

The term City-Sami was first used by the Sami themselves as the name for the Sami association in Helsinki. In the context of legal proposals, it was, however, used in opposition to "real" Sami living in the Sami region. In parliamentary speeches even the defenders of the legislation did not pay attention to the usage of the term "City-Sami" with its negative connotations. They merely denied the accusations that only the Sami elite and the City-Sami had been heard.

While those belonging to the Finnish majority accused the Sami of not being unanimous, the Finnish people were seen as forming one nation of which the Sami were part. In other contexts, though, it is obvious that the Finnish people themselves do not form a unanimous group. In the statements or speeches given by the Finnish majority, the Sami were not once called a nation. However, the idea of the Sami nation is strongly emphasized by the Sami themselves. Thus, the Finnish people relate the concept of the nation to that of the majority of the nation state while they relate the Sami to the concept of ethnicity.

Citizenship is the most comprehensive category in a nation state. The Sami people are full citizens of the states in which they reside. Thus, there is no problem in their acquisition of citizenship. However, the problem is how to combine

---

[35] The northernmost Lapland means the administrative unit called the Sami domicile region which consists of the municipalities of Enontekiö, Inari and Utsjoki and the northern part of the municipality of Sodankylä.

[36] Wetherell & Potter 1992, 153.

Sami identity with citizenship of the non-Sami state, how to be both Sami and Finnish instead of being either Sami or Finnish.

In principle, the idea of citizenship supports Sami claims for language rights. It is widely accepted that a mother tongue and the right to use it are intrinsic to the rights of a citizen. When commenting on the Sami language act proposal, some judicial organisations and regional state organs, nevertheless, claimed that there is no practical need for the Sami Language Act since the Sami already can speak Finnish.[37]

In the cases of land claims and cultural autonomy, the concept of equal citizenship becomes central. One interpretation of the liberal concept of equality between citizens denies all kinds of rights and benefits on the basis of membership in ascriptive groups. All group-specific rights are seen as morally arbitrary and inherently discriminatory.[38]

The idea of individual rights of citizens is so deeply embedded into the politics of Western nation states that the idea of collective minority rights is difficult to accept. In many cases, for example in Scandinavian countries, a strong universalist rhetoric of equality has been used when proposals for group-specific rights are introduced, and those proposals have also been dismissed. This is also the situation in Finland when discussing the Sami rights.

The category of citizen has been treated as self-evident for a long time but it has now become challenged in the discussions of minority rights. In the discussion of Sami rights, the defenders of the universalist version of citizenship base their arguments for example on the Human Rights agreement of the Council of Europe,[39] in the context of Western democracy which emphasises universal equality[40] and the needs of "our own citizens"[41].

However, there is another discourse emphasising that equality is not the same as similarity and that the needs of different groups of citizens should be taken into account. In this discourse, the Sami are also seen as "our minority" rather than a nation of its own, but this discourse does not exclude the possibility of specific minority rights. What remains unnoticed in the texts dealing with the rights of the Sami, is the fact that the Sami people live in the territory of four nation states and that citizenship of an individual state may not be as important an identity marker for the Sami as it still seems to be to those belonging to the majority.

---

[37] See for example the statements by the Land Court of Northern Finland 10.3.1088 and Finnish Lawyer Association 20.4.1988.

[38] Kymlicka & Norman 2000, 3.

[39] The municipality of Inari in the discussion on the Sami land rights, 25.2.1991.

[40] Leppäjärven jakokunta in Enontekiö, 14.12.1990.

[41] MP Osmo Kurola in the discussion on the Sami cultural autonomy, 19.4.1995.

Arguments Dealing With the Concept of Culture

Culture is an integral part of the narrative of nation. The project of constructing and maintaining the nation state seeks for cultural unanimity and common cultural heritage. The idea of preserving minority cultures is widely shared in Western nation states. The concrete application of this ideal is, however, suprisingly difficult.

When it comes to minority languages, the issue seems to be easy to deal with, at least in principle, since the right to one's own language is seen as universal right; still, there is not unanimity about the practical measures needed. The loci of quality and quantity are set against each other also in the language issue. When the locus of quantity favours what is considered to be unique and rare, then the locus of quantity is used to value what is seen as being good for the greatest number,[42] Although the preservation of the Sami languages is seen as important because of their unique value, the Sami Language Act proposal was nevertheless judged as "excessive" as far as financial investment was concerned.[43]

References to the opinion of the majority can be seen as part of the locus of quantity. In 1990, the Judicial Court of Lapland, for example, appealed to the opinion of the majority thus: "According to our understanding the majority of Lapps and residents of Lapland oppose the proposed law." However, the opinion of the residents has never been explored.

Linguistic differences appear nevertheless obvious, while other types of boundary between minority and majority cultures are questioned. Cultural differences and similarities are used to argue both for and against the rights of the Sami in Finland.

Lapland has been regarded as a mythical place not only by the Finnish people themselves but by Europeans at large.[44] The mythical North is a land of noble savages as well as a land of extreme landscapes and ways of life. In addition, it is not only distant in space but it has been regarded as distant in time, too. It is far from the spoilt and commercialised Western culture; it has remained pure and unspoilt.

As a mythical periphery Lapland is important for Finnish national identity. The nature of Lapland and Sami culture also form an important economic resource base for the tourism industry in Lapland and in Finland as a whole.

---

[42] Perelman 1982, 29-30.

[43] For example the statements by the municipalities in the Sami region (Inari 21.4.1988, Enontekiö 28.4.1988, Sodankylä 17.3.1988, Utsjoki 7.3.1988), the Regional Planning Association (26.2.1988), the Municipal Association (22.3.1988) and the Treasury (29.3.1988).

[44] Lehtola 1999.

The contested issues in the discussion of the Sami culture are firstly, the contents of the term culture, and secondly the differences and similarities of the majority and minority cultures.

When it comes to the concept of culture, the "traditional" way of defining culture[45] is emphasised by the opponents of the Sami bill and the Cultural Autonomy legislation. For example, MP Osmo Kurola from Lapland expressed his own definition of culture in his speech on cultural autonomy :

I have been very amazed by the beautiful Sami costumes on display here at Arkadianmäki. This strong emphasis on language, literature and this form of culture is the kind of traditional culture that I understand.

If culture is defined on a broader basis, then, according to Kurola, the result would be a self-administered "State of Lapland". The fear of the independent Sami state shows how deeply the nation state as the only form to protect culture is welded into our thought.

It was also perceived by the opponents of the 1990 Sami bill proposal that the Sami Language Act was enough to resolve the question of cultural protection of the minority:

The National Board of Forestry sees action to protect Sami culture, to preserve its language and to improve the social conditions of the Sami peoples as positive. This occurred when the law concerning the administrative use of the Sami language came into effect on 1/1/1992.[46]

The value of the Sami culture is not directly denied in any statement or parliamentary speech. However, after the protective attitude comes "but" which is often presented to separate principle from practice or to refer to the locus of quantity to overcome that of quality.

In addition to the concept of culture, the other contested issue is the uniqueness of the culture. Traditional livelihoods among the indigenous people, such

---

[45] There are innumerable definitions of culture. I base my reasoning mainly to that presented by Raymond Williams (1981). Williams regards that the concept is used in at least four different ways: 1) A general process of intellectual, spiritual and aesthetic development as in "she is a cultured person." 2) A particular way of life, whether of a people, a period or a group as used by anthropologists to describe different cultures. 3) The works and practices of intellectual and especially artistic activity:' music, literature, painting, and sculpture, sometimes including works of popular culture too. 4) The signifying order through which necessarily a social order is communicated, reproduced, experienced and explored: the post-structuralist understanding of culture as material practices in which identities, objects, and social rules are constituted. (See also Nash 2000, 274.) In the debate on the Sami rights the second and the third of the usages are presented as opposites.

[46] The National Board of Forestry 2.4.1991.

as fishing, hunting and reindeer herding, were regarded as an integral part of the Sami culture in the legislation proposals. The problem is that those "traditional Sami livelihoods", particularly hunting and fishing, are also regarded as an important part of *the Finnish national identity*. In the statements for the 1990 Sami Bill proposal, they were defined as a "Finnish way of life" and "the leisuretime activities of the Finns". The wilderness, as a symbol of freedom from authority and modern civilisation, is related directly to this view, and taking away this kind of freedom is seen as contraverting the idea of equality.

Thus, this kind of rhetoric consists of emphasising equality at the expense of minority rights and emphasizing the togetherness of all citizens.

The defenders of Sami legislation refer to Sami culture as a resource for Finnish culture and as an enrichment of the culture of the nation state. In this discourse Sami culture is regarded as a property of the Finnish people, which creates an obligation to take care of it. Thus, instead of emphasizing the intrinsic value of Sami culture, the nation state and national identity of the majority are also present in this more benign discourse.

Arguments Regarding the Institutional Dimension

If we speak about "the modern state" it conceals the fact that the state is not a uniform formation but a complex set of practices, as Foucault puts it. However, it is difficult to trace the way in which the state is produced from a plurality of institutional practices and discourses in which power is exercised and this makes it difficult to analyse how power works.[47] The state is nevertheless often represented as one institution and our images of the state generally assume that the state can be addressed as a relatively unified actor. While in many of the texts I deal with the Sami are regarded as an inconsistent group, the Finnish nation is made to look like a unitary one through the institutional dimension of identification.

The institutional dimension is related closely to that of continuity. It can be stated that the continuity of the nation state is crystallized in its institutions. The modern state can be seen as a number of organisations and collectivities which are related to the institutionalization of the political force. One form of this institutionalization has been legislation.

The rhetorical strategy of the established institutions is to give the impression that they operate in the field of logos only. They present themselves as objective and completely logical. However, this expressive style which tries to be purely logical, non-rhetorical, is actually part of the ethos of the administrational texts. It is a way to convince the audience of their expertness and neutrality.

---

[47] Nash 2000, 70.

The organisations related to the state administration try to convince the audience that the existing situation is the best possible. The administration is presented as flexible, non-bureaucratic and functional. Any change to the existing situation, in this case new legislation concerning the Sami, would mean deterioration. Through associative argumentation, the flexibility and functionality of the administration are regarded as inescapably threatened. Thus, for example, Member of Parliament Ossi Korteniemi, argues when opposing the legislation on Sami Cultural Autonomy:

> The municipalities estimate that the proposal in its wideness would paralyze the entire range of decision-making in the municipalities.[48]

The metaphor of paralysis refers to a disease, to something abnormal in the functions of an organism.

The efficiency of the government is mainly connected to the premise of quantity while it could also be interpreted in relation to the premise of quality. In that case efficiency would mean not time and money but the value of cultural uniqueness.

In the context of the discussion of Sami rights, the state administration was defended not only by the state organs but by the ethnically Finnish people in the Sami region also. This does not mean that the people in the region always appreciate the state. On the contrary, the National Board of Forestry, for example, has been strongly criticised by both Sami and Finnish residents in Northern Lapland. Now, when it comes to the land and cultural rights of the Sami people, the governing body of the state-owned lands is nevertheless regarded as a potential benefactor.

This change of rhetoric is remarkable especially in the issues concerning nature preservation. While the state has often been accused of founding too many nature reserves, in the context of the Sami rights the state is suddenly seen as the only possible guarantee for the valuable nature of Lapland. For example, one local resident claims that without the National Board of Forestry, there would be hardly any trees left in Lapland, and the lake and river coasts would be full of summer cottages and hotels.[49] The same viewpoint is repeated with different wordings in the statements by many other local commentators and also by nature conservation organizations.

The nation state seems to have retained its role as a significant nodal point in the network of power, at least when it comes to minority issues. The representatives of state power encounter a difficult dilemma. In minority issues, they have to define the state's relationship to the international community and to international treaties but, on the other hand, they also have to justify their

---

[48]   Korteniemi 9.2.1995.

[49]   Aira Partakko 21.2.1991.

decisions in the eyes of the national majority. However, the reputation of the state in the international community is important also to the "ordinary" people belonging to the majority.

The claims of the minorities question the status quo, and, in extreme cases, they are seen as secessionist and a threat to the unity of the nation state. Under that kind of threat, national identity seems to strengthen. Thus, the majority of the nation state is mainly concerned with the question of how far-reaching are the changes the state is asked to make in responding to the demands of the international community and sustaining its reputation as a tolerant state.

Concluding Remarks

In the texts I have been dealing with, the majority of nation state does not use the term nation when discussing the situation of the Sami, although the Sami see themselves as a nation without state. Little attention is also paid to the fact that the Sami people live in the territory of four nation-states. In Finland, as well as in Sweden and Norway, the issue is mainly handled as an internal one. Thus, although the preservation of this minority is a widely shared premise, the discussions of legal proposals show that it is not handled within the framework of multiculturalism or international relations but rather within the framework of nation state and national identity.

The rhetoric of nation works by citing established historical narratives, by referring to existing categories and legitimate institutions and institutional practices, and by assuming power to define what belongs to the sphere of culture and what does not.

Two strong discursive formations can be identified in these thematic bodies of national identity in relation to the concept of equality. One is connected with the formal idea of equality: it states that we are all equal individuals and there should be no special treatment based on group membership. This discourse is employed mainly by the non-Sami people who live in the Sami home region. The rationale of this discourse lies in the construction of common identity in order to defend the existing situation. When defending the existing situation, ethnically Finnish people use strong national rhetoric and give support to the national institutions instead of constructing identity on local basis. I argue that this deepens the gap between other residents and the Sami since the Sami do not have great trust in the nation state on the basis of the way the state institutions have treated Sami culture in predecing decades.

Identity politics is a multifaceted realm and different kinds of groups are claiming recognition. It is difficult to define ethnicity in the language of administration and legislation. Thus, the situation furnishes possibilities for challenging the ethnicity of the minority groups with new kinds of identity claims. That is what the ethnically Finnish group living in the Sami region has done, and their dissociative rhetoric has gained at least some success.

The other discourse states that certain group-differentiated rights or a special status for minority cultures is needed since these groups have been disadvantaged for so long. However, this more caring discourse is also limited. It makes concessions only as far as they do not threaten the unity of the nation-state or demand any sacrifices by the majority.

One of the most difficult questions is the role of historical knowledge. Appeals to historical facts in the rhetoric of both parties are especially problematic. The "objective expert knowledge" is regarded as a solution to the problem, and thus the possibilities of political negotiations on the basis of present situation are understated.

Study of the majority discourses of Sami rights shows that national identity, though it cannot be seen as particularly strong in everyday life in Finland, since overt nationalistic expressions are hard to find, becomes more important in a situation which is interpreted as a threat to the nation state.

National identity is maintained through omnipresent discourse and through the rhetorical power of the existing situation. Those belonging to the majority take the nation state for granted. In the case of the Sami in Finland, the question of land-ownership shows that the territorial dimension is extremely important for the nation state. Still, even the issue of language rights which is more congruent with the individual rights of citizens, is difficult to deal with. Those belonging to the ethnic minority also have to adopt the national rhetoric in order to make their voice heard.

References

Aikio, Samuli (1985): An overview of the history of the Sami people. (In Finnish) In *Lappi 4. The land of the Sami and Finns.* Karisto, Hameenlinna.

Billig, Michael (1991): *Ideology and Opinions. Studies in rhetorical psychology.* Sage, London.

Billig, Michael (1995): *Banal Nationalism.* Sage, London.

Burke, Kenneth (1989): *On Symbols and Society.* Ed. Gusfield. The University of Chicago Press, Chicago.

Calhoun, Craig (1997): *Nationalism.* Open University Press, Buckingham.

Castells, Manuel (1997): *The Power of Identity.* Blackwell Publishers, Oxford.

Couture, Jocelyne; Nielsen, Kai and Seymour, Michel (2000): *Rethinking Nationalism.* Canadian Journal of Philosophy. Supplementary colume; 22. University of Calgary Press.

Edmondson, Ricca and Nullmeier, Frank (1997): Knowledge, rhetoric and political action in context. In Edmondson (ed.): The Political Context of Collective Action. Power, argumentation and democracy. London, Routledge, pp. 210-238.

Foucault, Michel (1989): *The Archeology of Knowledge.* Routledge.

Greenfeld, Liah (2000): Is Nationalism Legitimate? A Sociological Perspective on a Philosophical Question. In Couture & al: *Rethinking Nationalism*; pp. 93-108.

Gusfield, Joseph R. (1989): Introduction. In Burke, Kenneth: *On Symbols and Society.* Ed. Gusfield. The University of Chicago Press, Chicago; pp. 1-49.

Hall, Stuart (1999): *Identiteetti*. Vastapaino, Tampere.

Hannikainen, Lauri (1991): The Status of Minorities, Indigenous Peoples and Immigrant and Refugee Groups in Four Nordic States. *Nordic Journal of International Law* 65; pp. 1-71.

Hobsbawm, Eric (1997): An anti-nationalist account of nationalism since 1989. In Monserrat Guibernau and John Rex (eds) *The Ethnicity Reader. Nationalism, multiculturalism and migration*; pp. 69-79.

Korpijaakko, Kaisa (1989): *Saamelaisten oikeusasemasta Ruotsi-Suomessa*. Lakimiesliiton kustannus, Helsinki.

Kymlicka, Will and Norman, Wayne (2000): Citizenship in Culturally Diverse Societies: Issues, Contexts, Concepts. In Kymlicka & Norman (eds) *Citizenship in Diverse Societies*. Oxford University Press; pp. 1-41.

Leerssen, Joep (1997): The Western mirage: on the Celtic chronotope in the European imagination. In Collins (ed.) *Decoding the Landscape*. Centre for Landscape Studies, University College Galway.

Lehtola, Veli-Pekka (1999): Aito lappalainen ei syö haarukalla ja veitsellä. Stereotypiat ja saamelainen kulttuurintutkimus. In Tuominen, Tuulentie, Autti ja Lehtola (eds): *Outamaalta tunturiin. Pohjoiset identiteetit ja mentaliteetit 1*. Kustannus-Puntsi and the University of Lapland, Rovaniemi; pp. 15-32.

Myntti, Kristian (1997): *Suomen saamelaisten yhteiskunnallinen osallistuminen ja kulttuuri-itsehallinto*. Raportti oikeusministeriölle, osa 1. Oikeusministeriö, lainvalmisteluosaston julkaisu 2/1997. Helsinki.

Nash, Kate (2000): *Contemporary Political Sociology. Globalization, Politics and Power*. Blackwell Publishers, Oxford.

Perelman, Chaim (1982): *The Realm of Rhetoric*. University of Notre Dame Press.

Perelman, Chaim and Olbrechts-Tyteca, Lucie (1971): *The New Rhetoric. A Treatise on Argumentation*. University of Notre Dame Press.

Seymour, Michel; Couture, Jocelyne and Nielsen, Kai (2000): Introduction: Questioning the Ethnic/Civic Dichotomy. In Couture & al. *Rethinking Nationalism*, Canadian Journal of Philosophy, Supplementary Volume 22; pp. 1-61.

Somers, Margaret R. (1994): The narrative constitution of identity: A relational and network approach. *Theory and Society*, vol. 23, 5; pp. 605-649.

Thompson, Andrew (2001): Nations, national identities and human agency: putting people back into nations. *The Sociological Review*, vol. 49, 1; pp. 18-32.

Thuen, Trond (1995): *Quest for Equity: Norway and the Saami Challenge*. Social and Economic Studies no. 55. Institute for Social and Economic Research, Memorial University of New Foundland, St John's.

Tuulentie, Seija (2001): Meidän vähemmistömme. Valtaväestön retoriikat saamelaisten oikeuksista käydyissä keskusteluissa. SKS, Helsinki.

Wetherell, Margaret and Potter, Jonathan (1992): *Mapping the Language of Racism*. Harvester Wheatsheaf, Hemel Hempstead.

Williams, Raymond (1981): *Culture*. Fontana Press, London.

Conclusion

Henry Minde and Ragnar Nilsen

The experiences

One of the main questions addressed in this book concerns the kind of connections that exist between "local resource management" and "global rights" in relation to indigenous peoples. Earlier research has confirmed the experience of indigenous peoples, namely that they need to state their case to *both* national politicians and institutions *and* in the international arena in order to be able to secure a local solution to their problems. As several of the articles in this book show, national state policies and the dominance of majority populations are obviously the main barriers to indigenous peoples' efforts to secure their own interests, which in their opinion is inclusive and universal. Or by their own wording:

> For this reason, our campaign is not an isolated struggle, and neither can we fight it alone. We must comprehend that to understand the nature of indigenous peoples and to fight battle means to participate and to come to grips with those problems which plague the whole of humanity. (Menchu Tum 1995 [1993]: 49)

As a response to these barriers, many indigenous peoples are together developing a global strategy to secure their rights and develop their own way of life. It is the interplay between these strategies towards the nation states and in the global arena that is the theme of this summarizing chapter. We shall focus on some of the outcomes of these processes, which may prove helpful to those who are practically or theoretically concerned with the issue of indigenous peoples' politics.

The articles in this volume demonstrate a variety of strategies concerned with putting forward solutions to indigenous peoples' problems in different nation states. An ever more tightly-knit global network is revealed between organized groups of indigenous people, which may be observed as an evolving superstructure over the way in which these groups organize themselves in their different countries (Jull, Chapter 2; Minde, Chapter 5). And a multitude of creative strategies and practical solutions are revealed, developed by people in "The Fourth World" in order to handle the considerable challenges they are facing, especially in the management of natural resources.

The problems defined by indigenous peoples are linked to two particular areas. In the first place, they are claiming rights of ownership of natural resources in their traditional settlement areas. Secondly, they are claiming the right to pursue their cultural expressions, particularly language. The most important means of securing material and cultural independence is through different forms of self-government, with increasingly stronger reference to the principle of the right of self-determination (see e.g. Daes 2000, and Chapter 4). During their participation in the standard setting process in the UN and from their land rights struggle at home, the indigenous peoples have learned that self-government (i.e. different degrees of regional or functional autonomy) does not guarantee the collective right of natural resources. Such rights can even be entrenched by political decisions since they are looked upon as a gift from the state. On the other hand the principle of self-determination concerning indigenous peoples is increasingly more and more accepted internationally (Thornberry 2000: 56-57).

Through increased rights over their own land and natural resources, and by establishing their own elected assemblies, some indigenous peoples' groups have progressed some way towards achieving stronger control over their own lives. The newly-established system of self-government for the Nunavut people (Jull, Chapter 2), the Sami Parliaments in the Nordic countries (Henriksen 1999) and the fishing rights of the Maori people (Hersoug, Chapter 7) are all illustrations of how the mobilization of indigenous peoples has led to concrete results. They are also examples of models of self-government working in practice, models that point beyond their principal restrictions.

Meanwhile, the chapters in this volume also reveal past and present obstacles preventing indigenous peoples' participation in national and global arenas. The catchwords for these barriers – as they are analysed in this book – are local identity establishment, top-down assimilation policy at the state level and economic globalization.

Identity and Visibility

Indigenous peoples have been dependent on mobilization, to a greater degree than other groups, in order to make their voice heard in the modern and post-modern world. They have been victims of colonization by strong nation states and dominating population groups that have conquered their homelands. And they have been dependent on acceptance by these majority populations and nation states, in order to put forward their general interests as national citizens and their particular interests as indigenous peoples. In this mobilization they have, on occasion, partly contested power structures where the ruling élite and the majority population have defined their culture and way of life as inferior. On other occasions they have not been acknowledged as a people in their own right at all.

The extensive barriers faced by indigenous peoples have not only included a set of structural positions and institutions formed by groups who are stronger than they are. This has also included the ruling power of definition, which has resulted in a lack of knowledge and awareness of the indigenous peoples on the part of civil and public authorities. Eythórsson (Chapter 8) and Nilsen (Chapter 9) show how the Sami people along the coast of northern Norway managed, by means of an uprising to secure fishing resources, to define themselves as a group in their own right. The consequence of this definition has been a dramatic change of political position for this marginalized ethnic group. Under pressure from the state assimilation policy, this group has found itself in a situation characterized by domination, as defined by Michel Foucault (1982) and earlier observed by Harald Eidheim (1971). Without self-categorization, the coastal Sami could not have a functioning relationship between themselves *as Sami* and the surrounding society at large. As a result, this Sami group were without any practical means to combat a state policy, which undermined their identity, as well as everyday Norwegian racism. Through Sami mobilizations against hydropower development (the Alta affair) and against the destruction of marine resources in northern Norwegian fjords during the 1980s, Sami-ness was redefined in Norwegian society. In the course of these two processes, the basis for mobilization changed, from opposition to hydropower development and fishing policy, respectively, to Sami mobilization. Thus, the Sami are an example of a general trend in the identity politics of indigenous peoples all over the world, namely that a disadvantage can be turned into a resource (cf. Jull, Chapter 2; Kingsbury 1998; Saugestad 2001:47-54; Niezen 2003:76-86). Mobilizations of this kind can result in changes of régime in state policy towards indigenous minorities – from assimilation to recognition.

The Indigenous Peoples' Network

Several of the chapters analyse the growth of the international indigenous peoples' movement. The presentations demonstrate that this has functioned as a meeting-place and laboratory for the generally hard-pressed minority groups. In a power perspective, it was important that a civil society-based global network should be developed: one that, to begin with, paved the way for the development of information and knowledge that secured reciprocal knowledge and support between many of the indigenous peoples. A transnational network was needed that would subsequently show itself capable of exerting international influence where the development of rights was concerned. This may be seen with reference to the UN's social and political convention of 1966, Articles 1 and 27, the ILO Convention 169 of 1989, and international conventions concerned with the environment and developments for indigenous peoples in more general terms (Jull, Chapter 2; Barsh & Henderson, Chapter 3; Daes, Chapter 4).

An important part of this work has been to create competing definitions of development and progress, compared with the ruling western capitalistic and social democratic development models, with their clear flavour of social Darwinism. These ruling models have defined the indigenous peoples as backward, as groups that must be assimilated within the encompassing society at large in order to secure growth and development. The fact that the indigenous peoples' settlement areas often house rich natural resources that are the basis for cultural traditions and identity has contributed to an aggravated level of conflict between societies of indigenous peoples and nation states. This is shown in Jull's summary of the conflict concerning the management of natural resources in the circumpolar regions (Chapter 2), and it is shown in the extensive conflicts concerning the management of fish and hydropower resources in the Sami region (Eythórsson, Chapter 8; Nilsen, Chapter 9; Davis & Jentoft, Chapter 10). From the meeting between Arctic peoples (Sami, Inuit, Indians and the Metis people) in Copenhagen in 1973, and up to the present-day UN's Permanent Forum on Indigenous Issues, it has been shown that the transnational network has been perhaps the most important instrument in promoting indigenous peoples' interests. What began as a necessary meeting place for marginalized groups in the world's peripheral regions has shown itself, in this field, to be an important agency in a globalized world. Nation states with indigenous populations have had to conduct themselves in accordance with this international legislation. The question now is how a formal endorsement of this legislation is followed up in practice by the individual nation states.

The indigenous peoples' transnational organization over the past decades must be seen as paving the way for a problematizing of certain aspects of important globalization theories. Here, local units and actors have been depicted, to a great extent, as victims of powerful global agents, whether these have been multinational companies or international organizations (e.g. the World Bank, World Trade Organization). It is expected that the local should be subjugated to global control and standardization, and that actors operating at a local level are losers in the era of globalization (Martin and Schumann 1996; Baumann 1998). Also, that a delocalization is predicted to take place by means of a growing separation between "place" and "space" (Giddens 1990).

The mobilization of indigenous peoples gives us a modified picture, at any rate, of such globalization theories. Marginal groups in the world's northern and southern peripheral regions have, from the starting point of their local situations, succeeded in individual instances in accomplishing a successful mobilization at a global level. Indigenous activists are both local and global. The message is that co-operation between these two levels is reciprocally fruitful, not that the local becomes marginalized. The opposite may be claimed: the local (in other words, indigenous peoples' identity pertaining to their location, or "sense of place"), and their opportunities to influence their own circumstances, are strengthened rather than weakened as a result of the indigenous peoples' global mobilization, and the subsequent regulation and legislation from international organizations (Jull, Chapter 2; Minde, Chapter 5). The conclusion must therefore be that the global, through learning by doing, can also empower local communities.

At the same time, it is important to emphasize that indigenous peoples' groups are victims of negative effects of the strategies of national and international corporations, especially where the management of natural resources in indigenous peoples' territories is concerned. During the 1990s, pressure on the natural resources in indigenous peoples' territories accelerated, partly as a consequence of private large-scale companies obtaining greater opportunities under the prevailing global trend of neo-liberalism (cf. Stavenhagen 1996). But the indigenous peoples' network is a functioning power contestant against these forces. An appeal for rights in their own traditional territory, based on internationally recognized human rights and reliable protection as indigenous people in international legislation, has functioned as a device for ensuring at least some rights and a certain kind of autonomy. But, as exemplified in Acosta's article (Chapter 11), this presupposes national state régimes with at least a minimal capacity, compatibility and competence to implement international human rights standards and agreements.

The Role of the Nation State

The actual accomplishment of internationally adopted rights and objectives for indigenous peoples at nation state level seems thus to be an important barrier for enterprises that further indigenous peoples' interests. Particular instances of such barriers include a state policy of assimilation, and a development policy based on social Darwinism, conventional development plans and new liberalistic ideology. This kind of politics has periodically contained racist overtones in many places: the indigenous peoples and their cultural traditions and lifestyles have been regarded as inferior and backward, compared to nation states' majority populations and compared to objectives of modernity and development, as defined by national power élites. It has been demonstrated that welfare and development have been defined in such a way that the need for indigenous peoples to renounce their own background and lifestyles has been promoted as a necessity. This kind of thinking, in the way that it has been formulated at the national level, has also been used to legitimize state and private capitalist venture expropriation of indigenous peoples' lands or natural resources. And it has been used as a legitimizing basis for top-down management régimes, where indigenous peoples have had little influence and, in the worst cases, have been rendered invisible.

Typical agents that have represented this type of repression or authoritarian management of indigenous peoples, with regard to the exploitation of local natural resources, include state administrative bodies, external private companies, and politicians or organizations that represent the majority population. The colonizing of indigenous peoples' territories also forms a part of this picture. New groups of people have migrated into the indigenous peoples' traditional territories. They have been agents in the national authorities' assimilation policy by means of state support and cultural dominance, and by competing with indigenous people in the exploitation of frequently rich natural resources in regions where indigenous people had previously been left alone to make use of these resources. The excessive exploitation and gradual destruction of natural resources may be the result of the increased and competing use of these natural resources. In Acosta's article (Chapter 11), we can see examples from Nicaragua of this type of state politics relating to indigenous peoples, e.g. through a large-scale railway development which hits the Rama Indians' territory particularly hard. In the coastal Sami region of Norway, the central state control over, and gradual privatization of, previously communally-owned fish resources is an illuminating example of state-stimulated undermining of indigenous peoples' resource rights. In the reindeer-herding Sami regions in Norway and Sweden, the destruction of pastureland through public and private construction developments stands out as a major problem (Riseth, Chapter 12). In Finland, the expansion of forest industry in Sami reindeer herding territories represents an equivalent problem (Nyyssönen, Chapter 13). And in Canada, the authorities are failing in their responsibilities with regard to the status of indigenous peoples' knowledge within the school curriculum, and with regard to the implementation of indigenous peoples' rights of participation in important decision-making processes affecting them (Barsh & Youngblood Henderson, Chapter 3). But here, at the same time, there seems to be an important breakthough for indigenous peoples' free harvesting of fish resources, through a judgement that was recently passed in favour of the Mi'kmaq people's marine fishing rights (Davis & Jentoft, Chapter 10).

In all these countries, the authorities have committed themselves to respecting the rights of indigenous peoples. And some of these states, e.g. Canada and Norway, have been in the vanguard of establishing international legislation relating to indigenous peoples' territory and self-determination (Henriksen 2000: 135-136). But in the past decade, in particular, a clear discrepancy has become evident in all these lands, between what is said in support of indigenous peoples' rights in official policy and what is often carried out in practical policy with regard to indigenous peoples' territories. In the analyses that are presented, the failure to follow up the state's obligations with regard to indigenous peoples, in any practical fashion, particularly affects the material cultural basis for indigenous people, i.e. their rights to land and water in their traditional settlement areas. Among the examples that are analysed in this book, this discrepancy between the support that is voiced for indigenous people and the policy that is implemented is strongest in Nicaragua. Here, there is an especial lack of state control with regard to heavy-weight capital interests which appear to have a decisive influence. But the discrepancy between proclaimed policy and practical enterprise is also clear in lands with strong state systems, such as the Nordic countries (Toulentie, Chapter 14) and Canada (Barsh & Youngblood Henderson, Chapter 3). This merits discussion in its own right.

Fragmented Policy and Variable Influence

Following the growth of modern democracy and welfare states, coalitions between bureaucracy, politicians and interest organizations within defined political territories have become the adversaries of indigenous peoples. But we can also observe individual examples where bureaucracy and politicians within a particular field have become the supporters of indigenous peoples. Relatively disparate political areas or domains of this type are obviously characteristic, to a greater or lesser extent, of contemporary political systems in mature nation states. These domains are generally linked to sectors concerned with political and legal matters, or economic activities, in public administration and other areas of society at large. In the chapters of this book, it is evident that, in some states, differences of this type appear to have developed in the policy pursued within different political areas, with regard to indigenous peoples. In Norway, the part of the indigenous peoples' policy that is connected to foreign affairs and the Ministry of Justice has been altered, so that the political area has changed its content from assimilation to recognition. The recognition has led to the establishment of a Sami Parliament which administrates constitutionally defined self-government (Josefsen 2001). This is a model of self-government that is also being copied in the other two Nordic countries with an indigenous Sami population, Sweden and Finland.

An indicator of the same relative separation of an individual political area is apparent in Norwegian reindeer herding. We can see how the Sami domestic reindeer herding managed to develop a sizeable structure of self-government within the Norwegian political system, which seems to be particularly based on co-operation between the organized reindeer owners and the Norwegian reindeer herding state administration (Riseth, Chapter 12). But at the same time, we can see how the one-sided, Norwegian-dominated and centrally-governed policy, with little breakthrough in influence where Sami priorities are concerned, continues to hold sway in other areas that are vital for the Norwegian Sami, for example within regional and fisheries policies (Davis & Jentoft, Chapter 10; Nilsen, Chapter 9; Eythórsson, Chapter 8). On the Swedish side, too, there appears to be little breakthrough in Sami interests within regional policies (Thorp 1992 and 2001). And in Canada, there has obviously been some kind of breakthrough for the rights of indigenous people within the fishing industry.

This diverse policy, with regard to groups of indigenous people within different state political areas in certain nation states, strengthens the assertion of a sectoral fragmentation or segmentation in politics (Niskanen 1974; Egeberg et al. 1978; Nilsen 1984). Consequently, it is necessary to conduct a further analysis of power relations between indigenous peoples and nation states, and also to focus more sharply on the control and influence within such defined political areas or domains. The influence of indigenous peoples within such areas appears to be dependent on both the relative strength they can mobilize within such areas, and on how the rights relationships with regard to the area in question are defined with reference, amongst other things, to the international rights of indigenous peoples (cf. Minde, Chapter 5). And this influence seems to depend on an interplay between the indigenous people, state bureaucracy, the political élite and interest organizations. The power of opposition, achieved by indigenous peoples' ability to define themselves as equal partners in politics and in everyday life, stands out as a necessary precondition in securing influence of this kind.

Self-Government –What Then?
The occasional breakthrough in matters of self-government and rights claims for indigenous peoples also makes it possible to start to analyse the effect of indigenous peoples' own strategies with regard to the securing of objectives such as participation and the sustainable use of resources. What seems to be the strongest example of a breakthrough in claiming rights with regard to natural resources is to be found in the Maori people's recently acquired property rights to a significant part of New Zealand's fish resources (Hersoug, Chapter 7), which has secured considerable influence for the Maori in different parts of the national fishing industry. In the meantime, experiences from New Zealand, Iceland and Norway indicate that the quota system that has been introduced into Maori fishing (individual transferable quotas, or ITQs) has definite harmful effects with regard to the distribution of rights. The ITQ system causes a division and privatization of resources that were formerly communal for indigenous people and other coastal people. With this system, the rights of use have become objects of sale and purchase, leading to a rapid concentration of users' rights in the hands of the few – especially those who are wealthy enough to buy up such rights. The consequence of this is the exclusion of indigenous fishermen and others who previously had access to these resources. Looked at in this way, the ITQ system in fisheries may be seen to be a breakthrough for a capitalized and excluding hunting régime, in accordance with the global tendency towards a concentration of capital and remote control.

In the same way, an analysis of reindeer herding practices shows that in one Norwegian region – inner Finnmark – a grazing practice is being developed that is resulting in considerable pressure on the winter pasturelands, thus weakening the basis of the income of the reindeer herding Sami families (Riseth, Chapter 12). This is in contrast to the organization of reindeer herding in another Norwegian-Sami region – the Røros district – where herding practices have managed to develop a grazing system on communal pasturelands that can be sustained on a satisfactory basis, in terms of pasture maintenance and herding incomes. On both the Finnmarkvidda [the inland plateau in the north of Finnmark county] and the Røros district, reindeer herders have an influence on the state reindeer herding policy. This is particularly true of the substantial, though partial, influence of the Sami reindeer herding interests organization. There is also an extensive co-operation with the local reindeer herding administration. But in these two regions, under the same national resource régime, Sami influence has thus resulted in different grazing practices, something that Riseth, amongst others, explains as being the result of a better co-operation with the local reindeer herding managements in the south than that which has developed in the north.

Increased influence and self-determination for indigenous peoples can therefore contribute to a process of democratization and a more responsible style of management. But this influence is accompanied by a specific responsibility in realizing the objectives proclaimed by indigenous peoples, to secure a democratic distribution of natural resources and sustainable management. We can see that increased autonomy and co-operation with state-run organizations, and inspiration from global capitalism, *can* lead to a policy on the part of indigenous peoples that may contribute to an undermining of such objectives. Here, both the nature of the co-operation between indigenous peoples and national state administration, and the breakthrough of a desire for large-scale herding, or a new liberalist mentality on the part of indigenous people themselves, are possible explanations.

A Global Experiment
In the course of the past generation, indigenous peoples have achieved important results in the direction of securing greater influence over their own lives, amongst other things the possibility of securing legal rights over the use of natural resources in their own settlement areas. The use of these natural resources consists on the one hand of an economic and political foundation for indigenous peoples' independence and their position in relation to the world at large, especially in relation to the nation states of which they are citizens. On the other hand, it is today precisely this relationship that supports indigenous peoples' claims for the security of their natural resources. The crucial question is whether the state has an obligation to respect and protect the resource base, which is a precondition for exercising culture rights, as stated in Article 27 of the UN Convention on Civil and Political Rights. This aspect of the equality discourse was elaborated by the Norwegian Sami Rights Commission, pub-

lished in 1984 (1984:18). The commission's legacy to this global discourse has, in the words of its chairman, Carsten Smith, been as follows:

> (W)hen a particular ethnic minority has a requrement for a special basis for its culture, such a basis must be secured if this minority is to have real opportunities of enjoying its culture. Like other rules of law, the article should be interpreted in such a way that it works efficiently (Smith 1995:67).

As Smith has shown, this conclusion was accepted in principle by the Norwegian authorities during the subsequent political process (ibid:67-71). But, as demonstrated in this book, even in the Nordic countries it has been difficult to carry through these principles, mostly because of heavy opposition from local "settler groups" (Minde, Chapter 5; Nyyssönen, Chapter 13; Toulentie, Chapter 14) and closed policy domains, especially within the fishing sector (Nilsen, Chapter 9).

The distinctive contribution in the political mobilization of indigenous peoples can be characterized as the conquest of the global. This is the question of mobilizing indigenous peoples' civil societies, in order to secure democracy and partial influence in nation states where they have traditionally held a marginal position, politically and economically. Claims relating to general rights as citizens and to special rights as an indigenous people have been put forward at an international level, especially by means of the UN system. The breakthrough in establishing an international legal system for indigenous peoples, and the nation states' obligations in living up to these rights as far as the indigenous peoples within their territories are concerned, stand out as the indigenous peoples' contribution to an international legal system in the twentieth century.

The indigenous peoples have, as shown, achieved different arrangements of self-government and have obtained various degrees of influence and success in some areas of politics. But even within the same nation states, the reviews of the historical developments have demonstrated public policies that stand out as relatively fragmented and often inconsistent. On the one hand, the complexity leads to a situation for indigenous peoples that is harder to perceive in overall terms. Not only must they cope with different experiences from the strategies at a global and national level, where there are important barriers to be overcome. They must also anticipate different policies concerning their own interests and claims from different adversaries in the same state administration. On the other hand, their experiences have shown that it is possible to achieve a breakthrough in terms of increased recognition of self-determination, both internationally and within each state. The obviously differing possibilities for influence in these various political environments show that, in certain areas, it is possible to attain a breakthrough for legitimate and worthy claims concerning increased self-control within nation states.

As indigenous peoples help to emerge new institutions to tame the globalizing processes, we can analytically use Oran Young's framework to depict the current developments. The cross-scale linkage of indigenous politics encompasses both horizontal (i.e. the same scale of level) and vertical (i.e. across different scales, from the local, through the national, to the international levels) dimensions (cf. Young 2003). Accordingly, it may be possible to draw on experiences from one political level where they have achieved results, and apply these to other vertical areas where they are hitting their heads against the proverbial brick wall. It is obvious for example that indigenous organizations creatively have used the "the politics of shame" in the human rights forums of the United Nation to influence domestic public policy (Minde 1996; Niezen 2003:179-192). In the same way, it has obviously been important to be able to draw on relevant experiences horizontal from other countries, not only between "settler" states within common colonial history, like Australia, Canada and New Zealand (Havemann 1999) or Latin-America (Brysk 2000), but also across such colonial regions, which now may even have emerged their own indigenous regions, like the indigenous Arctic region and the indigenous Pacific region (Jull, Chapter 2).

Herein, too, lies the importance of the network and co-operation beyond national borders and between indigenous peoples. The relatively similar positions of the groups, as oppressed minorities and marginalized inhabitants, obviously stimulates the kind of fruitful international mobilization that is demonstrated in this book. Disadvantage has been turned to their interest: it is, in fact, a contributory factor in shaping a transnational co-operation, in order to compensate for an isolated and difficult local situation (see cf. Smith and Johnston 2002). In other words, their relative success at a global level is used as a tool for indigenous empowerment at a local and national level. And a reciprocal development of knowledge about political strategies and practical enterprise has been part of the functioning international co-operation. But indigenous peoples' strategies in mobilization and problem-solving should also be examined in a critical light. The challenges seem, naturally enough, to have been particularly great when indigenous peoples themselves have to find solutions in a world where dominating trends conflict, to a great extent, with their own models of society and political objectives.

References

Bauman, Z: *Globalization. The Human Consequences.* Polity Press, 1998

Brysk, A: *From Tribal Village to Global Village: Indian Rights and International Relations in Latin Amerika*, Stanford, Carlifornia: Stanford University Press, 2000.

Daes, E-I: "The Spirit and Letter of Right to Self-Determination of Indigenous Peoples: Reflections on the Making of the United Nations Draft Declaration", in: Aikio, P. and Scheinin, M. (eds.): *Operationalizing the Rights of Indigenous Peoples to Self-Determination.* Turku/Åbo: Institute for Human Rights, Åbo Akademi University, 2000.

Egeberg, M., Olsen, J.P. and Sætren, H.: "Organisasjonssamfunnet og den segmenterte stat", in: Olsen, J.P. (ed.): Politisk organisering, Bergen: Universitetsforlaget, 1978.

Eidheim, H: "When Ethnic Identity is a Social Stigma". In: Eidheim, Harald: *Aspects of the Lappish Minority Situation*. Universitetsforlaget, Oslo, 1971

Foucault, M: *The Archeology of Knowledge and The Discourse on Language*. Pantheon, New York, 1972.

Giddens, A: *The Consequences of Modernity*. Stanford University Press, 1990

Havemann, P: *Indigenous Peoples' Rights: In Australia, Canada, & New Zealand*, Auckland: Oxford University Press, 1999.

Henriksen, J. B.: *Saami Parliamentary Co-Operation*. IWGIA Document No. 93, Guovdageaidnu and Copenhagen, 1999.

Henriksen, J. B.:"The Right of Self-Determination: Indigenous Peoples versus States", in: Aikio, P. and Scheinin, M. (eds.): *Operationalizing the Rights of Indigenous Peoples to Self-Determination*. Turku/Åbo: Institute for Human Rights, Åbo Akademi University, 2000.

Josefsen, E: "The Sami and the National Parliaments: Direct and Indirect Channels of Influence", in: Wessendorf, K. (ed.): Challenging Politics: Indigenous Peoples' Experiences with Political Parties and Elections. IWGIA Document No. 104, Copenhagen, 2001.

Kingsbury, B: "'Indigenous Peoples' in International Law: A Constructivist Approach to the Asian Controversy", in: *The American Journal of International Law*, vol. 93:3, 1998.

Martin, H.-P. and Shumann, H: *Die Globalisierungsfalle*. Hamburg: Rowohlt Verlag, 1996

Minde, H: "The Making of an International Movement of Indigenous Peoples", in: *Scandinavian Journal of History*, vol.21:3, 1996.

Menchu Tum, R: "Respect our Rights, Not Only Our Tragedies!", *Becoming Visible: Indigenous Politics and Self-Government,* Tromsø: Centre for Sámi Studies, 1995.

Niezen; R: *The Origins of Indigenism. Human Rights and the Politics of Identity*. University of California Press, 2003.

Nilsen, R: "Sektordynamikk og regional fordeling", in: *Tidsskrift for samfunnsforskning*, vol. 25, 1984.

Niskanen, W: *Bureaucracy and Representative Government*. Chicago: Aldine 1974.

Saugestad, S: *The Inconvenient Indigenous. Remote Area Development in Botswana, Donor Assistance, and the First People of the Kalahari*. The Nordic Africa Institute, 2001.

Smith, C: "The Development of Sami Rights since 1980", in Brantenberg, T., Hansen, J. and Minde, H (eds): *Becoming Visible. Indigenous Politics*. Tromsø: Centre for Sámi Studies, 1995.

Smith, J. and Johnston, H. (eds.): *Globalization and Resistance: Transnational Dimentions of Social Movements,* Lanham: Rowman & Littlefield Publishers, INC., 2002.

Stavenhagen, R: "The challenges of indigenous development", in: Ituralde D & Krotz, E (eds.): *Indigenous Peoples and Development: Poverty, Democracy and Sustainability,* Washington DC, 1996.

Thornberry, P: "Self Determination and Indigenous Peoples: Objctions and Responces", Aikio, P. and Scheinin, M., (eds.), *Operationalizing the Right of Indigenous Peoples to Self-Determination,* Turku / Åbo: Institute for Human Rights, 2000.

Torp, E: "Sami Rights in a Political and Social Context", in: Lyck, L (ed.): *Nordic Artic Research on Contemporary Arctic Problems*. Proceedings from Nordic Arctic Research Forum Symposium 1992, Copenhagen 1992.

Torp, E: "Traditional Sami Knowledge of Predators and Swedish Environmental Policy", in: *Acta Borealia*, 2001:2.

Young, O: "Institutional Interplay: The Environmental Concequences of Cross-Scale Interaction", in: Ostrom, E. (et.al., eds.): *Drama of the Commons*: Committee on the Human Dimensions of Global Change, 2002.

ABOUT THE AUTHORS

MARÍA LUISA ACOSTA is the Co-ordinator for the Center for Legal Assistance to Indigenous Peoples (CALPI) in Nicaragua. She is a lawyer, specializing on comparative law and indigenous law, with degrees from universities at home (Nicaragua) and abroad (USA and Spain). She was legal advisor in the legal claim for the land demarcation of communal lands before The Inter-American Commission of Human Rights (ICHR) of The Organization of American States (OAS), and Assistant to the ICHR before The Inter-American Court of Human Rights of the OAS in the case of the The Mayagna (Sumo) Community of Awas Tingni vs. Nicaragua. Amongst her publications are *The Legal Rights of the Communities and Indigenous Peoples in the Political Constitution of Nicaragua and the Implementation of the Autonomy Stature in the Autonomous Regions of Nicaragua* (1996), and "The Challenge of Diversity. Indigenous Peoples and Reform of the State in Latin America" in Assies. W. et al. *The State and Indigenous Land in the autonomous regions of Nicaragua: the case of the Mayagna community of Awas Tingni* (1999).

RUSSEL BARSH is Director of the Center for the Study of Coast Salish Environments, a marine research program of the Samish Indian Nation (address: 2918 Commercial Avenue, Anacortes, WA 98221, USA) He previously taught law and indigenous studies at New York University, the University of Lethbridge (Alberta, Canada), and the University of Washington (Seattle). His recent publications include: "Taking Indigenous Science Seriously" in *Biodiversity in Canada* (Stephen Bocking ed.): "How Do You Patent A Landscape?" in the *International Journal of Cultural Property*; "Driving Bison and Blackfoot Methodology" in the journal *Human Ecology;* and "A Social Theory of Fair Trade" in *Proceedings of the 96th Annual Meeting of the American Society of International Law.*

ERICA-IRENE DAES is a now-retired Professor of Law specializing on civil and human rights issues. She gained her degree from University Athens, Greece, and as a diplomat and UN expert has dedicated her professional career to the promotion of fundamental freedoms and human rights. She is especially known for her international work in strengthening the rights of indigenous peoples. Professor Daes is internationally best known for her work in The Working Group on Indigenous Populations since 1982. She

311

was Chairperson for The Working Group from 1984 to 2001. The mandate of The Working Group is to review developments pertaining to the promotion and protection of human rights and fundamental freedoms of indigenous peoples, and to give attention to the evolution of international standards concerning indigenous rights. On 28 March 2003 the degree of Honorary Doctor was conferred upon her at the University of Tromsø.

ANTHONY DAVIS holds the position of Full Professor in Anthropology within the Department of Sociology and Anthropology at St. Francis Xavier University, Antigonish, Nova Scotia, Canada. He is also currently directing a university-community research alliance entitled 'Social Research for Sustainable Fisheries (SRSF)' (www.stfx.ca/research/srsf). This alliance is dedicated to developing fisheries' social research capacity among indigenous and non-native fishing peoples and organisations. Born and raised in Nova Scotia, Davis has been involved in fisheries-centred research for over twenty-five years.

EINAR EYTHÓRSSON is a researcher at Norut NIBR in Alta, Norway. He has a Ph.D. in Social Science from the University of Tromsø. His research interests are the management of common property resources, and indigenous people's resource- and land rights. Recent publications include: "Voices of the Weak, Relational Aspects of Local Ecological Knowledge in the Fisheries" in Jentoft, Svein (ed): *Commons in a Cold Climate; Coastal Fisheries and Reindeer Pastoralism in North Norway* (1998), and "Stakeholders, Courts and Communities; Individual Transferable Quotas in Icelandic Fisheries, 1991-2001" in Dolsak, Nives and Elinor Ostrom (eds.): *The Commons in the New Millennium* (2003).

JAMES (SAKEJ) YOUNGBLOOD HENDERSON is Professor and Research Director at the Native Law Centre of Canada College of Law, University of Saskatchewan Saskatoon, Saskatchewan, Canada. He was born to the Bear Clan of the Chickasaw Nation and Cheyenne Tribe in Oklahoma in 1944. He is a law professor who created litigation strategies to restore aboriginal culture and institutions, and to protect indigenous heritage, knowledge and culture. His latest books are on Aboriginal Tenure in the Constitution of Canada (2000) and Protecting Indigenous Knowledge and Heritage (2000), and he is working on Treaty rights in the Constitution of Canada (2003). Currently he is a member of the Sectoral Commission on Culture, Communication and Information of the Canadian Commission for UNESCO; the Eminent Person Implementation Committee for Traditional Knowledge in the Biodiversity Convention Office; and the Experts Advisory Group on International Cultural Diversity.

312

Bjørn Hersoug is Professor of Sociology and a former Rector of The Norwegian College of Fishery Science, University of Tromsø, Norway. Throughout his career he has been occupied with fisheries management research. His Ph.D. research was on fisheries development. He has fieldwork experience from Norway as well as in Africa, Latin America and Asia, and has worked as both an academic and a consultant for the Norwegian Agency for Development Co-operation (NORAD). His two most recent books are: *Unfinished Business. New Zealand's Experience with Rights-based Fisheries Management* and *Fishing in a Sea of Sharks. Reconstruction and Development in the South African Fishing Industry*, both published by Eburon publishers (2002).

Svein Jentoft is Professor of Sociology at the Department of Planning and Community Studies at the University of Tromsø, Norway. He has published numerous journal articles, books and edited volumes on natural resource management, community development and industrial organization pertaining to fisheries and reindeer pastoralism. Among his books are *Commons in a Cold Climate: Coastal Fisheries and Reindeer Pastoralism in North Norway. The Co-management Approach* (1998). He is currently chair of the reindeer industry research program (SARVVIS) at the Center for Sami Studies, University of Tromsø, and co-ordinator of a collaborative capacitating and research program with the URACCAN University in Nicaragua, focusing on indigenous peoples.

Peter Jull is Adjunct Associate Professor at the School of Political Science & International Studies at the University of Queensland in Brisbane, Australia. He was an adviser on northern regions and indigenous policy for many years in Canadian prime ministers' and premiers' offices, and to Northern Canada's heads of government, and political and constitutional adviser to Canadian and international Inuit. He has also worked for Australia's Torres Strait Islanders and 'Outback' aboriginal peoples, and has researched and written on indigenous hinterland politics in Sápmi (Lapland), the North Atlantic, Greenland, and Alaska, and on related international comparative issues. His recent report, "Nations With Whom We Are Connected" (2001), was abridged in two parts in *Australian Indigenous Law Reporter* (2001).

Henry Minde is Professor of History at the University of Tromsø, Norway, where he specializes in Sami and indigenous peoples' cultural, legal and political history. He has received an award from the Government of Canada and has studied the history of the First Nations' people at McGill University (1990-91) and at Dartmouth College (1999). He currently works on and is co-ordinator of an interdisciplinary project called "The Challenge of Indigenousness: Politics of Rights, Resources and Knowledge", funded by the Norwegian Research Council. In English he has co-edited *Becoming Visible: Indigenous Politics and Self-government* (1995) and has published several articles that deal principally with the history of the Sami and indigenous peoples; some of these have also appeared in Spanish.

RAGNAR NILSEN is Associate Professor in Sociology at the Department of Planning and Community Studies, University of Tromsø, Norway. His main research interest is within rural sociology, regional development, resource management and small-scale fisheries and agriculture. He has published several books and many articles on Sami fisheries communities and reindeer pastoralist adaptations in Norway. He has also done fieldwork in Italy and Slovakia on small business management and flexible specialization.

JUKKA NYYSSÖNEN is a doctoral candidate and research fellow in the Department of History at University of Tromsø, Norway. Among his research topics is the environmental history of post-war Inari in Finland. He is currently preparing a thesis on the Sami notion on modernization and the mobilization of the Sami in Finland.

GEORGE L. PETERSON is a Senior Level (ST) research scientist with the USDA Forest Service Rocky Mountain Research Station in Fort Collins, Colorado, USA. His professional background also includes faculty appointments at UCLA and Northwestern University. His principal research interests include the monetary and non-monetary valuation of non-market goods and services, environmental resource damage assessment, the application of psychology to economic valuation, the integration of science and policy, cross-disciplinary collaboration in large-scale, complex environmental management problems, and outdoor recreation research and management. He has published numerous scientific and technical papers and has edited or co-edited several books.

JAN ÅGE RISETH holds a MSc .in Nature Conservation and a Ph. D. (2000) in Natural Resource Economics, both from the Agricultural University of Norway. His professional experience includes ten years in the Norwegian State Agency of Reindeer Management and another ten years as a college teacher in Environmental Engineering. He is currently a Senior Researcher at NORUT Social Science Ltd., Tromsø, and has an adjunct position at the Sami Institute in Kautokeino, Norway.

ROBERT SNYDER is a doctoral candidate in the department of Anthropology at York University in Toronto, Canada. He works concurrently as a project facilitator at the Island Institute in Rockland, Maine, USA. His research examines the political ecology of working waterfront access in Maine.

DANIEL R. WILLIAMS a research social scientist for the United States Forest Service, Rocky Mountain Research Station in Fort Collins, Colorado, USA. His research investigates the meaning and management of nature, particularly the application of environmental psychology and cultural geography to perceptions and uses of natural environments, public lands planning and policy, and ecosystem management.

SEIJA TUULENTIE has a Ph.D. in sociology and is a senior researcher at the Finnish Forest Research Institute in Rovaniemi, Finland, specializing in nature-based tourism. Her publications on indigenous questions include articles such as *Culture alone will not put bread on the table*, "The many facets of the debate on the preservation of Sami culture" in *Acta Borealia* (1999) and "National Rejection of the Saami Claims in Finland" in Karppi & Eriksson: *Conflict and Cooperation in the North,* (2002). The title of her doctoral thesis in sociology is *Our Minority. The Majority Rhetoric in the Debate on the Legal Rights of the Sami in Finland* (in Finnish) (2001).

315